I0137086

TELL ME ABOUT IT
3

A BOOK OF MEMORIES COLLECTED BY

ST SUKIE DE LA CROIX
&
OWEN KEEHNEN

RATTLING GOOD YARNS
PRESS
PALM SPRINGS, CALIFORNIA

Copyright © 2020 St Sukie de la Croix and Owen Keehnen
All rights reserved.

No part of this publication may be reproduced, distributed, or
transmitted in any form or by any means, including photocopying,
recording, or other electronic or mechanical methods, without the
prior written permission of the publisher, except in the case of
brief quotations embodied in critical reviews and certain other
noncommercial uses permitted by copyright law. For permission
requests, write to the publisher, addressed "Attention: Permissions
Coordinator," at the address below.

Rattling Good Yarns Press
33490 Date Palm Drive 3065
Cathedral City CA 92235
USA
www.rattlinggoodyarns.com

Cover Photograph and Design: Ian Henzel
Cover models Roy Alton Wald, Siouxzan Perry & Simeon Den

Library of Congress Control Number: 9781734146455
ISBN: 978-1-7341464-5-5

First Edition

To all the LGBTQ people throughout history who never had the freedom
or luxury to share their stories and experiences.

CONTENTS

PREFACE

As LGBTQ people, recording our history and our stories is essential. In sharing our experience with others, we are doing more than simply giving an account of our lives. We are saying that our experience, our lives, and our point of view have value.

From the outset, this groundbreaking series was intended to shed light on the lives and experiences of LGBTQ people by having a wide variety of folks share their responses to a specific set of questions. The content may vary in the series, but not the importance of capturing the answers.

Collecting our stories is a crucial component to claiming our space. As a group we have had our voices muted and erased from the annals of history for centuries. This conspiracy of silence and the redaction of our existence has had dire repercussions, which includes widespread isolation, misunderstanding, secrecy, and shame.

Tell Me About It is a way to help correct some of that legacy of suppression. This method of raising consciousness has the power to liberate, affirm, and connect us. Bonding over shared experience is key in overcoming social, cultural, and political oppression and strengthening community. Telling our stories connects us with others, and by listening to the experiences of others we deepen our understanding of ourselves.

Sharing our stories honors not only our lives, but also the lives of the millions of LGBTQ people who have walked the planet since time began. It is a means of paying tribute to those who never had the luxury of proclaiming their genuine experience or having their reality recognized. Given our history of LGBTQ suppression, the act of breaking the silence, sharing our stories, and revealing the truth of our lives is a political act. By speaking our truth, we are stating that we will not be silenced again.

As queer historians of the LGBTQ experience, we have been recording and collecting the memories, personal experiences, and anecdotes of queer folks for decades. The *Tell Me About It* series is a fitting extension to each of our life's work.

Response to our first two installments of the *Tell Me About It* series was so positive that we opted to do it a third time. With each progressive installment of the books our goal has been to widen and deepen the scope of LGBTQ experience we present.

Over the course of several months we collected responses for volume three and received dozens of honest, thoughtful, and funny answers from a great group of people. Choosing which responses would be included in the final edit of *Tell Me About It 3* was, by far, the most challenging aspect of the project.

We wish to extend our heartfelt thanks to all who shared a part of themselves. In doing so they have affirmed the importance of the sharing the personal experiences of LGBTQ people. The efforts of each and every individual who participated have resulted in an insightful, entertaining, and rewarding exploration of our community.

–   Owen Keehnen and St Sukie de la Croix

IS THERE A SONG THAT LIFTS YOUR SPIRITS AS A LGBTQ PERSON?

Chicago, IL (USA)

Oh Sylvester, *You Make Me Feel (Mighty Real)*. I hung around a lot before the Bistro ... I hung around a lot with Frankie Knuckles at the Warehouse. He was a good friend and I listened to a lot of house music. I like the funkier side of disco. I'm a musician, singer, and keyboard player, and I liked the funky stuff. *You Make Me Feel (Mighty Real)* was a good anthem. It seemed so liberating as a song. – James Scalfani

───────▽───────

Memphis, TN (USA)

(Your Love Keeps Lifting Me) Higher and Higher, as sung by Bette Midler. That concert was so exciting. There was a gang of us who got tickets the first day they went on sale, and we all sat in the middle of the front row. We dressed up in various costumes – that seemed the thing to do. I wore a one-piece, magenta jump suit, platform shoes, a ruffled shirt, and a rasta-style knit beret. Among the group was my boyfriend for a short time, Michael Jeter. He was known for his great talent, his many acting awards, and his gentle kindness to all his friends. May he rest in peace.

I've actually seen Bette Midler in concert five times: St. Louis, MO; Memphis, TN; Boston, MA (twice, once in an intimate cabaret setting – I could almost reach out and touch her), and, finally, Seattle, WA. During the other Boston performance in a theatre, she admitted she was sick with the flu, but she did a short show for us anyway. During one song she lay prone on the stage and gave it all she had. The audience was appreciative of her willpower and didn't resent her shortening the show. We knew a trouper when we saw one. – Oran Walker

—————▽—————

Midwestern City (USA)

House music in general. Reminds me of sitting around the pool at gay campgrounds/resorts and going out to gay clubs. – Anonymous

—————▽—————

South Bend, IN (USA)

I think the song that runs through my mind is *I Will Survive*. It was '79 or '80. I grew up in South Bend, Indiana, before I fled to Chicago. South Bend was not a place where our kind was welcome. I ended up having issues with my family and ended up living on the streets. – Steve

—————▽—————

Chicago, IL (USA)

I love *Together Again* by Janet Jackson. It's such a heavy subject, remembering friends who were lost to AIDS, but she makes it a celebration of them. It always brings me joy. – C'est Kevvie (Wilhelmina)

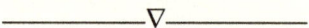

—————▽—————

Chicago, IL (USA)

Yes, yes there is. Way back in 1978 or 1979, my best friend Wesley and I had tickets to see Sylvester at Center Stage in Chicago. We thought of Center Stage as our version of Studio 54. We would get dressed in our Halston/Gucci/Fioruccio best whenever we went there, which was most Saturday nights. Sylvester had by then recorded two monster disco hits, *Dance (Disco Heat)* and *You Make Me Feel (Mighty Real)*. Both songs had a special place in our hearts because Sylvester was openly gay and it felt like those songs were for us! Well, the day came and we were ready. Outfits? Check. Coke? Check. A good, lively crowd was in attendance – Izora Rhodes and Martha Wash were every bit as good as we'd hoped, and then some. About a third of the way into the show, they slowed things down and performed the song that is my answer to this question ... *You Are My Friend*, a tune that had been a huge hit for Patti LaBelle in 1977. Believe me when I tell you they blew the roof off that motherfucking building that night! Sylvester used the moment to introduce Izora and Martha by telling the story of how they'd met. Then they each got a chance to show off their vocal range and when those three got together to sing the last chorus ... I get goosebumps and chills every time I hear it. A couple of years after that show, Sylvester recorded a live album at The San Francisco Opera House, including *You Are My Friend*. I cannot listen to the live version of that song without tearing up. For me, it defines that era, I see Wesley, who died in 1985, and I hear the thunderous cheering of Sylvester's hometown crowd (many of them also long dead) and instead of sadness, I feel nothing short of the jubilation that was palpable in that room that night. I live in San Francisco now and I pass by the Opera House frequently – and every time I do, *You Are My Friend* pops into my head and I understand what music can do to and for us. – Terence Smith (Joan Jett Blakk)

————▽————

Chicago, IL (USA)

There are probably a couple, but I'm more of a theater queen, so the best song ever is *Suddenly Seymour*. As a gay person there are all the usual ones, but my favorite song that's not supposed to be gay but is, is *Cell Block Tango* ... *He Had it Coming* from *Chicago*. – Mike

————▽————

Chicago, IL (USA)

I would say, *Lightning Strikes* by Klaus Nomi, the cover of the Lou Christie song. I just find it funny. – Xavier Bathsheba-Negron

————▽————

Nashville, TN (USA)
Birmingham, AL (USA)
Chicago, IL (USA)

Music has a unique power to stir the emotions. Among other things, songs can serve as anchors for emotional memories. That's especially true for me, as I was raised in a family of musicians and constantly surrounded by music and musical expression.

Nashville: There are many songs that lift my spirits. When you want to talk about specifically gay ones, the earliest I remember are the songs of Judy Garland. I do realize that's a stereotype. But I did not hear about the association of Judy and gay men until after I had come out in college. I first heard *Somewhere Over the Rainbow* as a preschooler, as part of the annual television showing of the *Wizard of Oz*. It has always been for me a song of hope amid despair, specifically I hope that the world doesn't always have to be the way it is, that somewhere, sometime, life can be different.

Along those same lines, the song *Somewhere* from *West Side Story* has always provided a feeling of hope. *There's a place for us, a time and place for us. Hold my hand and we are halfway there. Hold my hand and I'll take you there.* Even now thinking of it can bring tears to my eyes. I've always wanted a place where I would fit in, and be totally accepted. And for many years I've wanted to be part of an "us."

A song that thrilled me when I first heard it in my early teen years is Elton John's *Daniel*. It's a rare instance of a man singing a song about another man, a man expressing tender feelings about another man. At the time, I heard and understood the song as expressing romantic feelings, and took the phrase "Daniel my brother as a euphemism." I now know that the song was not written to mean anything of the kind, but has something to do with a war veteran, and furthermore, the lyrics were written by a heterosexual man, and not Elton. But at the time that I heard it, it was rare and precious, a validation for the feelings that I had.

Birmingham: I came out at the end of 1977. Elton had come out as bisexual in an interview the year before. This was a stunning admission. There were essentially no openly gay celebrities or public figures. This vitally important fact is often unknown or greeted with disbelief by young people today. It's so different from the life that they take for granted. But it's true. No one in public life could afford to be out, because it would be the end of their career. Ordinary people could not be out, because they risked arrest, getting fired from their job, being blacklisted from ever finding another job, being rejected by their families, and being insulted and assaulted by any heterosexual stranger or soon to be former friend. Some of these things happened to me.

For the same reason, there were no openly gay songs, or songs by gay celebrities. So gay people had to appropriate whatever was available from the wider culture. One song I remember from drag performances in the '70s is Shirley Bassey's hit from a few years previously, *This is My Life*. It communicates the theme of self-determination that is still important and is echoed in a number of other songs that are meaningful to me. Another drag number I remember from those years is Judy Garland's *The Man That Got*

Away. Hearing it still puts me in a trance, and lets me feel that someone else has shared my experience of constant longing for that ideal man.

Of course, the most meaningful and significant musical movement of the late '70s was disco. Disco is my life. I can't over emphasize the importance that disco had as the soundtrack of my life as a young openly gay man, the constant accompaniment to my every foray into the safe space of gay bars. In a sense every disco song is a song that lifts my spirits as a gay person. But I can mention a few specifically. *I Need a Man* by Grace Jones. *If My Friends Could See Me Now* by Linda Clifford. *I Am What I Am*, by the Village People. *Loving Is Really My Game* by Brainstorm, first, and then a cover version by Sylvester. *We Are Family* by Sister Sledge. All of these are songs I remember from my first years out. They express various aspects of my experience, and can lift my spirits even today.

Chicago: I moved to Chicago in 1980. Disco was still vital and relevant. Diana Ross sang *I'm Coming Out*, and we knew she had sung it just for us. There were so many songs and artists that lifted my spirits, it's hard to narrow it down. Donna Summer was the favorite and most popular. But the most special was Sylvester. He refused to be kept in the closet, and his unmistakable exuberance and joy of life that came across in every performance, made his body of work something apart from the often artificial and commercial minded songs that were popular at that time.

Showtunes became more relevant. Yes, another stereotype. Barbra Streisand *Don't Rain on my Parade* became the perpetual soundtrack to the vitally important annual gay pride parades. *We Kiss in a Shadow*, Rogers and Hammerstein's song from their 1950s *The King and I* has always had the theme of secret love, hidden from the world, but it became unforgettably breathtaking when I heard it sung by the all-male San Francisco Gay Men's Chorus in 1981. Openly gay Jerry Herman also wrote a song called *I Am What I Am*, carrying on the themes of self-determination and brave proclamation, for his 1983 show, *La Cage*. That same year, Gloria Gaynor sang it in a high energy dance version.

Gloria had already given us *I Will Survive*, among other songs in the '70s. But in the '80s that song took on new meaning as the perennial anthem for the community's determination to survive AIDS.

Openly gay Bronski Beat perfectly expressed the anguish and liberation of leaving an oppressive family of origin with their thrilling hit *Small Town Boy*, more recognizable with the shout of its opening line, "Tell me why?"

In various political actions in those years, I sang Holly Near's quiet anthem *Singing for our Lives*, with its first line, "We are a gentle, angry people." It's still true.

About every decade since has come an especially memorable meaningful song. *Pride (In the Name of Love)*, a medley by Clivilles and Cole.

Beautiful by Christina Aguilera. *Born This Way* by Lady Gaga. These are all songs that lift my spirit to this day. We are in great need right now of another one. – Bert Thompson

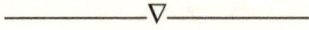

—————▽—————

San Francisco, CA (USA)

Although I wasn't much of a disco fan in the '70's (I was a rocker ... still am) I was living in the Castro when Sylvester rose to fame. My favorite song of his was *You Make Me Feel (Mighty Real)*. I had recently come out to myself and my new friends in San Francisco, and this song resonated with me. It was empowering! – Gary Borgstedt

—————▽—————

Chicago, IL (USA)

Well, I have to say that all of the Gay anthems of my youth are particularly lifting to me. When I am in a down mood there is nothing better than going back to the old days of disco and blasting that downer away. My all-time favorites that take me right back are, *We are Family*, *Disco Inferno*, and well if I really want to get it going I love, *Vertigo/Relight My Fire* Long Play... that build up to the vocals just gets me ready to party the day away. And then of course there is my one memory of riding in the Pride Parade in Chicago the year I won as American Leatherman in 2000. I was riding on the Hall of Fame float, I usually drove their car that carried the LGBT Mayor's Liaison from the Commission on Human Relations and an always Parade favorite Dawn Clark Netsch. But this year I got to ride the float, and as we pulled northbound on Halsted, the music on our float blared *I Am What I Am* and I could see the cheering crowds, it was breathtaking and yes, I did choke up a bit. What a magical moment, a real high point in my life as a gay Leatherman. – Dean Ogren

—————▽—————

Fayetteville, AR (USA)

The old Frank Sinatra song, *High Hopes*. I think a lot of times when things are really, really, dark and bleak, there's always hope. And as long as there's hope, I'm OK. – Renny

————▽————

Waverly, IA (USA)

Somewhere from *West Side Story* had special meaning to me as a gay person. During the AIDS epidemic *Bring Him Home* from *Les Miserables* seemed to be talking about gay men in the hospitals. During the '90s I discovered *Hold On* as sung by Bill McKinley. Finally, Michael Callen's *Let Me Go Home* about his readiness to pass from AIDS. – Robert Beck

————▽————

Chicago, IL (USA)

Hideaway by Erasure. It's a coming out story with a happy ending. – Drew

————▽————

North Carolina (USA)

Slave to the Rhythm by Grace Jones. Every time I hear that song it reminds me of the first time I went to a gay bar. Here I was, this 18 year-old kid from the mountains of North Carolina and I graduated college and I went to the big city. I became friends with a group of gay guys there. They took me to my first gay bar in Charlotte, North Carolina. They were having a drag show that night and there was this drag queen came out as Grace Jones who was just perfect, the look, the moves, it was just spellbinding. That was just incredible. That always gives me a happy memory every time I hear that song. – Randy

————▽————

(Bulgaria)

I don't really have an anthem that lifts my spirits, but I've always felt a particularly strong affinity for *It's a Sin* by the Pet Shop Boys. It came out at a time when I was struggling with family and religious issues related to my sexuality. For the same reason, *Losing My Religion* by REM also speaks to me at a fundamental level. – Louis Richard de Bourbon de Parme et de Savoie, Prince de la Pau

————▽————

Columbus, OH (USA)

Radical by Katie Curtis really grabbed me when I was still only several years being 'out' to myself and select friends, while I was living in hostile conservative Columbus, Ohio. Their daily newspaper had the NEWS headline: "Jesus Is Risen" on Easter for gods sake! I was younger, in-love, and scared and these lyrics really spoke to me as they still do:
"It's all right, we're gonna be fine
But let's give my mama and my daddy a little time
'Cause I've been good up 'till now
They see you and they think that I have changed somehow
But I'm not being radical when I kiss you
I don't love you to make a point
It's the hollow of my heart that cries when I miss you
And it keeps me alive when we're apart."
  – Lars von Keitz

————————▽————————

Chicago, IL (USA)

Being gay has nothing to do with good uplifting music. Music is universal and when at its best it uplifts the human spirit. Marvin Gaye's *What's Going On*. I remember hearing this song as a child and believing that one day in the future the things in this song would be fixed. Sadly, the lyrics are just as relevant, so we have not come very far since 1971. – Philip Bernal

————————▽————————

Rockford, IL (USA)

The song that lifts me up the most would be *Respect* from Aretha Franklin. I say this song because at my core respect is something I truly believe in. If you show me respect, I will return the same respect. Plus, as a community this is what we ask for from the wider world. And yes, there has been a lot of improvements the world over, but there are still many people and places that we need to gain respect. This is something as a community we should strive for. – Patrick J. Murphy III

————————▽————————

Seattle, WA (USA)

I have several songs that, to me, represent the LGBTQ experience. There is *I Will Survive* (Gloria Gaynor), *I Am What I Am* (from *La Cage Aux Folles*, the musical), *Smalltown Boy* (Bronski Beat – Jimmy Somerville). – Eric Andrews-Katz

—————▽—————

Frinton-on Sea, Essex (UK)

I suppose I'm supposed to put something cheesy like *Your Disco Needs You* by Kylie, or a standard like *Over The Rainbow* by Judy, or *The Man I Love* by Sophie Tucker, but for sheer depth, intelligence and lyricism, I'm gonna say *(Something Inside) So Strong*, by Labi Siffre. – Diesel Balaam

—————▽—————

Bellport, NY (USA)

I never really thought about it. You don't hear many LGBTQ songs in mainstream. That needs to change. You have to really search for artists that are LGBTQ. At least that is my experience. – Erin Michelle Miller

—————▽—————

Rancho Mirage, CA (USA)

Before writing this, all day I had the song *Freedom of the Heart* (Oodily, Oodily) stuck in my head, singing it endlessly. It's by Gwendolyn Sanford and the Good Time Gang (she's done music for *Orange Is the New Black*, if that helps). The song was featured in the unusual 2002 film *Chuck & Buck*. But THEN, while listening to a mix CD I made, a song from 1994 by Alphaville called *Apollo* came on, and that was it. That's all I could focus on. I always loved the song, but for some reason today it just surrounded me and enveloped me. Without trying to sound cliché, the chorus seems to grab you when Marian Gold belts out lines about rising from the ashes, growing like a rose from the ruins, having hope, and after all that, returning home. I believe he's just happier and feeling a bit clearer. I won't say reborn, that would be getting into the cliché realm. Believe me, I'm not into all the Four Agreements and self-actualization stuff. Yes, I do Reiki and have seen how it has helped cancer patients I've worked with, but ... I just don't walk around namaste-ing everywhere. I guess that's why some people who are more serious about spiritual/mystical things are baffled by me. And while the song *Soft King Kong* by Krister Linder is actually my anthem, *Apollo* by Alphaville is my song of hope and moving forward. Do yourself a favor and listen to that song. It builds, and builds, and BUILDS over its six minute 10 second length that you're belting out that song along with Marian that, well at least for me, I start to lose my voice a bit. It's like an emotional workout. And when I want to be reminded that I am incredible, the other uplifting song for me is *INCREDIBLE* by Gravitonas. – Todd Jaeger

—————▽—————

Hilton Head, SC (USA)

It would probably be *Wind Beneath My Wings*, just because it's very tough to go on this journey, no matter what the journey is, without support. When I do get a little down – which is rare, but I do – usually somebody is there to encourage me to keep going. So that's my wind, my friends and support system. – Andee

—————▽—————

Chicago, IL (USA)

Oh absolutely, *You Make Me Feel (Mighty Real)* by Sylvester. Hands down, every time. It's the embodiment of freedom. Sylvester was a non-gender conforming person before there was even a name for it. She just went out there and did whatever and killed it every single time. I go to Smart Bar every week – well, I did, before they shut it down temporarily – and any time I hear any strain of that song, like once I was getting ready to leave because I wasn't having a good time, and then I heard it and literally pushed my way through the crowd, something I never do … there was my friend standing there expectantly because he knew … he just knows. It's just the most beautiful uplifting song. I was in love once, just once, despite my many relationships. We met on the dancefloor and that's where it started … and that song reminds me what it's like to be in love, to have a partner in crime, and you're all in on that dancefloor. I lived those lyrics. I grew up in Chicago a rock 'n' roll brat in the 1980s. It was all that Disco Sucks nonsense. You were not to like disco and if you did you were a fag or a girl or whatever. I was aware of the song for a very long time, but it wasn't until I got into House music that I became super-specifically aware of Sylvester. For the longest time disco was just the Bee Gees but there's so much more than that. – Jeff Ramone

—————▽—————

Flint, MI (USA)

The theme from *Polyester*. It's sung by Tab Hunter and Deborah Harry. It's the opening of the movie *Polyester* with Divine. It's about suburban madness. It mocks suburbia and heterosexuality in general. "Polyester, this is your life, Francine." I saw that movie at the Butterfield drive-in theater in Flint, Michigan. I grew up outside of there before they poisoned the water. A lot of people think I have lead poisoning if they're around me long enough. – Jim

———————∇———————

Chicago, IL (USA)

Heather Small, *Proud*. It was already my feelgood song and then the Gay Games came to Chicago. I performed with the ROTC Chicago color guard for the opening ceremonies and during dress rehearsal we finished our performance on the field and were being guided off the field and I heard the music of this song start. I looked up and she was on one of the raised stages on the field. I stopped dead in my tracks. I don't get star struck, but I nearly geeked out. I was already swimming in endorphins from our performance and HERE SHE WAS! I stood there gobsmacked but as usual, dress rehearsals for singers are often just sound cues and level checks. She didn't sing. I left the field and already knew it would take a team of armed guards to keep me from stopping during the actual ceremonies. Opening ceremonies came, we performed, I stopped again by her stage and just watched. She was playing to the crowd but noticed me (I'm 6'7" and had a white sparkly rifle in my hands – I stood out) But she kept smiling at me as I must have had this dreamy goofball look on my face. As she finished I started walking away. She caught up to me and said how much she had been wowed at OUR performance. The experience cemented the song for me and THE Pride song. – Chris Grace

———————∇———————

Chicago, IL (USA)

Well, this is a loaded question. If you get me started talking about music, I'm likely to make you a playlist and go into deep discussions, but the song that lifts me and helps me flip the bird to the homophobes is *Family Affair* by Mary J. Blige. She sings:

"Don't need no hateration, holleration
In this dancerie
Let's get it percolatin', while you're waiting
So just dance for me
We don't need, don't need, no haters
Just try to love one another
We just want why'all have a good time
No more drama in your life
Work real hard to make a dime
If you got beef, your problem, not mine
Leave all that BS outside
We're gonna celebrate all night."
And I am off dancing – spinning into the music and almost believing that there is a world where people all feel like family and no one does anything just for drama. – andKevin

———————∇———————

San Jose, CA (USA)

The song that lifts my spirits is *Eye of the Tiger*. It gets you pumped, gets you ready for the day. And Dean Winchester does a rendition of it in *Supernatural*. I don't think it's got anything to do with LGB or trans but that's the answer I'm going to give. – Kelsey Brookes

———————∇———————

Palm Springs, CA (USA)

There are two, actually, that spring to mind immediately – first, the song *Proud* by Heather Small, and immediately on its heels, *Born This Way* by Lady Gaga. Both of these songs just scream "pride" to me. Another contender, from shortly after I came out, *Smalltown Boy* by Bronski Beat. The lyrics resonated deeply with me, as did the music video made by the band. This song still makes me feel a big tingle of pride even though it's more about homophobia and hate. It reminds me that, in retrospect, the rewards of coming out were far greater than the risks we took to be ourselves back when the risks were far worse than they are today, and it spotlighted for me the importance of our families-of-choice. – D. Warner

———————∇———————

Chicago, IL (USA)
San Francisco, CA (USA)

Of course, like 90+% of gay men my age, the immediate response would be *Somewhere Over the Rainbow* as sung by Judy Garland or Patti LaBelle, or maybe another song about another somewhere, *There's a Place for Us* from *West Side Story* written by the bisexual Leonard Bernstein and gay Stephen Sondheim. Always inspirational, even used for straight weddings, as the hope for that somewhere in which we as queer people can love freely and might have peace and justice. But a more "real" song, more related to my actually political-sexual coming out in San Francisco is the disco song *"Last Dance ...save that last dance, that last chance for love."* sung by disco queen, ironically later turned Fundamentalist homophobe, Donna Summer. As unfortunate as her betrayal was, I can't but be transported when hearing that song to almost any gay bar or disco of the late 1970s. The main memory of dancing in a Polk Street bar, where I first took to streets in a queer protest, to a neighborhood bar in the Mission District, at South Van Ness and 25th, the Phone Booth, near where I lived in a second-floor walkup flat. There's got to be a joke there, "How many dancing queens can you fit into a phone booth?" Many nights we knew it was closing time when Donna started belting out her cry for true love, as did we lip syncing "to hold me, to scold me," hoping to go home with that special "one for me" "guiding me," dancing out into the dark bay's night for that "last chance for romance, tonight." – David Hatfield Sparks

———————▽———————

Chicago, IL (USA)

When I was in my twenties, I was a big dancer at Dugan's Bistro, anything by Donna Summer you would find me on the dance floor and most any other song that was played. Probably why I have a hearing issue nowadays. Another favorite song was *So in Love with You*. Reminds me of my first lover. – Dennis Hardenstein

———————▽———————

West Lafayette IN (USA)
New York NY (USA)

Two, actually. I'm a musical comedy queen, so my favorite songs are from Broadway. Whenever I am feeling down these days, I recall a time in grad school, back in the '70s, when Sondheim's *Anyone Can Whistle* was my national anthem. This was a time when I was heavily closeted, a hollow intellectual becoming an expert in desiccated and obscure eighteenth-century literature but incapable of having a real emotional life: "What's hard is simple. What's natural comes hard." I have since learned to "whistle" – very loudly, in fact – but that song always reminds me of how much freer and happier I am now; hearing the song now is like looking at an old photo of myself as an unhappy, lonely, gawky teenager and thinking, "Look how far I've come!" Now, I'm the one who frequently teaches others how to whistle, how to let go, lower their guard, learn to be free. (Thank you, Mr. Sondheim!)

And of course, like every other card-carrying musical queen, I can NOT listen to Jerry Herman's *I Am What I Am* without goosebumps and/or tears: "I am what I am. I am my own special creation." I saw *La Cage aux Folles* in its original run in NYC and recall George Hearn blasting that song out of the park at the end of the first act. Every gay person in the audience (there were a few!) stopped breathing for the duration of the song, including me. And when Herne defiantly threw his wig at Gene Berry as he exited – Jesus! (Thank you, Mr. Herman). – William Demaree

————▽————

New Orleans, LA (USA)

Lady Ga Ga *Born This Way* or Bowie *Rebel Rebel.* – Terry Gaskins

————▽————

Palm Springs, CA (USA)

That's a hard one, and it's only hard because I listen to so much music. Being a musician, I look at things differently. Growing up, I listened to a lot of gay anthems. There's a lot of songs that touch me personally that aren't necessarily gay, because I'm into heavy metal. For gay, I would say *Born This Way* by Lady Gaga is uplifting. – David Vega (Lucifers Axe)

————▽————

New York, NY (USA)

Melina Mercouri's *Never on Sunday*. My parents had that kind of album when I was a kid. Whenever I could get to the hi-fi, when it was unattended, I would put on *Never on Sunday* and I would dance around the living room. – Keith Kollinicos (Missa Distic)

Song that lifts your spirits as a LGBTQ person?

————▽————

La Mesa, Tequendama Province (Colombia)

Champion from RuPaul. I actually downloaded it illegally and heard it on my desktop. I'd also say *Get Right* from Jennifer López, I heard it at a no ID party they used to throw for young guys who were not 18 yet, which is the age you become an adult here in Colombia. That song from JLo was the ultimate pussycat dancing hit for young queers back then. – Cristian

————▽————

Louisiana (USA)

I Got Life from *Hair,* the musical. – Katorri A.

————▽————

Hollister, CA (USA)

We Are Family, a typical one. I probably heard it on the radio. I think it was out before I came out. I think it was the late '70s that came out. I didn't come out until '83. – Spike

————▽————

Green Bay, WI (USA)

1978. There are three songs that come to mind and all three were released around the same time I worked in Green Bay, Wisconsin: The late 1970's.

    I Will Survive. At the time, I was married to a woman; an example of me doing what I thought was the "right thing" as a straight man. Problem was, I was a GAY man. Getting a divorce at that time was tearing me apart. *I Will Survive* became my anthem.

    Shortly thereafter, I fell in love. Or lust. Hearing Dionne Warwick singing *I'll Never Love This Way Again* spoke to me. I'd never felt the kind of euphoria I did when I fell in love with another man for the first time.

    Finally, there's *All the Time.* Again, Dionne Warwick, same album. It begins "All the time I thought there's only me … crazy in a way, no one else could be. I would've given everything I own … if someone would have said 'You're not alone.'" It summed up the loneliness and longing I'd felt thinking I was the only man who felt the way I did. I can hear any one of those songs today and they whisk me back to the earliest days of my realizing I was gay. – Steve Kmetko

—————▽—————

Grand Rapids, MI (USA)

Stars on 54, *If You Could Read My Mind* and Kevin Sharp, *Nobody Knows*. – Mark S

—————▽—————

Cleveland, OH (USA)

Anything by my divas – Cher, Dolly, Diana, and Madonna. The music of those ladies always lifts my spirits. – Roger

—————▽—————

Oxnard, CA (USA)
Los Angeles, CA (USA)

I would have to say Donna Summer's *I Feel Love*. It takes me back to a time when I was happy. It's a song you get lost in, it puts you in a trance and you feel good. It takes me back to that place of feeling good and feeling free. Feeling like it doesn't matter. Just be who you are, dance how you can, have a good time. It's always affected me that way. The first time I heard that song I was in a disco dance class with my mother. My dad wouldn't disco dance, so she took me to her disco dance class. At the same time, we were disco dancing to YMCA and things like that. Lots of fun. As to the first club I heard it in, it was a couple of years after that at Probe in Los Angeles. I remember being at this huge dance party with all these hot sweaty guys. When that song came on, nothing mattered. People were on the dancefloor and they had a really good time, screamed and yelled, threw up their tambourines … the club just changed. Everything changed, that's always stuck with me. For that moment I was the same as everyone else. – Crusher

—————▽—————

New York, NY (USA)

I have a million songs running through my head here, *More, More, More* and, of course, Judy Garland singing *Somewhere Over the Rainbow*. – Greg Day

—————▽—————

Chicago, IL (USA)

Friends Unknown by Donna Summer. Being a performer in the Chicago gay community for over 25 years, I am inspired by all the many fans who supported my ventures. This song captures the essence of my thoughts. – Mercury

—————▽—————

Salt Lake City, UT (USA)

I Am What I Am by Gloria Gaynor because it's an anthem of all of our lives. – David Hardy

—————▽—————

Cathedral City, CA (USA)

The only song that gives me a lot of spirit is by Elton John, sung by George Michael, *Don't Let the Sun Go Down on Me*. It was an Elton John original song, but Elton John and George Michael sang it together at an AIDS concert back in the '80s. He just took off with that song, I love that song. – Marcous

—————▽—————

Kansas (USA)
Albuquerque, NM (USA)

Going back to the disco days there were some songs that were fun. In the '70s it really was a good time for us. But a specific song? I don't have a specific song. I was in college from '73 to '77. I moved from Kansas to Albuquerque soon after that. It was interesting. There were a lot of gay bars there and a large drag queen population. I was surprised to see that. – Guy Seiler

—————▽—————

Chicago, IL (USA)

There are many, as music is a great place to go for a boost of energy or a nice pity party. I've just turned 60, so it's the songs of the past that warm my heart the most, because they bring me back to what was happening when I first heard them. Madonna's *Express Yourself* was an anthem. And a nice pity party wouldn't be complete with a few dozen spins of Janice Ian's *At Seventeen*. – MrZor

———————∇———————

Redwood Valley, CA (USA)
Tallahassee, FL (USA)

Collecting, supporting, and celebrating LGBTQ artists by sharing with friends and social media sites since the 1970s, I have been building a queer musical archive of vinyl, audiotape, and CD, which I intend to donate to GLBT Historical Society in San Francisco.

It's monumental to choose just one, but I'd start with the two that first excited me soon after my official coming out process that began in 1969: *Looking for a Boy Tonight*, by Chris Robison (Gypsy Frog Records, 1973), and *Glad to Be Gay*, by Tom Robinson (EMI, 1978).

My life experience was further fueled by discovering Sylvester in San Francisco in the mid 1970s. His song, *You Make Me Feel (Mighty Real)*, buoyed my being at the 1987 March on Washington for Lesbian and Gays Rights, which brought hundreds of thousands of us to our feet.

The music of historically-verified woman-loving woman, Hildegard of Bingen (1098-1179, a German nun) is the earliest verified same gender celebrating music I have found. Although I'm not religious, hearing her beautiful music celebrate the body of the mortal Mother Mary moves my spirit forward.

Other early recordings in North American culture that have spoken to me and my community include:
- *The Lavender Song* – Arno Billing/Mischa Spoliansky and Kurt Schwabach (1920), recorded in 1998 by Ute Lemper
- *Don't Ask!* – George and Ira Gershwin (1926, first known popular song to use the word gay to mean homosexual, from the musical *Oh Kay!)*
- *Prove It on Me Blues* – Ma Rainey (1928)
- *Green Carnations* – Sir Noel Coward (1929)

And, of course, *Over the Rainbow* - Harold Arlen and E.Y. Harburg (1939), recorded by Judy Garland

Cut me off if you need to ;-) but hopefully others will mention:
- *Secret Love* – Sammy Fain and Paul Francis Webster (1953), recorded by Doris Day, George Michael

- *Ooh! Aah! Oh! (This is Love!)* – Lee and Seelen (1955), recorded by Johnnie Ray
- *Somewhere* (From *West Side Story*) - Bernstein/Sondheim (1961), recorded by Barbra Streisand
- *A Time for Us* (from *Romeo and Juliet*) - Larry Kusik and Eddie Snyder (1968), recorded by Johnny Mathis
- *Lola* – Ray Davies (1970), recorded by The Kinks
- *Walk on the Wild Side* – Lou Reed (1972)
- *Looking for a Boy Tonight* – Tom Robinson (1973)
- *Leaping Lesbians* – Sue Fink (1977)
- *Ode to a Gym Teacher* – Meg Christian (1977)
- *We Can Dance if I Want to, I Will Survive* – Freddie Perren and Dino Fekaris (1978), recorded by Gloria Gaynor
- *YMCA* – The Village People (1978)
- *Singing for Our Lives* - Holly Near (1978, after the murders of Harvey Milk and Mayor Moscone)
- *We are Family* – Bernard Edwards and Nile Rodgers (1979), recorded by Sister Sledge
- *Go West* – The Village People (1979)
- *I'm Coming Out* – Nile Rodgers and Bernard Edwards (1979), recorded by Diana Ross
- *I Am What I Am* – Jerry Herman (1983), recorded by Gloria Gaynor, Shirley Bassey, et al
- *(Something Inside) So Strong* - Labi Siffre (1985), also recorded by The Flirtations
- *True Colors* – Cyndi Lauper (1986)
- *Be on the Safe Side* – Romanovsky and Phillips (1988)
- *Homophobia* – Chumbawamba (1994)
- *If There's a God She's a Queen* – Romanovsky and Phillips (1995)
- *I Kissed a Girl* – Jill Sobule (1996)
- *Rain* – Erasure (1997)
- *You Can't Take the Color out of Colorado* – from Howard Crabtree's *When Pigs Fly* (1997)
- *Gay, Straight or Bi* - Kinsey Sicks (1999)
- *Proud* – Heather Small (2000)
- *Beautiful* – Christina Aguilera (2002)
- *Freedom* – Yolanda (2004)
- *Everybody's Gonna Love Today* – Mika (2007)
- *Born This Way* – Lady Gaga (2011)

That brings us into the late 2000's when hopefully other responders will mention artists like Macklemore, Sam Smith, Mary Lambert, Ty Herndon, Ben Platt, Adam Lambert, Troye Sivan, Lil Nas X, Taylor Swift, Ricky Martin, Indigo Girls, Brandi Carlile, as well as pioneers like Phil Ochs, Holly Near, Chris Williamson, Bronski Beat, Pet Shop Boys, Ferron, k. d. Lang … OMG what a massive question to start with! – T. Lark Letchworth

─────────▽─────────

New York, NY (USA)

There's several but the one that does the most is *Knock on Wood*. I don't remember who sang it, but it was back in the disco days. – Juan-manuel Alonso

─────────▽─────────

Norfolk, VA (USA)

Believe it or not, Christmas songs. *Jingle Bells, O Holy Night* are two of my favorites. There's another song by Martha Stephens, I can't think of the name of the song. She's a gay songwriter and she had a song published and that song went to every songbook in the country. When these churches found out she was gay, they ripped out those pages in the book and mailed them to her. It was a very soothing song. I wish I could remember the title. – David Hayes

─────────▽─────────

Melbourne, Victoria (Australia)
Darlinghurst, New South Wales (Australia)
Sydney, New South Wales (Australia)

That would have to be Gloria Gaynor's *I Am What I Am*. Despite coming out in the late 1970s, I danced to it in the '80s at both Mandate in Melbourne, and the Midnight Shift in Sydney. It is a true "fuck you" song to everyone who tries to push their own hate and agenda onto anyone who is different, and just trying to live their own life in peace, and security. Even as I sit here typing this, I can zoom back to 1983s Midnight Shift, it's sunken dance floor with banks of speakers at each corner, overseen by the DJs box situated in the narrow area to one side of the floor called "the meat rack," as this is where you stood if you wanted to be picked up … or groped. At the opening bars "I am what I am, I am my own special creation, so come take a look, give me the hook or the ovation … " there would be a surging mass of males charging onto the dance floor. It was like a magnet! The floor would be vibrating from the bass, lights would be moving up and down on their rigs, flashing and swirling their coloured light through the dense swirling mist from the fog machine. Everyone was on the same plane, smiling, ecstatic. Naked, sweating torso's, some guys stripped down to jockstraps, amid a cacophony of blasting whistles, banging tambourines, amyl bottles screed to noses, or guys wearing a bandanna soaked in ethyl chloride. Others would be sprinkling talc, and fan dancers would gyrate from the tops of speakers. Everyone mouthed the words as they danced … this was our liberation anthem, the song that told the world exactly who we were, and we were proud of it! Hearing the track will evoke tears these days … not because it's sad, but because it invokes one of the most exciting, glorious, liveliest times of my life. One can never go back, and I know that … but oh … just for 10 minutes would be glorious! – Tim Alderman

———————▽———————

Chicago, IL (USA)

There are several songs that are standards, like *I Will Survive,* which was a very empowering song when I was coming out. I associated that with my background being in theater, a lot of friends were dying from AIDS-related complications. *I Will Survive* is about being strong and getting through. It wasn't only a gay anthem, but also it was a bigger picture. There are other songs back in the day that you took on, like *True Colors* by Cyndi Lauper. I love that song, about being yourself, showing who you are, come alive, be 100%, give the bountifulness of who you are. – Greg R. Baird

———————▽———————

Cathedral City, CA (USA)

Shining Star by Earth, Wind and Fire. This soulful song has helped me feel more grounded since high school. It celebrates all humans and our full potential no matter who we are. – Paul Harris

———————▽———————

St. Cloud, MN (USA)

Just one? Music has always been such a big part of my life, whether getting through good times or bad. I grew up in the 1970s-1980s and my musical tastes are still stuck there. I always dance to Diana Ross' *I'm Coming Out* and the Village People's *Go West*. I spent a lot of time as a kid with my older brothers listening to music with them. My oldest brother was an Elton John and Queen fan, and, somehow, he knew that all of them were gay before that officially came out. I felt it too from them.

Probably the queerest song/music video that had the most impact on me in my youth was *That's the Way I Like It* by Pete Burns and Dead or Alive. I was so socially awkward as a kid and felt like a freak most of the time, and here was someone who had wacked out hair like mine and was a woman and a man at the same time, working out, not going to take anyone's shit any more! I liked Pete Burns better than Boy George because of that. Boy George was all vulnerable singing *Do You Really Want to Hurt Me* and all girly, and Pete Burns was going to rip your face off. I could not verbalize it at the time, but at twelve-thirteen years old, that was the type of queer I wanted to be. A rip your face off, unapologetic queer person who could tower over people and beat them up if they had to. Keep that body strong. I lift my weights regularly because of that song.

I wish there were more lesbians out there who wrote music I could relate to. I feel like a bad lesbian somehow because I can't connect with most lesbian performers. Give me Pussy Riot's *Vagina*, though. That is the lesbian feminist anthem. They are the strongest baddest bitches of music because they are activists first and artists second. They will die fighting for freedom and justice for all, for civil rights, for the elimination of unjust incarceration and police brutality. I drove through a snowstorm to see them perform live in St Paul, stood right up front ... they have my heart, and if they told me to march somewhere with a firearm and a 50 pound pack on my back to some war I would. – Rachel Wexelbaum

---------------∇---------------

Napa Valley, CA (USA)

There is, it is the Cure's *Close to Me*. The first time I really listened to it, I was house sitting up in Napa. For the first time I was able to spend a little time, more than 10 or 15 minutes when my parents were gone, in female clothing. That song played and I felt free and alive and to this day it's remarkable, it's my favorite song. Saw them in concert, love the Cure, that whole gender spectrum, being able to see that in the '80s, with Robert Smith and goth that were happening when I was growing up. I always wished I could be that kind of dark and gothic, but never could. The moment you start breaking rules and going outside the lines, you might tip somebody off. – Serafine Sawyer

---------------∇---------------

(Germany)

Fucking Around the World – Astro Axolotl
Mein schönstes Kleid – Früchte des Zorns
Baby Revolution – Stereo Total
Dicks Sucken – Trailer Park
Wenn ich sing salambo und sie nennen much tunte k hoffmann irrenanstalt – Rio Reiser

– Cornelius Günther Körn

———————∇———————

Dallas, TX (USA)

Early '70s. *This is My Life* as sung by Shirley Bassey. When I first started going to bars, back in 1972 in Dallas, Texas, there was a bar called the Bayou Landing, there was a drag show every Sunday night (with $1.00 beer and hamburger buffet!) Anyway, among the most popular entertainers was a beautiful young black man, "Sajé" (I'm not sure of the spelling). He did great impressions of Diana Ross and Dionne Warwick, but his signature act was to Shirley Bassey's *This is My Life*, where he opened in a full black gown, wig, opera length black gloves and high heels and by the end had thrown off everything but his tight black pants. The crowd would go wild. It was a beautiful and powerful statement of what most of us felt, but dared not do – be who we were. – Michael Pickel

———————∇———————

Chicago, IL (USA))

Let Me Take You Dancing by Bryan Adams. – Mark Contornoc

———————∇———————

Cork, Munster (Ireland)

Mama Cass Elliot's recording of *Make Your Own Kind of Music*. It's the anthem of my life.
  "Nobody can tell you there's only one song worth singing. They may try and tell you, because it hangs them up to see someone like you. Make your own kind of music. Sing your own special song. Make your own kind of music, even if nobody else sings along." – David Clayton

———————▽———————

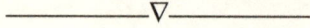

Milwaukee, WI (USA)

1977. *I Feel Love* by Donna Summer. When I "came out" in 1977, I went to a gay bar in Milwaukee, WI, called Kisses. I was shaking inside. It was new to me, all the flashing lights, people watching. When my date Tom arrived, this song played, and we went to the dance floor. I started to relax. I remember his goofy smile on his bearded face as we danced together. Maybe that's why it lifts my spirits. I associate it with freedom. – Tony Earl

———————▽———————

King, NC (USA)

Before I came out of the closet, I was in a traditional marriage with three small children. My wife and I both served and worked in a conservative church. The thought of standing up to the church and coming out back in the late 1970's and early 1980's seemed near-impossible to contemplate.

The one song that got me through this and makes me smile, even now, realizing how *right* the decision was to come out and be honest is from the movie, *Yentl.* The song is: *No Matter What Happens It Can't Be the Same Anymore.* It is no exaggeration that I played that song hundreds of times over and over during that time of struggle and it gave me the courage to do what I knew in my heart was the path to take. – Ron Cline

———————▽———————

Milwaukee, WI (USA)

Anne Murray, *I Just Fall in Love Again.* The first slow dance for me with another woman who ended up being my (now deceased) domestic partner of 33+ years. – Sherrie Howe

———————▽———————

Fort Lauderdale, FL (USA)

I have to go back to my youth and say the disco version of *I Am What I Am* from *La Cage Aux Folles*, it brings back that feeling of just coming out and feeling invincible. Currently *For Good* from *Wicked,* it's the song I want played at my memorial service because it will make people cry AND says exactly how I feel about the people in my life. – Rick Karlin

———————∇———————

Charlottetown, Prince Edward Island (Canada)

Absolutely *Heart of Glass* by Blondie from *Parallel Lines*, 1978. As a small town, closeted 14-year-old queer in Canada trying to figure myself out in the late 1970's, this timeless, ethereal track was my life preserver and spiritual escape to a New York City filled with sex, art, danger, acceptance, and opportunity, that may or may not have ever really existed, but that helped me deal with the ill-fitting life I was living regardless. – Dave Stewart

———————∇———————

Worcester, MA (USA)
(Pakistan)

For me, Hozier's *Take Me to Church* is a song that has always brought out the pain in me. I love this song for how it was able to shine light on the homophobic violence that exists in this world, which is often ignored by the mainstream cis/hetero society. –Salman

———————∇———————

New York, NY (USA)

As a DJ, music has not always been important, but it very often acts as, and serves as, signposts for moments in my life. As a young queen in NYC, I went dancing at the Gay Activists' Alliance Firehouse. It was one of the only places I could get into without showing ID. I was 13 years old. So many of those songs I danced to hold real significant memories for me but probably none more than *Ain't No Mountain High Enough* by Diana Ross. Folks would camp on the dance floor and act like Miss Ross and it was fabulous. My parents and their friends never acted out songs like that when they heard songs they liked.

Then later as a DJ I formed attachments to songs – actually many – and probably because of the influence of drugs on my disco psyche, sometimes I would experience sensations that were almost religious, so laden were they with sentiment and feeling. These songs are:

1) *My Love is Free* by Double Exposure
2) *Love Power* by Luther Vandross
3) *Don't Leave Me This Way* by Teddy Pendergrass
4) *Saturday Night/Sunday Morning* by Thelma Houston

5) *Changing* by Sharon Ridley
6) *Just Be Good to Me* by SOS Band
7) *I'm Coming Out* by Diana Ross
8) *Victim* by Candi Staton

And then there are those rock anthems

1) *Walk on The Wild Side* by Lou Reed
2) *Because the Night* by Patti Smith
3) *Glad to Be Gay* by the Tom Robinson Band
4) *TVC15* by David Bowie
5) *Sorrow* by David Bowie
6) *Ball and Chain* by Janis Joplin
7) *I Need a Man to Love Me* by Janis Joplin
8) *Lovers Will* by Bonnie Raitt
9) *Silver Lining* by Bonnie Raitt
10) *Cry Like a Rainstorm* by Linda Rondstadt
11) *Memo from Turner* by Mick Jagger (from the movie *Performance*)
12) *I Hope You Dance* by LeAnn Rimes

– Sr. Freida Peoples aka DJ Chrysler Sheldon

———————∇———————

DID YOU HAVE A MENTOR(S) IN THE LGBTQ COMMUNITY AND IF SO, WHAT DID THEY TEACH YOU?

Chicago, IL (USA)

I've had several mentors, some were partners I had over the years, one was a good friend of a partner. He was in the leather community, Master John. The lesson he taught me was not to be a dick. When you're young you can be very judgmental. He sat me down one day and said, "Don't be a dick. Everybody has their own issues and problems and their own preferences, take people as they are." I had other guys ... my first regular lover, who was 10 years older than me. He taught me a lot about how to have sex with men. The desire was there, but the mechanics weren't. Learning what your body can do, what it's happy to do, or likes doing. – Steve

------------∇------------

Chicago, IL (USA)

Yes, the Bearded Lady. BL and I danced at Coconuts. At that time, I was celibate, dancing, and questioning. BL used to call me his straight husband. He used to beat anybody that came within 10 feet of me, with his fan. He had a crush on me, an ongoing thing. He showed me the ropes. When I had a question, I went to him or Mother Carol. She gave me some good advice, saving me from getting picked up by Jeffrey Dahmer at Carol's Speakeasy. I was on my roller skates ready to go to Coconuts. It was about 1979. It was quarter beer night and this guy was buying me beers and I'd never been with a guy. He just seemed like a lumberjack, cute looking. I thought, "Oh I like that," he's not real queeny, blond hair, blue eyes. He started buying me drinks. Then he asked me, "I'm from Wisconsin, would you like to go up for the weekend after you're done dancing on Saturday." I'm considering it, "That's great, I can get away from the city, and this guy is kind of backwoods and good looking." I passed it by Mother Carol and she said, "I don't know what it is about him James, but I don't like him." I didn't realize it was him until 30 years later in a book. A policeman was very into all this and he showed me this book and it had a picture of him at the end of the bar looking exactly like he looked … I'm like, "Oh my God, that's him." I'm a little slow on the take. I didn't realize it was him until years later. So she saved my life. Like I said, there's always been a queen that I would ask. Even when I traveled to Puerto Rico, I would go up to the big queen at the end of the bar who knew everybody, and I'd say, "OK is this person good?" To me that's the role they fill in the community, at least in my life. I'm very happy that I've known some fierce queens who knew that I was a little naïve. – James Scalfani

————————▽————————

Memphis, TN, (USA)
Seattle, WA (USA)

There was a couple, whose names I would rather not share, who were very important to my growth as a gay man in a hostile society. I learned to be political, actively working against racism and homophobia. I also learned about music, all kinds of music. The two of them had a massive LP collection, and they shared many, many songs, well-known and obscure. I wouldn't have the appreciation for '60s rock, soul blues, and female vocalists that I do if it weren't for them. I've known them since 1977. One of them has passed away, may he rest in peace. The other is still patient enough to stay in touch. – Oran Walker

————————▽————————

Detroit, MI (USA)

Even though I knew people who were older and wiser, I didn't have a person who I could have considered my mentor. I would have to say that David Bowie came the closest to that role in my life at that time. Andy Warhol comes to mind as well, but I think I'm confusing mentor with influence, although the two things are similar. But, now that I've given it some more thought, I recalled someone who sort of took me under her wing while I was still in high school. My high school was in downtown Detroit, so we had lots of cool places to go after school. One of those spots was a 1950s themed eatery that was favored by us baby queens (drama dept, art dept and fashion dept). One of the waitresses there was a tranny that I became friendly with. Her name was Tara. I remember that other people just thought there was something odd about her, but not me. By that time, because of my love for magazines, I was a fan of Candy Darling, Holly Woodlawn, Hibiscus and, of course, Divine. Tara took me to my first gay bar. It was called the Casbah, and it was a dyke bar in Detroit that, now that I look back on it, was popular with men and women and everything in between. That's why Tara would go there. There were not many places where a pre-op transsexual could go and be accepted in 1974. Not long after we met, Tara was murdered by her pimp. Her murder was written about in the *Michigan Chronicle*, a black newspaper, because she was buried as a woman, something unheard of in those days. A beautiful person, gone too soon. – Terence Smith (Joan Jett Blakk)

———————∇———————

Midwestern City (USA)

Have had multiple mentors professional, spiritual, and personal. The most important thing I learned from them was to love and accept myself for all of who I am and to respect all persons unless they cannot respect me or others. – Anonymous

———————∇———————

Chicago, IL (USA)

I have to say I was fortunate to have many mentors in the community, that meant a great deal to me in my many circles of friends. Gary Chichester and RJ Chaffin were always good to take me under their wings and show me the fun side of our community, that was not all about the drinking, and party drugs and such, and just being kind of a "party girl" as I was in the day. Gary always made sure that I had things to do cause if I was busy or had a purpose or something I was doing, it kept me off the excessive over-drinking. He kind of says he pulled me out of the gutter and put me to work and showed me that being a part of the community was so much more than booze and boys.

Chuck Renslow was a great mentor and friend and lead me to see that being a part of the leather community was not just the play/hard SM side but there was a way to be a part of it and learn more from great men in that community that seemed to be, in my early years, more of an underground sort of thing.

Walter Klingler, who also showed me ways to have fun, and enjoy the world of leather, and be a leader in that community. Thom Dombkowski, who's love of leather and leathermen, showed me that you can love more than one, and not feel guilty about it. He also showed me that it is important to live that philosophy of each one teach one. – Dean Ogren

—————▽—————

San Francisco, CA (USA)
Chicago, IL (USA)

There were several. I worked for a law firm when I was going to college. Most of the guys who worked there were gay. It was right when AIDS was starting. They taught me it was ok to be campy but you had to know when not to be. Being gay didn't mean being a miserable bitch all the time to everyone. You certainly could be professional, and if you were professional, when you did tell someone you were gay, they had to stop and think before responding, they can't just dismiss you as being a fag or a queer. – Mike

—————▽—————

Columbus, OH (USA)

I used to have long talks with a Mexican transgender person called Nikki, living when she could as a woman in this conservative Midwestern town. I felt safe talking to her. She gave me the strength to be who I really was. If she could walk down the street in a dress, heels, and make-up, I could surely have the courage to be a gay man. Screw what all the townsfolk thought! – Lars von Keitz

—————▽—————

San Francisco, CA (USA)

In 1976, shortly after coming out, I was hired to work in the kitchen at a gay restaurant. I knew nothing about gay culture. The other guys working there were well seasoned queens, and they taught me all sorts of things about being gay. One day I asked one of them what a "queen" was and he laughed and told me that I was a queen. So was he! These fellow employees were truly supportive of me and humored by my naivete. The owner, "Uncle" Bert, treated me like a son. – Gary Borgstedt

—————▽—————

Fayetteville, AR (USA)

I kind of wish I had. The very first person I was with as an adult, the person I lost my virginity to … he showed me the ropes. He taught me that you need to cut loose and have fun. As far as anything to do with sex, I was pretty wound tightly. Just to relax and have a good time in the moment. I met him May 31, 1975 at a party. – Renny

————————▽————————

Lexington, NC (USA)

I had several. I felt very lucky when I was coming out. There were these gay men that I got to know in this tiny North Carolina town near Charlotte who showed me how to connect with other people and things to do. Then once I did, then I started volunteering for a gay newspaper based in Raleigh, doing simple news stories, interviewing people. The editor of that paper was a mentor to me. He offered me a lot of advice. Then I got involved in many community organizations and had several mentors there. I was really lucky to have a lot of people that I looked up to and admired and gave me good advice when I was coming out. That was in Lexington, near Charlotte, famous for its BBQs and their right-wing nutcase sheriff who was later arrested for operating a drug ring. He had his own reality TV show for a while and in the middle of all that he got arrested and several of his deputies were operating this drug ring. They were selling steroids and all kinds of crap to people. – Randy

————————▽————————

London (UK)

I never actually had an LGBT mentor, but one person who really made me feel at peace with myself and my sexuality was the late Ava Gardner, who was my neighbour in London. Although she was desperately ill and there was an enormous age gap between, she took me under her wing, introduced me to her friends – Vincent Price mainly, who was also an occasional neighbour – and she showed me how to simply not care what anyone else was thinking. Wonderful woman, much missed. – Louis Richard de Bourbon de Parme et de Savoie, Prince de la Pau

————————▽————————

Waverly, IA (USA)

I did not have a gay mentor. In fact, I had a recurring dream in which I was on stage and hadn't been provided with a script to learn from. Being in psychoanalysis at the time, I figured out it was about not having any gay persons to tell me how to live gay. A classic existential situation where existence precedes essence. After understanding that the dream disappeared. – Robert Beck

——————▽——————

Chicago, IL (USA)

I never had a mentor. I kind of winged-it. It's funny that you say that because most of my friends are a lot younger than me. I'm 46 and the crowd I roll with is in the 20s and 30s. There's one friend who specifically said that he looks up to me. I have a lot of spinning plates going on in my life and I do feel I have a responsibility to be a mentor if they want it. At a certain age you look at people and see their slow-motion car wrecks happening and you think, "Mmm! This looks very familiar" but they already have a dad, or an uncle, or a brother … you give advice sparingly. So I never had a mentor but I feel like it's my duty if they want my help to try to help people. – Jeff Ramone

——————▽——————

Rockford, IL (USA)

I had many mentors in both the LGBTQ community and from our Allies, they have taught me that being myself is the most important thing. They had stood by me when I was sad. They laughed when I was able to tell a joke. I am appreciative of the lessons they taught me. – Patrick J. Murphy III

——————▽——————

Chicago, IL (USA)

My mentor was my first lover. I noticed his piercing blue eyes and bought him a drink. That was 1982 at the lesbian bar Closet. We dated for over six years. He taught me about culture, the arts, he taught me how to have lively conversations even with those who we did not see eye to eye. He also instilled in me our obligation to pass on this education to the next generation of young men. Bob Fabino said, "One day you will be the guy teaching." I had no clue at that time, but I am now that "GUY." I have become the older dude younger men find desirable. At 58 I am fine with my new status as a Daddy! I am now that guy with several young men in their 20's. I hate it: We once had a real Tribe, we had clubs and venues, known only to Friends of Dorothy. We went there because society did not want us and to a large part they still don't. They will "accept" us only after we have become just like them. Being gay once had a certain cachet. It meant educated, cultured, wise, witty. Now with the whole "Metro Sexual Thing" we have become just as ordinary as the rest of the 90%. – Philip Bernal

———————∇———————

Gainesville, FL (USA)

I was very fortunate to meet my mentor "Bill" when I first came out at 15. He was 42 at the time, and while flirtatious, never hit on me. Instead, he gave me a sense of pride for who I am, and who I've become as a person. He handed me *The Front Runner* (Patricia Nell Warren's book) and told me to read it. He gave me many books by/about LGBTQ people so that I would know I wasn't alone, ill, or a degenerate. He was also the first person to tell me, "Use condoms, there is this weird illness going around" (it was Gainesville Florida, 1983). I credit Bill as to saving my life in many different ways. He has since passed but will always remain a vital part of my life. – Eric Andrews-Katz

———————∇———————

Chicago, IL (USA)

I definitely had a mentor. His name is Gil Herdt and he was a professor at U of C and when I was going to Horizons, they were doing a book called *Children of Horizons: How Gay and Lesbian Teens Are Leading a New Way Out of the Closet* and I ended up working for him, I was an undergrad at the time. We became fast friends and he was more of a father figure than my own father because my father was a bigot. We had no relationship at all. Gilbert mentored me a lot with my education and we've been fast friends ever since. He was the closest thing I had to a father figure outside of my father, who wasn't. – Drew

———————∇———————

Bath, Somerset (UK)

George Broadhead of the Gay and Lesbian Humanist Association (GALHA
– a UK-based organisation). He was (and is) my "Gay Dad" in many ways.
In a very long-standing relationship himself, with partner Roy, (now married
since the law changed in the UK), he taught me the importance of being a
bon viveur, as well as doing one's bit as an activist. He's very funny and kind –
queenly, rather than queeny – but that's always tongue in cheek. He's refined
and old-fashioned – or as he would put it himself, in 1960s gay lingo, "piss
elegant." Precisely what I aspire to be! – Diesel Balaam

————————∇————————

Bellport, NY (USA)

I have had no mentors. In fact, I had no one but books from a library to
explain how my homosexuality worked. I grew up on Long Island and was a
teenager in the early 2000s. When I was 18, I discovered a childhood friend's
mother was a lesbian and talked to her for a while. We haven't kept in contact
since, unless you count Facebook. – Erin Michelle Miller

————————∇————————

St Louis County, MO (USA)

I grew up in South St. Louis County in Missouri, particularly in the 1960s and
'70s. Knowing I was gay from at least five years old, it got increasingly
frustrating while in high school in the late '70s. In the Midwest where the
bathroom reading material on every toilet tank was *Reader's Digest, National
Geographic*, and Billy Graham's *Decision Monthly*, every parent was Republican,
and no people of color anywhere to be seen. There was no support system
for anyone LGBTQ. My only "news" were from *Honcho, Mandate, In Touch*
(the gay one before the celebrity one), etc. and once in a while a cover story
on *Time* or *Newsweek* about "being gay in America." The youth of today don't
know how hard it was particularly in schools where the counselors would not
have helped (they probably would have called your parents) and there was no
way to find out if there were ANY groups out there, because there was no
internet yet. But there was an art teacher named Harry at my high school. I
never took his class, never got to know him personally while I was a student.
But I heard things sometimes. Not bad things, but a rare mention of him
being gay. I heard of an incident where a student made a snide remark to him
in class, and I wish I could remember the very clever and classy comeback
Harry had for that student. Apparently, some students had a silent respect

for him over that. Nearly 20 years after graduating, through a former teacher who was very supportive to me and a former student of Harry's, I was given his e-mail and Facebook contact info. I wrote to Harry telling him that while back in school, knowing he was there and doing well as a gay man, that it gave me hope and I felt better about myself. When I went back to visit family in St. Louis, I called him and visited with him one afternoon and we had a wonderful talk. It meant a lot to him that I was inspired by his life (even though he had his tribulations, too) and we kept in touch up until he passed away several years later. He was perhaps just a man that had an ordinary existence in many ways, but he endured and a degree of happiness, which is all I really wanted as well. I figured I could grow from that happiness and go further. – Todd Jaeger

—————∇—————

Fire Island, NY (USA)

I was very young. It was on Fire Island. Just turning 15. I was fascinated. It was new to be around so many other gays. I watched the shows at the Ice Palace and one of the entertainers, Shirlena, was keeping an eye on me and I didn't realize it. I would hang out by the stage door trying to see what was going on in the dressing rooms. She came out of the dressing room one day and we started to talk and she invited me into the dressing room. From that point on it was that first gay family connection. She showed me the ropes, told me what to do and what not to do. If someone came around me that I should not really be around, she would say, "They're not good for you. Get rid of them." That type of thing. She left the biggest impression and she showed me how to be a stage entertainer. Everything that she taught me stays with me to this day. Shirlena was a trans back then. She worked at Pathmark under her sister's ID because it was very difficult in those days for the girls to get regular work, beside show stuff. – Keith Kollinicos (Missa Distic)

—————∇—————

New York, NY (USA)

If I had to pick a mentor, it would be a friend from college. He was one of the first people that I came out to. He took me under his wing and showed me the gay community, introduced me to his friends. I was not out before that. I did not experience anything. He was just a close friend. His name is Orlando, he was there for me at a time when I needed it, and vice versa. He showed me things I never knew existed in the gay world. – David Vega (Lucifers Axe)

—————————▽—————————

Forest Park, IL (USA)

When I was edging out of the closet in the late 1980's, I was motivated to come out by a friend who had revealed he had AIDS. Being the caregiver that I am, I wanted to find out how to support him, so I started calling support groups and educational meet ups to learn what I needed to do. Remember that this was early in the fight against AIDS. I had just had a medical doctor tell me I could contract AIDS by sharing a drinking glass with my friend. Idiots abounded.

One of those calls that I made led me to a man who happened to be a bartender at the Hideaway (a now-defunct gay bar in Forest Park, Illinois). Albert Nobile and I hit it off immediately – even before I put the phone back in the cradle. That night I met him at the bar, and he became my "fairy godfather – "the man who would help me make connections with quality men, and who would point me in the right direction as I stepped out of my closet and into the real world. (No, I don't mean he was pimping me – he would introduce me to men at the bar that he knew weren't jerks, that's all).

Albert was just there for me. When I was frustrated or scared; when I did not know what to do about any situation, I would walk to the bar, and spend all night talking to Albert and the others he would pull into the conversation. I had been raised a Fundamentalist Christian, and when it came to slowly dismantling every block of the foundation upon which I had built my life, Albert was there to hold my hand and dry my tears while he showed me a way to live that was more honest and loving and free.

I am 100% more authentic today as a result of knowing Albert in the late 1980's. AIDS took Albert from us in the early 1990's and I am here today because of what he taught me – and the great men he introduced me to. – andKevin

—————————▽—————————

South Carolina (USA)
Chicago, IL (USA)

I grew up in rural South Carolina. It may sound naïve but while I knew I was different growing up, I didn't realize what was different was that I was gay. Looking back, it would have been SO obvious had I even known a gay person. As it was, I was a senior in high school before I ever met someone that I knew was gay. Because of this and other things I didn't really embrace being out until I moved to Chicago and that's where my mentors came in.

Locally (Chicago):

Tracy Baim – I don't know if she ever set out or felt herself to be a mentor, but she should be the dictionary illustration for being an unapologetically successful and driven gay person. She taught me not to box myself in to being active in one way. I dove into the Chicago LGBT community through donating my professional event planning skills. Tracy got me involved in managing the hotel room block for the 2006 Gay Games. Then she came to me to help with a Chicago Gay History project. Then she found me to help with Illinois Marriage Equality efforts.

Nationally:

Elizabeth Birch – My first community activity in Chicago was producing the HRC-Chicago gala dinner in 2001. Elizabeth Birch was the CEO for HRC for my first three Chicago events. HRC's headquarters staff are always so busy but Elizabeth took time out to not only speak to me but remembered me and contacted me directly. She may not have been a direct mentor, but making that connection served as an ongoing example to me that kept me engaged. It's how I've looked at keeping volunteers engaged in all my benefit events since then. – Chris Grace

—————▽—————

Washington, DC (USA)

I suppose I had a number of mentors at different points in my life even though most of these relationships did not follow the traditional mold and some of these individuals may not have even been aware that they were filling a mentor role for me. I learned from them more by example than instruction. Two, however, stand out above the others. I had one mentor, a man with significantly more experience than I had at the time, in all matters of life and love, who taught me that, no matter what the right says, we are not damaged, and our sexual expression is neither aberrant nor wrong – and that we, too, had a right to pride. I had another mentor who showed me through her actions that staying informed and getting involved were the only ways to create the changes we desired, and that apathy and complacency within our own community were the surest routes to undermining all the progress the LGBTQ community had already achieved. – D. Warner

—————▽—————

Chicago, IL (USA)

Marge Summit took me under her wing when I first moved to Chicago. I had been out about a year and she showed me how to have fun. We became friends and she gave me a job at His n Hers. I started in the kitchen cooking those famous burgers and then behind the bar. I stamped $ gay money and we smashed cans to raise money for Chicago House.

Marge taught me to love all of our community. We went to all the bars, mostly boy bars and the Baton to see the "girls," Chili and Leslie will always be my favorite from those days.

We went to the Loading Dock and the Gold Coast and, of course, Augie CK's to try and find me a girlfriend. We lost so many friends in the '80s. I am so happy that we are still friends to this day and I consider her and her wife Janan family. They are grandmas to my two dogs. Marge Summit fought for all of us and I am so lucky she took me under her wing. – Terry Gaskins.

—————▽—————

Los Angeles CA (USA)
Chicago IL (USA)

I've been lucky to have two mentors, both early and late. In grad school and my early 20s, when I was waffling quite a bit – gay, bi, straight, WHAT? – I had a gay friend who would occasionally escort me through the gay community of southern California – plays, restaurants, bars. I have wonderful memories of the two of us dining at the sidewalk café of The French Quarter in West Hollywood. I felt so comfortable and FAB-ULOUS in and among the queer folks, drag queens, Joan Rivers impersonators, and teen hustlers that frequented that stretch of Santa Monica Boulevard. But I was exposed to the sad parts too: BMW-loads of tourists from Tulsa and Omaha driving slowly down Santa Monica, ashy-white faces pressed against the windows, gaping at the gay crowd as though "Seeing the Gays" was a sight-seeing event in LA, right up there with La Brea Tar Pits and Knott's Berry Farm.

More recently my friend Doug has been a mentor as I began to explore the Chicago leather community, a lovely community that I once avoided because I felt intimidated by it. I met Doug when the two of us performed at Outspoken at Sidetrack Bar, a monthly story-telling event. I was, frankly, daunted by Doug when he marched up to me in head-to-toe black leather to shake my hand and introduce himself. His story, though, was so sensitive and nuanced that I began to rethink my assumptions about leather men. (Ironically, MY story that night was about an event in my late teens that helped me overcome racial prejudice! And here, forty years later, I was still confronting my own prejudices.)

Doug helped me through that prejudice, and now my most pleasant memories of the last two years are visiting the IML, the Mr. Illinois Leather contest, the Leather Archive and Museum, Touché, Cell Block, both with and without Doug and other leather brothers.

Here's an experience I wouldn't have had if I had not met Doug: Some time ago, I tentatively slinked into Leather 64Ten, a leather shop on Clark Street, for the first time on a cold, sleety late November night to buy my first chest harness – a black asymmetrical chest harness, if you please! (I was so proud of myself that I had learned the terminology). After the fitting, I walked out onto Clark Street, bare chested except for the harness, on my way to Touché, the leather bar next door. With the faint sleet pinging against my bare skin, I stood outside in the cold Chicago night for a long time, feeling so goddam *alive* in a new and exciting way. When I finally entered Touché, I felt as though I finally *understood*. Who knew that a strap of black leather across a bare chest could have such an impact!

As a teacher who should have retired years ago, my proudest moments each semester are those days when queer students trust me enough to share with me the joys and fears of their queer lives and to sometimes seek advice, even if it's only asking me to recommend a good gay bar. The queer community is, among other things, a community of mentors, isn't it? – William Demaree

—————————∇—————————

Cleveland, OH (USA)

My first real boyfriend was a subscriber to *After Dark* magazine. He told me "this is the Bible of gay life." I read ALL of his issues. I took it from there. That magazine taught me a lot. – Roger

—————————∇—————————

Adelaide, South Australia (Australia)

I never did have any specific mentors within the community. The main thing was to be proud of who you are and not let others drag you down. Unless Drag is what they want to do then they'd better get a fabulous repertoire, etc. all happening. – Robert Verrall

—————————∇—————————

Louisiana (USA)

I haven't had personal mentors, but I have encountered members of the LGBTQ community, peers, older, and younger, who I have talked to, observed, and learned from by example of how they live, work, love, persevere, and continue to progress with the contributions to the community as well as their own lives. – Katorri A.

—————————▽—————————

Chicago, IL (USA)
New York, NY (USA)
San Francisco, CA (USA)
Indiana (USA)

Not unusual in 1976 when I finally came out at 27; having been hippishly bisexual and married for three years, there were few uncloseted mentors – even being a pianist, Liberace was not my choice, and Elton John remained iffy then about his gayness. I was, as they say, on the "down-low," having been exclusively queer before that, now living in a loosely wrought mélange with an ex-lover and his wife, a red haired French Horn player. My gay mentors were mostly those early activists I met in NYC and San Francisco who were the organizers of the burgeoning radical movement. I had arrived in Manhattan to attend a music conservatory in Fall 1970, when so much of the first political and consciousness-raising (the latter learned from our lesbian feminist friends) was going on. The Stonewall Inn was still boarded up and burned, but I went to see it anyway, with a sympathetic "girlfriend" as there was a meeting of the Gay Liberation Front, full of street queens and angry mustached boys in Levis, at a church near there.

But more personal level, my closest mentors were a gay couple living fairly openly in my small rural Indiana town! My parents had rented an apartment to them, and while, with good Midwest manners, nothing was ever said about why they were living together – the roommate excuse – we all, including my new wife were invited to their special gourmet candlelight dinners. They were not much older than me, but as the local hairdressers and artists/antique enthusiasts, they managed to have a life of which I, cautiously, took notice. My father, out of step with his heterosexual status, shared these enthusiasms, but not an attraction to men, he just didn't consider it a problem or concern. This couple, seemingly happy, creative, and enjoying life, were my first example of what life could be like. The closest we got to discussing being queer was their love for the mid-'70s folk rock singer Janis Ian, playing songs from her *Between the Lines* album, like *At Seventeen*, only later did I consciously catch on about its message of being a social "outcast," and living "between the lines," of accepted gender and sexuality. – David Hatfield Sparks

—————————▽—————————

Grand Rapids, MI (USA)

Sadly, no. Much stumbling and denial on my part. – Mark S

—————▽—————

Los Angeles, CA (USA)

When I came out all of my friends informed me that I didn't belong in a dance club, I belonged in a leather bar. I happened to go out to what was the Gauntlet, which is now the Eagle, in LA. I met a playwright called Doric Wilson and he introduced me to the leather world. He took me under his wing and taught me what it was all about. It was about accepting people, someone mentors you, you mentor someone else. Don't turn your back, accept and teach, let people make their own decisions. He taught me the basics like what to wear when you go to a leather bar. You don't have to wear leather, but when you buy leather, buy things that work for you, you don't have to spend a lot of money. Start off by buying small things here and there. Test the water, see how you feel, talk to people, be open. The first mixed drink I had, aside from a Cape Cod, was a Manhattan, and he gave that to me. He took me under his wing and kept me safe. – Crusher

—————▽—————

Chicago, IL (USA)

I always gravitated toward older men. My father's words of wisdom to me, I'll never forget. He emphasized how important it was to listen to people and that's what I did and really enjoyed doing up until this day. My mentors in gay life were all my older lovers when I was in my 20s. I learned how to talk and react to my older friends by enjoying their knowledge and life experiences that they shared with me. My older friends were my mentors, not just one but all of them. – Dennis Hardenstein

—————▽—————

Salt Lake City, UT (USA)

It depends on the aspect of the LGBTQ lifestyle that you're talking about. I had mentors in leather, mentors in sex, I had mentors in all things that made me who I am today. The leather one I had the head of a leather club who mentored me and taught me the proper way to act and how to do things properly, safely. To always consider the person you are with and … basically, it's etiquette. There's an etiquette to playing and ... just in life, there's an etiquette to being in life, that is not being taught anymore. – David Hardy

————————▽————————

Los Angeles, CA (USA)

1982. I was hired as a reporter by CBS in Los Angeles. It was around Christmastime and one of the first opportunities I had to meet the staff en masse was the company Christmas party. One of the staff directors played Santa Claus. He was outrageous and very obviously gay. Everyone knew him and his shtick and delivery was reminiscent of Paul Lynde – in the best possible way. (His name was Bob and we remained close up until his death several years ago.) It was then that I thought to myself, "I'll have no trouble being myself here."

There was some friction through the years – I was at KCBS for a decade – but by the time I left, I had no trouble telling my coworkers and colleagues that I was gay. It became a non-issue. – Steve Kmetko

————————▽————————

Chicago, IL (USA)

I didn't have a mentor per se. I will say that I was very, very, fortunate in that the guy I fell head over heels in love with after I came out, was a really solid guy. When he realized, after our first date, that I was a total newbie, he showed up on the second date that we had with two items. A book, which was *The Life and Times of Harvey Milk* and a box of condoms. He said, "This is your history, learn it. And this is what you'll be wearing every time you have sex." This was in the late '80s. – Thomas Stribling

————————▽————————

Atlanta, GA (USA)

I've had many mentors in the LGBT community from the very beginning. I had a really dear friend, a lesbian named Marcelina Martin, she was a baby butch. We were students in photography at Arts School in Atlanta, Georgia State University. Our professor had us do self-portraits and she did this portrait of herself naked with combat boots and somehow something happened when I looked at these photographs. I connected with the eroticism of the boots and the nakedness. One day Marcelina asked me, "Gregg boy, did you ever consider the fact that you are queer?" I said,

"Absolutely not, Marcelina!!" She said, "I'm taking you to Chucks." I said, "Oh alright." So she took me to this nightclub in Atlanta called Chuck's, it was a big dance club. It was the only place in Atlanta where same-sex couples and interracial couples could dance. She was part of a group called the Clifton Road Women, a collective of lesbians that were all in a group marriage, seventeen of them. They were witches and they danced in a circle. At that moment I realized that she was right. However, I thought I was bisexual at the time, I was actually dating my wife-to-be and also a very handsome gentleman who was an assistant to Ralph Abernathy. Marcelina wasn't older than me but she was way ahead in terms of her identity. That was in '69-'70.
– Greg Day

————▽————

Chicago, IL (USA)

Quite a few, but Dr. Ron Sable. He believed in me and we spoke often about my journey. He let me know that being a male dancer wasn't a bad thing and the way I reached out to my audience was magic. – Mercury

————▽————

Chicago, IL (USA)

My gay mentor was a hairdresser I met in my mid-20s. He was 40ish. As a kid from the suburbs, I was super naïve about being gay, esp. living in a big city for the first time. He introduced me to his arty friends, fine dinners, culture, fashion, design. I was a struggling actor, so he was very generous, and it was only later in life that I figured out he was most likely in love with me. We never had sex. I didn't feel 'that way' about him. He tried a few times, but I would always pull back. He was HIV+ and I was not. I had only been out for a few years. AIDS panic closed me sexually – mostly due to AIDS but also because I felt inadequate in the gay scene I had fallen into. He and I had a lot of fun together, but I always felt a lack of true intimacy. Neither one of us were truly able to let all the walls drop, there was always emotions that were held back. After years of living with HIV, the inhibitors came along and saved his life, pretty much in the nick of time. He regained his health, but the years of partying, cocaine, and taking expensive trips he couldn't really afford made it difficult for him to recover financially and emotionally. He was very surprised that it looked like he wasn't going to die anymore. Instead of being able to rejoice, he shut down and became someone else. Someone bitter, nasty, and lost. He died when he was about 70. By then our relationship had been over for a few years and he had moved out of town. I will always be grateful for what he taught me – how to have some class, how to have some fun, and how to take it one day at a time. – Mr. Zor

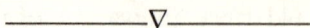

———————▽———————

Tallahassee, FL (USA)
San Francisco, CA (USA)
Santa Cruz, CA (USA)
Redwood Valley, CA (USA

Coming out in my Southern Baptist, Republican world at age 17 in 1969, I sought out older gay/bi men who had survived that environment, and who might have words of wisdom to share with my young, eager heart. And, also how to play card games, dance to early disco, be polite, avoid heartbreak, and use the correct fork. After moving to San Francisco at age 21 in 1974, my new-found peers became my mentors, who taught me about community, and "family," and social activism. When HIV/AIDS became a reality in the early '80s, my mentors were the ones whose lives were directly impacted by terminal diagnoses, including the non-infected but equally affected friends, who, like me, flew into political action to make politicians and society listen to what was going on around us all.

Today, my mentors are the straight allies, including PFLAG families and non-queer-identified Facebook friends, who speak out for our rights and existence, in my small, rural, NorCal community, and across the world. – T. Lark Letchworth

———————▽———————

(Germany)

Advisors, I guess I had, but never had a real mentor, kind of sad that I didn't, I'd say. – Cornelius Günther Körn

———————▽———————

New York, NY (USA)

Not really, I learned to do it on my own. I mean, my first lover, who loved me a lot, but it was a circus because he loved everyone else at the same time. There was a time when the bedroom was like Grand Central Station. Until I realized this is not what I want, but I didn't know anybody else. – Juan-manuel Alonso

—————————▽—————————

Mount Pleasant, MI (USA)

I didn't have any mentors in the LGBTQ community growing up, but when I got to college my theater professor, his name is Dr. Haushalter, I call him Uncle Bill, and he would not mind me mentioning him … I met him, he was the director of the theater at Central Michigan University, and I thought, "I could never talk to this guy," he put the fear of God into everybody. You knew he was gay. I was just coming out and understanding myself in college. So when I met him I was a little bit afraid. I had to meet with him at one time because I was working at a summer camp, directing a performing arts program, and I had to get extra credit. So I had to meet with him and report back to him during the summer. He used to smoke his cigarettes like this … "My dear Greg." He was very flamboyant and I loved every minute of it. He didn't give a shit what other people said. I remember in a speech class he taught – I got an A in it. And there was a girl that just didn't apply her work in the class. She got up and gave a horrible speech, it was not put together well. She sat down and he goes, "My dear woman, you have just wasted the last ten minutes of my fucking time." People were appalled but I loved the whole thing. He goes, "My advice to you is if you want to get a good grade in this class, apply the work and come back in here, so you're not wasting my sweet heart." So he had a relationship with a guy named David who worked in the library. Another year or so went by and I could not go home for the holidays, so he invited me over to his house for Thanksgiving. Also as we were drinking wine he had a guest room and wanted me to stay the night. By that time, I got to know him pretty well. He invited other gay people over. So I went over and he was telling me about gay history which I never heard about. He showed me my first gay film, *The Boys in the Band*. He goes, "Darling, you need to watch this film because these men are volatile to one another." We sat and watched that, he smoked a cigarette, we had our wine, David went to bed, but my fondest memory is sitting in his kitchen at this little table he had. The light was on above the table, music playing in the background. We just sat there and talked, and it was such a great memory of him. I'm still in touch with him to this day. He's retired, living in Las Cruces, New Mexico. My favorite story with him is when I worked at the summer camps in the Berkshires in Connecticut in this performing arts program. We would send each other raunchy postcards and I would find the most obnoxious rudest thing you could find on these postcards. I started off really mild with one that was different colored condoms hanging off a clothesline. This went on for years. He retired and I came back from student teaching at the end of '91 and he was retired by then. I went to say goodbye to him, and I was getting choked up and by that time we all called him Uncle Bill. Tim

Connors who was going to run the theater department after Bill – Bill had gone to the rest room – said, "Before he comes back you need to go to his office and look on the wall. He loves you." So I walked into his office and a whole side of the wall in his office were all the postcards I sent him. Like wallpaper. I laughed but I was really enamored. He came in and I said, Bill, you've kept every single postcard I sent you." And he said, "I loved all of them." We're still in touch. He calls me Brenda Baird Girl Tracker and the reason why he calls me that is because I used to have one of the Geo trackers, the shitty little small SUV. I got it in college and one time I was cruising in this park and his car was sitting there in the park. He pulls up and rolls down his window. "What's up Brenda, looking for cock out here." He was influential and he adores what I do for a living. He couldn't be prouder. I just loved how brassy and no bullshit he was. He was great. – Gregg R. Baird

—————▽—————

Norfolk, VA (USA)

My mentor was my husband, Clifton Banks. I had just left Pennsylvania and moved to Virginia with my brother. I was living in Norfolk. I was seeking out new friends because I was new in town. I found the new life MCC [Metropolitan Community Church]. The second or third week that I was there, I was standing in the corner watching everybody and this gorgeous black man was at the other side of this huge room. The Fellowship Hall at the church was pretty large. I noticed him looking at me and I nodded my head and smiled, and I just melted. We started seeing each other and eventually I moved in and started living with him. He was a Christian man, very sweet, very loving, he had a beautiful singing voice. He loved me. We were together 30 years. He passed December 4, 2018. – David Hayes

—————▽—————

Denver, CO (USA)

I had the pleasure of meeting Harry Hay and John Burnside in the '90's ... maybe 1996? My partner and I were in Denver. I was writing for a queer newspaper called *Preferred Stock* at the time and interviewed Harry, while John hovered nearby, asking him if he wanted hot tea. I just remember the gentle look in his eyes as he talked about "subject-subject" consciousness, which is the queer dynamic where we see each other as equals. The contrast was to heteros, who have a "subject-object" subjugation vibe. – Tony Earl

—————▽—————

Wichita KS (USA)
Albuquerque, NM (USA)

I grew up in Wichita, Kansas, on a farm. Probably the first person I talked to about being gay was a Catholic priest, who was gay also. I guess he was a mentor in that regard. What was taught to me? Just to be yourself and it's fine to be gay and don't be ashamed of it, which I wasn't. – Guy Seiler

————————∇————————

Chicago, IL (USA)

When I came out, the bar I went to (21 Club) was mostly guys older than I was (I was in my mid 20s, they early 40s and up). I learned so much about gay culture from them. Old movies, divas, how to avoid getting caught having sex in a public restroom (Bring an extra shopping bag and stand inside of it. That way when the cops look under the stall, they only see one pair of legs). And, "When doing a drag number, if you forget the words, make a dramatic turn and face upstage."

When I first came out, I was volunteering at Horizons, the LGBT community services organization in Chicago and so many of the "older" men there (they must have been in their 30s and 40s!) taught me how to give back to the community and gave me a sense of our community's history – Joe Loundy, Lee Newell, Greg Sprague and many more whose names I have forgotten. – Rick Karlin

————————∇————————

New York, NY (USA)
San Diego, CA (USA)

I didn't and I looked. In 2003 I was in New York City – I went through six therapists trying to figure out how to deal with this. I went to the LGBT center and they said, "Ok, you qualify as transgender." I thought, "Fabulous! Thank God." They said, "We have a transgender group." I said, "Perfect!" And we sat there. There were three of us and a facilitator. We all sat there, and we were all assigned male at birth, and we sat there in our male clothes. And we talked about the dysphoria, we talked about the misery. And then we looked down and thought, "What do we do with this?" … And she goes, "Well, we'll just keep talking about it." I looked up and said, "Is that it? We just deal with this until we die. Is this the way it goes?" This was in 2003. They didn't tell us about doctors. They didn't tell us about how to get good counselors. They didn't talk about other success stories. I didn't meet other trans-folks until I got to San Diego. Even then I would probably say it was Connor, a key person in the San Diego trans community. No, I didn't have a mentor. There should be more." – Serafine Sawyer

——————▽——————

Milwaukee, WI (USA)

Not really in the community, but when I told a straight woman I worked for about my dreams about being with other women, she said, "So what's wrong with that?" That kind of opened up the floodgates because I respected her so much and for her to say it was OK … so I went for it … and glad I did." – Sherrie Howe

——————▽——————

King, NC (USA)

I struggled to come out at a time when the AIDS crisis was just beginning to be talked about – this strange affliction of gay men. The Religious Right was gaining traction and I was entrenched in their conservative religious dogma. I'd been sequestered into that life and had never heard of Stonewall or the budding gay movement at that time.

My motivation to come out was not born from a mentor (although, I sure could've used one) but from a desire to stop living a lie and to end the crazy double life I lived and to begin believing myself to be a person of integrity and worth – something I could pass on to my children in time by example. – Ron Cline

——————▽——————

Charlottetown, Prince Edward Island (Canada)

Peter _____ is his name, and he's the first person I ever fell in love with. As long as I'd been aware of him (he's 10+ years older than I am), he'd lived his life openly as a gay man. I was still in the closet when we first met, but our sexual chemistry was so strong and intoxicating that I forgot my fear of being gay and was able to let go completely. Among the things that Peter taught me, and probably the most important, was to love myself as a gay man. Peter and I remain close friends today, almost 30 years later. – Dave Stewart

——————▽——————

San Francisco, CA (USA)

I have had three main mentors in the LGBTQ commUNITY and they were:
A) Harvey Milk – Who used to gladly develop our nude pictures when he worked at Castro Camera in SF. He taught me the value of political involvement and unflinchingly unapologetic activism.
B) Sr. Vicious Power-Hungry Bitch – my "mother" in the Sisters of Perpetual Indulgence, who taught (and teaches) authenticity and the continual possibility of evolution of personality.
C) Sylvester – Cockettes/chanteuse, who taught that racism and homophobia are always overcome by constancy.
– Sr. Freida Peoples aka DJ Chrysler Sheldon

—————∇—————

Melbourne, Victoria (Australia)

Not an individual, but a social group … without really knowing. I didn't come out until after my father's suicide in 1978. In late 1979, the company I worked for in Sydney sent me to Melbourne to troubleshoot their businesses down there. With my father now gone, no other family members interfering in my life, and no friends looking over my shoulder … I decided to use distance and anonymity to come out … at 25! The problem was … how to go about this. I knew no one, so nobody to introduce me to venues, to advise on how I went about being a gay man, no one to help me with the pro's and con's, the yes and no's of getting into a lifestyle I only knew through gay papers and magazines. I wasn't game to just turn up at a venue, in case there were protocols that I knew nothing about … thus giving my virgin status away. In other words, I wanted to come out BUT I didn't want anyone to know I was coming out. After perusing the local gay papers, I decided that the best way to go about this was to take advantage of something I knew about both personally … and through my work life in Catholic retailing. I would join a community group of gay Catholics called "Acceptance." One phone call, and I was off to a First Friday mass at a members home … conducted by the Servite Fathers, one of the few Catholic orders not under the jurisdiction of the local bishop, so able to cater to off-limits sub-cultures that were a no-no for the mainstream orders … and ready and rearing to go off into my new gay life. Turns out they were a wonderful group of people, very friendly, very accepting. Of course, unbeknown to me as I had no experience of gay life, a couple of the younger members already had me lined up as a conquest … a lesson from my mentors I was to quickly learn. After the mass and dinner, a group of us went to the University Club … a men-only venue … in Collins

49

Street in the city. My first gay venue! You have to realise that because I came from Sydney, there was an ASSUMPTION that I had been on the scene up there … and I let them continue to assume that. This was a real game of bluff on my part. So I now knew there were no secret rituals for getting into a gay venue. Inside, the music was pumping, and was wall-to-wall men. That eye contact was acceptable was my next lesson, though to be careful who you stared at for that bit too long. My first dance with another man … my first touches from another man … the first public kiss. What these men didn't know was that they were my safety zone, by listening in on their conversations, and observing what they were doing, and by following my own instincts when I realised there was very little that was off-limits, I was becoming the gay man I wanted to be. I was snatched up by a guy who I really didn't fancy … yes, someone older from that group … but I didn't know at that stage how to extricate myself from a situation I didn't want, so I just went with the flow (I later found out that a couple of the groups younger guys, who I did fancy, were a bit shocked that I went home with who I did). I ended up at his home. It was in many respects a bit if a disastrous encounter … but it was a learning experience. I hung out with the Acceptance guys until I returned to Sydney in mid-1982. Turns out they were more a social group than a religious group. I made some very, very, good friendships out of it, had my first partner, and had sex with a few members. I learnt quickly, and thanks to them I moved easily onto the scene, and launched my life as a gay man. To the day I left they never knew I had "come out" at that first meeting. I went on to become a committee member, then secretary of the committee. My big regret about leaving Melbourne was leaving these wonderful people behind. I will always have a soft spot for Nelboyrne, and the wonderful gay life it eased me into. – Tim Alderman

———————∇———————

(Pakistan)

I've always been a shy kid, for me I was about to come to take pride in myself after I interacted with many queer and transgender elders in Pakistan. The exposure to my community and moral support I got from them enabled me to take pride in my queerness and also explore my life and view my existence from a completely changed perspective.

If it wasn't for the queer exposure, I got I wouldn't have been able to come to terms with my queerness. I owe everything to the brave and beautiful queer and trans family and friends that I've made in all these years. Their support has enabled me to be where I am in life today. – Salman

———————∇———————

WHAT LGBTQ COMMUNITY ACTIVITY (SPIRITUAL, SPORTING, ACTIVISM, VOLUNTEER WORK, ETC.) GIVES YOU THE GREATEST SENSE OF CONNECTION AND WHAT ABOUT THAT ACTIVITY IS FULFILLING?

Chicago, IL (USA)

I'm a songwriter and I have some songs that are based – I've never defined myself as a gay person – but some of my songs are like that. I wrote a song called *This World* ... "Oh-this world-won't take this young spring love down. No-not this world. There's not enough hate in this world – to put out their love – someday this world will un-der-stand." ... it's about a gay relationship, actually about a lesbian relationship. I've done volunteer work in the schools as a music teacher, but not specifically gay oriented at all. I look forward to getting more involved in the gay community. – James Scalfani

————————∇————————

Memphis, TN (USA)
New York, NY (USA)
Seattle, WA (USA)

I'm pretty much retired now. In my Memphis and New York City days I was politically active, protesting against racial discrimination in the Memphis gay bars. Once I arranged to be a test case, entering a bar, making all kinds of noise, and was allowed in. Right behind me was a sedate African-American gentleman who was required to show several forms of identification. After that, we had a legal case. In NYC, I worked for about a year (1983-84) as assistant to the Broadway producers, Mr. John Glines and Mr. Lawrence Lane. I got there right about the time Harvey Fierstein was starring on Broadway in *Torch Song Trilogy* (I actually saw the first part Off-Broadway in 1978). Harvey was funny and kind and always spoke when he and I ran into each other at his favorite bar. John and Larry also were very kind to me, and I feel like I contributed to the running of their business as producers of Broadway and Off-Broadway theatre. Finally, in Seattle, I did doctoral work in dramatic theory and criticism at the University of Washington, under the mentorship of Dr. Sue-Ellen Case. I didn't complete the dissertation, but I was awakened like never before to the depth and breadth of late 20th-century gay ontology. Dr. Case changed my life. If I can think at all, it's thanks to her. By the way, I also directed stage plays and acted during the years I lived in Seattle, mostly work reflecting gay social issues. – Oran Walker

————————∇————————

Chicago, IL (USA)

Drag has always been my favorite part of the queer community. It's radical, it's political, and it's a celebration of what it means to be queer. – C'est Kevvie (Wilhelmina)

————————∇————————

Midwestern City, (USA)

I have been privileged to have had some opportunities to work in LGBTQI organizations and have greatly valued making a difference in the lives of my fellow LGBTQI peers. I am also grateful to be part of a LGBTQI affirming denomination and local congregation, which welcomes and values all persons. Being passionate about full inclusion of all persons, advocacy is an ongoing part of my life. – Anonymous

————————∇————————

Chicago, IL (USA)

It's varied a lot over the years. Now I do a lot of mentorship with younger men. Particularly around sex education and HIV testing, because I don't want them going through the same problems I went through. I want them to come away understanding that you have choices, and they can make their own choices based on their level of comfort. Their choices aren't necessarily somebody else's choices. Getting to understand one another, being able to see other peers in the community as being equal and valid, gives me some fulfillment. – Steve

——————∇——————

San Francisco, CA (USA)

I get my greatest sense of connection from what I'm doing right now. I had no idea that in my dotage I would be a kind of walking (ok, prancing) history book for our younger generation. That sounds a bit cocksure doesn't it? I am sure about cock! I have not been a "practicing" homosexual for decades. Those past decades are precisely why I am in the position I find myself. As a person who came out in 1975, I was never anyone's idea of the shy, quiet type. I could not be on the "down low" if I tried. I'm on the "up high." I've been around for every major shift in gay life in the modern age. To say it was a rollercoaster would be understatement. As I write this, we are in the midst of the first shutdown of the entire world, EVER. This last month and a half has changed everything. There's one gift being queer has given us that I'd guess we don't give it much credit for. Many of us have had to, for one reason or another, start our lives over again. Covid19 has ravaged our existence more thoroughly than anything before it. No war, no illness, nothing has put a halt to the whole Earth. So we will see what is on the other side, if there is one. It is odd to say that, out loud, with even the tiniest bit of heft behind it. However, we, you and I, are the next generation's history. We didn't have time to write it down because we were busy living it as it could disappear at any moment for any reason. Now we also have some strange form of PTSD as a result of all the death, brutality, and cruelty we've seen mixed with all the joy we crammed into our lives too. No regrets my dear. It has been a richer, fuller life. – Terence Smith (Joan Jett Blakk)

——————∇——————

Chicago, IL (USA)

For 25 years I was very active in two different LGBT Christian congregations, Good Shepherd Parish Metropolitan Community Church, in the gay identified neighborhood Lakeview, and in suburban Oak Park, Metropolitan Community Church of the Incarnation, which left MCC and changed its name to New Spirit Community Church.

Over the years, this involvement catalyzed a great deal of my own personal growth as a gay man and was one of the primary ways I interacted with other LGBT people in the community. I transformed from my somewhat closeted, somewhat fearful, and definitely guilt-ridden young man to maturity as a confident proud strong open adult man. I met a great many people I would not otherwise have met, people of different genders, races, and walks of life. Many of the people I came to know were impacted by AIDS, including some longtime members. And others who only became involved in the church after their diagnosis and at the end of their lives. I served in a variety of formal leadership roles, including officer, board member, choir member, and worship leader. I was one of the founders of the Oak Park church. Through length and depth of involvement, I was able to welcome newer members and facilitate their involvement and growth in the church community. I also engaged in the graduate study of the Christian religion, earning a Master of Divinity degree from Chicago Theological Seminary in 2000. At CTS I not only learned a great deal but became a member of another community and was able to serve as an example of someone who was both gay and committed to Christian community for the non-gay students at the school. – Bert Thompson

—————▽—————

Chicago, IL (USA)

Homolatte is Scott Free's long running queer performance series. I have been going and helping out since the very beginning after Chris Piss from the band Three Dollar Bill told me I should meet Scott. I was new to Chicago, a refugee from Ohio, and before that a veteran of the Washington, DC punk rock scene who was looking for his new tribe. I was just starting to write songs again on my acoustic guitar. At Homolatte I met many other queer musicians and poets who were participating in that big conversation with the universe called art. I have played there, been inspired there, and met many new friends there. – Lars von Keitz

—————▽—————

Chicago, IL (USA)

I have to say that the one area of community activity that has always brought me great satisfaction is the years that I have worked with Lori Cannon with Open Hand/Vital Bridges/Heartland Alliance, probably because of the nature of the leadership that Lori has shown over the years. This organization, and the grassroots nature of it, always gave me such joy to be participating in. I hardly remember how I got involved, but do remember the early first years of meals prepared, first at the hand of Lauren Verdich and then at the kitchens of Ann Sathers with Tom Tunney driving the workers. I remember at times the chaotic nature of how it would roll, and the changes over the years from home delivered meals to groceries picked up once a month at the start to then the grocery program it is today. But what was most striking to me about it and what brought me such great satisfaction was the fact of the simplicity of it. When I started my gift was my time, and what we were doing was we were feeding people. So simple yet so necessary. – Dean Ogren

—————▽—————

Chicago, IL (USA)

In the past it was activism. In Chicago, up until 15 years ago, you couldn't get a government official to say "Gay" without saying "Die Fag" in the same breath. But now, I have a group of friends who get together once a month to discuss comic books and graphic novels, all with a gay bent to it. We go to a place that's not necessarily gay but most of the waiters are. It's a way for us to get together and not be all about sex. We're a group of gay men who show up and talk about things besides who's doing who and what's the latest gossip in the gay community. – Mike

—————▽—————

(Bulgaria)

I have never been involved in any LGBTQ community activity, simply because I've never stumbled across such a community. It's something that seems to exist – at least for me – only as a chimera. I've never seen it, nor have I ever known anyone who ever felt a part of it. – Louis Richard de Bourbon de Parme et de Savoie, Prince de la Pau

—————▽—————

San Francisco, CA (USA)
Palm Springs, CA (USA)

Activism. Participating in marches and rallies focused on LGBT issues. I enjoy the sense of common ground with the other participants and the sense of belonging and standing up for issues that are really important to me. – Gary Borgstedt

—————▽—————

Waverly, IA (USA)

I served for a few years as the Iowa gay liaison to the National Association of Social Workers. A friend and I lead a Gay Men's Support Group for many years. I also co-facilitated an AIDS support group for several years. – Robert Beck

——————∇——————

Greensboro, NC (USA)

There was a point in my life when I was volunteering for a lesbian and gay crisis hotline in Greensboro. About that time, I got involved in the Tarheel Leather Club. Through both of those organizations I felt so connected to the community. Both of them really reached out to a diverse group of organizations and other people to work with to raise money to help people who were in crisis. Fundraisers for people who had a fire or were dealing with AIDS. I got to meet and know so many great people being involved in both of those organizations. Both of them are focused on making a difference in the community. I know a lot of people think a leather club would just be about sexual stuff and be insular, but the Tarheel Leather Club was a little different. It was that but it also wanted to reach out into the community to overcome a lot of stigmas about what leather people were like in the days before the current cultural acceptance of people being kinky. – Randy

——————∇——————

Rockford, IL (USA)
Chicago, IL (USA)
Columbus, OH (USA)

Marching in Pride Parades. I have marched in three Pride Parades, twice in Chicago, IL and once in Columbus OH, and this activity has made me want to continue to march. Getting to see the support of the community and our allies is what drives this passion. Being part of the excitement, music, dancing, love, support, and the community makes me smile and feel so happy. And I want to share this happiness with as many people as possible. For this reason, I will continue to go to pride, and help start pride parades where I can. I especially liked marching this past year, the 50th parade, because this made me feel like I was part of a major event in history. And I will tell people that I was part of that for the rest of my life. – Patrick J. Murphy III

——————∇——————

Bellport, NY (USA)

When I was 18 I used to attend LIGALY (Long Island Gay and Lesbian Youth) once a week and met people just like me or at the very least who had some similarities. It was then I walked in my first pride parade and held the rainbow flag. I also volunteered at a local lesbian bar to sell raffle tickets for breast cancer awareness and participated in the 50/50. I won the 50/50 and donated all of it back to breast cancer research. This was back in 2005-2006. I admit I could be more proactive in volunteering for LGBTQ organizations in the present, once the quarantine is over. – Erin Michelle Miller

——————▽——————

Chicago, IL (USA)

That's an easy one. That's Chi-Town Squares. I started doing it after my spousal equivalent passed because I wanted something social that wasn't in the bars. I've made friends through that in a big way with Chi-Town. Now I travel all over North America to different square dance events that are predominantly LGBTQ. It's just super-silly fun with a bunch of super-silly odd people like me. It's something I do twice a week. – Drew

——————▽——————

Frinton-on-Sea, Essex (UK)

I'm not really a joiner or "clubbable," so tend to avoid large groups of gay men, or any large group composed of one constituency of people – as I find behaviour always tends to deteriorate in such monocultures. I enjoy the meaningful connection found in small gatherings, whether social, cultural, or political. I like working (voluntarily) for the Pink Triangle Trust charity, as it is able to do some good via its funding of vulnerable LGBTQ people. – Diesel Balaam

——————▽——————

Seattle, WA (USA)

Oddly enough networking with other GLBT writers/authors/publishers. I very much enjoy the written word and all the powers it possesses. I learn so much about how different we all are around the world, and how similar that makes us at the same time. "Gay" isn't restricted by skin color, age, gender, nationality etc. ... and so our experiences in dealing with our own sexuality helps us to see that we are not alone in the world, even if we are from very different places. – Eric Andrews-Katz

——————▽——————

Chicago, IL (USA)

I'm not really involved on a community level. I've never been a joiner. I wouldn't say that I'm a lone wolf necessarily because I have a lot of connections, I have a lot of friends. But for me being involved in the house music community, doing event photography, just being part of that world ... I guess you would say that's the answer to your question. I found myself a family on the dancefloor. I found the next version of myself, the next era of myself. That started happening around 2014 -2015. So the person I was before that was not the person I am now. – Jeff Ramone

——————▽——————

South Carolina (USA)
Chicago, IL (USA)

ROTC Chicago (Righteously Outrageous Twirling Corp) All male (at the time) color guard/rifle corps that performed for all the Chicago Gay High Holidays (Pride, Market Days, MidSommarfest) as well as traveled to other cities for their Pride parades. Almost like drag, I was able to become another person when I performed with ROTC. I/We entertained crowds and while I was active we were applauded and recognized. While that may sound self-serving (and yeah, a little bit it was) I felt fantastic that someone recognized me and enjoyed me doing something that I would never have been able to do growing up. I was in high school in rural South Carolina in the early 1980s. I was in the rifle corps in band, but it was just precision performing to the music. ROTC was MUCH much more.

Event Production. I am a convention & event planner by profession. When I first moved to Chicago I couldn't afford to give to causes for Equality but I thought I could volunteer. In 2002 I emailed the local HRC (Human Rights Campaign) planning group and told them I was a professional planner and asked if there was anything I could do to help. Twenty minutes later I was on the phone with one of the co-chairs. I managed the production of the HRC-Chicago gala dinner for the next six years. My first dinner had roughly 800 attendees. I remember looking through the curtains just before the show started and the feeling of "There are this many people here either like me or in support of me" and it was a very moving moment for me. I ended up branching out to volunteer the same for TPAN, Windy City Rainbow Alliance of the Deaf and other charities. – Chris Grace

——————▽——————

St Louis, MO (USA)

I went to college just over the Mississippi river into Illinois, just a few minutes from St. Louis. Back in 1981 there was no great LGBTQ support on campus, one student group actually set up a table to get signatures to STOP the possible formation of a gay student union. That particular group got a lot of the funds and didn't want any going towards a new one, especially if it was GAY. So, no gay social life for me there, and the few LGBTQ students I did know that were in the dance and theatre departments didn't seem to let me in at the cool kids table. I was super lanky and a bit awkward though people said I was a really nice and funny guy. Through a student I knew (but never knew he was gay until years after we graduated), he got me in contact with someone at a Midwest LGBTQ newspaper called *The Gay News Telegraph*. Since I did cartoons for fun that had a Kliban-esque quality, they were interested in having a cartoon in each edition. They didn't pay me, which I felt totally fine with. I was just thrilled that my eclectic humor would be seen all over the Midwest. That went on for some time, and I kept clippings and a few editions of the cartoons. I look back on those and it still makes me smile because I was really contributing to the LGBTQ community with my personality and creativity, not just helping on the sidelines. One cartoon I did which I really would like to share with (I was so proud of its naughtiness) was in the first frame one man says to the other, "I do NOT lift my legs for every guy." In the second frame he continues, "I sometimes rest them on their shoulders." The other guy has that 'oh, gawd' expression, of course. – Todd Jaeger

——————▽——————

Chicago, IL (USA)

I've recently started attending a private Gay BDSM club. Stop what you're thinking! I mean, yes, it's exactly what you're thinking, but it is also just about the most caring group of men I have ever had the honor to meet. For example, at the last event, I met a man who put me through a most extreme "scene." Details might not be necessary. Let's just say that I was pushed to the limits in ways I had never considered before, and wasn't sure I would endure. (No, it's not THAT). When it was done, and I was freaking FLYING on endorphins (I mean, I was pretty much out of my body at this point), this man who had been a stranger to me three hours earlier, sat next to me and held my hand until I could sit up. Then he pulled me to himself and cared for me until it was clear that I was "back." Example of this type of caring behavior was all around me. I saw dozens of men caring for each other. I do not think I have ever felt such a strong connection to a group of men as I did on that night.

When I walked into this clubhouse at the beginning of the evening, I knew only one man. When I exited six hours later, I had a new family. – andKevin

—————▽—————

Cathedral City, CA (USA)

I've given to the community in a very underhanded way. I go to the bathhouse and blow 10 people. – Jim

—————▽—————

New York, NY (USA)

For me it's walking in Pride because so many thousands of people go. We get to see those people, the interaction with them, it's like that love energy is in the air. It really affects me deeply. That would be the event for me. People want to hold you and touch you; it becomes very personal, very close. As many people as there are at those type of events, that closeness always comes into play. That one-on-one looking into somebody's eyes. That one person who says, "I came because I wanted to see you. Because of what you represent." That's very personal to me. – David Vega (Lucifers Axe)

—————▽—————

New York, NY (USA)

The Gay Pride events. I've been marching since the late '70s. No matter where I've lived, or where I've traveled, I've never missed one. It's the outpouring of love from everybody, all different aspects of our community, all different walks of life, different religions, and everybody gets along and supports each other. I'm able to connect with them on different levels. There are so many personal contacts, people who are intrigued with the way I look, so they'll come over and talk or they want a hug. All the ones my age and older will talk about our history and younger ones coming up don't know our history. I'm able to put a thought in their head and they can go Google it and see what they were unaware of. It's nice also that I'll get feedback. I'll get a Facebook message, or a Twitter message, or an email, where they are letting me know that they did go look. They found out about Sylvia Rivera or Marsha P. Johnson or Miss Major, any of the events in our past and they thank me for it and stay in touch. That is fantastic. It's the best type of family we have, is our LGBT. In my opinion. – Keith Kollinicos (Missa Distic)

—————▽—————

Louisiana (USA)

Social engagement in general is most fulfilling. It can be a neutral setting for opportunities of congregation, camaraderie, sharing personal stories of setbacks, achievements, celebrations, both offer and receive valuable information, and potential for collaboration towards common goals. Within these settings is a chance to plan for activities that may be spiritual, sporting, activism, and volunteer work. – Katorri A.

—————▽—————

Palm Springs, CA (USA)

My regular attendance at events planned by the Among Friends LGBTQ social group in the greater Palm Springs area has to be the most fulfilling activity in which I engage at present. Among Friends sponsors LGBTQ interactive movie nights, cocktail parties, singalongs, happy hours, cruises and other LGBTQ travel, etc. in an effort to establish and strengthen relationships within the LGBTQ community and to promote solidarity among participants. Everyone in our diverse community is welcome at Among Friends activities and everyone is made to feel both welcomed and included. – D. Warner

—————▽—————

Chicago IL (USA)

Every year, the Chicago Pride Parade becomes more and more important to me, a barometer of how fulfilled I am becoming in my life. The first time I went to the parade, I felt like an outsider. It was right after the shootings at the Pulse Nightclub in Orlando. I was shaken to see armored guards with rifles atop a building across from me. My dominant emotions for the afternoon were fear and guilt – fear that "something" might happen, and guilt that I had been playing it "safe" in the closet for so long. I don't think I talked to anyone for the entire day, except for a very friendly Chicago policeman who directed me to the right train on my way home.

At the most recent parade, the 50th anniversary of Stonewall, I felt a part of the community, both intellectually and emotionally. I stayed in Chicago for the entire weekend and did the gay Grand Tour: the Chicago Diner, Sidetrack, Touché. At the Parade itself, slightly hungover, I knew nearly every organization represented in the parade and felt proud that I at least financially supported many of them. I felt *connected*. I was proud that a former student and his boyfriend chose to stand with me for the parade: I felt like a mentor. Standing in front of me was a seven-year-old girl who had been brought to the parade by her mother; there's a little girl being introduced to diversity in a positive way at a very early age. Watching the parade through the eyes of an innocent little girl is quite an experience! – William Demaree

————————∇————————

Adelaide, South Australia (Australia)

In 2018 I did the Out, Loud and Proud thing for Coming Out Day. The videos are done by Rainbow Roo, the Aussie gay pride clothing company. I didn't do it for the free T-shirt, though, I did it so I could hopefully give advice to those who were on the threshold of coming out, weren't sure or whatever. I've done many of the Equal Love rallies, too. I'll always take part in those as I think we need to be seen when things directly affect us.

I'm with the Adelaide Gay and Lesbian Qwire and, if anyone has seen us, I'm the one who bounces around the most. People like to see that but it's all natural. I'm not a show pony with it and I know the audience can tell the difference. I love to sing and that certainly comes across. Problem is it's so genuine you can always tell a song I don't like. I'm one of the main tenors and I help out that section where I can. I like the feedback I get from people where, to see me up there, it makes them feel happy. I like knowing I can do that for people. – Robert Verrall

————————∇————————

Palm Springs, CA (USA)
San Francisco, CA (USA)

Of course, my favorite LGBT activity is the Arts. My entire life I have sought to be part of a community of artists. I have moved from one community of artists to another across the country. Queer artists in particular, but all artists have been my inspiration. Everything I do is activism. I am really inspired by art that has a positive impact on social justice. With the LGBT community

I've been an activist in many organizations. I'm a founding board member of the Queer Cultural Center in San Francisco, for example. To me, the greatest inspiration is queer artists as activists. Their focus on some aspects of social justice, their identity, and the building of a queer identify. When I started out in life, queer public identity was a travesty. It was a negative putdown to say the least in all the media. We had no self-images, we were in the closet, we didn't know who we were. My work as an activist and a photographer has been not only to change the law to be more inclusive for LGBT people but also to define who we are. Because we were an outcast community then that definition is ours to create and we have created it over the last five decades piece by piece, as more and more people have come out and as the community itself has emerged from the shadows. And my colleagues in the Arts have been key, at the very front of that. Also, in journalism and photojournalism as well. I worked for over 30 LGBT news organizations at one time or another. – Greg Day

—————▽—————

New Orleans, LA (USA)

I think the Pride Parade is amazing. It brings us all together and these days all our straight friends are right there with us. – Terry Gaskins

—————▽—————

Palm Springs, CA (USA)

That's something that's changed over time. Most recently, it's been outreach to LGBTQ teens and pre-teens. Most often I'm working with transgender. It's rewarding because they're in a place of finding acceptance of who they are. To have someone they can speak to who accepts them, when friends at school don't accept them, when parents don't accept them. They need someone who can help them get coping mechanisms, to help them get through this period of time. It really helps. Many I speak to are suicidal, so it helps me to help them, make them feel like they do belong, they do matter, that it does get better and the best revenge is success and not death. – Crusher

—————▽—————

Grand Rapids, MI (USA)

Political activism, and helping young LGBT people learn basic reading, math. – Mark S

—————▽—————

San Jose, CA (USA)
Palm Springs, CA (USA)

The Pride Parade. My first parade was in San Jose, probably the summer after I came out in 1984. I was already out and going to the gay bars and that's how I knew about it. The first one was on a little street where the gay bars are. I was probably with a group of friends, but I wasn't with any organized group. I wasn't in the parade. Then a year later we got part of the downtown which was a little work to do because it was still controversial back in the early '80s. Then eventually it turned into a big thing at the park … it got a lot bigger then. I've been in the parade in Palm Springs a few times, either with the rodeo or the leather community. I was Mr. Palm Springs Gay Rodeo 2014. – Spike

—————▽—————

Cleveland, OH (USA)

Volunteering. The best cure for depression is to just get out of your own shit and do something for someone else. – Roger

—————▽—————

Chicago, IL (USA)
San Francisco, CA (USA)

Probably a combination of two or more of these spirituality + social/political activism, more often than not, reflected in my writing about the global historical presence of LGBTQ people in religion and spirituality – and actively supporting other LGBTQ writers in publications and events. For me these are intertwined from lessons learned from my childhood Quaker influence, that also was echoed in the various rights movements of the late 1960s and 1970s. This transferred into the LGBTQ movement in various ways depending on locale and community. In the San Francisco Bay area, where my activist and awareness coalesced, there was no holding back in bringing out one's spiritual beliefs as a foundation and motivation for one's political stance. From the Radical Faeries to Starhawk's Wicca-centered Reclaiming Collective, to the antics of the San Francisco Mime Troupe, the glamour drag of the Cockettes, and the politics of Harvey Milk and gender queer Teddy Mathews, the dynamics between daily life in the avant-garde psychedelic Haight-Ashbury and hard sex driven SOMA, and openly queer Castro districts, LGBTQ activism evolved and flourished from such diversity found in new radical America. All this shaped my personal politics and spirituality. – David Hatfield Sparks

—————∇—————

Los Angeles, CA (USA)

I suppose volunteering at AIDS Project, Los Angeles, gave me the greatest sense of connection. I answered phones at the Geffen Center, I collected sundries for APLA's necessities of life program in Gelsen's parking lot in Silver Lake, and I distributed toys to the children of AIDS patients and participated in a number of fundraisers. – Steve Kmetko

—————∇—————

Palm Springs, CA (USA)
Chicago, IL (USA)

I would say that today what that is, is the amazing connection of friends we have in Palm Springs. So it's not a particular organization, but the fact that it's a close-knit community and I feel a lot of support from that group and my close network of friends. Some people who have moved here I knew somewhat before. We all ended up in this little bubble. And I love my little bubble. In my earlier days when I first came out, my lifeline was the Frontrunners running group. I had come from a very religious background, so I didn't know about drinking or any of those things, so the bar scene was very foreign to me. I was fortunate that I latched on to that group and they were able to bring me in and teach me a lot of things. Not only about running club type stuff but a lot of activism and community activities and how to negotiate in bars and everything else. Just a connection of friends. – Thomas Stribling

—————∇—————

Chicago, IL (USA)

My charity work of being able to raise monies for different HIV/AIDS organizations starting in 1982 (Direct Aid, Children with HIV, Chicago House and others). – Mercury

—————∇—————

Long Beach, CA (USA)
West Hollywood, CA (USA)

I grew up in a very tight Catholic home where even talking about homosexuality was a no, no. When I was 16 some friends that I had secretly were gay. We all went to Long Beach Gay Pride. Just seeing everyone so happy and joyous and alive. It was an eye-opening experience for me. I no longer wanted to dismiss or hide or lie about who I was. Right after that we did the West Hollywood Gay Pride. So every time I do a Pride, however small or big, it always brings a part of me alive. I get to meet all these people and get to call them family for a day and that makes me very happy. – Marcous

———————▽———————

Salt Lake City, UT (USA)

What is most fulfilling for me is my art, but that's more than just the LGBTQ world. Just lately, I've delved into the sexual nuance. Most of the time I've played it pretty safe in my artwork. Now I'm opening new avenues of painting, things were not considered mainstream, things that were sexual. Like nudes. Things I had not done in my younger years. Now I'm old, not like I have anybody to answer for anymore. Nobody's paying my bills, except me. – David Hardy

———————▽———————

Chicago, IL (USA)

Well, for many years it was the bars. It seemed to be the easiest choice for community bonding, no matter how superficial. I think gay spirituality groups are wonderful, but I usually end up cruising them. I like gay men's reading groups and I'm currently in a Queer Men's Therapy Group at the Center on Halsted. I have learned not to just allow men I desire to become friends – I look now for guys who make me laugh or seem sane, or have a different perspective on life than I do.

Perhaps the most time-consuming community activity for me have been online chat rooms. I never thought I would spend so much time living out sexual fantasies (things I would never do in 'real' life) with strangers. Strangers who are posting photos that look even faker than mine. I've had a fake profile for about 10 years. It started when I didn't feel like going through all the effort of looking for real sex. It was new, and erotic, and fun, but I knew all along it was a chickenshit way of avoiding real men, real sex, and real feelings. Still, it was fun and exciting to create a whole different person to be. It appealed to my sense of play, and adventure. It was freeing to be someone else. I am pretty bored with it now, but I will sign on every now and then to see if any of my 'regulars' are online. It's silly, but I have a true connection with a handful of them – we have shared a certain intimacy even if it's just chatting and based upon lies. I trust them with my most private sexual desires – they know things about me that even my closest friends do not. – MrZor

—————∇—————

(Germany)

I love to cocreate with the radical faeries as well as demonstrate on lefti emancupatoric autonomous queer (pride) demonstration (blocks) and I love the feeling of doing something that's good, right, and needed, to be done and also to see the flow of this social dynamic. – Cornelius Günther Körn

—————∇—————

Albuquerque, NM (USA)

The biggest connection was when my previous partner owned a book publishing company. He published 23 gay books and wrote three. So that connection. The book that sold the most that my partner published was *What the Bible Really Says about Homosexuality*. It was written by Daniel S. Helminiak, a Catholic theologian. I've had three more printings done since my partner passed away six years ago. So there's still that connection. Most of the books dealt with religion or gay issues. It was called the Alamo Square Press. – Guy Seiler

—————∇—————

Redwood Valley/Mendocino County, CA (USA)

Gotta be our annual Pride celebration. I helped start the first several in Mendocino County soon after moving here in 1998, and continue to provide support. Not only do our volunteer, non-commercially sponsored, events bring out the local LGBTIQ folks from the hills and neighborhoods, our straight-identified friends and neighbors also show up to remind us what community, and love, are all about. Also, the rainbow art, and the ever-younger queerfolk each year at Mendo Pride feed my heart and soul. – T. Lark Letchworth

—————▽—————

Norfolk, VA (USA)

When I was in Virginia, I was delivering food boxes to poor people at the New Life MCC church. We made deliveries to people and we would sing Christmas carols at elderly homes. Also, participating in what they called Out in the Park, all the groups getting together and setting up booths. Our church had one too. – David Hayes

—————▽—————

Chicago, IL (USA)

My career being a national lecturer on LGBTQ civil rights and equality. What I love about it is, I feel it's my legacy, what I'm doing. I also feel that a lot of the audiences I'm reaching out to … I wish there had been someone coming to my school when I was younger to tell me, "Hey, I understand you." It's that reaching out. I don't have a doctorate or written several books. I've been included in some, but I haven't written any of my own. I have a lot of credentials in different ways. It's just seeing the discovery, the joy, the encouragement to go out into their own community and be a mentor and do something with your life, do something for other people. Just to have that ripple effect out into your community. So that causes me great joy, especially years later when I've heard former students tell me, "You made a difference." I was in New York City about four or five years ago with friends and we had gone to Marie's Crisis, a piano bar not far from the Stonewall Inn. At that point, I'd never been to the Stonewall. So we're in Marie's Crisis and everyone is sitting around the piano and it was a Monday night. A lot of the Broadway performers were there because they were off that day. My friend Paul goes, "Girl, don't you know the Stonewall is across the way," I said, "We've gotta go, we've gotta go." So while they were out front cruising the Black hunky security guy, I went in just to use the bathroom. It was two o'clock in the morning. I'm walking out and there's two young guys, about 24, 25, sitting at a hightop table on my left. This one guy goes, "I know you." I said, "There's no way that you would know me." He said, "No, I know you." He's looking at me and says, "Chicago." That perked my ears up, "Yeah, but how do you know me?" He thinks, "Is your name Greg Baird?" I was floored. Then he got really teared up and said to the boyfriend, "Honey, don't you remember this guy in college that came to speak? We were at Slippery Rock University in Pennsylvania and we saw you come to speak. I've always wanted to tell you what an influence you had in my life. Your message was great, you're a storyteller. Instead of talking at us, you were talking with us. I've never forgotten it." I got really verklempt and said, "I can't believe I'm at the Stonewall Inn and you two are sitting here." Sometimes the universe speaks to you and tells you you're doing the right thing. – Greg R. Baird

—————▽—————

St. Cloud, MN (USA)

I am a Wikipedian and a member of Wikimedia LGBT+, a global thematic user group devoted to improving and creating LGBTQ+ content on Wikipedia and other Wikimedia projects, as well as using Wikimedia spaces for LGBTQ+ community engagement and information activism. I work with LGBTQ+ people from all over the world through this organization. People who don't know any better would say they're all just queer nerds but they are true warriors. They are doing this work in countries where LGBTQ+ visibility is not protected and where the government sometimes monitors your Internet activity. They get harassed online, and sometimes people make death threats against them or their families, for creating LGBTQ+ content in their languages or about LGBTQ+ people or issues in their countries. And this work is so crucial because not everyone has free easy access to libraries or objective LGBTQ+ information – especially in languages other than English. So this Wikipedia work is crucial to our survival. Whatever I can do to lift my comrades up I will do. – Rachel Wexelbaum

—————▽—————

Davis, CA (USA)
Sacramento, CA (USA)
San Diego, CA (USA)

Political activity has always been my lifeblood whether it's an environmental, civil rights, or economic justice issue. Speaking and writing and organizing for just causes is therapeutic and reflects the morals that my folks instilled in me. – Paul Harris

—————▽—————

Darlinghurst, New South Wales (Australia)

I never considered myself a street protester, waving signs, confronting antagonists. Sure, I always had a considered opinion on what was going on around me, but pretty well kept it to pub discussions with friends. Although

I seroconverted to HIV in 1982 … yes, I'd learnt to be trashy since coming out … I never developed AIDS until 1996. In the interim period, the closest I'd got to any form of activism was going on trials for HIV drugs, and therapies. I ended up in Prince Henry Hospital (at Little Bay) in mid-1996. It was the closest to dying I could possibly get. Chronic CMV retinitis, chronic anemia, chronic wasting, chronic candida, and 10 CD4s. If it wasn't for the introduction of new HIV drugs right at that time, I probably wouldn't be here now. I did recover, and a long process of rehabilitation followed. Part of my own recovery process was that I started doing volunteer work for a leading HIV community organisation called PLWHA (NSW) Inc (People Living With HIV/AIDS … now called Positive Life). It was here that I started putting my talents as a writer to work, using the organisations monthly magazine *Talkabout* as my mouthpiece. The magazine was designed to be a voice for HIV people, by HIV people. It was through here that I could document my own HIV/AIDS journey, criticise services, and dispel myths and fears. As an adjunct to this, I joined the magazines Working Group, thus having a voice in what was … or wasn't … included in the magazine. Through the same organisation, I also joined the Positive Speakers Bureau, which was a group of trained speakers who went out to schools, colleges, medical and nursing organisations, community groups and health care professionals, telling our personal stories of life with HIV and AIDS, as a way of not just passing on our communitie's history of HIV, but the personal impact on our lives, and those around us. It was a very cathartic and fulfilling experience with the bureau, and I also ended up on it's working group. I spent 12 years as a speaker for the PSB, and 15 years writing for *Talkabout*. The most fulfilling aspect or both these activities, for me, was the imparting of knowledge, and the sharing of strategies to cope with life with HIV. As for the PSB, education was the primary fulfilment, which was particularly helpful for nurses who had to deal with HIV patients. Knowledge of the, often depressing, history of the HIV battle … discrimination, stigma, misinformation etc. … gave them an empathy for those they had to treat. It also led on to me assisting in reconstruction programs for those looking for advice and alternatives for moving back to work after often debilitating encounters with AIDS. Between 1996 and 2000 I also participated in some paid work through community organisations: The Positively Working Project, through the AIDS Council of NSW (ACON), who compiled a report on the return-to-work needs of HIV+ people; The AIDS Research Initiative, for whom I did database work, and the HIV Prescribers Project, who trained doctors in all aspects of HIV, and how to prescribe HIV medications. These days I run a blog primarily focused on Gay History (with a tiny bit of HIV thrown in). I try to avoid the known bits of gay history, such as Stonewall, Harvey Milk, Gay Pride etc., and closing in more on the obscure, weird and eccentric side of gay history that most wouldn't know about. By doing this, I hope to give all my readers a broader view on being gay and making them aware that many aspects and people in our history go back many centuries ... that it is not just a product of "now." – Tim Alderman

————————▽————————

Brunswick, ME (USA)

Sadly, I confess that I have spent too much time on the "sidelines" of the LGBTQ community and have not done enough to support it. – Michael Pickel

————————▽————————

Bratislava (Slovakia)

The great gay author, Armistead Maupin, once wrote about how his experiences in bathhouses were some of the most powerfully spiritual moments he has ever had. I know exactly what he means. I have traveled extensively in my life and in every country and culture, I have tasted at the well: hamams in Turkey, termasin Brasil, saunas across Scandinavia. And in every one of those places, I have sent Jesus a thank you note for the men I have met there.

I have also marched in gay pride parades around the world: Chicago, NYC, Madrid, Dallas, Rio de Janeiro, etc. I remember attending Bratislava's first gay pride march (along the Danube river) in 2010. The government was unsure of the reception that the small group of queer activists would receive, so they called out the army and had soldiers positioned all around the capital, with helicopters flying overhead. While there were a few jeers and catcalls, the overwhelming response from the good Slovak people was one of warmth and welcome. And the struggle continues. – David Clayton

————————▽————————

Palm Springs, CA (USA)

I live in the Palm Springs, CA, area and enjoy the annual Pride Parade and Festival. I love the flipped reality where queer people are everywhere! I am in my 60's now and this parade welcomes men and women of all amazing ages. It's my tribe. – Tony Earl

————————▽————————

Chicago, IL (USA)

I volunteered for the Howard Brown Center back in the early '80s when the AIDS crisis hit. I went through training and started working in the lab once a week. Later, I answered the phones and directed calls. I then started to work on maintaining records in the database. That amounted to three nights a week. It was fun; I was learning something new; and I met people. I felt that I was making a contribution. I didn't have any fear back then, probably because I kept up to date with the latest knowledge about HIV and other sexually transmitted diseases. – Yehuda Jacob

—————▽—————

Washington, DC (USA)
Jacksonville, FL (USA)
Denver, CO (USA)

Over the years, I have participated in numerous Pride Marches – two of them in cities that was their first such march of its kind. I marched in the 1993 March on Washington – the first time ever in my life (or since) that I felt like I was in the majority.

The one thing that has given me much joy in this regard is having been involved in three gay chorus'. The first of which was in Jacksonville, Florida. Our first concert was at the Jacksonville Landing next to a Hooters restaurant. It took a fair amount of guts to walk up on those risers to perform as the Jacksonville Gay Chorus next to a bunch of beer drinking straight men and sing our Pride Songs. The last gay men's chorus I was involved with was the Denver Gay Men's Chorus. The night that we performed at Red Rocks Amphitheater to a sold-out crowd gave me immense pride – especially when the entire audience stood and cheered at the end of the performance. – Ron Cline

—————▽—————

Charlottetown, Prince Edward Island (Canada)

As I've settled into middle-age, I've found that the need to take part in organized community activities has diminished significantly. Typically, a dinner party with friends takes care of whatever needs I have currently for community. Having said that, I was asked to co-judge and read at an LGBTQ Poetry Slam a couple of years back, and this past summer, I attended as part of the audience. I've found the talent of the people taking part in these slams, mostly young queers, and the energy of the events themselves, has really

rejuvenated my interest in being part of queer creative projects. Additionally, whenever I'm travelling, I like to check out local gay bars that are to my tastes.
– Dave Stewart

—————∇—————

San Francisco, CA (USA)
Des Moines, IA (USA)
New York, NY (USA)

Certainly, having been a Sister of Perpetual Indulgence for the past 38 years is a thing, perhaps the main thing for me. Our HIV-AIDS activism, fierce opposition to oppressive church doctrines and our continual lifting up of the human spirit feeds me every day. We continue to grapple with gender issues which seem to be paramount these days.

I also, here in Des Moines, Iowa, work as a volunteer with ONE IOWA, a LGBTQIA legal advocacy group. This continues the work of the Gay Activists' Alliance that I joined as "chicken" in NYC. – Sr. Freida Peoples aka DJ Chrysler Sheldon

—————∇—————

(Pakistan)
Worcester, MA (USA)

I've taken it to be my life's purpose to bring global awareness to the plight of the LGBTQ+ community in Pakistan. I've been an openly queer activist for years in Pakistan and I've faced much discrimination, bullying, and even death threats for that.

Due to the mounting risks to my life, I was forced to relocate myself to the US and seek political asylum there. Even in the USA, I've continued my activism. I came here on a Human Rights Campaign (HRC) conference in 2019, being based in Massachusetts I've been volunteering for Boston and Worcester Pride. I've also been an elected member of the Massachusetts Commission on LGBTQ Youth.

Activism is something that comes naturally to me, I've always had a rebellious nature but I was also shy and feared the world around me as a queer kid. For someone who had to fight many other battles like racial injustice for being an ethnic minority (Urdu speaking Mahajir), class inequalities for coming from a low-income middle-class family and for rejecting the religiosity of his people and be an atheist, it wasn't easy and I believe I must be the voice of those who are voiceless and are too afraid to speak out.

Through my activism work, I have been able to inspire the next generation of queer activists and community leaders, I'm extremely proud of myself for the community work I do and the visibility I have given to the plight of LGBTQ+ people in Pakistan. – Salman

—————————∇—————————

WHAT ARE YOUR THOUGHTS ABOUT THE SOCIAL AND CULTURAL ASSIMILATION OF LGBTQ PEOPLE?

Chicago, IL (USA)

I think it's great but I still see a level of self-hatred in the community. Actually, kind of projecting some of the prejudices people have given them onto each other. I've always noticed in my experience that hateful remarks come from the type of people with insecurities. They come from small towns and they come here and gravitate to the urban gay environment and then they become their own little rarified exclusive environment. To me that works contrary to the community. For example, people like Miss Foozie, who has always been a super positive, happy and light and no bitchiness. I didn't like the bitchy part of the community. I like the real sense of humor and all being together. For example, Berlin, everyone met there. It wasn't that you had to have a certain style or look a certain way. I feel there needs to be a little more diversity within our community. – James Scalfani

———————▽———————

Chicago, IL (USA)

As a fat disabled tr*nny, assimilation is not an option for me. I am a radical queer, and we need to keep fighting for those of us who *can't* assimilate into cishet culture. – C'est Kevvie (Wilhelmina)

———————▽———————

Oxford, MS (USA)

I believe in sustaining one's personal identity as one who is LGBTQ, and living openly to quicken the normalization of LGBTQ people as fellow human beings to those who run the world, namely, mostly straight (white) people. – Oran Walker

————————∇————————

Midwestern City (USA)

I am concerned about assimilation, believing we as queer folk have lost our capacity to be prophetic about relationship structures and possibilities for mutual, faithful and life-giving forms of intimacy and relationships. We have often accepted heteronormativity as a default and seem to have lost our ability to challenge its limitations. – Anonymous

————————∇————————

Chicago, IL (USA)

It's a double-edged sword. It's odd because in some ways AIDS changed the face of everything. When I first came into the community it was rising, then everybody left the bars. Then we all came back to the bars and community centers to help one another. Then in the '90s and 2000s you have the whole online thing, which I don't get to some degree though I use it all the time. That whole thing with assimilation, I think we've lost gay culture to a degree. The culture that we would build in bars with one another or tea dances or in the parks and alleys … guys don't know how to cruise each other physically anymore. The references, the language, the body movement, how we dressed was all encouraged by that. That's all disappearing and I think that's sad. I am not of the assimilationist mindset. I don't think we should assimilate … but that's me. – Steve

————————∇————————

San Francisco, CA (USA)

Frankly, I'm nauseated. I'm baffled by people who discover their difference only to lock it back up as soon as they realize what that really means. Are you prepared to think and act differently? That, my dear, takes courage and commitment. Forging a new zeitgeist isn't easy, but boy is it liberating!

Everybody can't handle that, they'd rather just go along with the program doing things as they have always been done. That way they feel a sense of comfort I suppose. But us queers, we don't have that luxury. If we are to indeed be our true selves, we can't play that game at all. Fuck a yellow brick road. – Terence Smith

───────▽───────

Chicago, IL (USA)

It's good and bad. It's good that people are recognizing that we are aren't horrible creatures that lurk in corners waiting for husbands and small boys to come by. But at the same time, it familiarizes people too much with us as a community. So things like bookstores and gay bars, restaurants that cater to gay clients are becoming dinosaurs, things of the past. I worry that in Chicago you have Sidetrack and Touché, but there are no small gay bars left. They're all owned by corporations, or conglomerates, and there to make a profit rather than this is where you can go and hang out and be yourself. – Mike

───────▽───────

Tulsa, OK (USA)

What I like, as opposed to when I came out 40 years ago, I see less and less of a need for gay bars. A lot of the younger people today, they don't give a rat's ass who you are or what you are. We're not gay people, we're not straight people, we're just people. I like that. One thing I think is interesting is when you talk about gay marriage … marriage is a private thing, I believe. I've never been married but I would not want to model my marriage after that of a straight couple. I would want to cultivate that with my partner, what was good for us, because when you have two men, two women, a man and a woman … a man and a dog, whatever … you're going to have a different energy. I think it's great that we have some of the same things but they don't have to be what people traditionally think of as a relationship. – Renny

───────▽───────

Chicago, IL (USA)

I never wanted to assimilate with a non-gay community. Assimilation was never the goal. The goals were freedom, self-determination, basic safety, civil rights, and the ability to live our own lives and make our own community. I wanted to be part of a healthy happy and strong gay community. Not necessarily separate from straight people, but not submerged within them either. We need our own social circles, and our own distinctive spaces, so that we can live our own lives according to the patterns that we choose and we decide.

Not being able to distinguish between gay and straight people, not having any separate gay institutions, organizations or spaces, leading the same lives as straight people ... these are not goals, these are nightmares. That would be a return to the bad days of the 1950s. That's the closet.

That's not what I want, or have ever wanted. I'm greatly saddened that there are LGBT people who do want that. In my opinion, what they need is less shame and more self-esteem. – Bert Thompson

—————∇—————

Chicago, IL (USA)

I don't know. I used to think a particular way, that we were losing our identity. Now though ... I think a part of the problem is that I don't feel a part of the community anymore. Not really. I feel like I've aged out of the community. It pisses me off. I've put a lot of things into the community and now I feel I'm being pushed away by kids. I'm glad that young people have it easier than I did. I think that's great. Maybe I'm a little bit jealous. It's good really, but now I find it dull. There was something a lot more interesting about the struggle. People still struggle but it's not like it used to be. While I'm happy for young people, I miss the struggle and now find everything so dull. – Xavier Bathsheba-Negron

—————∇—————

Chicago, IL (USA)

I guess in the early days I always thought that it was kind of a good thing that we strive to be assimilated in to culture and society, but now I don't know that I am so happy about that as a whole. I mean, do I really want to have to fit into the constructs of what others tell me is normal, or right, or the way to live? At the end of the day, I have to say no. We all have our path in life to live and no one should have the right to determine if that is correct, or standard, or normal, or necessary. If it is right for me and does not impact those around me in a negative or degenerative way then I say live and let live. I don't see that relative standards that you force people into necessarily improve conditions. – Dean Ogren

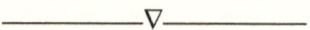

—————∇—————

78

Chicago, IL (USA)

It is a good thing to normalize homosexuality as just a part of the diversity of the animal kingdom of which we are a part. So I understand that some of us have to wear suits to hoidy-toidy functions to show that we can do that. But many of us are truly freaky people who do not fit into 'normal' society. We need to be recognized for the creative freaks we are and celebrated as such. We don't all fit into the big corporate money-making machine. – Lars von Keitz

$$\nabla$$

San Francisco, CA (USA)
Palm Springs (USA)

My opinions are mixed. I enjoy the freedoms we now have, such as being able to get married and being affectionate publicly. In San Francisco, I witnessed the Castro District gradually become gentrified by straight people to the point where it isn't a gay ghetto anymore. The straights complained to City officials about the fact that people were allowed to walk around naked in public. A battle ensued at City Hall and public nudity was officially banned from the streets of San Francisco (except for certain celebratory events). – Gary Borgstedt

$$\nabla$$

Waverly, IA (USA)

I don't feel that assimilation should be the main goal for LGBTQ people. Marriage equality is important but not more so than job and housing equality. I would not want to give up my freedoms as a gay man to like the arts including opera and showtunes. Most straight men can only talk about sports and business – how narrow. Watching grown men chase a ball up and down a field or court does not hold my intellectual or artistic interest. So I don't agree with the current party line, "No one would choose to be gay." And I don't agree that we are all "Born that way." Wainwright Churchill's cross-cultural studies prove that "sex positive" cultures produce more bisexuals than our "sex negative" Western culture. Also, Latin straight men can accept blowjobs without it threatening their machismo. – Robert Beck

$$\nabla$$

Mebane, NC (USA)

I think that works really well for some people, but there are other people who are on different journeys in their lives. Different places where they're at with who they are, be it gay, or lesbian, or transsexual. Sometimes you need that acceptance in settling into a routine and just going into a melting pot. I think there needs to be room for people with a stronger sense of a unique identity of being gay, or lesbian, a bear, or transsexual. To have spaces where you can express that. Not just in the way you dress, or the people you date or socialize with, but really part of it is kind of a mindset. It colors your outlook on how you see the larger culture, the way you might see politics, the way you might see spirituality. Someone like the Radical Faeries. I think there's not one answer. I think there needs to be a range of ways for people to express themselves. The gay people who look for that acceptance and the assimilation of culture, those people are valuable to our movement too because it shows that we can be your next-door neighbor, we can be a Mayor who's running for President who's gay and has a partner. At the same time, it is important to acknowledge that there are radical queer artists who are making statements in the street. There are leather people who look very intimidating. There are Radical Faeries who go out and get in touch with the Earth and the spiritual side of the world around us. – Randy

—————▽—————

Chicago, IL (USA)

Oh boy, I have many thoughts on that. Being gay or queer used to be a rebellious thing. Even that we existed at all was a rebellious thing. Now it's like we're a target market. A lot of people in our community have this idea of who and what we're supposed to be. I feel like my least favorite kind of gay man, it's always a male, and it's always someone who identifies as gay … my least favorite kind of gay man is one who has a concrete idea of what it is to be gay. If you draw outside the lines, they have nothing but criticism. It feeds on itself. There are some people who exist within the stereotypes, the cultural mores of what it is to be gay, but I found my life, my people, on the outside. I've never cared about what the gays are doing, or liking, or listening to, I've always done my own thing. Being a rock 'n' roll kid, growing up and working in rock radio and going to school for radio, that was not a very queer thing to do. I feel that the mainstreaming and homogenizing of gays is making a lot of people boring. It's no longer a rebellious act. Oh look, two guys kissing on TV whoop-de-do. – Jeff Ramone

—————▽—————

(Bulgaria)

I can't speak about Western society, because I've been living in Eastern Europe for decades. Assimilation of LGBTQ people in Bulgaria is not something that is ever going to happen. There is no political will to even introduce legislation protecting gay people from hate crimes, and there's certainly nothing on the horizon that would even contemplate civil partnerships: marriage is regulated by the constitution as "between one man and one woman" and that is never going to change. The left and right wings of the political parties are a sham: the socialists are just as fascist about LGBTQ and women's rights as the Far Right, which has been in power for several years.

In Bulgaria, over 80% of people surveyed felt uncomfortable around LGBTQ people and nearly 90% don't want them as neighbours or co-workers. Support for marriage equality is below 10%.

LGBTQ culture barely exists in Bulgaria and, the one time somebody tried to highlight it at an exhibition for the "Plovdiv – European City of Culture 2019" events, the public outcry was deafening. Politicians from all parties condemned it, and it was removed "for the sake of public morals and protection of children." Bulgaria is a synonym for bigotry. – Louis Richard de Bourbon de Parme et de Savoie, Prince de la Pau

$$\nabla$$

Seattle, WA (USA)

I think that it is a good thing to assimilate the LGBTQ community into the rest of society. That doesn't mean we have to lose our individuality (being LGBTQ) or compromise who we are. I think that LGBTQ books/authors should be mixed in on the shelves with others of that genre, but also should have a small LGBTQ section to themselves. Our history both shows our uniqueness and commonalities around the world, but that doesn't mean we need to surrender our differences. – Eric Andrews-Katz

$$\nabla$$

Rockford, IL (USA)

I think the assimilation is critical for the survival and continuation of our community. When we can get the majority of society to accept us then we have less to fear. With the progressive policies of former presidents, and the strides of the marriage equality movement I believe we are moving closer to a greater acceptance. The more our community can be seen the more that we will continue the need to be vocal. We will be able to go about our daily lives. Plus, as acceptance grows then it grows more for those who are still on the outside of society. Assimilation is also good for the younger generation because as they see more acceptance, they feel more able to express the same feelings. – Patrick J. Murphy III

——————▽——————

Chicago, IL (USA)

I'm torn. It's really great, but I don't think I want to see a woman in a backroom cruise bar. There are certain venues like that, such positive ones, that I really don't want women, or straight woman, at all. It kills the mood. So that scenario I think I want to keep like that. But as far as mainstream gay bars, I don't mind it. But there are certain places where I just don't want to interact outside of my own tribe. – Drew

——————▽——————

Palm Springs, CA (USA)

I look at it from a lot of different angles. On the one hand, I never thought that in my lifetime I would see some of these things happening. It makes me happy to see commercials and movies and books, because that stuff didn't exist before. It existed but it was in the background. It wasn't a part of mainstream society, a part of the world the way it should be. So that type of stuff makes me happy. At the same time, I always go back to the fact that within the gay community itself, there's so much division, there's so much separation. Unfortunately, that's always going to be, because that's human nature. To separate themselves and want to put them into groups. I wish that wouldn't happen, but it does. – David Vega (Lucifers Axe)

——————▽——————

St Louis, MO (USA)
Rancho Mirage, MO (USA)

Well, instead of something especially insightful, profound, and essay-like, I'm going to vent a little because this has bothered me a bit all my life, even up to this day. While I'm grateful that, in many ways, LGBTQ people have progressed a lot and we now get to see and experience all facets of being LGBTQ – so many things people just weren't aware were going on, like trans acceptance and more. But ever since I was a kid back in St. Louis, I was pissed that SO many people equated gay men with being a stereotype of swishy and weak. When society keeps perpetuating gay stereotypes it slows down the complete acceptance and assimilation. You had the gay character on *Barney Miller* that was always getting arrested for cruising, who was played queeny for laughs (although later a fellow moustachio'd cop who acted like an everyday guy turned out to be gay, which shocked and made me hopeful). You had Billy Crystal's character on *Soap* seeming to have non-stereotypical mannerisms, but then they had him cross-dressing and wanting a sex change. I felt so let down when I was told "Oh you MUST see *La Cage Aux Folles* and then I just sank further into my chair in disappointment when there wasn't just ONE gay male character that was ... AVERAGE. I had to sit by silently while I would hear people and relatives go on about "look at them, so effeminate and embarrassing." Of course, I don't believe men that have feminine qualities are bad nor wrong, it's exciting to see so many different elements to people. But this was me as a kid up through into college in a place where it was believed all gay men want to be women (they didn't realize that saying "You throw like a girl" is just saying women are second class and weak) and something HAD to be mentally wrong with them. I was average. I looked average, talked average (despite my sense of humor). I wanted to know that gay men were of different personalities, mannerisms, lives. I remember when John Goodman starred in a sitcom on Fox called *Normal, Ohio*. His character Butch Gamble (Butch? Okay, that was a bit of ridiculous obviousness, but ah well) who was gay and moved back to his hometown Normal, Ohio (Okay, the town's name was a bit of a stretch too, but hear me out). The thing is, he was just an average joe. The only way you knew that he was gay was that once or twice in each episode something was said to let you know he was gay. He was ... "normal." Gay and normal. I thought wow, it's a start. I roll my eyes whenever someone tells me that it takes baby steps, like after all these years we still get to see big fantasy lesbian make-out scenes a la *The Hunger* and *Atomic Blonde*, but rarely see anything like the two bearded men in series two of *Midnight, Texas* seriously kissing in a pickup truck or outdoor shower. "Baby steps, Todd. It takes a while."

Bullshit, I say, SOMEONE just needs to do it, make it happen. Not excuses, that it "takes time." You can argue that *Normal, Ohio* wasn't exceptional as a show, but when I actually read reviews that said Butch and the show "weren't gay enough," I just shook my head in disbelief. I mean, it IS possible to have gay male characters in a comedy that aren't stereotypes for laughs. I don't go for the examples in *Will & Grace, Superstore* and *Modern Family*. At least in the Wayfair commercial where Kelly Clarkson appears in a gay couples' kitchen portrays them as everyday guys (the situation may be vague of who they are, but come on, it's a gay couple). I had hopes for the comedy film *Booksmart*, but while the lesbian characters were regular cool gals, the two guys were screaming queens. Of course. I want something I can feel is relatable to me. There are TONS and TONS of TV shows and movies that cover the wide array of LGBTQ life and yes, mannerisms. Just give me an average joe. A main point about assimilation? I feel we can't totally assimilate and be respected when there are people who try to hold us back by consistently enforcing stereotypes. There. Thank you for giving me your time to get this out. Whew! – Todd Jaeger

————————∇————————

Frinton-on-Sea, Essex (UK)

Acceptance is a two-way street and requires some compromise on both sides. Some very out-and-out queers can rub people up the wrong way. For example, I remember travelling back from a Pride parade in south London some years ago, in a carriage that was very mixed (i.e. straight and gay), with some silly queen shouting repeatedly at the top of his voice how he loved to "take it up the arse." It was intended to be provocative and made everyone feel embarrassed, but had some straight guy slapped him down, he'd no doubt have started bleating on about "homophobia." Some gay people are their own worst enemies. That said, I feel it's important to stand your ground in a dignified way and insist on consideration as well as respect from our straight friends – but you have to be prepared to earn that. We are, in some ways, different – we need gay-only and men-only/women-only spaces, not least so other LGBTQ people can find us, be supported, and get their various gay needs met. So, assimilation should be confined to the general public sphere (shopping, banking, the workplace, mixed nightclubs, etc.). Our lives shouldn't just be inferior copies of heterosexual lives. – Diesel Balaam

————————∇————————

Bellport, NY (USA)

We have always been here, even in history. As a teen and in my 20s I did a lot of research on LGBTQ and can recite a lot of stories even before the Stonewall riots of 1969 in New York – Erin Michelle Miller

————————∇————————

Chicago, IL (USA)

Early in my life I learned that I could not be me and be acceptable. I had to be some clone of what others thought was acceptable – to play the roles they wanted me to play. I went along with it because I wanted to fly under the radar. I experience a lot of "inculturation" through years of torment and bullying at the hands of school mates who recognized that I was different and thought that gave them license to break me into pieces.

So for the first 60 years of my life, I never did or said ANYTHING without first running it through a filter of "what is expected/acceptable?" Or "what will they think?" As I got older, I started taking the risk of being more authentic after deciding that this was a risk worth taking. Still, that is still a part of me, and a couple years ago, I realized I didn't even know who I am anymore.

I think assimilation is dangerous. It makes a society full of clones who thinks that everyone is just like them or SHOULD be. We miss out on all the fabulous variations we could have because variations are crushed. I do not believe that LGBTQ folks should be trying to assimilate and "pass" for whatever is considered "normal" in the society around them. If you are one of a kind, then fuck it! Live your one of a kind way! Be you! I can't really know all that is possible in this life if I don't see your particular variety.

So I've been joining groups that turn their backs on what is heteronormative. I have dear friends who are gender fluid and dear friends who are in polyamorous relationships. If the way it's always been done is not YOU, then do it your way! The pressure to be conformed to someone else's' idea of who you should be is a life-sucking lie. We should be helping each individual find their individual way to becoming fully themselves.

So, Kevin, how do you REALLY feel? I turned 60 and still wasn't sure who I was. I mean I knew a lot – I was that man who "x" in his own home and liked "y," but wouldn't let anyone know. Don't try to make me be who you think I am, cause, honey – I am going to be ME. – andKevin

————∇————

Denver, CO (USA)

I think it's said that we've lost our ghettos. I lived in Denver most of my life and we had a great gay downtown neighborhood. I miss the fact that we all had to hang with each other in the same area. But there was a lot of oppression that came with that, there was a heavy price tag. – Jim

————∇————

Palm Springs, CA (USA)

Sometimes I get very angry because I'm seeing things that were ours, part of our LGBT community and they're being taken over by the straight community. To the point where we're starting to get shoved aside at our own events. I find it disturbing that we are allowing this to happen. I think the progress we've made is great, but like every other culture, you don't just let somebody else take it over to the point where you become erased from it. Some of the things I see, that's the direction it's going in. It really concerns me very deeply. – Keith Kollinicos (Missa Distic)

—————▽—————

Chicago, IL (USA)

Nowadays I think it is very important for us to be more vocal and seen as members of the LGBTQ population. When I was young, we had to fit in the closet that we made for ourselves. – Dennis Hardenstein

—————▽—————

Louisiana (USA)

The current generation is by far the most assimilated as it should be. They are the most connected worldwide thanks to social media. In their lifetime a sitting president recognized the right of LGBTQ people to marry if they choose and the Supreme Court agreed. As social media has provided multiple platforms for them to express their right to quality of life in all areas, career, family, community involvement, and recreation, unfortunately there are also platforms with opposing views. With the support of a number of different organizations – Human Rights Campaign, GLAAD, Lambda Services and local community-based agencies – they are able to empower themselves forward in spite of opposition, building on a foundation that was set for them by previous generations. – Katorri A.

—————▽—————

Chicago IL (USA)

I saved this question for last, for I find it the most difficult to answer. I live and work in a predominantly straight environment in the Chicago burbs. I am out to all my friends, colleagues, students, baristas, bartenders – everyone who matters knows who I am and together we celebrate that. So many of my straight friends know so little about the queer community and listen with great interest to my stories about gay bars, and parades, and plays, and Boystown, and queer writers' conferences. Many tell me that I am their window to a world they would otherwise know nothing about. I am out in my classroom and help my queer students learn about who *they* are and help my straight students learn about who *others* are.

And yet, as happy as I am in this environment, there are times when I must – *must* – walk away from the "non-queer" world in which I live/work to spend an evening or a weekend in a clearly segregated queer environment. Once a month or so, I feel the need to hang out in a crowded rowdy gay bar until it closes at 4:00AM. Every spring, I feel the need to celebrate leather at IML in Chicago. Once a year, I feel the need to attend Saints and Sinners, a weekend conference for queer writers in New Orleans. I don't really understand why these excursions into strictly queer environments are necessary, but I know that they are.

And I get irritated when the non-queer world intrudes. Recently, at Second Story, a Chicago gay bar, a group of drunken "Bachelorettes" (often called "Whoo-girls") invaded the bar and began to hit on the guys. Yeah. I know – straight women *hitting* on gay men: "Are you sure you're gay?" "What would happen if I let you touch my breast?" No one said anything to them, but when these nitwits left, you could almost hear the men heave a collective sigh of relief. I was extremely angry that my bar-world had been invaded. And when I left at 2:30AM, other men were still bitching about it as well: "Can you believe that they actually . . . ?"

As happy as I am in my daily straight world, I would not want the clearly defined "gay world" to disappear. I would not want to feel that I am being assimilated out of existence. – William Demaree

───────────▽───────────

Cleveland, OH (USA)

First off, unless everyone is invited to benefit from LGBTQ gains, I don't want to be a part of it. Second, why the hell would I want to be like everyone else? Sometimes great gifts come from being an outsider. – Roger

───────────▽───────────

Palm Springs, CA (USA)

I'm of mixed mind on this issue. On the one hand, I keep thinking that I should be eternally grateful that it's now possible for LGBTQ people to take their rightful place in society and be accepted broadly as an equal member of society – after all, isn't that what we've been fighting for all of these years? But I also can't help feeling sad and angered by the fact that the more we assimilate, the more we lose many of those special things that made being a member of the LGBTQ community so special. Our bars and other queer meeting places are quickly disappearing or becoming overrun by curiosity seekers and other onlookers, our bookstores are virtually gone, our newspapers and other publications are slowly going under, our parades and festivals have become spectator events for curious heterosexuals, and whether or not they are allies, we are now even being crowded out of those few safe spaces that used to be LGBTQ havens. Our gayborhoods are virtually gone. Even our dating apps (something else which I'm of mixed minds about) are becoming just one more place for non-LGBTQ people to seek hook-ups. So much of what was once fun, exciting, and special about our community is slowly but surely disappearing, as well as the desire for us to continue to be a unique group now that we've invited everyone else under our umbrella. Gone are the places where community and solidarity were forged in a cauldron of struggle and rebellion. Most sadly of all, there was a time when just by virtue of coming out of our closets, we were making a political statement, living on the edge and being a rebel, and taking an extreme risk that could cost your family, your job, or even your life. It was exhilarating to be a member of something so powerful, so important, and so revolutionary. People really felt connected. Now, there is so much apathy about being a political *anything* within the community, and everyone walks on eggshells for fear of offending someone. What disturbs me the most is that every day I encounter LGBTQ youth that have absolutely no understanding of what came before or how hard we had to struggle to get where we are today – and how quickly it could all disappear because way too many can't even be bothered to vote. – D. Warner

––––––––––∇––––––––––

Chicago, IL (USA)

Another complex topic was that of "assimilation." When I came out among the radical activists, assimilation was considered, in early activist Harry Hay's terminology, "hetero-imitative." This included what were called 'male-identified" men, straight-acting and straight-dressing; even the idea of "gay" marriage was considered anti-revolutionary. Gay men in particular were tending to explore their "gender fluidity," a positive manifestation of being a "sissy," a "faggot," as now part of being male. Many referred to themselves, including myself, as a "not-man," to protest the social programming that boys receive, and usually not even acknowledged. Gay and lesbian rights were conceived of in opposition to "straight society," and the perceived enemy of this more radical struggle was the national Human Rights Commission, seen from the left as a sinister self-promoting group of wealthy queers. Certainly, the very concept of gay marriage was antithetical to the struggle of civil rights, the institution being referred to as misogynous and hetero-imitative, concepts and labels borrowed from lesbian feminists.

This criticism has not born out in reality once it was realized that neither the Democrat Party, nor any third party could be relied upon to forward our LGBTQ agenda. Queers needed to organize on the local and national levels to elect queer representatives or verified allies. My own thinking about gay marriage remained either critical or ambivalent until the more recent struggles for legalization in California and then nationally. We asked our daughter, a radical bisexual public-school librarian-teacher, what she thought. With tears in her eyes, she reminded us that if we had been legally married and could have legitimately gotten full custody of her at six years old – out of the question for two queer working class artists in 1980 – that her life would have been very, and more positively, different. She knew that we loved her and would protect her. But from her birth mother and step father, with whom she was forced by the courts to live, mistreated her, her step-father mentally and sexually abusing her, while her clueless, and complicit mother, ignored all the warning signs, eventually sliding off the scales into mental illness. So hearing this, we got married in San Francisco in the court house next to the bust of Harvey Milk, and she was our "best daughter" standing up with us during the ceremony. –David Hatfield Sparks

———————▽———————

Chicago, IL (USA)

I'm undecided. In some ways, I think it's great. I like seeing us represented in television shows, movies, and commercials. On the other hand, most of those representations feel like sanitized versions. We're stripped of some of the qualities we possess as a group of people. Then again, I'd be the first to cry "foul" if we were stereotyped, which still happens. I guess there's no pleasing me. Best example of a good, recent film with a gay theme would be *Moonlight*. – Steve Kmetko

———————▽———————

Hollister, CA (USA)

Whatever floats your boat, that's what I say. I'm not too keen on merging too much. I mean, I'm not going to go out and adopt babies for one thing. I might have considered it way back when I was a lot younger. When I first came out, I might have for a very short time. My partner and I don't see eye to eye on pet-rearing, let along child-rearing. So, it would be a source of friction if we did. I remember when California first had domestic partnerships, and we registered right away. Then we got married in that window of opportunity in 2008 also. We were down at the courthouse in our hometown in Northern California because we thought there would be a long line to get the marriage license but we were the only ones there. They did a big front page and back page story, with pictures and everything, of San Benito County's first gay couple to get married. – Spike

————————▽————————

Palm Springs, CA (USA)

I think it's great that we are being incorporated into the mainstream. The youth now have things that we didn't have. They have resources we didn't have, but they also have problems we didn't have. The assimilation is good, it makes people aware of what's out there. We didn't have that. We had to remain in the closet. Now it's giving them a label, and everyone is trying to fit into a label instead of being themselves. I find that's giving a lot of people a lot difficulty. It's tough and it's what puts people on the edge. – Crusher

————————▽————————

Atlanta, GA (USA)
Geechee Coast, SC (USA)

I studied cultural anthropology in a desire to understand humans. My original field of study was architecture at the Georgia Institute of Technology. I discovered that architects, especially at that engineering school, knew absolutely nothing about human behavior, or about how the building would be used by humans, or its effects on humans. So I took a class in anthropology at Georgia State, another branch of the university system there. I got hooked and I was fascinated by the culture of stigmatized communities. Communities stigmatized by race, gender, sexual practice. My entire life I've documented those communities, sometimes as a member of the community and sometimes not. To me, assimilation is a very dangerous thing. It's a double-edged sword, we want to be accepted as a community, but we don't want to be like everybody else. Obviously, some of us, as a reaction to our discrimination, become more conformist. Conform to straight mainstream ideals. This is a phenomenon that's going on all the time. This is the downside of assimilation, that you are giving, or camouflaging, your queerness. For me art that has a queer content and has a statement about our identity is a very powerful tool for change. Fortunately, in anthropology, I started studying African-American history and culture. Everybody should study that. It should be in every public school. African-Americans led the way, fighting against discrimination and being isolated from the economy and the acceptance of the country. If you look at the way African-American culture has been a major source of American culture, even of British culture. We have a lot of white people doing black culture. This is the problem with being popular in the popular culture, is that people appropriate. Mainstream appropriates minority culture. From the very beginning, my work has been about the queerness of things. One thing that is true for African-Americans, and other minority and discriminated groups, is that we take from the mainstream culture and re-appropriate it. Gender-queer is not simply taking on the culture of an opposite gender but redefining gender from a queer perspective. When you think about it this way, you're talking about how the queer-eye sees the world differently, as does the African-American eye, quite often. These are not mono-cultures, there's a lot of diversity in the African-American and the LGBT community. But there is this tradition of, since we are not accepted as we are ... of defining ourselves by taking things from the larger culture and changing the meaning of them and putting them together in different ways. To me, this is the most important aspect of queer culture. Just being like everybody else is not a personal achievement in my view. Another phenomena is to make it in your career, in your family life, in America, requires a ... if you're a minority in America, black, women, Latino, LGBT, you develop a strategy of survival that includes a development of other personas or other identities of self-presentation as a survival strategy. This is a great art form. I learned this from my work with the African-American basket makers in South Carolina. To them, art is the blood of life, it's in every breath that you take. It's not a separate thing. You can't separate it from life. It's essential for success in life and it's essential to be somebody. To present oneself in different social contexts differently. It's an adaptation, to make that into a performance art form. So, identity, just like gender and all the aspects of identity, are performed in every culture. To me that cannot be given away, simply for equality. – Greg Day

———————∇———————

Chicago, IL (USA)

I was just a little too young to experience the sexual freedom of the '70s. It exists as a kind of Gay Disney World in my imagination – the orgy ride, the fisting ride ... AIDS got its name the year I officially came out. It almost made me go right back in. But I was interested in gay history and researched Stonewall and talked to older gay men who experienced the days when sexual freedom was a sign of pride. It was so different for me, coming out in the face of AIDS. I came out and fell in love with the guy I came out to. We were together for two years, and both monogamous. Navigating the field after we broke up was very difficult, so I sort of just stopped having sex with anyone at all for a few years. I didn't only want the sexual freedom of the '70s – I wanted to know what it felt like without having to worry about death, or judgement or isolation. I became somewhat militant about fighting AIDS, which led to an internal pride because as least I was doing SOMETHING. It helped me get in touch with how I felt about the brotherhood of gay men, not just their dicks. The way the gay population fought for their health rights and took care of each other, was inspiring. Now, with legal marriage, it seems this generation wants the exact same things as heterosexuals do. I'm all for equal rights, or course, but I do hope young gay boys appreciate the rich history of the past 50 years. I hope it makes them better men, more compassionate lovers, and still ready to experience the freedom of gay sex especially the flexibility of what creating a loving gay relationship can be. – MrZor

————————▽————————

Palm Springs, CA (USA)

I take a view that probably most people don't. And that is, I think it's an incredibly good thing. I think that in some ways if the whole LGBTQ just becomes a piece of history, I'm ok with that. I feel that we're getting to a point in progressive society where people are just people. And sexuality is fluid, gender is fluid. We look at each other more as individuals instead of a particular type. For me I think that there's an incredible LGBTQ history that needs to be preserved and understood, so people can learn from our experience. But in terms of actually living it out, I hope that it's just a non-issue going forward. I'm scared, given the politics of the day, that we may be fighting this battle for a lot longer than I thought. Hopefully, someday down the road, this will just be a total non-issue. – Thomas Stribling

————————▽————————

Joplin, MO (USA)

Personally, I think the way society understands those of the LGBTQ community is a bit under par: not exactly clueless to their existence but not on terms when it comes to classifying specifics such as gender and sexuality. Even with the availability of quick access to new information and terms the community brings, there's still a lot more to share to the cis-hetero normative population. I believe that there's a lot of support for the rights of those in the community such as transgendered individuals, but not a lot of action being brought up. Aside from the negative news posts of those that are sadly murdered for whatever, there's not a whole lot of positive news to be seen.

The only ones I've noticed were just those that came out as transgender or genderfluid. Nothing is wrong with the news of people coming out as that is always really cool to see, but I would like to see at least a good few that would inspire more than just action towards preventing negative impact on the LGBTQ community but also positive impact as well. There's not a whole lot of light that shines on them that basically screams "we're just human beings like you" and places us as deviant individuals. Needless to say, though, we have come a good way along since at least the 1970s or so when being homosexual was considered a mental illness. The addition of "they/them" pronouns into an online dictionary was another major positive. Even now, there are still a lot of information that has been shared online but has yet to be brought into the public eye or more individuals that are in the LGBTQ community that could find it useful such as how anyone that could be genderfluid and still identify as a female. To me, that bit of information really shined more light on the genderfluid term as a whole to where I felt more in sync with it to use it for myself. As for a cultural stance, I think it's really interesting to see such identifications like two-spirit coming into being. It seems like depending on the culture a person originates from, the view on those that identify as "queer" in one aspect or another is different from another while still retaining specific key points. – Julie W

—————▽—————

Cathedral City, CA (USA)

Before gay marriage was legal it was always my escape route when I was in relationships because I knew I could never get married. Yes, I got engaged a lot, but we never crossed that line, my safe line. Then they made it legal and at that time I was with the most awful, nastiest person you ever wanted to live with, or even be with. They made it legal and he was pushing for marriage … so marriage for me is not a good thing, but I'm glad that people who have been together for a long time can marry. I'm all for it, but for me personally, no. – Marcous

—————▽—————

(Germany)

It makes me sad. l really think we shouldn't have fought ourselves outta the closet to then immediately try to fit into their old school frames and patterns. I think that we can create our own concepts of social interaction, society, and culture. It's one of our most important most unique things we inherit and it is foolish to not try to unfold at least some possibilities of new paths to explore that might suit each individuals situation. To give this opportunity up to cope with people that are not respectful, full of understanding and support, is really not a good move at all. – Cornelius Günther Körn

—————————▽—————————

Santa Fe, NM (USA)

I think it's wonderful. We're equal, all the same. We are all relating in one way or another. I don't understand discrimination in any way. I believe that if people just relaxed a bit, it will be better for everyone. You don't have to have a feather duster to be gay, you don't have to be super butch to be gay. I've never understood why we segregate ourselves into a ghetto. That I've never understood. Maybe I'm a strange kind of gay person but I always have not just gay people around me. I don't feel comfortable when it's all gay people because the world is not that. If I wanted to be in a gay movie theater, a gay restaurant ... it's too much gayness and it breaks the stability of being a human being. I believe that anyone in private do whatever they want. Whether it's a male or a female, as long as they don't hurt anyone. – Juan-manuel Alonso

—————————▽—————————

Santa Fe, NM (USA)

In New Mexico, where we live, it's a live and let live community. People know we're a gay couple where we live, and nobody bothers us at all. There are places that are much more prejudiced against gays but where we are at in New Mexico it's safe. – Guy Seiler

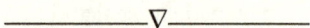

—————————▽—————————

Redwood Valley/Mendocino County, CA (USA)

It's necessary that today's young people grow into a world that knows they are equal, valued, welcomed, and treasured, regardless of sexual identification. It is also necessary that LGBTIQ youth, as well as queer-identified folk of all ages, and society in general, know our roots, our specialness, our heritage, and our rights in this society and this world. There is nothing contraindicative about being assimilated as a queer person into the straight world. Gaining marriage, military, civil and social rights are not about assimilation, they are about justice and equality. In fact, it is what our world needs right now. It strikes me that today's youth and their pop icons are proclaiming a world where queer identity is, in essence, the assimilation at question. All that being said, I will forever claim the specialness that labels me queer and continue to refer to my legally wed companion as "partner," rather than using the negatively derived and assimilated word "husband." When our specialness has been assimilated, we will be validated. – T. Lark Letchworth

———————∇———————

Petoskey, MI (USA)
Travis City, MI (USA)

I think we've been in a rough spot since 2016. I feel there's a few of us doing the work for a lot of people. I think we've become very passive with our devices taking action. We can comment on Facebook and we can write a paragraph and send it off and some people think that's all you need to do. It's just got to be a lot more, for our community to be out there. I go to different parts of the United States and there are some areas where assimilation is still behind the times. Then there are some communities, I'm shocked how embracing they are. My small town of Petoskey, Michigan is going to have their first Gay Pride this year. Travis City, Michigan, I was there in June of 2019. When I lived there at one time, it was a very conservative area, but they painted the crosswalks rainbows colors and a lot of the stores had rainbow flags. That was a surprise to me. So we've made some great advancements, but there's a lot of work to do. I think we've gone back a lot politically in a lot of different ways. – Greg R. Baird

———————∇———————

Davis, CA (USA)

My thoughts have varied on this topic depending on the time in our historical struggle and the location and particular environment. From my personal standpoint I'm pretty much a believer that one should be able to do whatever he/she wants as long as one doesn't physically hurt another person or put them in danger or slanders someone. If you want to walk around naked go for it. If you want to cover yourself up in religious garb go for it. Freedom to be transforms our full creative potential. Mass conformity stifles personal freedom and often subtlety uses fear to keep individuals from challenging the status quo in art, politics, religion, and health issues, to name a few.

That said I believe there are times when conformity to the norms of a locale may be the best strategy for achieving social change. In the 1980s in the rural college town of the University of California at Davis lesbians who normally wouldn't be caught dead wearing a dress, much less a nice dress and makeup adorned these "costumes" when making formal appeals for LGB equality at City Council meetings and community forums. Had they chosen their daily "dyke" clothes realistically they probably wouldn't have reached as many towns persons.

I can't count the numbers of times I've heard out gay people say, "I just wish those guys wouldn't dress so provocatively" or "I wish they wouldn't act so nellie." When we dismiss these important parts of our community we lose a part of what I feel is a mission of our movement: to embrace all folks to their fullest positive potentials and let personal freedom grow.

As a teen I was terrified of gay men like Liberace. Even though he wasn't publicly out he represented a stereotype that I didn't recognize in myself. My internalized homophobia wanted gay men to look and act like John Wayne or Robbie Benson and women to look and act like Elizabeth Montgomery or Dianna Rigg. I of course fell into a self-limiting trap of hoping we all could just be the same, fit in, be accepted, and live happily ever after.

Those old enough to remember may recall a hugely successful campaign in the '60s and '70s to encourage more women cigarette smokers by the tobacco industry. Disgustingly hopping on the slogans of the Women's Liberation Movement these multinational corporations invited women to be independent enough to have their own brand of cigarette. They proclaimed, "you've come a long way baby, to get where you've got today, you've got your own cigarette, you've come a long long way."

So women were invited to assimilate in order to be a part of society's club, without a worry that now women too could be killing themselves off more quickly, just like men.

I am thrilled we know that LGBT folks are everywhere, are diverse ethnically, politically, etc. Where I draw the line is though when assimilation means that we become such conformists to a societal belief system that begins to prohibit our special characteristics and creative spirit. That same line can be applied towards the assimilation of ethnic minorities into mainstream society. Yesterday's mainstream society denied marriage equality, allowed/allows job discrimination against us based on arbitrary grounds. It's that same assimilation that frowns upon black, female, gender fluid and Hispanic equality to name a few.

Log Cabin Republicans may be the ultimate example of gay assimilation on steroids but personally I think anyone who supports the politics of inequality or exclusion should not enjoy the fruits of our hard fought labor and we should boycott sex with these folks. – Paul Harris

--------∇--------

Chicago, IL (USA)

Speaking as a gay man, I feel that the social and cultural assimilation of LGBTQ people has been a great step forward for my community. When I came out in the '70's I never expected to see such gains in my lifetime. I pray that our simulation into the mainstream will continue to grow and flourish; however, given this current administration we must be vigilant and not become complacent. We are not in the Obama years anymore so we must not take for granted how far we have come.

That said I have to admit that there's something I miss about being gay in the '70's when I came out. Though one had to more or less hide their homosexuality for fear of being harassed, losing one's job and a whole plethora of acts that could be waged against you, there was also something exciting and titillating about being gay. You were different. You were special and having sex with a man was so hot because it was taboo. It wasn't mainstream. – Mark Contorno

—————∇—————

(Australia)

I had often wondered about the social acceptance of LGBT people in Australia, and when the Same Sex Marriage vote happened in 2017, I was surprised … pleasantly … to see that about 62% of people voted "Yes" to it being passed into law. Certainly general acceptance tends to be a generational thing, with people up to about 40-50 being more likely to accept it. There is still a lot of discrimination and prejudice amongst our older populations, though there are many exceptions even with them. Cultural is another matter altogether … and no surprises that religion in these cultures is the main instigator of discrimination, prejudice, intolerance and stigma. Let's face it … who'd be openly gay in the Islamic world! Considering what religion is supposed to be about … it certainly manages to promote a lot of hate under many different names – Islam, Hindu, Christian, Fundamentalist … the list rolls on! It is never easy to come out, but certain cultures have such a strong lineage of what they consider "male roles" within their society that coming out as gay is just a form of cultural alienation. Greeks, Italians, Lebanese, Muslims, Turks, Egyptians, Jamaicans are particularly harsh on those coming out as gay. Here in Australia we have seen a vast shift in the social acceptance of LGBT people over the last few decades. I do a seniors' gym class three times a week. At 66, I'm probably the youngest there, and I'm often the only male. I've been doing the classes for nearly 12 months now and have made a couple of friends over that time. I've never been openly gay within the class … though I personally think it's pretty obvious I am, though at this stage of my life, it's not something I feel I need to make a big song and dance about. Over coffee with a couple I've become close to, I've mentioned that my ex-partner "him/he" lives nearby. No one batted an eye. I feel that with the strong movement away from organised religion, that the realisation that most people interact with gay people on a day-to-day basis through shopping, accessing services, at work, the gym, and within their own family and friends' circles that the incidences of discrimination are quickly declining. There is also a realisation that in reality, our lives are really no different to anybody else's. The same sex marriage debate here showed a strong movement towards social justice, and despite the high volume of "No" vote publicity from churches and religious organisations, people as a whole saw through it, and ignored it. I think there is hope for us yet, as an integrated society. – Tim Alderman

————————∇————————

Brunswick, ME (USA)

Certainly, same-sex marriage and openness in many facets of life have made a great improvement in life. Unfortunately, we still have so far to go, so many anti-LGBTQ groups and politicians, so many young LGTBQ people bullied, raped, committing suicide. It's still "not easy being gay." – Michael Pickel

————————∇————————

Glenview, IL (USA)

I think it is empowering on one level to see the social and cultural assimilation of LGBTQ people. Where we live in Glenview, people don't think twice about our sexuality or marital status. We live in a multi-religious, cultural, social community. We are friends with everyone we meet. From another perspective it is sad to see some organizations, whose purpose was to promote the LGBTQ community, struggle to stay in existence. Some have even disappeared as they don't seem to be needed. The younger generation has no memory of what life was like before assimilation started so they may not think twice about their current state of affairs.

However, abuse and harassment still exist. The lack of common social interactions which was offered by some of these organizations is still needed. It is important to have something like this in place to help those who are struggling. I know there are some agencies that help the abused, the homeless, and the harassed. Social connectivity is important too, so the LGBTQ individual does not feel isolated. The bars or baths can only do so much. One such organization that no longer exists is NSG or North

Suburban Gays. It was a strictly social organization for gays in the North Suburban Chicago area, but it was one that provided an important outlet for men (and women) to socialize once a month with each other. We established friendships there, which we maintain to this day. – Yehuda Jacobi

—————∇—————

St. Cloud, MN (USA)

So far the socially/culturally assimilated LGBTQ+ people are white, affluent, able bodied, of Christian Western European backgrounds, in monogamous relationships. They are gatekeepers, and the mainstream media and LGBTQ+ media hold them up as a standard for everyone else to conform. I am not for it. Equal rights for LGBTQ+ people, to me, does not mean we aspire to live like heterosexual people. We have to live as we believe and as we love, and we have to know our history. A lot of that history remains lost due to colonization, slavery, and genocide. We have always existed, and in our own way, in our own spaces. We need those spaces back more than ever now. – Rachel Wexelbaum

—————∇—————

New York City (USA)

I came out just six years after Stonewall and I remember going to GAA meetings in New York and the ENDLESS debates about whether queer folk were better off remaining outside the cultural mainstream or working to demand a seat at the table. Well, the assimilationists won (Kameny, Gittings, et al). But what a price has been paid.

So much queer spirit has been either lost or Disney-fied. I would rather cast my lot with queer liberationists (Ginsburg, Grahn, Lourde, Reich, etc.). In the end, I don't know that it matters. The planet is unlikely to survive anyway. – David Clayton

—————∇—————

Palm Springs, CA (USA)

I grew up in the Midwest. I don't think of LGBTQ people being assimilated at all! Heteros can't be trusted! I have felt marginalized and trivialized in every job and city I have worked and lived in. I have been fired for being gay. I rarely trust people these days.

What I believe is queers do everything heteros do. It's just when we

have lots of sex, or play kinky, or push the norms, somehow queers are trashed up over it – whereas if it's a hetero man or woman, it's promoted as a trendy hip norm. – Tony Earl

————————▽————————

King, NC (USA)

It is my observation as an older gay man that it seems to me that the young generation of LGBTQ folks take it for granted that they can express themselves so freely in today's world with a plethora of social choices, APPS, and situations to connect with each other.
In the days before the internet and the embracing of some of the main religious denominations as we have now, many of us found our tribe in dark seedy bars, cruise parks, and bath houses. Those environs are far from the norm now – which is a wonderful thing. I just wish that the young generation could realize and appreciate the struggle it took to get us here. – Ron Cline

————————▽————————

Charlottetown, Prince Edward Island (Canada)

I think it's vital that we continue to fight to obtain all of the rights given to our straight peers, but at the same time, I think it's crucial that we stand apart as queer people and remain visible that way. Equality does not mean being the same as. It's all about having options and protections. Sure, there is overlap between straight and queer lives, but there are also differences. We were forced to form our culture, diverse as it is, and we've made something with meaning, a history and hopefully a future. By no means should queers disappear into straight culture. – Dave Stewart

————————▽————————

San Diego, CA (USA)

I'm torn about it. It shouldn't be a big deal. Theoretically we should be able to fuck whoever we want to, whenever we want to. We should all be like this, all the time. But there is a history and there is a culture. That oppression and the remembrance of all those people who went through that shit, as we continue to do. So, I think it's different now in so much as we don't need gathering places, the lesbians in San Francisco don't have a bar anymore. That's hard, but that's because they CAN go anywhere. It used to be that you COULDN'T. But that remembrance is still important, and we need to keep that alive. When we lose the places and the history, that's a problem because there were millions of people before us who never got to come out and died." – Serafine Sawyer

—————∇—————

Scottsdale, AZ (USA)

I find there are a lot more open-minded people who are very inclusive now, but on the other hand, there are many more evil hateful ones that were "hidden" and are now out of the homophobic closet due to the POTUS. – Sherrie Howe

—————∇—————

Des Moines, IA (USA)

I have to answer the major part of this as a queer man of 65 years old. For some years now I have noticed and spoken about our abdication of our leadership in many areas. It is not only in the entertainment industry and fashion that I speak but culturally as well. It used to be that we were on the forefront of many areas. Besides entertainment and fashion, there were also literature, politics, design and let's say cultural trend. We did it first and better and the rest of the world took our cues and interpreted them in their way.

While the benefits of same sex "marriage" are obvious, I can't help feeling that we dropped the ball. The two-partner model, while being acceptable by some and tolerated by others, I feel doesn't go far enough. I won't go so far as saying that those who choose this model are also choosing heteronormativity, but I suspect that our wanting acceptance has caused us not to call the whole institution of "marriage" into serious question.

We have, instead of agitating for forms that are elastic to include all of the humans who choose them, have selected instead to settle for tolerance and acceptance. The two-partner model sadly excludes bisexuals, polyamorists as well as everyone who is gender non-conforming.
Marriage is about commitment and bonding – period. Humans of all types ought to have their commitments and bonds protected by law. For me, this is major.

In addition, we have made no inroads into eradicating racism, sexism, ageism and classism and continue to be sadly lacking in those areas. The whole "no blacks, no fems, no fats, no little dicks" craziness of "dating sites" is a scandal. As a group so hurt by prejudice, we long ago needed to eschew prejudice ourselves. We have not and I find our insistence on rationalizing and making lame excuses for holding on to prejudice ("it's a personal preference") frankly appalling and shameful.

The fashion industry's embracing of "plus size" models and the use of a wider variety of "types" has outshone us and we should have led in this area as well. – Sr. Freida Peoples aka DJ Chrysler Sheldon

―――――∇―――――

Fort Lauderdale, FL (USA)

It's what we worked for isn't it? But I miss the sense of community there used to be. I also miss being someone outside mainstream society, being a bit of a rebel. – Rick Karlin

―――――∇―――――

(Pakistan)
Worcester, MA (USA)

When we normalize our existence as LGBTQ people, we normalize our lives and our rights too. I see that a lot in the US and its media. Representation and visibility of LGBTQ+ matters, the more social and cultural assimilation there is in the mainstream cultural, socio-political discourse the more our rights would gain prominences. – Salman

WHAT ARE THE BEST AND WORST PARTS OF GOING OUT TO THE BARS/CLUBS?

Chicago, IL (USA)

I think the best is that there is still great music and I love to dance. You can always communicate to me much more through movement and music in a way that breaks barriers, that brings people to together, and a sense of humor. A lot of the negative things are ageism, stereotyping and this and that. But it's been perennial like that and I wish there was a bit more diversity. Embracing everyone a little bit more. It's a turn off. – James Scalfani

————————▽————————

Memphis, TN (USA)
New York, NY (USA)
Nashville, TN (USA)

Best part: camaraderie, drag performance, healthy buzz, and, back in the day, I'm not ashamed to say, an exhilarating hook-up.
Worst part: incipient alcoholism, STDs, AIDS, alienation.
I think my favorite bar was The Bar in NYC. George's in Memphis had drag performance art *par excellence*, not just drag, but performance art. And for the sake of personal history, I came out at 19 at a bar in Nashville called The Jungle and had some of the best times during my early sojourn in Memphis at The Front Page, affectionately called The Frog Pond. – Oran Walker

————————▽————————

103

Chicago, IL (USA)

I love going to gay clubs because it's one of the few places where I can see my queer friends. I have a hard time with the loud music and lights though. I usually won't go to them unless it's for a show and I leave as soon as the show is over. – C'est Kevvie (Wilhelmina)

———————▽———————

Chicago, IL (USA)

The best part is cruising a guy and watching him move. I guess it's like hunting. You either wanted to hunt or be hunted. That whole atmosphere, that whole vibe, that whole physical movement. As well as being able to talk to people and know this person is one of us. When I grew up, particularly in my teens, I had no idea that gay people even existed. I didn't even know if there was a word for what I was. I just knew I was strange or different, somehow wrong. Being able to go to the bars gave me a place where I was not alone, I'm with other guys, there's a community here. There's more of us than I thought. The worst part of the bars is the drunks. I can't abide a sloppy drunk. But that's just me. – Steve

———————▽———————

Midwestern City (USA)

The best part is spending time in queer space with other queer folk. The worst part is attitude when it is present with its curse of excluding and looking down on others. – Anonymous

———————▽———————

San Francisco, CA (USA)

Well, I never thought I'd say this; I don't miss going out EVERY NIGHT at all. There were thousands of moments of bliss, when the company, the crowd, the music, your high, it all mixed well and we danced, danced, danced. Then at other times, not so much. One went out to see and be seen, that was the unspoken agreement. We effortlessly straddled genres and styles. We'd be doing the hard-core disco stomp on Saturday, and Monday night we'd slam dance at a punk club. Often, we'd end up at a White Castle or some such thing, stuffing our fucking faces, or we'd go sex-hunting, (the baths, a park, empty churches ...). We had the best music, the best clothes, the best drugs. I have no idea what people do in clubs now. You know, it's funny ... I'm dancing (well, seat dancing, anyway. It's hard to dance and write.) to some James Brown now, a song I spent considerable time dancing to when I was oh, fourteen-years-old. I seem to have come full circle, cutting up the same old rug that I did back then, and it has lost none of its magic. Clubs are crowded, too many stupid, drunk people spending too much money, and not having that much fun. I'm sorry. We took all the fun with us when we left. We either smoked it, lost it, spent it, or spilled something nasty all over it. In any case, that's why we have all these tales to tell. – Terence Smith (Joan Jett Blakk)

―――――∇―――――

Chicago, IL (USA)

The best part is to see people, hang out, and be in your own element. The worst part are the crowds and the people who are dismissive, like "We don't want someone to be old, or someone to be ugly. We don't want somebody too fat. We don't want someone to have this skin color, or that ethnic background." There's a whole lot of that, especially among younger gays, they are very sectional and compartmentalized. I don't know if that's a function of being older and having the sense that everybody belongs and they don't yet. Or if they've just simply ... I don't want to say they've had it too easy ... but that's what it feels like sometimes. They just expect everything is owed to them. – Mike

―――――∇―――――

Birmingham, AL (USA)
Chicago, IL (USA)

Birmingham: Gay bars were not just the most visible but the most important part of the gay community. A gay bar was where I first came out. A gay bar was where I met friends and sex partners. Gay bars were where I came to love disco, where I was transported out of myself and out of my painful daily reality to a fantasy world of love and joy. Gay bars were safe spaces, where I knew I would be safe from straight people, from their prying eyes, their hateful words, and their hurtful fists.

I did have to put up with a lot of secondary smoke, but that's no longer a problem.

Chicago: The gay bars no longer attract an exclusively gay crowd. Many people see this as a positive development. I do not. I do not feel safe around straight people. I need a space where I can count on being myself without fear of rejection or assault. Gay bars used to be that space. That's been taken away for me, and nothing has replaced it. – Bert Thompson

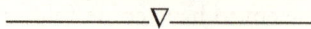

———————▽———————

Chicago, IL (USA)

I don't do that anymore, but I can tell you what I thought of it years ago. I liked it for the most part, it was fun meeting all kinds of new gay people. Of course, I was a lot younger. I had a lot of good friends, that was the best aspect of it. It was wonderfully social. I don't even know if people go to clubs anymore or if they just hook up online. When I was young everybody went to discos. The bad side of it was, the music was usually so fucking loud you couldn't hear people talking. You had to leave the club to have a conversation with somebody. Even then, I didn't like the fact that a lot of the younger gay men were mean to the older ones. It seemed to cruel. I wasn't attracted to them but I always tried to be nice to them. Basically, I was raised to be nice and I'm a gentleman. That bugged me, that vindictive cruelty that young people have. It wasn't acceptable behavior. – Xavier Bathsheba-Negron

———————▽———————

Tulsa, OK (USA)

I moved here eight years ago after I retired. I lived in the Dallas/Fort Worth area for 20 years. While I was in Dallas/Fort Worth, 18 of the 20 years I lived with someone and we didn't go out. I really have not been out to clubs since then. So, I don't have an answer for that. My idea of going clubbing, it's that it's not much fun. I did that and it was fun, but it's not much fun anymore. In gay years I'm 195 years old. – Renny

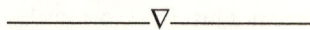

———————▽———————

Chicago, IL (USA)

Well I think that we are starting to recognize what we miss about them now that we are held out of them in the times of social distancing. The best part was the act of socialization and of being with others. Of course, a major part of the bars/clubs was the cruising, and the interaction of "the hunt." I certainly miss that the most, even as bars/clubs have changed over the years that cruising activity has changed as well. I feel bad for those in the community that have grown up with the internet as the first point of contact and outreach. Sure, there are many things that are improvements, like you generally get what you are really looking for, well that is if the profile is accurate. I just miss that hunt. The going out for the evening, making the efforts of what you think will get the look from someone, or just the release of getting on the floor and dancing with your friends to the latest songs that drove the community wild.

The worst part was working in the bars/or clubs and have to deal with those that could not "hold" their liquor ... never a pretty time. – Dean Ogren

————————▽————————

Chicago, IL (USA)

It is nice to stand in a bar and feel comfortable eyeing and kissing other men. What I do not like feeling is being judged solely on my looks. I also do not like the pressure to keep drinking bad brands of alcohol. I hate the loud repetitive dance music. I once went into Hydrate on Halsted street by myself and no one would talk to me. I thought "This music is terrible. What would I rather be listening to?" At that moment I wrote a rock song in my head, while the beat went on in the background. I still play that song to this day. It is called, *Bless Me Father for I Have Sinned, I've Been Drinking Again* – Lars von Keitz

————————▽————————

London (UK)

I wouldn't know. When I was living in London, I was wafted by friends from one exclusive private club to another on a regular basis. I've never gone to a public gay club. – Louis Richard de Bourbon de Parme et de Savoie, Prince de la Pau

————————▽————————

North Carolina (USA)

The best part is being with other people who are like you. If you are a professional like me and you go to work every day, you have to put on a bit of a mask to deal with being a professional. You don't really bring a gay identity to work. People may know that you're gay and you might be out at work, but you're not going to use gay slang, or reference gay culture very much. It's not a part of doing business with people. So the nice part about going to the gay bars is just being around other gay people where you can be yourself and be immersed in gay queer culture and shut out the outside world. Honestly, the worst part about it is the cliquishness that can happen, where identity groups get into their own things and they don't mingle with each other. There are some bars and clubs that foster that attitude and some that don't. – Randy

———————▽———————

Waverly, IA (USA)
Chicago, IL (USA)
San Francisco, CA (USA)

I used to enjoy going to gay bars, especially those that featured male strippers. The first time I saw a drag show was at Kitty Sheon's in Chicago. I asked the guy next to me if the drag performer was going to strip at the end of the act. He replied, "God I hope not." Early drag performers would pull off their wig to prove they were actually men. I don't think today's piss-elegant queens ever do that. I actually thought that drag would disappear with liberation, when gay men would no longer have to pretend to look at women. Boy was I wrong. I have no problem with cross dressing in everyday life or transgender persons. I just don't consider drag an art form. I spent many summer vacations in San Francisco and liked the gay bars there (the clone years) because the customers didn't have to look gay, be bitchy or camp. I also thought that camp would disappear with liberation but unfortunately it seems to be making a comeback in the Midwest. – Robert Beck

———————▽———————

Chicago, IL (USA)

Honestly, I only go to one bar and that's Smart Bar. I have family there, they know me, they treat me very well, I treat them very well. The sense of community and home and family that I've found there, that's the best part. I've been searching for that my whole life. I finally got it after a very long time. I've been living in Chicago for 27 years and it's taken a long time to find my tribe. That's the best part. The worst part is the younger gays who don't have a perspective or the historical wherewithal to fully appreciate what they have. No-one ever believes me when I tell them how old I am because I roll in a different way. I'm just not your typical 46 year old, whatever that means. The hardest part is just people who have preconceived notions of how it's supposed to be, what you're supposed to be doing, what you're supposed to be wearing. That's always bothered me, and it's always been extremely boring.

I have no interest in what is popular or in, I just do what I do and I don't really ... I don't appreciate when somebody gives me shade who doesn't know me. At the end of the day I don't give a fuck. Too old for that. – Jeff Ramone

—————▽—————

San Francisco, CA (USA)
Palm Springs, CA (USA)

In my younger days, I frequented bars a lot late at night, for the booze, music and dancing; and especially for the opportunity to get laid. The downside to all of this was that I would binge drink at these bars. I don't do that anymore. I've been fortunate to live in cities with large gay populations with enough bars to cater to old men as well as younger. These days I mostly go to bars that cater to old farts like me, but only for happy hour, to enjoy a drink or two (usually two). I do this 2-3 times a week. There is a lot of camaraderie at Streetbar, my favorite bar in Palm Springs. I can walk into the place and know that I will see many friends and acquaintances, including the bar tenders. I have so much fun when I'm there that I feel like I'm in high school again, except that we can drink legally. – Gary Borgstedt

—————▽—————

Chicago, IL (USA)

The best parts used to be actually meeting people. I once worked at Clarks on Clark the best dive gay bar on the Northside. I was there when the whole cell thing hit. I would often bribe the patrons with shots to turn off their cell phones and actually talk to men they were sitting next to. Now when I am well rested "naps" and I do go out, I am so sad. Sometimes crowds of men are all gathered and not a single one is talking. They are all staring into their phones pretending to be engaged and they go home alone. I'd rather invite friends over for dinner and drinks at my house. – Philip Bernal

—————▽—————

Rockford, IL (USA)

When I was younger the best parts of going to the clubs was that fact that it was a place that I go with my friends and we could dance, laugh, live, love, express ourselves, and enjoy our shared company. We liked the loud music, having fun with our bodies, seeing strippers/drag queens etc. And while I don't like the loud music and pumping bass, and crowds anymore, I still like being able to go to drag bingo, stripper shows, and again being part of the community. I do think that in some instances the community can be a bit harsh to those who might not fit the mold, so that's something that I don't like about going to the bars. But with the right amount of confidence I know I can overcome this issue. – Patrick J. Murphy III

—————▽—————

Seattle, WA (USA)

The best parts are seeing the culture survive in this form. Bars/clubs have always been a part of the LGBTQ society, either illicit or legitimate. There is a certain bonding to seeing your 'tribe' releasing their inhibitions as one, pulsing unit on a dance floor, or the feeling of power to see that community congregating as one.

The negative aspect of bar/club life is that it represents a ghetto for us. We feel that it is the only place for us to meet and congregate in safety. It also, unfortunately, confines us to an atmosphere that pushes drug and alcohol usage onto our community. That can be a deadly cycle. – Eric Andrews-Katz

—————▽—————

Frinton-on-Sea, Essex (UK)

At my age (late fifties), the worst bits are the noise, the crush, being invisible when trying to get served at the bar, inadequate or dirty toilets, over-priced beer. The best bits – a decent laser or light show, a male stripper or two, occasionally the music. Sex clubs can be fun. The democracy of nudity and the absence of some of the problems listed above, means there's a refreshing honesty as to why we're all there and you can just get down to it! I's not about "finding Mr. Right," it just fulfills a basic human need. Hey, don't judge me, I'm a busy guy! – Diesel Balaam

—————▽—————

Bellport, NY (USA)

Honestly, I no longer frequent bars/clubs. There needs to be more hangouts for LGBTQ people aside from bars/clubs. Not every LGBTQ person is into that scene. – Erin Michelle Miller

——————∇——————

St Louis, MO (USA)
Rancho Mirage, CA (USA)

When I first started going out (yep, before I was 21), I was so overwhelmed and THRILLED that there were so many people like me. It all felt so right. And to this day, I benefited from getting to meet more and new people and establishing new friendships. Okay, and some much-needed sex. I know for some that as they age they still want to go out and get some, or just love getting out to be social. I, however, started becoming less interested in going out and standing around. For a while there, too many were too focused on looking at their phones, which negated being there. While I can be very open and chatty, I'm not good at approaching people. Not because of rejection, but just the fear of dealing with attitudes. At work, people are basically thrust at me and I have a great time and love to interact (I'm always recommending what I call "frontage road" films, the ones that are just off to the side, away from the processed mass-audience ones). About 10 years ago I started feeling less interested in going out and hanging around. If I am meeting up with friends, then that's a different story. A friend of mine who lives "on the other side of the mountains" as I put it will drive over at least once a month and we'd go to a bar here that always has a big Sunday afternoon crowd on the patio to see friends (a certain author of this book is one of them). It's a joy to be there and talk with our friends, I usually wind up losing my voice because of trying to be heard over the music and people (I'm also having vocal cord issues, but that's for another story). While I'd rather just hang out at a friend's shindig/wing ding/get-together and socialize that way, it's still nice to be in a bar like the one we sometimes go to, to be reminded that we're all still here and experiencing BEING. – Todd Jaeger

——————∇——————

South Carolina (USA)
Chicago, IL (USA)

I wasn't comfortably out until I moved to Chicago. Once I was gaining comfort in South Carolina I would try to go to a gay bar and would circle around a bit, find a parking spot where no one could recognize my car (as if anyone would recognize my car).

I moved to Chicago June 5, 2000 so it was Welcome to Chicago! Here's a Pride Parade! I hadn't really been into the Halsted Street bars until then so my first real time going in it was like parting water. My ass was grabbed so much that day I finally thought "When in Rome…"

After I came into myself and made friends the bars were either a location to meet friends, or a tool to use for fundraising. I've never been much of the type to go to any bar alone and that didn't change after I came out. The handful of times I did happen to go it was uncomfortable for me. I wasn't going there to hook up. If I ran into someone I knew that was great. But being Southern I smile at pretty much everyone. Not to be cynical but more often than not I got the not-too-subtle brush off when I hadn't even done anything more than smile at someone because they walked past me and we made eye contact.

I did notice two interesting effects the gay bar scene had on me though:

- I had a lot of deaf friends and we'd meet at a bar (usually Sidetrack) and get a table back in the corner and chat the night away. I wasn't paying attention to people that passed by as I was watching their hands. But on these nights when I wasn't paying attention to the crowd, often some in the crowd paid attention to me. I was approached more often when I was there with groups.

- I grew up playing it straight and went to bars through college and my twenties. (straight obviously) and had a great time with friends, etc. After about six years living in Chicago some straight friends of mine came to visit and we ended up in one of the Wrigleyville bars and I found I was uncomfortable. Not like I was in danger uncomfortable, but I felt like I did not belong there. I don't think I've been entirely comfortable in straight bars since.

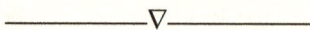

– Chris Grace

——————▽——————

Chicago, IL (USA)

The best part is going to Touché to get my rocks off. Going with friends is great. However, I'm 52, which means if I go to Roscoe's or the more dancey bars I get looked at as if I'm made out of glass because of my age. So I just don't go to those venues because it's not good for your ego, dealing with a crowd that's considerably younger than you and they look right through you.
– Drew

——————▽——————

Palm Springs, CA (USA)

The worst part for me as a trans-person is the reception that I get. It could be very friendly but sometimes gay men can be very difficult to be around. They can criticize you and tell you to pick a sex. It's rare but it happens, so I think it's the anticipation of going in a place where you feel you're being stared at. I always wondered myself, some of those men, if they went into a straight bar would probably get upset if straight people were staring at them. To me that's the bad part of going to a gay bar. That, plus, quite frankly, in the past three or four years, I even think about what could happen. Somebody doing something in the bar like shooting, or fire bombing. It just doesn't feel as safe, although nothing has happened to me. I never felt that way years ago but I think about maybe something could happen. I think that's the negative way I feel about gay bars. I'd say the positive part is just the opposite, the camaraderie. I find that when I went into a bar as a gay man, I blended right in. Nobody noticed you unless they were interested in you. If I go into a friendly gay bar as trans, I feel almost a welcoming, that a protection is around you. That's just completely the opposite of what sometimes happens. That's the good news, you feel that it's family and that people realize that we are all vulnerable, perhaps trans people are a little bit more vulnerable. You kind of feel the protection when you go in and that's a great feeling. – Andee

—————▽—————

Palm Springs, CA (USA)
San Jose, CA (USA)

I am not a big bar and club girl. I actually lived most of my life in isolation. I was extremely depressed and dissociated most of my life. Not coming out as trans caused a lot of dysphoria and I was unable to function properly. I also had an undiagnosed fatigue disorder, which I recently fixed. So I didn't have a lot of energy to do anything, so I never really went out until just recently. I mean, I've been going to clubs. The best part in Palm Springs is that it's accepting and there's no worry that you're going to be discriminated against. At the same time there's an uplifting of all cultures within the LGBT community. Everyone seems to be very supportive, even if they may not understand your particular struggles. They just take it as is. If you tell them you identify as a woman who is sexually attracted to women, it's "Ok, that's cool." But if I were to go back home, people would probably argue with me a lot more. Try to contextualize it or understand it better. At the same time not want to listen. – Kelsey

—————▽—————

Cathedral City, CA (USA)

The best part is the sense of community. The worst part is to see the alcoholism, it's really depressing. – Jim

113

—————▽—————

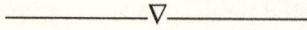

Palm Springs, CA (USA)

The best part, of course, is being among other gay people, having a good time, drinking, laughing, getting to see people we haven't seen in a while, because they're family to me. I think of everyone as cousins, some are brothers and sisters, a little closer. But we're all family. It's always great to see people and have a good time. The downside would be running into people who are too drunk, or that don't know the concept of soap. Their human body odor is just the way they are. I respect them for being themselves, but it bothers me. It always happens when we're out. It's a shame that one of the worst bad things now is that when you go into a bar or nightclub, especially if it's someplace new, my first thought is, "Where are the exits?" God forbid something happens, we need to know how to get out, how to keep ourselves safe. The constant scanning of the crowd, "Everybody is cool, nobody's fighting." That's the negatives of going out. – David Vega (Lucifers Axe)

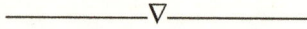

—————▽—————

Palm Springs, CA (USA)

I love going out, even if it's only once in a while or seven nights a week. It's like seeing family, family you like, family you want to be around. People you want to catch up with. People you accept, just for who they are. Their best parts could be their flaws. We have so many people we know in our lives that we are blessed to see them. It doesn't matter which venue you go to, which circuit party you go to, it's like time never lapsed in between. That feels so good. The worst part is the first thing that I look for are the exits, for safety issues. It's just a fact of life now that we have to deal with that, and we do. We're careful. I do not leave the house without pepper spray or a taser. I carry it everywhere with me. That's how it is, we have to be safe. It's not any different than it was back in the '60s and '70s, the Upstairs bar that burned in Louisiana … it's no different now from then. It's just that the press coverage has changed. – Keith Kollinicos (Missa Distic)

—————▽—————

Palm Springs, CA (USA)

The best parts of going out to the bars/clubs for me is that they are still the best places to go with friends to celebrate, to put a tough week behind you, to enjoy good music (and perhaps some dancing), to spend time with like-minded people, and to just be yourself without fear of reprisal. The worst parts are that so many of the bars/clubs are no longer our very own safe spaces like they once were. Men-only, women-only, gay-only, bisexual-only, and mixed events and spaces, etc. once served a real purpose in our community by giving people at a very precarious time in their lives places where they could meet and connect with others that they could relate to at a very intimate and personal level without fear. Now we're so mired down in gender politics and absolute inclusivity that those needs are no longer being met for people who are just coming to terms with their sexuality and gender identity. In addition, every weekend our local nightclub is overtaken by the new trend of straight bachelorette parties being held in gay clubs – the participants often drink too much, manhandle the dancers and other patrons, and generally they don't tip the bartenders very well at all. This can completely ruin the experience for people coming out to experience the good things I listed above. Additionally, in certain cities (not so much in Palm Springs), we have met certain younger patrons who have been completely disrespectful and often downright rude to anyone over the age of 40. And, of course, there is always the chance that someone will overdo it or just can't handle their liquor, and who likes being around a messy drunk? – D. Warner

———————▽———————

San Francisco, CA (USA)

Community and acceptance, but now being older, not so welcoming with overt and silent critical assumptions, and insults about age. The best bar, without dancing, is still the Twin Peaks at the corner of Castro Street and Market. With its large picture windows, the first gay bar to have such a bold element, one can sit, talk to friends, and watch a very queer world sashay past. – David Hatfield Sparks

———————▽———————

Louisiana (USA)

Worst is always self-image. We know that we shouldn't live by the standards set by our media consumption but media is media because of its power and sometimes control. Sometimes alcohol can bring out the least desired characteristics and that can be a party pooper for me. The best is humans, conversations, flirting, the joy of someone dancing, shared excitement over a tasty drink, hopping from one bar to the next, creating memories to be able to reminisce. – Katorri A.

———————▽———————

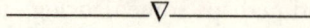

Chicago, IL (USA)

The best in my youth was that this might be the night that I meet "THE ONE." The worst was that it never happened. – Dennis Hardenstein

———————▽———————

New Orleans, LA.

The older you get you realize what older people told you is true. Kids these days … I think yeah I was 21 and skinny and cool once too. – Terry Gaskins

———————▽———————

La Mesa, Tequendama Province (Colombia)

Best parts are the music, the guys ... the hormonal relief. Worst part is the transport back home and the feeling of insecurity – Cristian

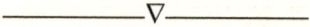

———————▽———————

Cleveland, OH (USA)

The best part is the camaraderie, with the feeling I am among my people, dancing, and fun. The worst part is that sometimes there can be cliques, or nights where I spend lots of money at the bars and end up having my self-esteem take a hit. – Roger

———————▽———————

Grand Rapids, MI (USA)

I like seeing others at bars, being happy, enjoying the music, dancing. I don't like when they aren't busy/crowded or only busy very late at night. – Mark S

———————▽———————

Palm Springs, CA (USA)

I haven't gone to the bars for four or five months. The camaraderie, to be

around my own kind is the best part. The worst part is probably not hooking up. That can affect your self-esteem. And it can get catty sometimes. That was back when I was young. I don't care too much about it now. – Spike

———————∇———————

Chicago, IL (USA)

Well, it depends on the bar. In my favorite bars, the best part is having adventurous conversations with the bartenders and the patrons. If I go alone to Touché or Second Story in Chicago, for instance, I can always count on a long interesting conversation with whoever happens to sit next to me. For instance, in the past year, at these two bars, I have had long, long, long conversations with these strangers:

1) A refugee artist from Afghanistan who subsequently gifted me with one of his extraordinary paintings.
2) Another college English teacher from out of town (I teach college English too), with whom I talked philosophically about being "out" in the classroom and with whom I adjourned to the local Taco Bell at 2:00A where an itinerant artist did a caricature of me in Crayolas. (The caricature now hangs on my office door.)
3) A younger musical comedy queen with whom I sat in the rowdy backroom of Touché and, wearing chest harness and bar vest, analyzed *Follies* and *Once on This Island* for two hours.
4) A member of Onyx with whom I shared a sensitive and surprisingly sad conversation about the various forms of bigotry – from both within and without the gay community – directed against black gay men who are into leather.

In each of these cases, initial barstool chit-chat with a stranger became a meaningful conversation with a brother. Whenever I finish any of these unexpected encounters with strangers, I always feel more "woke." As Kio Stark says in *When Strangers Meet*, "When something unexpected happens it calls you to full attention, turns your awareness outward to the world. You are awake." Most of my recent "awakenings" have occurred on barstools, holding a rocks glass of Templeton, watching the ice slowly melt into the dark amber rye, and listening to the life story of the stranger next to me unfolding against the ambient sound of a gay bar on a Saturday night.

On the other hand, there are bars that seem to be closed systems – places where nobody knows your name nor cares to know. I have found these bars in both Chicago and New Orleans. I shudder to recall the night when, feeling low, confused, and lonely, I went to Sidetrack just to be distracted by idle chatter with bartenders and bar patrons. As I sat at the bar, I noticed that every single patron was staring at his phone rather than engaging with the men around him. This went on for an hour. I finally left, discouraged, after one drink, the only time in my existence when I left a bar after only one drink.

On a happier note, I once sat in the front bar in Touché surrounded by two men on their phones. I was on my phone too, texting a friend that I was going to meet there later in the evening. One of the bartenders saw us texting, spread his long arms along the bar in front of us, and literally yelled at the three of us: "I cannot believe that three attractive men are sitting by themselves at a bar on a Saturday night and you are all staring at YOUR FUCKIN' PHONES! Put them away and talk to each other!" We all did as we were told.

There's a bartender who takes the purpose of a gay bar very seriously. I wish they were all like that. –William Demaree

———————▽———————

Chicago, IL (USA)

Being a 67-year old alcoholic, I avoid them. – Steve Kmetko

———————▽———————

Palm Springs, CA (USA)

The best things about going to the bars and clubs is to be with the tribe. It's a tribal thing, a gathering, it's our sacred spaces. That and the streets and the gutters, the public toilets, the bus station lobbies, you name it. These are the public places where queers have gathered. Queers have been excluded from mainstream culture and my partner and I often go to the beer bust on Sunday just to feel the tribal beat, to feel a part of the community, something you can't really experience on a screen. A screen is helpful for communication but it's not the full ambience that you would get in a public setting. The sociability of it and also the performance aspects of it. If you go into a queer bar, or club, you're going to see queers perform and this is a really great gift in our culture, a joy. Performances are not fixed, they are constantly changing, there is a permission for constant remaking of oneself or creation of new characters. This is a very important theme in African-American culture as well. I read about the work of this African-American artist, whose exhibit I saw at MOCA in LA. He has these huge paintings of his people in very elaborate costumes and he said, "I am fascinated by how as African-Americans we spend hours preparing our appearance before we go out." Well … duh! You're talking about every gay man I ever met. So, what's going on here – this is an important point – if we are given a less than fair or equal identity in American culture then we have to create our own. And we have.

Just because you can have marriage now, it's no reason to give up the other aspects of our queer identity. These public spaces are very important and we're very fortunate here in Palm Springs to have leather bars and Jewish delis, things that are vanishing from the American landscape. The worst thing about the gay bars is you see the damage our people sometimes wear on their faces from having survived from when being queer could cost you your life and your family. There are still people trying to murder us every day. But that too has an upside because in a gay bar today it doesn't matter what color you are, what age you are, what gender you are. As we have come out of the closet, we've discovered who we are. We are a much larger and more diverse community than we ever imagined. It's a bit overwhelming. At the same time, it's a great achievement for that to happen. In these gathering places we get to see ourselves and our diversity. That tribal spirit goes on and you can flaunt it and you can be as queer as you want to be and it's on your own turf. – Greg Day

————————∇————————

Cathedral City, CA (USA)

The best part for me is … I like to call myself a fashionista. I like to see what's new, who's wearing what, how it's worn. The downside of that is that I've learned over the many years of going to gay bars, you have to belong to a clique. If you're not in that clique you pretty much don't exist at all. A lot of those cliques will not accept outsiders or even invite you into their clique. So you have to be beyond rich, beyond hung, or beyond a perfect tan, or just looks, just to get into those cliques. I don't qualify in any of those because I'm more realistic. I like everybody, till they prove otherwise. So I'm in my, what my sister calls, "the grungy clique." I hang around with people who are not socially acceptable to everyone else. – Marcous

————————∇————————

Palm Springs, CA (USA)
Chicago, IL (USA)

It's really easy in Palm Springs. It's just so easy. In the earlier days when I was going out, I was very strategic about things. I was all about the sex, and so I had this deal going where there were two leather bars in Chicago in the '90s. One had a two o'clock license and the other had a four o'clock license. I knew that if I took a little nap and got up at two in the morning, all those guys who struck out at the first leather bar would be in the second leather bar and they'd be quite hungry. It was like shooting fish in a barrel. So that was my MO at the bars was to figure out a way of negotiating all of that. But today in Palm Springs it's just easy. I think I've come to a point in my life – I'll be 63 this year – that I really don't care anymore about what people think. So I can just be myself and if they like that, that's great, and if they don't they can move on to somebody else. There's much more of a comfort level than when I was in my thirties and terrified. – Thomas Stribling

———————▽———————

Chicago, IL (USA)

For me the cost of going out to bars is a bit expensive. A good and sometimes bad part for me is the recognition. Some guys who desired me on stage come on strong then there are those who are happy to remember the good old days and when they first saw me perform. – Mercury

———————▽———————

Cathedral City, CA (USA)

The good part is meeting friends. The worst part is trying to meet new friends, to have new conversations. Also not being a drinker is a real problem. When you can't drink and be relaxed, uninhibited, it's a problem. I choose not to drink. I just decided in 1984 to stop drinking. I was a three-beers a month drinker, so there was not much to give up. – David Hardy

———————▽———————

(Germany)

I think the bitchiness between allies, as well as when you start to realize that a lot of those social interactions are caused by long term trained coping mechanisms. That's the worst, along with cheesy music. The best things about it are honest conversations and encounters that crop up out of nothing, as well as the enormous number of possible great sex available. – Cornelius Günther Körn

———————▽———————

Chicago, IL (USA)

I enjoy going to a sex club sometimes, just for the experience of knowing a place like that can still exist. I don't go to bars anymore. I used to love them

– worked hard to be known by the bartenders and get special treatment and who to go to and get the drug I wanted that night. I liked closing Berlin. Most of all I loved the "dance." Not just TO dance, but the dance of being in a crowded, smoky, sweaty room with hot gay men. Flirting, grinding, testing limits – all very fun. When I got older, I didn't need that anymore. I remember very well, a gay pride day many years ago, getting up on the dance floor at Circuit and realizing I just didn't have it anymore – that specific rhythm was gone for me. The animal drive, the quest for sex. I'd lost the beat. So, I learned to dance to a different beat. Not one where you feel you have to compete to be 'in the game,' but one where you can be yourself no matter where you are. It feels good not to feel like I need to compete to be in the game – the game actually seems silly now. Fun, still, I'm sure, but silly. – MrZor

―――――∇―――――

Santa Fe, NM (USA)

You really want to know? Staying away from all of them because they're fucking crazy. Drunken alcoholics. I don't like bars. I have problems with people who have more than four or five drinks and getting sloppy. I can't deal with it. – Juan-manuel Alonso

―――――∇―――――

Cathedral City, CA (USA)

The best is seeing all the eye candy and seeing some genuine people. The bad part is the non-acceptance from some people. All the circuit guys hang together because they go to sex parties. If you're not part of that group they don't want to talk to you. Actually, when you go to the bars everybody is in a group. How can you break into a constant conversation without being rude? Leaving alone can be a defeating feeling. If I'm going there and I'm trying to meet someone and I get my hopes dashed, I leave for home. I'm a sensitive guy, so I'm hurt inside because the people I'm interested in aren't interested in me. – David Hayes

―――――∇―――――

Redwood Valley/Mendocino County, CA (USA)

I don't get around much anymore, but I love hanging with other men (especially), and women at a friendly, huggy, neighborhood bar. Nothing like the smiles, touch, and chat real time. The (racy) videos and music can be fun, too. Outside of California, the smoky environments can ruin my evening, as well as the way too loud music, unfriendly elbows, and unhappy drunks. – T. Lark Letchworth.

―――――▽―――――

Chicago, IL (USA)
Palm Springs, CA (USA)

Going on 59 next month. I think it's different being here in Palm Springs, you meet people from all over and they're more my age. It's easier to talk with people. When I'm in Chicago – I live in Boys Town – and going out there is a huge divide on ageism, a lot of isms going on. I think a lot of the Latino and Black community have some trouble being in the bars. It's the younger, the ones with the best bodies from the gym, drinking top shelf, Grey Goose instead of well. There's a lot of pressure going out. I used to hang out with friends, brunching and drinking on a Sunday, the parties. Now I can't keep up with that. I'm going to be me and not what somebody wants me to be. – Greg R. Baird

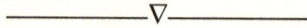

―――――▽―――――

Chicago, IL (USA)

Though at my age I don't go to bars and clubs anymore, I remember the time when I did. The best part was being in a space with men that shared your same sexuality. The worst part was going home alone after a night of drinking and cruising. – Mark Contorno

―――――▽―――――

St. Cloud, MN (USA)

There are almost no lesbian bars now. When they did exist, I did not frequent them because they were too far away from where I lived at the time, I did not drink, and I was very shy. No one taught me how to seduce women and I wish someone did. I remember the one time I got my courage up to ask a woman to dance with me and she turned me down. I had to accept it … but it really hurt at the time. Asking is important. I remember when I was very young the first time I went to a ladies' night, and a woman grabbed me and had a dance with me without even asking. I didn't like it at the time, but afterward I did. I felt validated somehow by that experience, that I was an attractive woman to someone. I realized that maybe I should have done that with the woman who turned me down instead of ask her. My rejector could have done that out of shyness too. The woman who grabbed me and took me for a spin wasn't gross and didn't do anything dirty or anything – she just gave me a dance. Now that I am older, I realize why she did it. I respect her for it. She didn't ask me for anything after that dance either. No one is teaching us how to overcome our shyness, how to court women. I read a lot of lesbian fiction and watch a lot of lesbian television shows and films, and admire the characters who are so smooth. I am an old lady now, in a committed relationship, and there are women who look at me longingly … and I freeze up when they approach me. I may be old enough to be their mother, and I just can't with them. Probably the boldest lesbian who ever hit on me in a bar was a deaf Asian woman who was determined to have sex with me in the bar's restroom. I need to take a few steps with you before getting to that point. – Rachel Wexelbaum

───────▽───────

Sacramento, CA (USA)
San Diego, CA (USA)
Tijuana, (Mexico)
Palm Springs, CA (USA)

Best: Maybe finding the love of your life. Having heavy philosophical discussions about LGBT assimilation while under the influence. Observing the diversity of our community (depending on the bar). Fascinating observations about the stalking/hunting behavior of human animals tracking one another for possible encounters.

Worst: Lack of diverse music in most venues. Sometimes racism and sexism on display. Reminder of how I could have been more assertive in my pretty youth. Overpriced drinks, cliques, and body shaming. – Paul Harris

───────▽───────

Darlinghurst, New South Wales (Australia)

What bars & pubs! Lol. The heady hey days of Darlinghurst's gay Golden Mile are long gone. Only three out of eight pubs left … and one of them not exclusively gay anymore … and two nightclubs left. I'm glad I lived the glory days of the '80s & '90s. The worst thing about the current "app culture" is that we no longer have bars to go to, to pick up. Used to be that you'd go out for a drink, meet up with friends, sit somewhere and cruise your surroundings. You'd catch somebody's eye, buy them a drink, chat, sum each other up over several more drinks, then head off to one or the other's place. It was fun, interactive, and pretty safe. I … and many others my age … miss it! I'm sort of at the stage of life where I've pretty well removed myself from the "gay community" as such, and tend to be more active in just "the community." I interact as much with straight people as gay these days. I've also moved to a much quieter life in an area that is a 90-minute drive from Sydney. It is a coastal village, and as such has no obvious gay life … and certainly no gay bars. There is a joke in the community that once you're over 40, you may as well not exist. The trouble is … it's not a joke! You do notice, as you get older on the scene, that the times you are actually cruised for a pick-up is rare. You could go to a bar, and if no friends were there, you could spend all night sitting on your own! Now, well into my 60s, I really don't think I'd stand a chance. Certainly if the apps are anything to go by … and I've now deleted them all … I may as well not exist in cyberspace either. – Tim Alderman

——————▽——————

Brunswick, ME (USA)

I can't speak for contemporary gay life. I seldom, if ever, go out. I've been in a relationship for thirty years and married to my husband for over six. We might stop at a gay bar for a drink, when we're traveling, but neither of us was ever into the "bar scene." – Michael Pickel

——————▽——————

Amsterdam (Netherlands)

The best part is the thumpa-thumpa tribal spirit that exists wherever you go in the world. The worst part is the stench of tobacco. – David Clayton

——————▽——————

King, NC (USA)

Since my husband and I are looking at being seventy years old right around the corner, we are not part of the bar/club scene. We live in a small, rural town in North Carolina. The nearest gay bar/club would be, maybe, an hour or so away from us. Personally, I would imagine that if we were to enter a bar/club it might prove to be a humiliating experience to try to engage in conversation with others much younger than we are.

My relationship prior to my current one was with a man who was an eternal club kid. He was also an off-and-on DJ and he was a performing drag queen. We spent many nights throughout our twelve years together in bars and clubs. My experience throughout those times was mostly feeling like a broken spoke in a wagon wheel. Being naturally a shy person, I was connected with a very gregarious man who knew no strangers and someone who felt like the proper time to be thinking about going to a bar/club was 11 pm. Now, I feel as though I have turned into my former in-laws (who I used to make fun of) – *Wheel of Fortune*, *Jeopardy*, bedtime. – Ron Cline

——————▽——————

Palm Springs, CA (USA)

The best parts of going out to bars and clubs are the sense of shared space, of delicious potential, of some sense of "safety in numbers."

The worst parts? It's painful to be a marginalized minority! So, I see so much drinking and drugging that I wonder how people are numbing themselves ... just to make it through the day. – Tony Earl

——————▽——————

Charlottetown, Prince Edward Island (Canada)

Best: Energy, eye candy, community, music, going home with someone when you want to.
Worst: Going home alone when you don't want to. Not chatting with anyone.

– Dave Stewart

——————▽——————

San Diego, CA (USA)

When I came out, I lost my biological family, I lost my wife, I lost the family I married into. They all stepped back. I lost absolutely everyone. Now they were very kind and understanding and caring about it, but that divorce happened like that. My world was upside down. So, going to the bars in the community that was there – and San Diego, I'm blessed to have such a great community – became my second family. It's become a lot of our second families. We see our friends there. You can sit there and lament. I can tell you when I got my divorce papers and I went into Mo's Universe and I saw my favorite bartender and he knew I was sad, and he said, "Are you ok?" I said, "Well, I just got the divorce papers." And he looked at me with the most heartfelt eyes and said, "Chardonnay?" I said, "Yes." He said, "Chocolate cake?" I said, "Yes." He said, "Kamikaze?" I said, Fuck yes!" Because he knew that this is our family. I can go in any bar down in Hillcrest and I can run into somebody and we're having a bad day we're supporting each other, because it's not easy out there. It's still not easy." – Serafine Sawyer

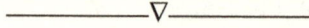

———————∇———————

Milwaukee, WI (USA)

Years ago, it was the thing to do ... meet people ... we were all ONE family in the late '70's. After 1990, they appeared to just be places to get drunk and pick up strangers. Not my cup of tea ... although, I have no qualms about meeting friends there for "a" drink. – Sherrie Howe

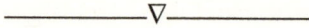

———————∇———————

Des Moines, IA (USA)

I have to answer this both as Sister Freida and as Chrysler:
BEST as Sr. Freida – I like going to bars. The press of people. Doing a bit of networking and needs assessment/"bar ministry"– all that nun stuff.
WORST as Sr. Freida – drunks pulling on my veil, groping my naughty bits without consent and really, though I am sex positive, I am careful not to associate my nun-persona with sexual activity in habit.
BEST as Chrysler – tribal rites and disco
WORST as Chrysler drunks and drunk bullshit.

    –   Sr. Freida Peoples aka DJ Chrysler Sheldon

———————∇———————

Karachi, Sindh (Pakistan)
Bangkok (Thailand)
Washington, DC (USA)
Boston, MA USA)
New York, NY (USA)

Despite being a bit reserve and introverted person, I have always been a party animal. Now in Pakistan, we do not have gay bars/clubs but the underground gay scene is booming despite societal restraints. We have parties at farmhouses late night on the weekends outside the city in Karachi, which are frequented by lower-middle-class segments mostly. The elite and upper-middle-class gays have their own parties in more private and indoor posh settings in Karachi and the rest of the country.

The best part of venturing into such queer spaces was to meet, hang around and party with your own kind and also to feel the empowerment that one would not be able to get in such spaces that are not present in more cisgender and heterosexual spaces. The worst part has been the classism that exists within gay spaces, the "rich queens" tend to hang out in their own spaces, while us "struggling queens" …

I've also had a chance to meet with queer folks in Colombo, Sri Lanka in 2016, and in 2017 I was able to enjoy the queer nightlife of Bangkok, Thailand. The most interesting experience so far of my queer journey has been in the US, I am quite new to the culture here but the sense of empowerment and freedom are what had changed my mind.

I have frequented many gay bars in Washington, DC, when I first landed here. I did notice a bit of a divide that exists within the gay bars and the clientele they serve. Certain gay bars are frequented by the cis white middle-class gay men, while others were exclusively black. Some were for bears while others were for lesbians. I am not against that, us queers are not exactly one big happy family that the rest of the society thinks of us. We have racialized, class, bodily and gender differences … in all this I've struggled as a brown and as South Asian person is to find a place where I can belong.

I have spent most of my time in the US in Medford, which is a suburb of Boston. Boston was a historic city with a known as an intellectual heart of the US too. I'd frequented the gay clubs/ bars there but always felt out of place. I felt I didn't belong there. I was more able to find good queer folks, who were able to understand me and empathize with me in queer POC spaces. In Worcester, I don't go to the gay bars here too … I did once or twice but since I do not know people it is a bit awkward to go to such places on your own. But through my activism and community outreach I have been able to find amazing queer folks and allies in both Boston and Worcester prides.

The most fun I had was in New York, only had three chances to visit that beautiful city. I've to say the queer life is quite vibrant and diverse. I knew so many friends and allies there. I had the chance of showing her New York in November, 2019 … I'd visited Stonewall Inn but we went there for a special transgender event and my sister, Aradhiya Khan was able to perform there on the stage which was a memorable experience. When New York Pride was there earlier I'd a chance to attend the Sholay Bollywood queer party and also a grand queer POC party at the end of the pride with some friends. I wish to visit New York more and enjoy the beautiful queer scene there. – Salman

———————▽———————

WHEN WAS THE FIRST TIME YOU REALIZED YOU WERE DIFFERENT?

Chicago, IL (USA)

I think it that wasn't only connected to sexuality. I felt intellectually different, I felt artistically different, musically different, other things. I was really late on the take, really late to discover who I was ... bisexual to a late age, all through college. Then I had a period of celibacy. And interestingly enough it was at the time that I was unobtainable and didn't do anything with anyone, it insulated and protected me, until I was ready to have a real relationship. I kind of realized who I was and took ownership of it. I was in a 17 year relationship that was in the closet which I didn't want to be, but he did. That stilted things for a long time. I'm just happy to be more honest to just be who you are. It took me a long time. I guess everyone goes through it and it in a completely different way. I realized I was different when people stared saying, "Oh don't do that. Boys don't do that." How can a piece of cloth have a sexuality? I just didn't get it. But it does. There are certain norms. I worked within the norms, I guess. I feel more on the masculine side and I didn't like being denied a man just because I was gay. And I had a punk attitude. "Yeah, I'm a gay guy who's going to kick your ass." – James Scalfani

————▽————

Fulton, KY (USA)

It must have been when I was about 15 years old. There was an older scout who, on looking back, I clearly see was gay, and who enticed me into mutual

128

masturbation. He went out of his way to seek me out and initiate the activity. I was scared and a little disgusted, but I didn't say "no," so there must have been some attraction there. In years prior to that, I had had crushes on boys, but there were no realizations about them. There were many incidents of homoerotic camaraderie and titillating dares to oral intercourse, but I feel that such things are a staple among adolescent boys. They did exert a great attraction to me though. – Oran Walker

—————∇—————

Texas (USA)

Growing up in a rural area I was intrigued by other boys from preschool forward and experimented with male peers out in the countryside until junior high when I began to realize that my attraction to my male peers was considered "wrong." – Anonymous

—————∇—————

Chicago, IL (USA)

I have no idea when I actually realized I was different. My memories of childhood are mostly missing, so I couldn't tell you what happened in the gaps. One thing I do remember is that in middle school I was the lone "boy" in a friend group of girls. They started to call me an "Honorary Girl," which I appreciated immensely. In 8th grade, when I first suspected I was gay, I was filled with concerns. The one silver lining I distinctly remember was that being gay was close as I could get to being a girl, so it didn't take me long to embrace it. – C'est Kevvie (Wilhelmina)

—————∇—————

South Bend, IN (USA)

I remember looking at other boys and having feelings, particularly around the genital area. I mean you watch television and realize you're supposed to be attracted to girls. I like girls, girls are nice, they're fun to dress up, kinda pretty. Girls are lovely but I'd rather be with … I was sexually aroused by the idea of boys. I didn't know it was sexually aroused at that age but it occurred to me later on that it was. – Steve

—————∇—————

Detroit, MI (USA)

When I was fifteen years old, I saw a picture of David Bowie, and my entire world flipped upside down, inside out and backwards. I had never seen any human being more beautiful and I was confused and delighted simultaneously. Never the same after that epiphany in the Inkster Public Library, I half expected to look different, sound different and be totally unrecognizable to my family. Silly me, however, because I saw the words ayndrogyne, and gay, and I thought they meant the same thing. It took me a couple of years, but I finally understood that "gay" meant having sex with boys, something I had not even considered. The whole idea of sex, pushing one's genitalia close to someone else, was repulsive to me. Then. – Terence Smith (Joan Jett Blakk)

—————∇—————

Fayetteville, AR (USA)

When I was born, I had cerebral palsy. At a very early age in life, I had to wear leg braces on my left leg. In the day I wore a brace and at night I had to wear a heavy brace that had a stainless-steel plate through it. I was probably about five years old at the time. I remember we had just built a house and we had hardwood floors and mother said, "If you have to get up and go to the bathroom at night, hop to the bathroom because I don't want you scouring up my floors." So I would wait until everybody was asleep and I would get out of bed and hop to the bathroom and lock the door, sit on the commode and look at the men's underwear in the Sears catalog. I was just obsessed with the hairy chests … oh I wanted a hairy chest so badly. So I was about five years old. I remember at the time thinking … how a five-year-old brain works … "Why I am doing this? And why do I feel compelled to have to wait until everyone else is asleep?" I don't know. It was just something I couldn't broadcast to the world. – Renny

—————∇—————

Charlottesville, VA (USA)

Even in Catholic high school I was beginning to doubt I fit into the Catholic and mainstream world. When I landed at The University of Virginia, all of a sudden I was in Preppie-land filled with stuck-up wannabe rich kids. I definitely did not fit in. I used to blast Black Sabbath records out of my dorm room to torment them. I was drinking, doing drugs, and mad at the world. I was starting to hear some interesting underground music on WTJU our college radio station though. Then one day I saw a handmade flier on a light pole advertising a Hardcore Punk show. I said, hmm, what is this? I should go to this. It was in the dank basement of a lesbian bar in downtown Charlottesville called Muldowney's Pub. There was a band called Lackey Die that was making a god-awful racket and cursing at the top of their lungs. I was shocked. But I kept coming back to the shows with the foul mouthed hot sweaty guys who I quickly realized were writing songs about their own lives and how fucked up the world was. I did not know you could do that. They played with such abandon that it became apparent anyone could do that too. I met another band called The Landlords whose lead singer John Beers was the Hardcore DJ at WTJU. I started hanging out at the station while he DJ'd late at night. I was introduced to a whole international underground scene of misfits like myself. Here were people being themselves in a hostile world and singing about it. I had found my tribe! (More recently on Facebook I found out that my friend John is Gay. Who knew? Did he know about me?) – Lars von Keitz

———————▽———————

Chicago, IL (USA)

I think that I would have to say when a good friend of mine in high school who was very open about being in a relationship with a man, confronted me with the fact. I think before that I never really thought about it as a concern but as he pushed me to be true to myself, I think then it was well time to be your true self. It was kind of a tough, but fortunately short blip for me. – Dean Ogren

———————▽———————

Waverly, IA (USA)

I realized I was different at a very young age, but I guess I had a strong ego or was somewhat autistic, because I thought I was right and everyone else hadn't discovered how good a relationship with another boy could be- – even before my sexually awakening. I couldn't understand how other boys wasted their time fantasying about girls and getting laid. I had "played doctor" and "played house" with some neighbor girls but considered it a phase I went through. Now I look at straight couples and think they are "playing house." – Robert Beck

———————▽———————

North Carolina (USA)

When I was very young and Steve Reeves movies started coming on television. I thought, "You know, I find these very interesting. I'm not sure why but I find these very interesting." I grew up in a tiny little rural town up in the mountains in North Carolina. When I was growing up there back in the 1970s there were no gay people around. Gays were something you heard about in whispers or were heard about on the TV news. It was shocking to me when I was a kid when *All in the Family* had a character, a friend of Archie's, that came out. I was completely shocked by that. Gay people weren't around where I was … of course, there were gay people there but very closeted, very quiet. What I found out later is that many of the gay people who live up in that corner of the state, at weekends would drive two or three hours to go down to the gay bars and get a hotel and spend the night. Then drive all the way back up there. That was very common. So they led a double life where they were trying to fit in in a small rural town then take the weekend to go courting. – Randy

—————▽—————

Rockford, IL (USA)

I think I first realized that I was different when I was about 10 and started thinking about the guys in my class. I know we had started talking about the changes we would experience going through puberty, and I could only think of my male classmates. I wanted to ask about my feelings but being in Catholic school, I never got to ask those questions. One of my friends (who will remain nameless) would come up to talk to me and I always felt that I was looking down. So thinking back on those instances I think that's where it began for me. – Patrick J. Murphy III

—————▽—————

Seneca, SC (USA)

People debate me when I say I truly didn't know I was gay. I remember around 7th or 8th grade when boys and girls were not just "going together" in name, they were starting to make out and more. I knew I was not like most of my guy friends, but I also knew straight guys were not all alike either. There were those hyper-masculine guys who cat-called, bragged, hit on, dated girls left and right and there were guys who were respectful, didn't kiss and tell, etc. I figured if they were on a scale of 1-10 I was WAY down on the 1 side. I dated some but never really did anything.

I can honestly say I never met a person that was out as gay until I was a senior in high school. He was in a play I worked with at the community theater. I learned he was gay during the show. I learned a few months later he was in the hospital due to the new HIV crisis that was just beginning to hit rural South Carolina. He lived at least until I went away to college, but I don't know what happened to him after.

Looking back, however, if I'd had a gay man that could have been a role model that so many kids have today, I would have known I was different far earlier. When I look back on my childhood, I'm surprised I wasn't farting rainbows by the age of six. Things I liked, things I looked for (Sears Catalog, Men's underwear section) would have been big flags to my being different. – Chris Grace

―――――∇―――――

Chicago, IL (USA)

I think l, like many people, when I was very, very young. I always knew. I specifically remember saying to myself at 14, admitting to myself that I was gay and that there was no way I was going to deal with this right now. Never had any self-hatred, never had any denial, I was never suicidal or any of that. I knew it was a thing and I knew at the age of 14 at junior high or high school that that was not the place or time to deal with it. I came out when I was 19 and I was living in the city finally. – Jeff Ramone

―――――∇―――――

Chicago, IL (USA)

I knew I was different at about five years of age. My family was very much involved with sports. I knew the first time I went into a men's locker room. I was mesmerized by the smell and the men walking around naked. I knew I wanted to be there and often took my time getting ready. – Philip Bernal

―――――∇―――――

Menton, Côte d'Azur (France)

I think I was about eight years old when I realised that I was gay. My great-aunt, who supervised most of my upbringing, had a young chauffeur who, during the summer in Menton, South of France, used to wash the Hispano-Suiza in just a pair of tight shorts, and I remember I couldn't take my eyes off him, even though I wasn't even sure what my desires and sense of attraction were actually about. All I knew was that I thought he was the most beautiful guy I'd ever seen. – Louis Richard de Bourbon de Parme et de Savoie, Prince de la Pau

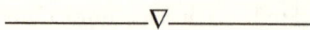

—————▽—————

Bellport, NY (USA)

I think deep down I have always known but it wasn't until I was 12 that I pieced it together. I had tried to tell my Mom at the time, but she didn't take it well. As a result, I didn't officially "come out" until I was 17. – Erin Michelle Miller

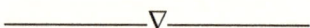

—————▽—————

Chicago, IL (USA)

I was a young kid. My earliest homoerotic thing I can remember is watching the original *Star Trek* with my mother. She was a big Trekker. It was a virtually naked Captain Kirk. "Oh well, that's interesting." But even before that I knew something was different my entire life, but that was the first moment where the light went on. – Drew

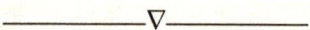

—————▽—————

Detroit, MI (USA)

I always thought I was special. Remember *Leave It to Beaver*? I looked and acted just like Beaver Cleaver. Yeah, I said "Yes, ma'am, No, ma'am", I played the organ at church, I got good grades, I wore big bookworm glasses, I was terrible at sports. Yeah, I was probably pretty obnoxious and cloying. I didn't know anything about being gay – I didn't even know what that meant – but I'm sure everyone around me knew that I was. Amazingly, I didn't put it together till I was well into my 20's. All those wasted years. – Brian T

—————▽—————

Rome, New York (USA)
Indiana (USA)

I would have to say that I sensed it when I was a teenager because I played, sexually, with other boys more ... at the time I did not think it was more than everybody else ... but when I was in college and we started talking about experiences in high school, I got the sense I was doing it a lot more than everybody else was. And I enjoyed it more. Everybody was like, "Oh guys do that, you do this, you do that." But I sensed I was doing it more. I also sensed that my attraction to men wasn't just because I was a boy, I felt I was different and that's why I was attracted to them. I really didn't think I was gay because that was way back in the '50s and '60s. I didn't think of it that way. I just thought, "Well I'm attracted to them because I'm a little different." I felt more connected to my sisters that I did my brother. I was closer to my sisters. So, I thought my attraction to other boys was because I had more female in me … if I can say that. That for me was when I was nine or ten years old. I realized there was something different, then when I got to college it became even more … But in those days coming from a small town, I went to a large university. In those days when you were talking about things like that it was always followed up with, "Oh that person's weird, he's queer, he's a faggot." So you wouldn't pursue it and say, "Gee, I kind of feel a little bit that way." I knew I was a little different and I knew I had to suppress it and keep a low profile. – Andee

—————▽—————

Springfield, OH (USA)

I love this question. I have a specific memory that I always go to when asked this question. 1962. I was seven years old. That December, my brother gave me a western wallet for Christmas. It was one of those brown plastic wallets – pressed to look like leather – with white whip stitching around the edges. Inside the wallet was a flip-file for photos. What photos did I have as a seven-year-old? I put my siblings' school photos in the cellophane pockets and filled the rest with photos I cut from magazines. At the back of the pages, I put photos of men without shirts I had cut from my mother's *Better Homes and Gardens* magazine. These were ads for men's swimsuits or (my favorite) men from old Charles Atlas body building ads. At seven years old, I knew two things – that these photos did something to me and excited me in ways I could not yet describe, and that they were never to be shown to anyone else, because this was clearly not "Normal." – andKevin

—————▽—————

San Jose, CA (USA)

I had gender dysphoria from a very early age. As soon as I could walk, as soon as I started forming thoughts. I have very specific memories that I understood that I was not a girl. I had two sisters and my older sister and I, we liked to take baths together. I saw what she had, and I thought, "That's not what I have." I got really mad and I started kicking her. And mom was like, "We're not doing bath time anymore with you, you can't be controlled." I was so angry. It was persistent throughout my whole life. Even when I was five years old, I was a ring bearer at my aunt's wedding. I was told at the last minute that was what I was going to be doing. I was told to go stand next to the flower girls. From my five-year-old standpoint of understanding, I was going to be a flower girl. When they called the flower girls, I tried ... and they were like, No, no, no, you're not a flower girl." I thought, "Oh I'm not them, I don't get to wear those pretty dresses." So I started crying. There are pictures of me crying the entire night. "Oh, I'm not a girl." Apparently, I ruined my aunt's wedding. Whatever, she's over it ... maybe a little bit. But my mom's getting married in two weeks and I get to be a flower girl. So I get my redemption. I know I'm thirty, but I still love it. – Kelsey Brookes

————▽————

Morrice, MI (USA)

I was probably six years old. I had a crush on a kid in 1st grade and I thought, "Well, that's not the norm, so don't say anything or I'll get the shit beaten out of me." So, I kept it to myself. – Jim

————▽————

Louisiana (USA)

I'm not sure if it was a moment of realization but I recall wanting to recreate the *Wizard of Oz* on the playground during recess and after lunch in kindergarten. I remember the other boys in the background playing basketball and me in the grassy field as the cowardly lion, or the scarecrow, or the tin man, or maybe Dorothy, she was the lead. – Katorri A

————▽————

Indianapolis, IN (USA)

Realizations of this sort are always made in hindsight. Had I known as a kid what *queer* meant, I would have seen the signs, I guess. As a youngster I hated the typical sports crap the other boys on my street seemed to live for. I preferred sitting by myself in my room listening to 45s on my cheap little record player from Montgomery Ward. I remember spending hours trying with no success to figure out what was going on behind that "Green Door."

Other boys seemed obsessed with baseball and racecars (this was Indianapolis, after all); I was more interested in music, art, books, and the comedic timing of Bob Hope and Jack Benny.

My first inkling of *sexual* difference occurred in late elementary school, right before junior high. While the creepy boys in my class seemed obsessed with all things mammary, I found myself more focused on the huge bulge in the crotch of the jeans worn by some late-teens fellow who helped keep kids lined up to get on the bus at the end of the school day. Away from adults, the boys in my class did not hesitate to crow about the huge tits on early-developing female students or on whatever sultry singer appeared on Ed Sullivan the night before. Even then, I knew not to say, "Well, yeah. But did you see the huge bulge in that guy's crotch yesterday?" – William Demaree

———————▽———————

Wisconsin Rapids, WI (USA)

I think I always knew I was different, but I just didn't have a word for it until I was about seven or eight years old. I was playing in the yard with my sister when she called someone in the neighborhood a "queer." I asked her what that word meant, and she told me it meant a boy who likes other boys in an unnatural way and that it was, "the absolute worst thing you could ever call someone." I didn't really understand but I was pretty sure that was me, because I had always had fantasies about other boys and tended to identify more with the feelings of girls. After that, I was very careful not to let anyone know that I was one of those "queers." – D. Warner

———————▽———————

Cleveland, OH (USA)

When people started telling me what I should like to do and play with and how I should be as a boy ... but I knew I was not that way at all. – Roger

———————▽———————

Adelaide, South Australia (Australia)

I'm sure many have answered with the same: "At school." I have an interesting way of thinking and/or putting things that is apparently quite individual. I'm never aware of that until it's pointed out to me. I knew something was there and I knew I was attracted to bigger guys – chubbies –

and there was a guy at school I got a bit "ooh ... that's niiice" toward. I never acted upon it, though, as I knew that would be a no no. But I was age twelve/thirteen when that happened. Plus, it didn't help that I was one of the bullied kids, but they didn't like that I would stand up for myself if I had to. – Robert Verrall

———————▽———————

La Mesa, Tequendama Province (Colombia)

I was having a pillow fight with a friend of mine (straight guy) and then realised he was turned on by such game. That sort of changed the way I looked at him and other guys. And it felt so nice, it gave me a power I never had before. – Cristian

———————▽———————

Chicago, IL (USA)

The minute that I developed the ability to remember. – Dennis Hardenstein

———————▽———————

Cincinnati, OH (USA)
San Francisco, CA (USA)

Being different seemed part of my DNA, as from age five I studied dancing in recitals and musicals, wearing glittery costumes and pancake makeup. Spending half my day at the library helping my Grandmother, who was town librarian, gave me a lot of positive attention. Living in an extended family with parents and grandparents, in a very small town offered me a lot of freedoms, boyish and otherwise, that I would call gender fluid.

If I did not have an old battered black and white photo of me about age five, one might attribute my memory of this permissiveness to wishful ones. In this photo I'm sitting in the living room, our fox terrier sitting at my feet, in front a 1950s style children's record player. With it on the short table are picture books and records in hard cardboard covers. I sit in my Lone Ranger tee-shirt, a long calico skirt, ruffled at the bottom, and moccasins. I remember the game well. Tippy had to sit still beside me and listen to my favorite records to which I would sing, and she would howl.

I remember the outfit, especially the moccasins – perhaps I was Tonto to my imagined Lone Ranger, and that I wore them constantly, only forcibly having them removed for washing up. But consciously probably it was when we moved from this ancestral home to Cincinnati, Ohio for my father's new job. He was a designing engineer who was to work on a large federal project, of all things, a nuclear-powered airplane! But the tragedy was leaving my, unbeknownst to him, best boy friend Jimmy. I now realize how in love with him I was, and when I was told we were moving, I became very upset and ran to find and tell him. His response was a deflating, noncommittal, "Ok," he said. I was devastated and balled my eyes out. My mother was very angry with me, but I think that both my parents already knew I was very different.

The most adult realization was about a year after getting married. There was one T.V. special "movie of the week," that spoke, if quietly and tastefully, to bisexuality and being "homosexual." *That Certain Summer* (1972) starring Hal Holbrook as a divorced dad and Martin Sheen as his lover. Somehow my whole family, including my pregnant wife, ended up sitting and watching this television movie in its entirety, during which many awkward and painful silent moments were experienced – mostly by me – but the story's impact was felt on all as Holbrook's ex-wife, teenage son, and extended family and friends discovered his secret. It was a terrifying and profound moment of realization of my difference, and that difference was not just my individual quirks or flaws, but part of lived human existence. By 1976 I was out, divorced, and headed to San Francisco. – David Hatfield Sparks

———————∇———————

Oxnard, CA (USA)

When I noticed I was different was when I was on the swim team. I was 12 or 13 years old. The coach would always squat in his Speedo when he talked to you. I would find myself trying to look deeper into his Speedo. It was at that point that I realized I wasn't interested in what everyone else was interested in. – Crusher

———————∇———————

Hollister, CA (USA)

Probably in the 1st or 2nd grade. My mother had a couple of ballgowns from the '50s that she bought at Goodwill for my sister to play dress up. She was a year younger than me. I would play dress up with my sister with those two. She was closest to my age, so I used to hang out with her. That was back when I was younger, not so much when I got a little bit older. I was in a play in 2nd grade in my Catholic grade school. I had the lead role in the play and I remember to make us show up more on the stage they put lipstick on us and

I realized I liked that. So I wore it home, walked home from school with the lipstick. I remember some man calling me a sissy because I had the lipstick on. Of course, I wiped it off on my shirt right away. I didn't want to be picked on. It didn't work. I had very few friends in grade school – Spike

―――――――▽―――――――

Grand Rapids, MI (USA)

When I was in about 3rd grade, I got a hard on, when talking with a friend's friend. I thought he was so cute, and I never saw someone as great as him. – Mark S

―――――――▽―――――――

Cleveland, OH (USA)
Chicago, IL (USA)
Green Bay, WI (USA)

When I was six years old, the neighbor boy and I examined each other's anatomy in a broom closet in the kitchen. My sister put a stop to that. I was made to feel ashamed. That was when my family still lived in Cleveland, Ohio. 1958 or '59.

Next time I had a same sex experience was in elementary and high school after my family moved to Chicago, in the '60's. But even then, I enjoyed the experience, but I didn't think of myself as gay. I had girlfriends and even got married for the sake of appearances and adhering to my Baptist upbringing.

It wasn't until I moved to Green Bay, Wisconsin, in the late '70's and met a guy by the name of Cary.

Here's what I wrote in a memoir I may finish some day: Like me, he was a reporter at the television station where I worked. Meeting him was the point at which I first started admitting to myself that I was gay since lust struck me like a lightning bolt. Clichéd but true. It started innocently enough. Doesn't it always? He walked into the newsroom carrying a cup of coffee. He accidentally spilled it on himself and announced in a loud voice:

"Good thing this suit is wash and wear!"

"Too bad it's not flammable," I said.

It stopped him dead in his tracks. He shot me a look as if to say, "You'll regret that remark."

A split-second later we both sucked in our cheeks, pursed our lips, and laughed. I was smitten. Personality-wise, I would soon learn, we were mirror-images of each other. Each of us had met our match in the other.

There's a fine line between thrilling and frightening and I was about to cross that line. Before long, he was someone I wanted to spend every waking minute with. Again, clichéd but true. Spending a lot of time together wasn't hard to do since we worked together. Confirmation of our mutual admiration society came at a Halloween party when we found ourselves alone together, not by accident. We were in a dimly-lit room adjacent to where the revelers were reveling. I can't remember if I made the first move or he did, but we kissed. Not a peck on the cheek but a full on the mouth "I'm crazy about you" kiss. With my wife in the very next room. And we were off to the races. I divorced my wife and Cary and I set up house together. 40 years later, we're still in contact. We were too young and inexperienced in the beginning to know how to handle being in love with each other. – Steve Kmetko

————————∇————————

Madison, WI (USA)
Washington, DC (USA)

I was a very small child. I was the first grandchild on one side and the first grandson on the other. I was born during World War II after D-Day and before Hiroshima. My father was in the military when I was born. I didn't really see my father until I was a year old. I was raised by my grandparents and extended family and my mother's family in Madison, Wisconsin. I was treated very differently in that situation. In my grandparents' house, my mother had a brother and a sister that were married that lived there. It was a big house, divided into small apartments. I was the center of attention. I never really got over that. I found that I could make people laugh as a young child, so I was an awkward clownish kind of child. My grandmother, when I was about seven years old, my father's mother, said to me, "It's too bad you were born a man." I said to her, "Grandmother, what do you mean?" She said, "All men are fools. A man is like a wild critter, like a dog that doesn't come in out of the rain. It takes a woman to make a man sane." Later I realized what she was saying, and I heard this from my relatives, that I was a very effeminate child, and androgynous, up into my teens. From the very start I felt like I didn't fit in. As a small child, four years old, when my parents got together after the war and brought me back to Washington, DC – they both worked for the government – every time my parents had guests over, other young couples, I would go upstairs and pack my bags and I would be waiting at the door with my bags to leave with them. My parents thought, "Oh isn't that cute. Little Gregory is so cute, he's ready to go." But that is a feeling I've had for the rest of my entire life. When I came of age, I couldn't wait to escape from the nest. I felt like I didn't belong in my family. In more recent times, looking back on it, there were other people like me in my family. Not queers but eccentric individuals. That's why I studied anthropology because I could not find my place, I felt like an alien. I didn't realize until early adulthood that that was because I was queer. – Greg Day

————————∇————————

Raytown, MO (USA)

That was a very specific time. I was in 5th grade, in elementary school, at recess, and one of the kids on the playground – one of the boys – said, "Hey Johnny found a page out of a *Playboy* magazine, let's go look at it." So all these guys pile into the boys bathroom to look at this picture. On one side of the picture is this woman laying out naked by the pool. In the background of the picture there were these three guys standing behind her naked, but you could barely see them. On the flip side of the picture was more of a close-up of the guys and you could see them clearly naked. The boys were all looking at the close up of the woman, and I kept flipping the picture over, saying, "No, no, no, let's look at that picture." They were saying, "Are you weird, what's wrong with you?" Ding! I knew I had to be quiet about this, I had to be careful. Obviously, I'm very different. By the next year, in 6th grade, I was reading a newspaper article and there was some mention of some sort of activity ... it was a criminal report about two guys having some sort of sexual contact and they called that homosexuality in the paper. I just put the paper down and thought, "I guess that's what I am." – Thomas Stribling

————————∇————————

Cathedral City, CA (USA)

I was around five or six. I started noticing things on TV because back then we only had five TV channels because in our age TV wasn't a big thing back then. Watching Hanna-Barbera and certain characters like Witchipoo was my favorite. I loved her from Living Island. The dark side of me wanted to be that flamboyant and that loud, that vivacious. Wear whatever the fuck I wanted, and nobody would care. In reality, I couldn't do that. Then as time goes on the characters change. You had *Bewitched*, where everyone was gay but playing straight. *The Brady Bunch*, the husband was gay playing straight. Then Paul Lynde was my role model. Vincent Price was my role model, though he wasn't gay. Those characters were the ones I wanted to gravitate toward. Love those characters. – Marcous

————————∇————————

Cathedral City, CA (USA)

Probably at age three or four. I actually had sexual dreams at three and four and acted them out with neighbors. That would be the first and I have no idea where it came from. It became more sexual in my early teens. – David Hardy

—————▽—————

Chicago, IL (USA)

When a neighbor boy and I played doctor at six years old and I was the only one who got hard. – MrZor

—————▽—————

(Germany)

I guess in beginning of elementary school. People started using gay and fag as swear words and I didn't even know the definition of these words but felt insulted by their use. I brought those new swear words home and my mother was getting upset. She told me we need to talk and explained to me that most times men love women but sometimes it's different but being different is not making gay love less valid. That she'd love me anyway if I turned gay even if she wouldn't wish so for me. Parents always hope for easy ways for their kids and because some people are blind to see that love is love. She thought this way would be less easy. I was so glad hearing that and was wondering why it had such an impact on me to hear her say that. – Cornelius Günther Körn

—————▽—————

Joplin, MO (USA)

Ever since I was at least 12 years old, I always knew how different I was when compared to my peers – but that is only in the sense of being a part of a different minority group. In terms of being a non-binary individual, it really didn't take off until around the 2018 fall semester (my second semester at Missouri Southern). One of the pieces I was given the chance to work on was one personal piece – and at that point, I decided to do one over me questioning my gender. Prior to then, I considered myself mostly asexual and an ally of the LGBTQ community (somewhat questionably good due to how many characters I've personally made that was either a girl or a boy that was bisexual or gay/lesbian) so I had some exposure to at least a portion of the

143

terminology for identities. At that point, I began to question more of my gender rather than sexuality. I was stuck between the general "non-binary" and those that involved the fact that I still felt associated with my gender at birth like genderflux and genderfluid. Even to this day, I still haven't been able to finalize the fact that I'm a genderfluid female that is still an ace as she already knew for the past few years. There are times to where I doubt that and feel like one of those people that are just "faking" it to be part of a group but at the same time, I know that if I was cis-female I wouldn't be questioning it. – Julie W

—————▽—————

Lawton, OK (USA)

I was watching *The Green Hornet* and I was interested in Kato, Bruce Lee. Also, Jim West on *The Wild Wild West*, Robert Conrad, the hairy muscular perfect looking guy. I was afraid to tell my parents. That and I found myself beating off to the musclemen magazines. – David Hayes

—————▽—————

Carmichael, CA (USA)

In terms of having a same sex attraction it was when I was five and my best friend mooned me through his bedroom window. Of course, I didn't know what gay was but I imagine I was aware those thoughts were wrong. As for the first time I really pondered the idea that I was different was when my family was visiting Manhattan. I was a naive nine-year-old in 1965 and my 12 year old brother called me a queer. All I knew was that it was bad and different. Ironically it turned out to be a case of "look who's calling the kettle black." – Paul Harris

—————▽—————

Tallahassee, FL (USA)

I knew I was different from other boys before I was three years old and wanted a teddy bear for Christmas. I knew because my dad responded, "No son of mine is going to have a doll!" My two grandmothers came to my defense, and I still have my cherished Teddy. Some years later, I demanded a boy doll, who I named Timmy (after my first crush on the TV show, *Lassie*), and my Grandma Essie made him pajamas and underwear out of flour sacks and socks.

Around about age eight or nine, I heard my older brother and male cousin throwing around the word "queer" in my presence. When I asked what it meant my brother said, "It's one of the Ten Commandments." I searched the scriptures for the reference and decided it must be the one about adultery. It was three decades later, in the '80s, when I owned the word "queer" as my own.

I think I always knew I was a sissy. It was one of my mother's favorite words, while my dad used the more toxic label "queer." When I was 13 or 14, I had an erotic fantasy on the bouncy bus ride to school, when I realized my sissyness was also about sexuality. "OMG, I'm homosexual! That's why I'm fascinated by the other boys' crotches in the hallway!" That's the year I began to search out books by James Baldwin, Gore Vidal, and Walt Whitman. I wanted to know my difference.

I no longer consider my Self "different," so much as special. – T. Lark Letchworth.

———————∇———————

Chicago, IL (USA)

The first time I realized I was different was when I was 12 or 13 years old. I started to find men so attractive and started to fantasize what it would be like to have sex with a man. I didn't know that there was a name for what I was feeling and I thought it was just a phase of "hero worship" or whatever. I was a guy. Why would I be attracted to other guys. I even got married to a woman thinking that's what guys do. Eventually I figured it out. – Mark Contorno

———————∇———————

Sylvania, New South Wales (Australia)

I would have been about nine years old, and in Year 4 of Primary School at Sylvania Heights Primary School. This would have been 1963. I had sort of always felt that I was different to the other boys around me, but this was the year … along with an early kick-in age for puberty … that there was something about me that was really at odds with the accepted norm. I had a creative streak that came out in my composition writing, was good at inventing science fiction scenarios, could copy writing fonts and a lot of other things. I loved reading and loved nothing more than burying myself in a corner with a book. I avoided sports at all costs … you could get both dirty … and hurt, so that was a no-no. My father tried to get me to play soccer with the Gwaley Bay Bunnies around this time … that was a disaster! I just ran up and down the sideline, avoiding the ball as much as humanly possible. I got my mother to buy me dolls … yep, that should have been a dead giveaway … because I liked dressing them up. Women's clothes were so much more interesting than men's! Mum made sure they were kept hidden from my father. I liked playing jump rope and a French skipping with the girls at school, than playing with the boys. This was despite the boys often giving me stick. I secretly collected newspaper advertisements of men in underwear … these, when I see them now, were exceedingly unsexy at that time, but a budding gay boy just had to make do. At the beach, a lot of young guys ran around in nylon Speedos, which were big in the '60s. My eyes were magnetically drawn to their bouncing bulges in the very clingy swim briefs. I still have fetishes for nylon swimwear, and classic Y-front briefs. Funny that! Of course, I didn't have a name or label for this "different" … it just was. There was certainly no one to guide me through it. I recollect very clearly being in the car with my father, and a mate of his. They passed this guy on the footpath who was wearing nothing, a pink shirt. Uncle Peter rolled the window down and the both yelled "Poofter" at him as they drove past. I remember thinking to myself, "I wonder if I'm one of these poofter people! If I am, I'd better keep quiet about it!" My mother left home when I was 11, and I just sort of naturally fell into the "looking after the house" thing without really thinking … "why"? I do remember my brother and I getting caught in our back yard, dressed up in some clothes my mother had left behind. And early drag career, perhaps? My father ordered us to take them off, but he was with a neighbour who said to him, "Just leave them … they're kids playing dress-up!" My father had a violent streak, and I sort of instinctively knew that I was to have a difficult time with him, trying to express who I was. I wasn't interested in dating girls, and only did in later days to fit in with my group. I certainly never saw them as potential sexual partners. After my mother left, my father got in a housekeeper. She was an absolute bitch, and a bully, and there was mutual hatred on both our parts. She was largely the cause of my younger brother, Kevin, having a very traumatic death at my father's hands in 1965. There was massive news coverage of the event, including the court case. When I went to university to get my writing degree in 2001, I researched and wrote up the event, which had never been spoken about since the time it happened. In one of the newspaper clippings I found, regarding his court case, it mentioned that when the housekeeper had been questioned, she had mentioned that I was a "rather effeminate child." I had never realised until then how obvious it was. Funny thing is, her 21year old son used to stay at our home, and slept in what had been Kevin's bed in my room. I used to feign sleep to watch him getting undressed so I could catch a glimpse of his cock. He used to wear "Bonds" S'port Briefs, and every opportunity I got, I'd nick them and put them on. They got me hard, and so I came to a realisation at a very young age that underwear could be erotic. And … he knew I used to do these things, and he played up to it. On one occasion he said to me, "I know you watch me getting undressed!" I was sent to a Catholic boarding school in 1967 (where I saw a lot of things that I probably should never have seen!). I was in the pool one day ... wearing blue Speedos, as was the fashion ... and this kid in my form – Graeme Turner-yep, I remember his name – was swimming under water, and grabbed my bulge as he swam past. He surfaced a bit further on, just turned and grinned at me. I remember wishing that he'd held onto my cock a bit longer! It was at this stage that I was well aware of just how sexual guys could be, and there was a lot of secret crushes ... and wanking ... going on. My father killed himself in 1978, and life suddenly got a lot easier for me, though coming out was still a couple of years down the line. I was 25 before I had my first full sexual experience with a guy. – Tim Alderman

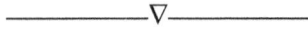

————————▽————————

St Cloud, MN (USA)

The first day of kindergarten. I was four. I could already read and crack jokes. The other kids were crying and peeing in their pants and needed to be taught how to string beads. I knew something was very wrong. – Rachel Wexelbaum

————————▽————————

King, NC (USA)

My first stirrings that I felt of being different or gay was probably when I was five or six years old. I met the girl who would eventually become my wife when we were both eight years old in Sunday school at church. By the time I asked my girlfriend to marry me at age seventeen, I realized that I had attractions for guys – particularly the strong, silent, brooding ones but I felt like us getting married and starting a family would make all of those feelings disappear – and they did for a while. – Ron Cline

————————▽————————

Palestine, TX (USA)

Oh, I'm not sure, maybe when I was about eight or nine? I recall being in a Sears store in Tyler, Texas and seeing the most beautiful young man, except that "he" was a mannequin. I kept slipping away from my mother to go back and gaze upon him. I was active in Boy Scouts and I loved camping trips, where, after the Scoutmaster went to bed, some of us would pack into a tent and talk about sex and sometimes share in group masturbation. Sometime in high school, the rest of the boys no longer wanted to share these moments and I realized I was different, but I also found others like myself and throughout high school, I had a few close male friends with whom we shared sex, but none of us would have been comfortable identifying as gay. – Michael Pickel

——————▽——————

Delavan, WI (USA)

My Aunt Carol and her husband ran a Boy Scout camp. One summer they invited all the family for a summer picnic. I must have been nine or ten years old.

I'll never forget cousin Mark, who was probably about 16 or 17. He simply stripped off his shirt and climbed up to a diving platform. Something inside me melted by just seeing his beautiful self. He dove into the pool. I was so gobsmacked by his beauty. I had not felt that way before! And at the same time, I realized how I felt was not normal. He climbed out of the water and smiled. I was both in love and terrified at the same time. – Tony Earl

——————▽——————

Charlottetown, Prince Edward Island (Canada)

I don't remember a specific first incident, but I do remember knowing that I was attracted to other boys when I was about six years old. That, and I developed a big crush on David Cassidy. Somehow, I learned early that this was something I had to hide. – Dave Stewart

——————▽——————

San Diego, CA (USA)

I was probably four. I knew way, way, early. I also knew it was wrong, because little boys didn't get to be little girls. I think it was at my cousin's wedding, if not sooner, when some family member – she was in this beautiful green velvet dress – and all I wanted was to be in that beautiful green velvet dress. From there on out it wasn't an option to dress however it is I wanted to. I was born mid-1970s and in the '70s and '80s, even as creative as it was, you still had boy side and girl side and I knew enough to know that nobody switched sides. I felt so alone for so long. Our pets know when we're going out, they just instinctively know. I don't have to say a damn word. They've got the leash, they just know. Something triggers them. The entire world around us falls into two camps and when you know you're on the wrong side, you look around and nobody is switching sides, you have enough instinct to know, "I'm very different from anybody else." And in my family "different" wasn't allowed. – Serafine Sawyer

—————▽—————

Minocqua, WI (USA)
Milwaukee, WI (USA)

I didn't know I was different, but I felt things I didn't understand going back to the early '70's in High School. Like feeling all warm inside watching *Police Woman* ... LOL. It was never talked about back then in a tiny town, so I hadn't even heard of a lesbian until I was a senior in high school and never connected the *"Police Woman* warm feelings" dots. 1977, I started dreaming about being with women ... all the time ... then I knew I was different. I was 22. – Sherrie Howe

—————▽—————

New York, NY (USA)

My queer self was a non-issue when I was growing up at home. (My parents were more concerned about grades). But I was called "faggot" for the first time in 4th grade. This coincided with having my first boyfriend – a classmate who held hands with me up until 8th grade. – Sr. Freida Peoples aka DJ Chrysler Sheldon

—————▽—————

(Pakistan)

I always say this that I was born gay, I realize I was different and in fact I say special when puberty hit me and the sudden change in the hormones had aroused my interest in men. It felt different, I wasn't able to discuss about my queerness with anyone around me, nor my friends or my family were that understanding or tolerant. I'd to hide myself for years and coming to terms with my queerness was the most difficult period of my life. – Salman

TELL US ABOUT THE ONE THAT GOT AWAY?

Chicago, IL (USA)

There were a few and it was because of my timidity. I was so close with Frankie Knuckles and I had such a crush on him and he really liked me. I didn't go there because I couldn't wrap my brain around it. I was infatuated. Same thing with Michael Serafini, I had a crush on him. I never had the balls to do it, be that person. We all have regrets, but I guess everything is the way it should be. – James Scalfani

—————▽—————

Boston, MA (USA)
Provincetown, MA (USA)

Well … there was one hippy boy during my years in Boston. It started behind the scenes unknown to me. I attended a party of friends of my gay landlords (I lived in a gay rooming house on St. Botolph Street behind the Christian Science cathedral.). Apparently, the hippy boy was also at the party, and I must have made an impression on him, because mysteriously he appeared at my door one night after I'd already gone to sleep. One of the landlords must have let him into the house; otherwise, he couldn't have come to my room. I opened the door, and standing backlit in the hall was the hippy boy. He said, "Quick, get dressed; you're coming with me." I didn't hesitate and found myself in a cozy apartment in ice-bound Provincetown. I don't remember getting there. The hippy boy was a gentle, lovely young guy. There was a never-ending supply of wine and marijuana and all kinds of talented, fascinating people sitting around his table in the kitchen. It was all a bit much for me. I became quickly, severely infatuated and broke down crying (after everybody had left). The hippy gently said I needed to return to Boston immediately. I think he was perceptive and knew that a break was necessary, both quick and complete. I never saw him again, but I've remembered him in vivid detail ever since, and it's been about 45 years. I remember his name and know that he lives in Boston and Provincetown, and that through the years he has been a productive and active member of the Provincetown community. He has worked in all aspects of theatre, acting, designing sets, etc. I would like to see him again, but to what end, I haven't the faintest idea. He wouldn't remember me – he was a lover of poets, and I was just a freaky kid, much younger than my years. One fun memory: we went with a lesbian couple to see the first release of movie *Carrie*. Stoned to the max, we sat in second row center of a sparsely attended theatre, and we all jumped and screamed at all the easily imagined moments. It hadn't all been bad. And I still have that infatuation for the hippy. – Oran Walker

—————∇—————

Midwestern City (USA)

I was very close to a work peer and friend. Around the time I was divorced and coming out, he was also going through a divorce. We loved and supported one another during that time, and, perhaps, could have had a life together. Though, he never came out, called himself a metrosexual and continued to date butch women. We are still dear friends who love one another. – Anonymous

—————∇—————

Chicago, IL (USA)
San Francisco, CA (USA)

Boy, did I fuck that one up. For about a year before I left Chicago in 1993, I had been going out with a fellow named George. We had a wonderful time together and saw each other frequently enough that our friends considered us a couple, although we hadn't said anything about it one way or the other. After I moved to San Francisco we kept in touch but we didn't attempt a long-distance thing at all. In 1994, I fell completely in love with a new friend named Jon. Jon and I spent a great deal of time together, going clubbing and just hanging out. We got to know each other pretty well and I thought, wow this is going somewhere. Then in early 1995, George landed a job in San Francisco. We kind of picked up where we left off, as George was now rooming with a good friend of mine, but I was conflicted. I finally had to say something to George about it but what I had not done was tell Jon about my feelings for him. George and I cooled things a bit, and one night after we had done some ecstasy, I got up the courage to speak to Jon. Well, as fate would have it, Jon did not have the same feelings toward me. While our friendship was solid it was not going to evolve into anything else. So, there I was, having pushed one man away only to be pushed away myself by another. I say pushed away but that isn't what really happened in either case because I remain good friends with them both to this day. – Terence Smith (Joan Jett Blakk)

—————▽—————

Chicago, IL (USA)

There were definitely men that I hooked up with that I hoped would last longer and didn't. Either they decided we weren't a good fit or something happened and it just couldn't work out. There was a guy named Stefan … I've had three relationships with a variation of the name Stefan. He was a cute red-headed boy. We spent a few weeks together. He was very smart and lovely. Then he decided he couldn't be gay. It was frustrating and disappointing and I was pretty angry about it for a while. – Steve

—————▽—————

Chicago, IL (USA)

There was a cute Latino boy walking down Addison by Wrigley Field. It was the summer of 1986. He was wearing shorts and bare-chested, absolutely gorgeous. We chatted a bit but it didn't go anywhere. But I've been thinking about him for 30 years. – Xavier Bathsheba-Negron

—————▽—————

Fayetteville, AR (USA)
Springfield, MO (USA)

I was in college and I played piano and a lot of the time people would contact me to play at social events. There was this florist convention, and these florist dudes hired me to play at a cocktail party. There was this florist from St. Louis and he sat down at the piano and started talking to me. I was just enamored with him. Spent the night with him at his hotel that night. Then a couple of weeks later I met him in Springfield, Missouri, kind of halfway between Fayetteville and St. Louis. We had a couple of rendezvous like that. Then he said he had a job offer in Laguna Beach, California. I just knew he was going to ask me to go with him and we would live happily ever after. I didn't go. He never asked me, I never got the invitation. I would have gone. My favorite memory of all that was the first time we went to the Howard Johnson in Springfield. He registered us as Mr. & Mrs. _____. We were there late at night and the night person was a gay guy. We got up the next morning, went down for breakfast and this dude was still on shift. He looked at me as I walked by ... I was a 20 year old ... He said, "And how did you sleep Mrs. _____?" And I looked him right in the eye and said, "Oh I didn't sleep at all." – Renny

————————∇————————

Chicago, IL (USA)

When I was in high school, there was a boy who treated me terribly. I spent three years pursuing someone who actively gaslit me, going out of his way to make me believe he had feelings for me, then telling me it was all in my head. While all this was happening, there was another guy I thought was pretty cute. I was in theater and he was a techie, and a couple times at rehearsals he said a few sweet things that seemed to indicate he was interested. Sadly, I don't remember what he said; I don't even remember his name. Occasionally I'll think about him, and ponder what could have been if I gave him a chance rather than sticking with the one who kept hurting me. – C'est Kevvie (Wilhelmina)

————————∇————————

Chicago, IL (USA)

I don't think any of them actually got away. I have had the ones I wanted ... for what I wanted them for ... and then have moved on. – Dean Ogren

————————∇————————

Chicago, IL (USA)

I was dating this really hot guy for several months. He was very unreliable and would not always keep dates. After one of the best fucks of my life I did not hear from him for a while. One day I came home to an answering machine message that said, "I think I'm falling in love with you. I have some demons. I'm sorry. I have to break up with you." I called back and he had lost his job and been kicked out of his house according to his roommate. I did not put two and two together until later that he was probably an alcoholic and wanted to spare me. He did always have a vodka in his hand. It's a shame he never got to hear the beautiful song I wrote about him. – Lars von Keitz

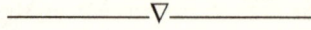

————▽————

Waverly, IA (USA)

Looking back, I had some surprising success for an average looking guy in having sexual partners that I had at first considered above my level. At age 50 I counted almost exactly that many sex partners. I did fall strongly for a few very handsome straight men who unfortunately continued to be unavailable to me even though I thought all of them were cock teasing me. Two of them were married but that wouldn't have mattered. – Robert Beck

————▽————

Chicago, IL (USA)

I've had many boyfriends. I can honestly say that until the last one I've never known what it was like to be "in love." I mean I've loved plenty, that's easy, loving is so fucking easy, being "in love" when you're just in it … that's a whole new thing for me that I didn't learn until I was in my mid-40s. The one that got away was much younger than me. It went against every instinct in my body, everything that I've ever practiced, which is to not even conceive of dating somebody 21 years younger than me. I know, I know, you'd think I would know better. I feel like wisdom is a chosen behavior sometimes. It didn't last very long. It was very intense. I was very much in love with him. He was in love with me, but as the young so often do, it's very easy to fall out of love, and be scared, and whatever. So, I got dumped and he broke my heart and the hardest part about it is having to see him all the time. Having him still be a part of the community, a part of the scene. Having everybody I know still know him and still be friendly with him. That was fucking rough. I was super-depressed for a year and a half. Therapy, anti-depressants, good friends, house music, got me through that. But it's funny you ask about this because I recently had an incredible epiphany. That is, I don't speak to him directly, he barely has a social media presence, we know a lot of the same people, so I hear things here and there. He's changed quite a bit since we broke up. I don't like the things I'm hearing … well, I won't say I don't like them, but I don't recognize those things. Two epiphanies I've had, you can't date somebody when they're in the larval stage and expect them to remain a larva. But the real epiphany was that the person I was in love with doesn't

154

exist anymore, so that for me was like ... "OK well that's the nail in the coffin." During this whole stupid pandemic ... if this had happened a year ago, I think I would have made poor choices. I would have reached out to him. But now I'm like, "I hope he's well, but it's none of my business." I guarantee he doesn't spend time thinking about me. It's a hard lesson to learn and at a weird age, but I don't regret being in love, I don't regret being with him. – Jeff Ramone

—————▽—————

(Bulgaria)

As with so many of us, the one who got away was straight, even though we had been in a semi-sexual relationship for two years. He was a lovely guy, a very dear friend, and stunning to look at. His only drawback was that his dick was tiny – amazing for a man who was 6'5." He couldn't cope with being bisexual, so we split up amicably and kept in touch. A few years later, he was happily married with children. – Louis Richard de Bourbon de Parme et de Savoie, Prince de la Pau

—————▽—————

Chicago, IL (USA)

The one that got away: his name was Mr. K. we had been dating a very short time and he was just being kind and generous. I had just left a very unhealthy relationship and took his generosity as a control issue. I dumped him flat. I did reach out to him years later to explain that he had done nothing wrong and it was all my shit. He now lives on his 1000 acre plantation in the Philippines. – Philip Bernal

—————▽—————

Rockford, IL (USA)

I was dating a young guy named Zach. It was a long-distance relationship. We were very close and loved each other dearly. We would talk everyday. We knew what seemed like everything about each other. While we never met we talked, skyped, texted all day, every day. I moved closer to him and we had plans to meet, and things kept happening that prevented us from meeting. In October just three years after we started talking, he went into the hospital. I had known that he had health issues and that things could be rough for us going forwards. I was so worried about him. I wanted to do everything I could to help him. His parents didn't want me to visit. They didn't want me to send a card. Two weeks later I found out that he died due to complications. I thought my life was going to end. I cried and cried. Even typing this up now I am sad about his passing. I wanted to marry him and spend our life together but alas that wasn't meant to be. – Patrick J. Murphy III

—————▽—————

Seattle, WA (USA)

I met a man many years (25) ago when I first moved to Seattle, at age 27. I was hit by the "thunderbolt" when we met, and I told people that I found the one I was going to marry. Unfortunately, this person "M" was too insecure with himself to allow someone as gregarious, opinionated, mouthy, and driven (all of which I tend to be) into his life. He preferred to listen to his enablers and we never dated passed the third date. He DID call me every time he was between boyfriends, wanting to hook up, until he found his footage again, and then I'd be dropped like a rock in the ocean. After many years of this cycle, I fought to have a friendship with him, that eventually formed. It wasn't fulfilling. What I realized was although he is a good person, "M" and I would NEVER have worked out as a couple because he would compromise every desire to not make any waves in his relationships, and would NEVER stand up for himself. I would have walked all over him waiting for him to push back, which was definitely NOT in his personality. We'd eventually have a bitter breakup and would never have had a friendship afterwards. – Eric Andrews-Katz

—————▽—————

Bellport, NY (USA)

I have been told before that I was the one that got away. When it comes to romance, I am still looking for whoever that person might be. – Erin Michelle Miller

—————▽—————

Frinton-on-Sea, Essex (UK)

Two or three "got away." You kinda think you're on a similar wavelength with a guy, in a similar league looks-wise, have similar interests (not just, or even mainly, sexual), and within an acceptable bandwidth of age – I'd say within 10 years of each other. Sadly, two or three prime candidates for being "the one" had other ideas. The main stumbling blocks were their residual Catholic guilt, or the fact they wanted someone 30 years my junior, or they just couldn't see how fucking fabulous I am. Sometimes all three at once! But I did alright in the end. More than alright. – Diesel Balaam

───────▽───────

Chicago, IL (USA)

I was at a square-dancing event in Washington, DC and this guy hit on me like a ton of bricks. We ended up having a really good time, but he was already married. I fell hard for him, really hard. That wasn't easy and now 10 years later I'm pretty good friends with him and his husband. But at the time I was a wreck. It's kind of the guy who got away but we're good friends now. – Drew

───────▽───────

Ozarks, MO (USA)
St Louis, MO (USA)

In the late 1980s I went to something called the Midwest Men's Festival that took place each summer in the Ozarks in Missouri. For the first time in my life I earned a week's vacation from work and took that time to go to this gathering. The first day there, while I was unpacking things in a cabin I chose (there were at least four to each two-bedroom cabin), a man named Ken walked in and when our eyes met I can tell that's when he decided to stay in that room. We clicked instantly. And while I let him have his room to breathe and experience the time there and meeting others, he would usually spend the evenings snuggled up with me. He left a few days earlier than I did, and I felt sad. Turns out he lived in Chicago and visited me in St. Louis a few times. We'd talk on the phone once in a while, but while it was not a torrid affair, we felt something despite living in different cities. And now here's where you're going to go "Ohhhh. Here's the wrench thrown into the situation." Ken was still married and had a wife and a kid. Had I known that right off the bat I would have hesitated with him. It just seemed like not the ideal situation for me. Apparently, he came out to her, and she accepted it. To keep things good for their child they stayed together and he slept in a different bedroom. I guess the child was young enough to not think that different bedrooms were odd. With the distance and his work, it just was not easy to keep things flowing, though he always looked forward to the music cassettes I'd make and send (mine were custom productions with me being a DJ of sorts on each one). One winter he came to town for a business function

157

and was going to stay at my apartment. Murphy's Law set itself in motion and it was one of the fiercest winters in St. Louis, and the radiators in my building stopped working. It was FREEZING in my apartment. I feared for my two cats. He had arrived while I was at work, and he had a key to let himself in. When I got home there was a note from Ken saying how unbearably cold it was in my place and that he was going to check into a motel somewhere. I could have understood that easily, but he didn't ask me to join him nor said anything about calling me later to meet up. It was weird. His wife had even called to see if he had arrived, I didn't know he had given her my number! I told her about the radiator issue and that he had checked into a motel but didn't give her the info yet. He tried to call the next day, but I didn't answer. I felt a strange vibe about it. I got my key a few days later from a mutual friend he had given it to before he left the city. I didn't hear from him again, and about a year later found out from the mutual friend that Ken had passed away. This is the part where I'm just not sure how to conclude the story with a sense of closure. I'll never know if that winter I was somehow at fault for something. – Todd Jaeger

---------▽---------

Lansing, MI (USA)

There were 10,000 that got away. There was a guy when I was coming out. I was 20 years old. I had a crush on him, and I threw myself at him, but he wasn't interested. He moved on. I think that's happened to all of us, right? All of us fall for someone and they're not into you. So he got away. I'm still in touch with him. We're friends. – Jim

---------▽---------

Chicago, IL (USA)

Because I never really dated growing up – where straight kids get to work out their awkwardness and hone their skills – coming out late meant that I had to do all that awkwardness with adults. They were also usually adults that were farther along the timeline in their outness compared to me.

Then I met David. We weren't supposed to meet but as I walked through Sidetrack one night he was getting animated in a story he was telling, extended his arms with one of those slushie glass mugs in his hand and smacked me right in the mouth with it. I was mad, he was apologetic. He was trying to fix it, I wanted him to leave me the fuck alone. My lip was bleeding and I wanted to leave. He followed me out and wouldn't stop bugging me until I agreed to let him make it up to me. We dated for just over a year. I never had thought I would find someone I would marry, but even though this was before Marriage Equality passed, he was the candidate. Unfortunately he wasn't the one that 'got away' as much as he was taken. He traveled around the world for work and died in a car wreck in Germany. I lost him and if I'm honest I lost part of myself. I've not dated, nor really wanted to date someone since. – Chris Grace

———————▽———————

Salem, OR (USA)

I had just graduated from a Fundamentalist Christian college. For my first year out of college I traveled as a singer in a group representing the school and giving concerts at churches, youth camps, schools etc. Along the way that first summer, I met a man from California and we hit it off. I mean, he was everything I would ever want. But of course, I had not yet admitted to myself that I was gay. So even though I lusted after him and even though we did everything we could for the next year and a half to spend time together, it never went anywhere.

I could cry thinking about him right now. I moved across the country and he stayed in Northern California. We lost touch. I haven't spoken to him since 1984. When I first came out, he was the first man I thought about. What would he say to me if I told him? Would he be interested in me? Would he reject me as evil incarnate and break my heart? So I left him to his world and started to build my own life.

I still wonder about him. – andKevin

———————▽———————

Florida (USA)

When I was younger, I felt I had a very soft heart. So, in my mind, there were a lot that got away even though they were not the one. At the time I thought they were the one. So, it's hard for me to say about THE ONE that got away. There's a lot that got away. But if I had to pick one, a friend of mine that I knew in Florida – the person knows who this person is – he was the one that got away. Only because he eventually came on to me, but I said, "No." I thought he was too young and I didn't want to be his first. As much as I wanted it to happen, there was that little voice inside me that said, "Don't do this David, because it's not right." – Dave Vega (Lucifers Axe)

———————▽———————

Palm Springs, CA (USA)

I never had that scenario, because anyone I wanted, I got. I started to learn when I was young, from friends … I had a bad self-image, but they made me see reality. Once I was comfortable in my own skin, there was not one person … if I wanted somebody, I got them. – Keith Kollinicos (Missa Distic)

---------∇---------

Chicago, IL (USA)

There have been so many. They were all unique in their way and I was hopelessly in love with all of them. –Dennis Hardenstein

---------∇---------

Cleveland, OH (USA)

My time with him was all consuming. When I remember that time I don't think of specific things, I recall our block of time in a big chunk. It was intense and maybe a little too much for me at the time. I was stupid and listened to my friends. I didn't realize at the time that they were more bar acquaintances than real friends. I think I had happiness and love and that was something they wanted. They were jealous. I believed them when they said I could do better. Better than love? I was an idiot. Real friends would want me to be happy. I should have realized that. The one that got away is dead now. Maybe it wouldn't have worked out, but I wish I had the chance to say that I tried. – Roger

---------∇---------

Louisiana (USA)

In college, I met someone and knew them briefly. I wasn't totally comfortable yet with the idea of identifying as gay/queer and I wouldn't recognize my feelings for him. He was smart, charismatic, assertive, articulate, attractive, and a good listener. My attraction to him scared me and I couldn't think straight when trying to talk to him, idiot speech is not the way to go, and I unfortunately started avoiding him. He wasn't even gay but I admired him and a friendship would have been just as appreciated if not anything more intimate. – Katorri A.

---------∇---------

Washington, DC (USA)

There's only one that really stood out and ever made me wonder what might have been. His name was Bill and I met him when I was in graduate school. We met in a bar in Washington, DC just before Thanksgiving and the attraction was immediate and powerful. We were both born on the same day and we were both studying the same thing (at different universities) so it seemed sort of fated at the time. Our first few dates were hot and heavy, he talked seriously about spending our lives together, and then shortly after Christmas he pretty much ghosted me and told me in very brief phone call that he "met someone." I never knew what really happened between us until I ran into him about two years later. He told me he'd lied about meeting someone because he was too afraid to tell me the real reason that he broke it off with me. Basically, he confessed that he was so deep in the closet – and not out to his family – that the very idea of having a real relationship with anyone was frightening. His family would eventually figure out that we were more than just friends and he couldn't face that. The silver lining is that the last time I saw him, about 10 years later, he hadn't evolved at all and was still stuck in the same rut he'd been in since the late-'80s. I was relieved to have been spared that. – D. Warner

———————▽———————

Adelaide, South Australia (Australia)

There was a guy at school I quite liked. He made it obvious he was interested "like that" but I was quite naive as well, so I really did not know what he was up to. Problem was that friendship bit the dust after Mum thought she caught us smooching when in fact that wasn't the case at all. She went ballistic and threatened to call his grandmother and stuff like this. I'm sure that did him no favours in regard to his sexuality. It would have been nice to see if we would have stayed in contact and had anything happen. – Robert Verrall

———————▽———————

Chicago, IL (USA)

I met her at His n Hers – she moved back to San Francisco, I waited and waited. I got involved with someone else and then one Saturday night she came into the bar. By then it was too late. – Terry Gaskins

———————▽———————

San Jose, CA (USA)

There really wasn't one that got away. I was only out for about three months when I met my husband. There were a couple I fell hard for. One was quite a bit younger than me. He lived with his mom and sister in Decatur and he was from El Salvador. The first time I was on the receiving end of sex we got caught by a sheriff at a reservoir outside of San Jose, shining the flashlights. Of course, it hurt like hell because I didn't have any lube. What happened with that? He met somebody else. We went out a few times, I would see him at the local gay disco. He was 21 and when he was 40 he committed suicide. I don't know why, he was such a successful and well-liked person, I don't know why. Then there was another guy who worked as a bartender. I was sick with the flu and I'd only known him a very short time. We never went out. In fact, I never had sex with him. But I remember he came over to my apartment and made homemade chicken soup when I was sick. Actually, maybe we did have sex. That was the sweetest thing. He was a night shift bartender, so he was a night person and I was a day person. So we both realized that wouldn't work out. Then I met my husband and I wasn't really attracted to him at first, but I could tell he loved me a lot. I decided to stick with him for a while and I grew to love him. It's been 36 years. – Spike

———————▽———————

Chicago, IL (USA)

There have been several men who "got away," men with whom I was obsessively in love. Fortunately, each time they "got away" I realized that my feelings for them were actually a warning sign that something inside me needed to be fixed: I needed to bring into my life something that they had that was missing in me. I'm actually grateful that they got away. – William Demaree

———————▽———————

Oxnard, CA (USA)

It was a guy from Australia. We had a whirlwind affair and it was quite apparent where things were going. I was too young to know what I had. I was too young to take a chance. I was 30 at the time. We had this great affair. A year later he announced that he had to go back to Australia and offered to take me with him. He offered me a lot to take me with him. I said, "No." I got a call at work saying, "Please come, I've already left but there's a ticket waiting for you." I never returned the phone call. Never contacted him. I was so in love but so afraid. I'd always been that I would never be good enough, nobody would love me, I wasn't worthy of love. If anyone loved me, there was something up and not to trust it. I've regretted it every moment of my life until I met my current partner. – Crusher

———————▽———————

Grand Rapids, MI (USA)

I can't say this happened to me. I have been left my many, but usually realize it is for the better. – Mark S

———————▽———————

Chicago, IL (USA)

I don't feel that way about any one man. I have regrets. I was with one man for 17 years. Another for three years. And still others for shorter periods of time. I didn't let them get away, we moved in together until the passion waned. Either they went their way, or I went mine. – Steve Kmetko

———————▽———————

San Francisco, CA (USA)

After coming out and living San Francisco, it was still a little scary for me to have an ongoing, conscious boyfriend that I "dated," introduced to friends and co-workers, and took to their parties. But one I met by accident in 1977 at the tryout of a play, the title of which I forget. He was working for ACT, the American Conservatory Theater, creating ads and, being an artist, drawings. His specialty that was avant-garde and popular at the time was paintings on canvas created from projected images and photos. Using this as a basis, the finished paintings looked very realistic.

He was also writing a play about Stonewall that focused on the fact that the riots followed directly after the death and funeral of Judy Garland. There was one reading at a fancy party in Marin, across the bay from the city. I read one of the parts and was toying with the idea of setting it to music in a musical play styled after the 1960s *Fantasticks*. But things went downhill from there (I don't think I was that bad), he began almost never returning my calls. I began hearing rumors from mutual acquaintances (ok, I was stalking him a little) that he was planning to move back to his hometown of Seattle, and to an old boyfriend he had left. Well, several "bumpy" nights and screaming phone calls later, it was over. He and the city's theater scene were surgically removed from my path. I never heard from him again, though in the plague-time of HIV/AIDS, I did wonder and pray for his health. – David Hatfield Sparks

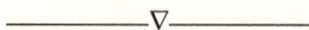

—————▽—————

San Francisco, CA (USA)

I had a boyfriend in San Francisco that I was infatuated with. He was a radical fairy and an artist. We had a relationship that lasted many years, but we were very close for a year. We spent all our time together. I wanted that to evolve into something more sustainable. But he would never agree to it and that caused us to break apart. He just didn't want to make the commitment to anyone. This was after the AIDS epidemic. I have to say that the AIDS epidemic had a profound impact on everybody but also on our community in San Francisco. A lot of people rushed to get a partner because they felt that would help them survive. That was not true by the way. That was the biggest false lie of the entire epidemic. When the epidemic started in San Francisco people in the medical profession, social workers, were trying to think of something to do … nobody knew what to do. You couldn't even identify the source of the disease at that time. So they said, "Have one partner, get married. And only have sex with that partner." Well, the truth of the matter was that by that time a large percentage of the population was infected and didn't know it. So if you had one partner and either one of you were positive then those couples died. The other reaction was that people didn't want a partner because they were losing people all around them and they were afraid of loss. That was my case, I was afraid of attachment followed by loss. Which is a very traumatic psychological state. All humans have it, but especially when all those young people were dying. I think that a lot people I dated and wanted to become partners with didn't feel like they had time left, that their future was uncertain. They didn't want to be in a relationship with one person. – Greg Day

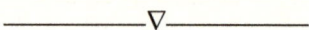

—————▽—————

Chicago, IL (USA)

I guess that would have to be my first ever falling in love experience. His name was Tom and he has now become incredibly successful, he owns a high rise in Manhattan. I missed out on that … I still stalk him on Facebook, after all these years. I was so new that I totally scared him off. Basically, I was a 30 year old man that had no sexual experience to speak of. Especially not with a man. So when we first got together I was just like this junior high school girl. I was writing Tom + Tom = Love and Little Hearts. It was just disgusting. It was funny because I was aware of how stupid I was acting but I couldn't help myself because it was all emotion that I couldn't control. I would go to his doorstep and hide little presents for him, so he would walk out the door and find presents. Well this was all over the top and very stalker-like. He had enough of that after about two months. He basically said, "You gotta find somebody else dude." I went into a period of major grieving, crying and all that. This is going to sound strange but at the time I had just bought a building in Chicago, so I was renovating it. I remember that when my grandfather died – my grandmother was a widow from a pretty early age – she locked herself in the garage and restored antiques for an entire year. In my mind, this was like a death to me, so I threw myself into renovation and I renovated an entire apartment to try to get over him. The addendum to that story was that I found another guy to date and then I got dumped pretty quickly by him because he started dating my first boyfriend. – Thomas Stribling

————V————

Chicago, IL (USA)

There was a guy who went to the high school near my elementary school, that I would see on the bus and we chatted and eventually hooked up. When he graduated from high school, I graduated from elementary. For several years when he returned here, we would meet up. I don't know how to reach him or if he is still alive, but to me he was my first love. – Mercury

————V————

Spokane, WA (USA)

It wasn't that he got away, but we had a tragic event that changed everything about us. His name was Rick. He had a beautiful nine-year-old son who had major allergies. He was pretty much allergic to everything that was normal. He passed away three years into our relationship. He died on a school field trip. Once that death occurred and dealing with the media and the school district and the whole nightmare for a year, it just separated us. I regret the fact that we never stuck it out. But once you lose a child, it's pretty over. He's always in my thoughts even today. – Marcous

————V————

Cathedral City, UT (USA)

There were many that got away, but the most important one that got away, that I fucked up, was 10 years ago and he was perfect, everything I wanted. We had so much in common, we were very compatible, but I had a panic attack and I confronted him on the fact that we weren't having sex, we weren't touching each other anymore, kissing each other. It blew up in my face. I lost him for that, but he's still the love of my life. – David Hardy.

—————▽—————

Chicago, IL (USA)

You're gonna make me cry. I have a habit of falling in love with men who are not attracted to me. I mentor them, I support their efforts, but have yet to find a peer. The guy that comes to mind, I loved the minute I met him. He had a boyfriend, but I didn't think it would last. It didn't. He still didn't' want me. I had 'the talk,' told him I was in love with him and he said he didn't' feel that way about me and never would. This after a 10-year close friendship. I tried to stay his friend, but it was just too painful. I felt kicked in the stomach every time I was with him. After a few years of therapy, I realized I was not in love with him – I was obsessed with him. I wanted him only because I couldn't' have him. I had to break off the friendship. We exist now as friends on Facebook. He still haunts me. – MrZor

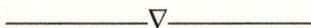

—————▽—————

Cologne, North Rhine-Westphalia (Germany)

My gosh there were kinda tons of these stories. I guess I'm terrible at timing. One time there was this (like I was as well back then) dreadlocked boy from Berlin who was studying Polish history and language, coming over to Cologne for a social media date. It was spring '05 so we met Friday. I picked him up from the station Friday midday. We immediately crashed into each other couldn't keep our hands off each other at the station, tram, street, house floor 'til we got home. But I promised my roommate to join him at a party in a town nearby. We went there and were so occupied with each other that we even got complaints that we shouldn't behave like that in public. So then we went home after the party. My roommate kindly arranged to stay somewhere else after the party. We were having 24-30 hours of great sex until I brought him to the station. I was supported by friends as I had a breakdown at the station. Crying like hell, putting drugs and even alcohol in my system. My friends dragged me to another trance party in Cologne. I danced all night to stop me thinking about him. When I stopped dancing, I left the party and immediately ran into the phone booth in front of the party venue to call him. He told me with weak voice that he cried all the hours in the train. He got away. The bad timing part of the weekend was when I was asked by a friend to help him promote a free open-air trance party in Hamburg. On the way back, police stopped and searched us. Found loads of drugs on one of my friends and a tiny amount of stuff on me. I was arrested for three months because of the investigation, and because I didn't register at my new home officially at that point, I couldn't inform him for three months. He thought I screwed him over. I learned from someone else I met 4-5 years later, that he was with another person, but didn't seem to be too happy. But our moment was shattered and gone ... Roland ... I'll never forget this moment. – Cornelius Günther Körn

————————▽————————

Santa Fe, NM (USA)

Honestly, I don't think anybody got away. I just put the snake to work ... – Juan-manuel Alonso

————————▽————————

St. Cloud, MN (USA)

I don't go hunting or fishing. – Rachel Wexelbaum

————————▽————————

Chicago, IL (USA)

When I first moved from Northern Michigan to Chicago, I dated a guy named Jay. I had to be near a major airport to fly in and out for my work. I decided to make the move and a month later I met this guy named Jay. I met him in Charlie's ... he was hot. Tall, younger, good-looking. I got Chicago but Jay was the Ginsu knives. Like on QVC I bought the product, but I got the Ginsu knives with it. We started dating and I was all about him. Nice guy but then he started having conversations on the phone with somebody else. It was his ex-boyfriend. His ex-boyfriend was luring him back ... "If you come back to me, we can have an open relationship. You don't have that with Greg. If you come back to me, I have a larger home, you're living with Greg in a one bedroom." I have the shittiest time dating people because they always leave right before the holidays. I think people lose their shit during the holidays. Two weeks before Christmas and he decided to go. I tried to lure him back but, I learned a lesson, you can't force someone to like you, or love you. I let him go. He's married to the guy he left me for. It's fine, but I was tragic, heartbreak and crying. – Greg R. Baird

—————————∇—————————

Tallahassee, FL (USA)
Redwood Valley, CA (USA)

His name was Gerald, a Latino graduate student who chose to go by the name Jerry. I was an entering freshman at Florida State, during summer orientation the weeks after high school. I had been with only one man, briefly, at a cruisy rest stop I read about on the local mall bathroom wall and had never even tasted alcohol. Jerry chatted me up at the campus pool and we showered together. He taught me about cooking, Joan Baez, uncut penises, and the importance of dignity and family. He soon got accepted to law school in California, and encouraged me to move with him, describing the wonders of Northern California. I was torn by my young existence and the thought of such a dramatic change when so much change was already flooding my life. Four years later, I was ready to leave Tallahassee for San Francisco, but have yet to catch up with Jerry. – T. Lark Letchworth

—————————∇—————————

Lawton, OK (USA)

I met this guy named Keith in Oklahoma, an American Indian, huge broad-shouldered Indian. I want to say he was Apache or Cherokee. He always gave me warm hugs and I was in bar called Atomic Annie's in Lawton, Oklahoma, and there was a lot of drag shows, a lot of beers. I was actually a DJ there because nobody else would spin records. I was not very good. I didn't know how to blend them, later I found out. I met Keith and he was so sweet, but my friends said, "Oh you don't want that, you want a white guy." When you're first coming out, you're very vulnerable to peer pressure. He was a kind spirited person and that would have been the one that got away. I was a matchstick and Keith was a big guy, broad shoulders, thin waist. Back then in Oklahoma, to stay in the popularity of the crowd I had to stay with white people. I was taught to be prejudiced but deep down inside I think he would have been it. He's the one that got away. – David Hayes

—————————∇—————————

Honolulu, Hawaii (USA)
Davis, CA (USA)

Just one? When I was 13 I went to Oahu to visit an old childhood friend who had moved to Hawaii Kai with his family. I quickly joined my friend as a Junior Camp Counselor at the Rec Center. After a few weeks a fellow counselor invited me to join him in using the small sauna at the center. He was cute, and somehow I knew that he was just enticing me to go in there and play around with him. Being a virgin as well as a very late maturer and very self-conscious of my body, I totally chickened out and made some excuse not to. I regretted that for years and years.

Having not learned my lesson I repeated this in college. For fun I took a general acting class. I was out of the closet then and no longer a virgin. This one Swedish looking blonde piece of sweetness in the class asked to hang out with me. We didn't really know each other, and he was shy, but I suggested he come over and we smoked some pot. I so badly wanted him and I assumed he did as well, but both of us became even more shy and introverted and we hardly said a word to each other. What could have been a beautiful time or more fizzled like my veterinarian career. – Paul Harris

—————▽—————

Bondi & Darlinghurst, New South Wales (Australia)

Ah … Paul _____. My heart breaks every time I think of him … which is perhaps more often than is healthy for me. Amongst those who are close to me, it is no secret that I've always been in love with him. To add to it, he's on my Facebook friend's list … so, except for a long break of about 20 years where I lost contact with him, he's still there like the proverbial carrot waved in front of me … still single … still married to his job, which was, for me, always the problem … the stumbling block that held me back. He's still got those beautiful eyes that seduced me on many occasions. I met Paul around 1988. I'd been single … again … for about a year or so. I was sitting against the wall in the bottom bar of the Midnight Shift, in Darlinghurst, just watching two guys chatting at the end of the bar in front of me. Then Paul came in and joined them. I thought "What a cute guy … younger than me by a few years, so probably out of my league!" Then at one stage he turned around … and our eyes locked! It was almost like destiny stepping in. Yes, we did go home together … yes, we got along like a house in fire. We went home together many times over the next eight years … I guess you'd classify it as a fuck-buddy situation, but there was always a lot more to it than that. There was a very definite deep affection between us, and it was always a relationship that I felt comfortable in. I think I fell in love with Paul early in the fuck-buddy thing, but I never stated it, even though I don't feel he would have been shocked to know I was. There were occasions where I thought of a relationship with him, but the thing that held me back was our differing approaches to life and work. I have a very casual approach to life, and work. My ambitious days were behind me at this stage, as I couldn't see the sense in it. I worked jobs I wanted to work, instead of jobs I had to work. I was very much a "scene" person and loved my social life. Paul, on the other hand, took his job very seriously, worked long hours, overtime, weekends. He went out, but nowhere near as much as me. On the occasions I ventured to imagine a life with him, this was always the wall I came up against … would our social and work lives always be clashing, and would it lead to friction. It was one thing to be fuck-buddies under these circumstances … but partners could paint quite a different scenario. So, then Paul met someone he had a relationship with for a couple of years. In the interim I contracted AIDS, and that robbed me of about 18 months of my life. Then I met David. In the 18 months of recovery, Paul and his partner had moved, and I hadn't seen him. David and I went out to the Midnight Shift one night … and there was a Paul … and on his own. I introduced him to David, and we got to chatting. I realised as soon as I saw him that my feelings hadn't changed. We fell back into conversations so easily, like we'd never been apart. When we left the nightclub, David said to me, "You're in love with him, aren't you!" It was that obvious. David and I were together for 16 years, and in that time I glimpsed Paul only on one occasion in a pub after a big party. I was a bit out of it on an "E", and decided it was better not to say hi in that condition … as one tends to speak one's mind. But in the 16 years I was with David, and in the six since we've split up, Paul has never been far from my mind. About 18 months ago my housemate ran into him in Darlinghurst, and got his phone number, which he gave me. First phone call was like 20 years had never passed. We just fell back into what used to be. But there is distance now. He still lives in the city, and a I'm 90 minutes away on the Central Coast. I'm severely vision-impaired as a result of AIDS, and on a disability pension. He single, but still married to the job he's working, which involves him being overseas a lot of the time. A brush with cancer hasn't chilled him out. I'm still in a quandary as to whether to mention the "L" word, or just leave it lie this far down the line. A great unrequited love. I don't want to lose his friendship by frightening him off, and he's talking about living in Italy when he finally retires. As much as I find Italy a beautiful place, I really don't want to leave home. So even now … it's all a big question mark. Maybe we both need to get pissed, and have an openly honest phone conversation … maybe … – Tim Anderson

―――――∇―――――

New York, NY (USA)

When I lived in New York in the '80's I met a waiter who worked in an Eighth Avenue bar/restaurant that I frequented. For me, it was love at first sight. We spent many a night romping thru Hell's Kitchen where he lived as well in his tenement apartment with the bathtub in the kitchen. Then the day came when he wasn't as interested in me as I was in him. He was definitely the one that got away. When I think back and see his face in my memory, my heart still pitter patters. – Mark Contorno

———————▽———————

Brunswick, ME (USA)

So many men ... but unfortunately, in my twenties, I traveled a lot, working for an international airline and had hundreds of sexual partners. I met a lot of nice guys, but none of them nor I were ready for anything permanent. Who knows where they are today, which ones made it safely through the AIDS crisis of the '80s? I was fortunate and in the late '80s met the man with whom I'm married and still share my life. I have no regrets, but I wish I'd taken the time to get to know more of the men with whom I only shared some "recreation." I think about some of them even today. – Michael Pickel

———————▽———————

Aspen, CO (USA)

I hit on a sweet very rich guy in Aspen, CO. I had gone to dinner with him and his friends as part of a business deal with the Aspen Gay Ski Week. I liked him and after dinner I propositioned him. He put me off, saying I wouldn't understand why.

Years later I wonder if the rejection was that he was white and I was brown ... or he was rich and I was poor ... or if sex would spoil the business deal I was trying to put together. – Tony Earl

———————▽———————

New York, NY (USA)

The year was 1993. My first partner and I were in New York City to see a few shows. We had been together about ten years by that time. After seeing a show on Broadway, we took a taxi to a gay bar that he'd read about. I can remember how seedy that area of town seemed to me. The car parked along the sidewalk a block or so from the bar with its missing wheels having been ripped off sometime during the night testified to this.

My partner loved to have anonymous three-ways and even orgies when he could arrange it – something that really had little appeal to me. When we walked through the door of the bar, it was a cavernous warehouse of a building filled with men, loud with laughter. Cigarette smoke filled the air. A fistfight broke out in a far corner and there was a large TV playing *Hello Dolly* with Barbara Streisand. Men in leather sitting on the floor watching Dolly.

As we entered, my partner told me that if I met someone and I liked him, to go home with him and he'd do the same. This angered me and really hurt my feelings, but it came as no real surprise either.

As my partner stood in the long line of guys lined up at the bar twenty across waiting for their drinks to be poured, I stood watching the throng of activity surrounding me. As he walked up and handed me my beer, I noticed a young man on the opposite side of the room smile at me and lift his bottle to give me a salute. I did the same and smiled. My partner whispered in my ear, "It sure didn't take you long, did it?" I ignored him and walked towards the young man across the room still angry by his suggestion of finding someone else – but angry enough to do just that. Our eyes locked and his smile broadened. We tapped our bottles together as I stood next to him. He said that he'd noticed me when I walked through the door just now. I said something like, "How lucky for me." He asked me if I'd like to go back to his place that he didn't live far – only a few minutes by taxi. Without hesitation, I said, "Sure." It turns out, he lived on the twentieth floor of a high-rise with a guard sitting at a desk in the marbled lobby and everything. I remember seeing his closet of clothes, the cowboy hat on the shelf above two full-length fur coats – one black, one gray. The most notable thing about the bedroom, besides me standing next to a total stranger, was that the window was open and frigid air had been filling the room all evening. His bed was piled high with numerous blankets. He told me that he loved to sleep with the window open. From that distance, you could still hear the life of the city far below.

His small, smooth body felt nice next to my larger, hairy one and we had passionate sex throughout the night. We also talked and shared for much of the night and I don't really remember going to sleep at all. This was in the days before cell phones, so I knew that my partner had no idea of where I was or if I was okay or not. This seemed to please me somehow. Now, I was holding the cards.

When sunlight was filling the room, Peter turned towards me, kissed me, and asked me if I would like to stay with him for the day. I knew that there would be a price to be paid if I said yes, but I said it anyway. We talked and shared for hours and hours. We made love again and by afternoon, it seemed like a bit more than just sex. I was beginning to feel something.

By the time the sun was starting to go down, I knew that I had a decision to make. In my coat pocket was my ticket for that night's show. I could leave Peter and go to the show and sit next to my partner or I could stay another night.

As I walked the long twenty or so blocks to the theater, I thought about all the events over the past – not even twenty-four hours. As I walked into the theater doors, I wasn't sure what I would expect to find sitting in the seat next to me, or if it would be empty. I saw my partner's profile in the semi-darkness as I made my way to my seat. His head was stiff, and he didn't turn to look at me. At intermission, he immediately got up and left – no words were spoken. After the show, he quickly sprang up and left.

I made my way through the exiting crowd and walked out of the theater. It was snowing now. If I turned left, I would be heading back to our hotel. If I turned right, I would be heading to Peter's apartment. I looked both ways and then I turned right and the snow falling on my face felt good as I smiled thinking about the night ahead.

When I got to the lobby of Peter's building, the guard saw me standing out in the cold and I asked him if he could ring Peter's apartment. He allowed me to sit in the warm lobby next to the elevators. Peter wasn't at home. I began to think that maybe Peter would arrive with someone else on his arm if I waited. I decided to wait anyway.

About an hour later, Peter walked up and when he saw me sitting there, he jumped up in the air and ran over and gave me a kiss on the cheek – even with the guard watching. In the elevator, we kissed all the way to the twentieth floor.

That night, in the cold of the bedroom, and with the lights turned out, Peter shared that he felt a very real connection with me. He knew that my partner and I had just opened a new restaurant where we lived. Peter told me that if I would consider coming to New York to be with him that he had the resources and connections to help me open a restaurant there. He even knew of a vacant building not far from where he lived that would make a fabulous restaurant. My head was swimming. If it hadn't been so very cold in the room, I would've thought that I needed to pinch myself to see if what I was hearing was really real.

The next morning, Peter got up to get ready for work. He said I could stay as long as I wanted. He told me to call him and he gave me his office number. He knew that I was needing to head back home that morning and my flight left in a few hours. My thoughts about all of this were spinning like some carousel – round and round.

When I got back to the hotel, I found our room empty of my partner's belongings. My plane ticket was sitting on the dresser. I took a taxi to the airport. The flight back was without my partner on board. I fell asleep in my seat and woke up with the plane touching down on the runway in our city. I took a taxi home. The house was empty, but I noticed my partner's suitcase in the foyer. I called Peter's office number. His secretary told me to hold on that he was expecting my call. He sounded genuinely happy to hear from me and told me to call him that night, which I did. I went upstairs and decided to unpack my things in the guest room, and I laid down on the bed. I heard the front door open downstairs. I heard my partner mount the stairs and I heard the door to our room shut behind him. The large house was eerily silent now.

The following week was peppered with numerous calls to Peter. I had this new little device that I could store phone numbers and other information of my friends. This is the device where my partner found Peter's number. I didn't understand why when it became clear that Peter was not taking my calls at his office. His secretary telling me that he was always "in meetings." My calls to his apartment were left unanswered.

After a week or so of no conversation with Peter, I made the decision to fly to New York and to wait in his lobby for an explanation. The guard, again, let me in to sit and wait. At around 6 pm Peter arrived at the lobby. He seemed shocked to see me. This time there was no kiss on the cheek. No jumping up in the air with excitement. When the elevator doors closed, he asked me what I was doing there. He said that I couldn't be there. He told me that my partner had called him and threatened him. I tried to imagine my partner threatening anyone. Peter said that he didn't want to be in the middle of this. He asked me where I was staying. His question stunned me. Peter agreed for me to stay the night with him. If it wasn't so sad, it would've been amusing to see him place all those blankets between us on the bed so that there would be no physical contact. Peter was gone the next morning before I woke up.

I returned home to a silent house. My partner's new Cadillac was in the driveway. The door to the bedroom – our room – was closed. I fell asleep on the guest bed, exhausted and shocked and even angry at all that had transpired – but mostly angry at myself.

I awoke to my partner hitting me with his fists in a rage. Two of my ribs were fractured and then, lying there, stunned, I heard the front door slam and the wheels of his car screech out of the driveway. The beginning of the end between my partner and me had started. – Ron Cline

---------▽---------

Charlottetown, Prince Edward Island (Canada)

I'm very happy that I'm married to my husband, so I tend to think of "the one(s) who got away" as unmet sexual opportunities. I can think of two examples, both of which will most likely never happen, but Mark, Michael, if you read this, give us a call. – Dave Stewart

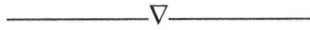

————————▽————————

Milwaukee, WI (USA)

One never got away. The only woman I was with was my first and it lasted 33 years, five months, until she died. That was seven years ago. She still communicates with me. I have enough material to write a book about it. – Sherrie Howe

————————▽————————

Des Moines, IA (USA)

I wish there were only one. That phenomenon is a constant even until now. I usually credit people to be better than they are really, and I have no problem extending trust. I don't mourn or pine for any one of them but for all of them. – Sr. Freida Peoples aka DJ Chrysler Sheldon

————————▽————————

Fort Lauderdale, FL (USA)

There hasn't been one. My one relationship before the one I'm in now (27+ years) would have been great if I was ready for a relationship and he wasn't an alcoholic, but those are two big issues. – Rick Karlin

————————▽————————

(Pakistan)
Worcester, MA (USA)

I wish I had someone in life, I always wish to fall in love and live happily ever after like they do in the storybooks, but relationships are hard in the queer world. Worst is when you're struggling and new to a country as an asylum seeker or an immigrant and your experience is completely different from the lived experiences of those around you which makes falling in love and being with someone even harder. – Salman

————————▽————————

DO YOU EXPERIENCE PREJUDICE IN YOUR DAY-TO-DAY LIFE AND IF SO, WHAT FORM DOES IT TAKE?

Chicago, IL (USA)

Interestingly enough, I found a little bit of prejudice when I lived in Humboldt Park in the Puerto Rican community. They had a tough time wrapping their brain around me. In that community there's a lot of closeted nature, someone's either on the down-low or they're a drag queen. They wanted me to be more what they thought gay was. I remember they would be in shock when I wasn't dressing in drag or I wasn't the most feminine person there. They had a problem with that sometimes. I thought that was really weird. – James Scalfani

—————▽—————

Oxford, MS (USA)

Yes. I live in Oxford, Mississippi, the last hole in the Bible belt, surrounded by Christians who have certainly lost their connection with any of Christ's teachings. There are a couple of responses that I get. I'll be interacting with some straight guy, like a contractor who has come to the house for some repair, for example, when suddenly the realization that I'm gay hits them. I can feel them retract themselves into themselves and, invariably, they get very nervous. I don't know exactly what they expect me to do. I've learned simply to continue with the interaction in a friendly, polite manner, and it's soon over with. The other reaction is the hostile stare. I've come to believe the person staring at me isn't aware that I can see them because, again invariably, they are startled if I smile or lift an eyebrow or respond in some way to the stare. Then, they become nervous and/or mean. When it's younger people in a group there is often sniggering and elbowing. I am sure they know, in that case, that I do indeed see them. Sometimes, I confront them in a non-aggressive way, which scatters them like "leaves before the wind." – Oran Walker

——————▽——————

Chicago, IL (USA)

Probably. But I probably don't notice anymore. I've gotten to a point where I'm old enough and curmudgeonly enough and I've built up enough of a work reputation … you know what, I'm not going to hide who I am. I'm not going to be something that I'm not going to be. The only prejudice I see … well, it's not really a prejudice … there are people who make assumptions about me that are incorrect. But otherwise, there's nothing that comes to mind that affects me on a day-to-day basis. – Steve

——————▽——————

Chicago, IL (USA)

Mostly it's ethnic, because I'm tall and large, and I don't always come off as openly gay. Although, I've never made it a secret. Mostly the prejudice is because I'm Latino and I look like it. I frequently have people trying to speak to me in broken Spanish. They're absolutely appalled when I answer them in French. – Mike

——————▽——————

San Francisco, CA (USA)

To be a black man in America means that at any moment, prejudice could rear its ugly head. To be a black man in present day San Francisco means that most of that prejudice you won't see or hear. Should the subject of race come up, and I'm with a group of my (mostly white) friends, I will sometimes mention the old saying that a nigger is a black gentleman who has just left the room, making them squirm just a tiny bit. I doubt that anything like that has happened a lot, but I'd bet that it has happened. And then there are the guys who will insist on saying to me, as we are having sex already, or about to, that they "want to suck that big black cock" or some form of that. I usually allow them to get away with that once, but it does not bear repeating. It is a deal-breaker if it is mentioned more than the one time because, while that kind of objectification can be fun, bringing it up like that can really sully the mood. – Terence Smith (Joan Jett Blakk)

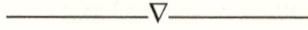

————————▽————————

Texas (USA)

In my earlier life I experienced a lot of prejudice, growing up in the rural Southwest. The religious, political and cultural atmosphere was toxically anti-gay. That's why I did not come out until as an adult I had moved to a major Midwestern city where I found peers like myself. At this point in my life my major experience of prejudice is in the context of the current toxic national political situation and how our rights as queer persons are consistently being eroded. – Anonymous

————————▽————————

Chicago, IL (USA)

Many straight men don't like me. I see it less now as I have gotten older and become less threatening. But I still get challenged and insulted by straight men, either because they notice my mannerisms and guess my sexuality, or because they noticed me noticing them and consider that an attack upon their masculinity. Yes, even now, even this week. – Bert Thompson

————————▽————————

Chicago, IL (USA)

I'm an older disabled gay man, so I'm pretty much ignored when I go to Boystown. I hardly ever go there anymore. Nobody wants to talk to me. They see my cane and think I'm defective. When I was younger, I used to get harassed by the cops a lot. Never quite figured out why. I had a lot of black and Latino friends and I'm part Native American. I had long black hair. I also have ethnic facial features. I would get harassed along with these other people. It happened on a fairly regular basis and didn't stop until I got much older. – Xavier Bathsheba-Negron

————————▽————————

Tulsa, OK (USA)

I'm very sensitive when someone helps me, or waits on me, or serves me in a store, a restaurant. And they say, "OK sweetie, we'll let you know when it's ready." If I was a 65 year old man who was straight, more butch, I wouldn't be called "honey" or "sweetie." ... Bitch! I got a hairy chest, look at this. I don't know if that's prejudice but it's a source of irritation. – Renny

———————∇———————

Chicago, IL (USA)

I think that even today there are those that will still call out degrading names or make a derogatory remark to me. But prejudice no. I think I worried about that in the workplace in the past but I think most times that they were unfounded. – Dean Ogren

———————∇———————

Columbus, OH (USA)

Living in a gay-ish neighborhood in Chicago I do not experience prejudice from day to day. But when I lived in Ohio in the 1990s I would just walk down the sidewalk and people would yell "Faggot" and threaten to beat me up because of the way I walked. I do not think I walk especially gay. I just walk. – Lars von Keitz

———————∇———————

North Carolina (USA)

Back in the 1990s I had a very difficult time. I was working at a university and had a boss who was very anti-gay, anti-women. There were a lot of evangelicals around. I decided I would be out and let the chips fall where they may. I would get crank phone calls from people telling me I was going to hell. There were people who put nails in my parking space at work, so I'd end up with flat tires. The guy I worked for was constantly trying to intimidate me, mentally and physically. It was just awful. Now the main thing that I see, once in a while, if I'm out with some gay friends, I might see a conservative waitress in a restaurant give me and my friends a dirty look. But mostly nowadays what you see are just constant evangelical billboards bullshit everywhere. It's as irritating as ever. But I don't really have it directed at me personally the way I did in the past. I think it's more of a general lashing out that some extremists do. There's been some protests near here of neo-Confederates, and there have been threats made against our local Pride event. The police are very cooperative in watching it very closely. – Randy

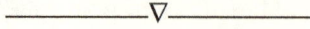

——————▽——————

Chicago, IL (USA)

I don't think so because I'm a white male. Our very existence is heaped with privilege. I couldn't tell you the last time I was discriminated against because I was gay. Again, a lot of that has to do with how I look, who I am, and also, I don't put up with any shit, that's the other thing. All I want to say to anybody is, "Try me, please, go ahead and we'll see where this is going to take us." Again, it's white privilege, male privilege to not be fucked with. But I will say this, I have lots of friends who are people of color, friends who are trans and younger than me and that has been an incredible eye-opening learning experience. The one thing I learned was don't ever, ever, question someone's experience. If someone says they have been messed with or discriminated against, the details of their story are their story and if you love them and care about them, no matter if there's some remaining part of you that doubts it, believe them. That is the way you support people of color, by believing them, listening to them. Listen more, talk less, that's the key. – Jeff Ramone

——————▽——————

(Bulgaria)

I don't experience much prejudice on a personal basis, but I do experience institutional prejudice. – Louis Richard de Bourbon de Parme et de Savoie, Prince de la Pau

——————▽——————

Chicago, IL (USA)

It's nothing direct. You still get the side-eye. I was walking with my boyfriend at the time on Michigan Avenue and we were holding hands. Somebody shouted, "Don't hold hands." Then somebody said, "Oh they don't know anything about love." That's the most direct that I've experienced in a very long time. Micro-aggressions … I see that regularly. – Drew

——————▽——————

Chicago, IL USA)

Absofukinlutly I experience prejudice most from the gay community if you're not white, young, wealthy or at least appear wealthy, the community ignores you. I am also sick and tired of white dudes who only date Hispanic men. We are often nothing more than a fetish to be exploited for their own shallow narrow-minded agenda. I now no longer trust white men and mostly only date men of color, it's a cultural thing. People of color seem to be more honest. – Philip Bernal

————————▽————————

Rockford, IL (USA)

I think as a cis white gay male, I would say that I don't experience that much prejudice. So, I can't say if it takes any form in my life. – Patrick J. Murphy III

————————▽————————

Seattle, WA (USA)

Not usually. I'm self-employed on two levels, so my clients pretty much know what they are getting from me as a person. Anyone that doesn't know I identify as "gay," figures it out within a few moments of meeting me. Helen Keller could walk by me, point and yell "Gaaaaaaaayyy!" – Eric Andrews-Katz

————————▽————————

Frinton-on-Sea, Essex (UK)

It tends to be low-grade background prejudice, sometimes when people are ignorant of who (i.e. what), I am. Silly and crass comments from work colleagues, not hateful, but just lazy and stupid. For example, one colleague was poring over the *The Sun* newspaper one lunchtime and complained that the word "faggot" had been printed with asterisks, i.e. "f****t." "Can't we even use the word faggot anymore?" he protested loudly. I told him "No – and we can't use the equally offensive word "Nigger" either." That shut him up. Moron. – Diesel Balaam

————————▽————————

Bellport, NY (USA)

Between the years of 2007-2008 I was assaulted by a group of men because I am a lesbian. I won't get too detailed about it, but the men were wearing crucifixes around their necks ... There are small things even today, but they are too numerous to mention. I guess we still have a long way to go. – Erin Michelle Miller

————————∇————————

Chicago, IL (USA)
South Carolina (USA)

The bitch of coming out when I did was that within a year of moving to Chicago and finally coming out fully, I was diagnosed as HIV positive. I come from a healthcare background so my acceptance of it was different than many. After I adjusted to what it was, I decided it was part of me and I needed to move forward. That would have been all fine and good except that after finally coming out of the closet as gay and having that done, now I have to come out over and over and over. In Chicago it was there, but there were also plenty of people who didn't care that I was positive and it was a non-issue.

Now I live back in rural South Carolina and even though I'm next to a medium/large city and right between Charlotte and Atlanta, the bigotry of the LGBT community is there and the stigma of being HIV+ is rampant. When I was in Chicago you could drive down the street and know right where TPAN and AIDS Foundation Chicago were because of their logos on the doors. When I came to SC I find that AID Upstate can't even put their initials on their front door because clients are too afraid to be seen going into such a place. – Chris Grace

————————∇————————

Rancho Mirage, CA (USA)

Not really. I don't go around talking about my being gay, there are just no reasons nor situations to do so. I'm gathering that people don't assume anything with me because I don't act a certain way nor have any mannerisms (as stereotypical as that is) that would give them reason to think I am. It's like when people criticize actors for not speaking out so much – well, they're people first, being gay is not first and foremost about being a person. So, for me, it's having to hear people say hateful things, particularly in the time of Trump. I'm appalled at how I've heard customers at work even say terrible things in passing about LGBTQ people, and know those who think they're devout Christians yet blame "the gays" for everything wrong in the world. Though it was years ago, I'll never forget when I was a PBX operator at a hotel and my co-worker had a habit of shutting down her board, leaving her post for chunks of time, and leaving me to do everything. When I turned her board back on one time, she came back in yelling at me. A manager came in and she yelled at him to "tell that faggot to leave my board alone." When I shot back and said to "tell that bitch to do her job," the manager looked at ME and said, "now there's not need to call her that. When I asked him why it's okay for her to call me a faggot but not okay to call her anything, he just said to calm do and let's get back to work. That's something I never forgot. I try to not let people get to me. But now when someone can't seem to shut up, I usually get them to shut up by letting them know the people who keep being the loudest about how bad gays are, are usually the biggest closet cases themselves. And you know, that always works, at least when I confront them. – Todd Jaeger

———————∇———————

Chicago, IL (USA)

I work with teenagers, so every-once-in-a-while I get the teenager who calls me "faggot" or dismisses me as useless. But mostly I experience prejudice from the common discourse on the street. Hatred is still out there. There is still the pressure to be something I am not, and the more I resist that, the more I feel rejected and devalued. – andKevin

———————∇———————

Cathedral City, CA (USA)

I'm going to give you a very unusual answer and that is ...yes, I could, but I avoid it. I typically do not make eye contact with anyone when I'm walking in public places. Because I realize that when I do go into a public place, especially without a wig, I get looks, some of them are curious, some of them are negative, hateful, I can feel it. I've come to learn that if I don't acknowledge them, in my mind it goes away. Considering that I try to avoid interaction in public spaces, I would say I don't really feel it on a daily basis, but certainly every week something happens. Typically, it's non-verbal, it's a look of disgust. If not verbal, then it's a "Tsk." I try to avoid it, but I've been out with friends and family and had them get irritated, "Oh that person's staring at you, I'm going to go over and ask, 'Why are you staring?'" I say, "Oh it's fine, just leave them alone." I try to avoid it, put my blinders on, but people with me when they do spot it, because they're such good people to me, they get irritated. It probably happens more than I acknowledge it because I try to avoid it. – Andee

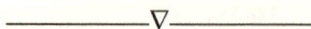

—————▽—————

New York, NY (USA)
Palm Springs, CA (USA)

I wouldn't say in my day to day life, but yes, I've experienced prejudice in different ways. Being Hispanic and growing up in New York City in the South Bronx, there's that side of being a part of a poor society. Where you get pushed to the side and you experience all that negativity that comes along with it. But as I got older, I changed physically, my appearance changed. Now, I get a weird thing that happens where people don't realize I'm Puerto Rican and they'll start talking in Spanish in front of me. Let's say they're talking in Spanish about someone else, something negative. But they don't realize I'm Spanish. So I let them go on and let them say what they have to say. Let them have their little joke, their fun against that other person. When they're done, I always come up to them and say to them, in Spanish, "Be careful what you say, because you don't know who's listening. But I see that as a form of racism because it's affecting me too. They're Hispanic and they're doing it to somebody else. "You didn't receive enough hatred in your own life against you? Now you're doing it to someone else." – David Vega (Lucifers Axe)

—————▽—————

New York, NY (USA)

As far back as I can remember, within the family, I would hear things at home, between my father, my mother, my uncles, my aunts. In four different languages I knew derogatory names by the time I was in elementary school. Then in school, discrimination against gays – I wasn't the kind of kid that could hide. I was a rather unique didn't blend in kind of character … that's polite for screaming queen. It escalated. I did not like school. In my high school there was an Acceleration Program and if you had enough credits, which was 64, you could accelerate – one year and you were out of school. By the time I got to the first year of high school I had 68 credits … I wanted OUT! We came from a predominantly Jewish neighborhood. I do not have a Jewish last name. I have a very long, very Greek, last name. So when I applied, it was declined. My mother went up the school and she fought with the dean of students. "The list is full this year." My mother went through the list for the last I don't know how many years. There was not a child on that list that did not have a Jewish last name. So my mother fought for me to the point where she called up *Newsday*, a big newspaper on Long Island. Finally, because there was so much ruckus, the school allowed me to accelerate and get out. I was not going away quietly. In life, I've experienced different types of prejudice, not just LGBT. You can't let them crush you. You have to crush them – Keith Kollinicos (Missa Distic)

—————▽—————

Chicago, IL (USA)

I have always been out and open in my work and home life and never have I experienced prejudice not even in the all-boys high school (Lane Tech) that I went to. I was very fortunate in that respect. – Dennis Hardenstein

—————▽—————

Chicago IL (USA)

I experience very little prejudice in my life, though I hear horrific stories about bigotry from my students. I'm lucky, I guess, to live in an enlightened urban environment and lucky that I no longer travel to less enlightened areas to visit relatives. Prejudice happens to me rarely.

Once, though, I had a rather pleasant experience of bigotry in my local Starbucks. One of the Bux patrons was a crazily conservative woman who frequently insisted on bending my ear for a long time, even on those times when I was clearly engrossed in a book or grading student essays. I tolerated these intrusions for several months. One afternoon I was at Bux reading a book about queer issues; I have forgotten which book, but the rather garish cover yelled the word QUEER in fluorescent pink ink. I had the book face down on my café table when local crazy lady approached; I gritted my teeth. "Whacha reading?" she asked and grabbed the book, turning it face up. When she saw the title, she paled, reeled a bit, mouthed a silent "O!" replaced the book face down, and walked away. Since then she has seldom acknowledged my existence. That's all it took? Really? If I had known that being overtly queer would have stopped her from annoying me, I would have started showing up at Bux draped in a rainbow flag and yelling to the baristas across the room, "This latte is FAAAABulous!" Sometimes prejudice is our friend. – William Demaree

—————▽—————

Chicago, IL (USA)

Over the years this prejudice has ranged from homophobic violence, experience even in such gay centers as Los Angeles, San Francisco and Austin, Texas, to being fired from jobs (e.g. a health food store in Los Angeles), evicted from apartments, or refused rentals (sorry, we don't have any vacancies now). Now living outside of the city center of Chicago, prejudices range from daily "micro-aggressions" from neighbors and co-workers on the community college campus that we teach at, to threats and exclusion from holiday parties and block parties. At one point both our next door neighbors were actively hostile, one family moved, the mother used to herd her children into the house while giving me the evil eye when I said "Hi!," and the remaining one who started a fist fight with the man helping me shovel snow, stopping just short of hitting me during the irrational argument. This neighbor works for the Chicago police, so threats of calling the police are met with laughter – this being Chicago, the police are themselves still a potential danger and threat to queers and people of color. – David Hatfield Sparks

—————▽—————

New Orleans, LA (USA)

I do not feel any prejudice in New Orleans except when I interviewed at a gay bar. I was floored. – Terry Gaskins

—————▽—————

Palm Springs, CA (USA)

Unfortunately, I still do experience prejudice in my day-to-day life but not nearly so much as when I was younger, and not nearly as aggressively. Even in Palm Springs, which is one of the most gay-friendly towns in America, you still hear the word "faggot" from time to time, usually shouted out of the window of a passing car along the gay strip (Arenas Road) by some coward who is too afraid of the huge volume of us to use that slur on the street. We still see religious right hypocrites protesting many of our events and parades, and there are still incidents of gay bashing from time to time. It's pretty common here for us to get dirty looks, sneers, laughs, and sometimes pointing fingers, from tourists when my husband and I are shopping together or holding hands on the street. When I added my husband to my retirement health insurance and as beneficiary for my investments and health insurance, the HR department demanded a certified copy of my marriage license from

186

me, unlike my straight coworkers who were not required to provide one. Much of the prejudice now is also more subtle, and at times, I don't think many of the people perpetrating it would consider their comments and action prejudiced. We've had heterosexual acquaintances ask us stupid, homophobic questions like, "who is the man and who is the woman in your relationship." I've had friends and acquaintances who know full well that we're married refer to my husband as my "friend" or my "plus one" because they just cannot equate the value of our marriage with their own. – D. Warner

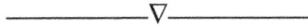

———————▽———————

Cleveland, OH (USA)

Not so much anymore; years ago, yes. I was never really out, but I didn't quite fit in the closet either. In the town where I grew up (that I am not going to name) there were a couple restaurants that would not serve me. Not blatantly, I was never told anything. They just never came to my table. I was alone the 3-4 times it happened, and there's that horrible moment when you realize what's going on and you have to get up and leave. There was no point in saying anything; people who do stuff like that don't listen. I eventually left town. – Roger

———————▽———————

Grand Rapids, MI (USA)

Yes, some. I am not totally out, so I hear others make negative comments/remarks about gays. – Mark S

———————▽———————

Palm Springs, CA (USA)
In mid-air (USA)

Do I ever? I get it at work for my race, for being a nurse, for having a beard, for having piercings, and because I'm gay and muscular and hairy. For some reason having any of those traits means I'm not as capable as everybody else. Ordinarily I can speak and prove to people that I'm educated, but on one occasion I flew to Missouri from Palm Springs. It was my first trip to meet my partner's parents. I thought, "Oh God I'm going to Missouri. A black guy in Missouri! What the hell's going to happen to me. But I went to Missouri and had a wonderful time. They proved me wrong. On my flight back … I got on my flight. It was open seating, so I chose my seat, an aisle seat. There were plenty of empty seats and a plus-sized white woman sat down beside me. She chose to sit next to me. About half an hour into the flight she kept punching me, fidgeting, pulling her sweater out and huffing and puffing. It was just like a two-year-old having a temper tantrum. Finally, I turned to her, "What is the problem?" She called the flight attendant and said, "I need you to move him, please." I turned to her, "What is the problem here? You chose this seat. Is it because I'm black, I'm gay, or both? This is your issue, not mine." She continued to fidget, and the flight attendant said, "Listen lady, it's Christmastime, the flight's full. I can't move him." ... "Then move me. His shoulders are too broad. He should have to pay for two seats." And she's oozing over the arm rests. So I was forced to endure her behavior for the next four hours. I wanted to lash out and say horrible, horrible things to her. But I knew that it would not be the right thing to do. As my grandmother always said, "There are paybacks. When you least expect it, you will get your rewards." When the flight landed, I thought, "Let her get off first." So I backed up and let her go. When she stepped out, they held up the rest of the plane. And there were marshals out there waiting for her. She was arrested as soon as she got off the flight. So I got my reward. I was thankful I hadn't done anything, because had I said something, I would have been the black aggressor, because I'm male and I have muscles. Go figure! – Crusher

———————▽———————

Adelaide, South Australia (Australia)

I occasionally wear a rainbow cap and sometimes a snide comment will be uttered at just the right volume for me to hear. Work wise there's no hassle. I work as a carer and the people I go to have no problem with sexuality and the office don't know. Have they got me picked? Probably. I can sometimes be a bit flamboyant with the humour so I suspect at least a couple have picked it. They like the style of humour, though, so that probably does help. There's a mild sarcasm that is said in the correct way they like. Again, I'm not aware of the way I say it which I'm told is why it's funnier. Okaaaay ... – Robert Verrall

———————▽———————

Chicago, IL (USA)

The only prejudice I had in life was being told all strippers are hoes. In my current life, I have none. – Mercury

———————▽———————

Chicago, IL (USA)

A daily dose of prejudice? Not really. I've trained myself to walk away if I sense anything I'd identify as prejudice towards me. Can't waste my time. Been there, experienced that. – Steve Kmetko

———————∇———————

Palm Springs, CA (USA)

I really don't, especially here. I wish I had an incredible answer to that, but the fact is even if it's there, I feel at my age, I'm confident enough to say, "If you don't like it, shove it." – Thomas Stribling

———————∇———————

Palm Springs, CA (USA)

Even today walking down Arenas, you still get people shouting out, "fucking faggot." Really, this day and age we gotta do that. Especially in Palm Springs where there are so many of us. Why would you want to be prejudiced here? So yes, there's still prejudice today. – Marcous

———————∇———————

Chicago, IL (USA)

I gratefully do not feel a lot of prejudice. I've always been in the arts and/or academics where being different was more celebrated than questioned. I'm sure it's different if you don't live in a big urban city. I think a lot of people don't realize I am queer, at least not at first. I usually take it for granted, I do realize however, that I don't advertise it either. – MrZor

———————∇———————

Rancho Mirage, CA (USA)

Slightly at work. I'm white and I'm the only white person in my department at work. A lot of Mexicans and a lot of Filipinos. I don't fit in because I don't understand what they're saying, so they talk freely about me in front of me. I can pick out certain words that I remember, because in Pennsylvania I found out some Spanish words from a Puerto Rican group. They were calling me maricon which is faggot and pato which is like a duck. They compare the walking of a duck, as if you just got fucked. So they call me pato. I did tell my manager and her boss the reason I'm here, that I lost my husband. I'm sure that trickled down to the supervisor, the one who picks me out and chooses the worst word for me. – David Hayes

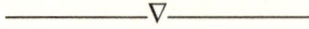

—————▽—————

Santa Fe, NM (USA)

No, not in my day to day life. I see a lot of prejudice but not to gay people only. If I experience it, I don't notice it. Sometimes we have had incidents when we're riding on the road with the top down on the car and were holding each other's hand and some people don't feel comfortable with that. – Juan-manuel Alonso

—————▽—————

Michigan (USA)

A couple of things have happened. This is based on Donald Trump being president. He literally stuck a stick in a hornets' nest. I have a former student of mine kept in contact and I've seen him over the years. He lives in Michigan. I became good friends with him through his divorce, the birth of his kids. The boy is 17 and the girl is 15. I've known them forever, from seedling on. They call me Uncle Greg. I would go up north in the spring and summer and see them. He was always fun. But after the 2016 election he started sending me some horrible transgender pictures of people in transition, those gif video files. The one that really struck a chord with me –he knew I voted for Obama – at Christmas time a picture of a Christmas tree and an ornament on the tree had Obama on it and the caption read "This won't be the last time that a black man was hung on a tree." I was horrified. Then there were some anti-gay jokes that he thought was funny. I said, "You know the work that I do why would you think I would find humor in that kind of thing." I called him out a few times and I guess he got offended by that. Then there were gaps of time I didn't hear from him. Then those times got longer. And now I've not heard from him since May 2019. It's been over a year since I saw his kids. I sent them well wishes at Christmas, their birthday. I sent them popcorn from Chicago. I don't know what kind of influence he's had on those kids but he's brought them to my lectures and now he's done this 180. His first wife was a big supporter of my work, then she started going to a church, a holy roller church. The minister of the church advised her not to be friends with me anymore. She no longer speaks to me. That hurts because she was a big supporter of me and my work. All of a sudden, she was coming to Chicago with the kids, they wanted to see their uncle Greg and stay with me. She changed her mind and stayed in a hotel because she didn't want them staying with me. That's horrible, it makes me feel like I'm a pedophile. I'm normally pretty blessed but here and there, even when I lecture, people will come with their own agenda. I had a woman show up in Iowa with *People* magazine with the holy bible in it. She started to read to me, and I stopped her in her tracks. But the most hurtful one is my friend up in north Michigan I've known them all their lives and I feel that's been cut off. – Greg R. Baird

————————∇————————

Redwood Valley, CA (USA)
North Florida (USA)

After twenty plus years in Mendocino County, I am so blessed to say that prejudice is not a part of my daily life. Until I go on-line, that is, or interact with blood relatives who still live in the South and put religious politics before relationships.

When I first moved to the Ukiah, CA area, in 1997, there were signs of right-wing reactions to the progressive evolution of our county, a redneck vs hippy kinda tussle. More than twenty years later, there's overwhelming support community-wide for all things loving and liberal. The haters have been shamed into submission. Love wins when all else fails. – T. Lark Letchworth

————————∇————————

Cathedral City, CA (USA)

Since I have been out for 42 years, I definitely have seen a huge evolution in society's acceptance of LGBT folks. I have endured death threats, prank calls, and probably the loss of a promotion in my past. As for presently, I can't read people's minds so I go on the assumption that most of those who know me treat me with goodwill and would help me in an instance. Still there is always a part of me that is on alert, especially if I'm in a strange area or politically conservative area where I know someone might verbally attack me due to their own insecurities. I imagine women endure this often when they are walking alone in an unfamiliar environment or at night. For me, I often may not be able to completely relax and let my guard down unless I am out in nature, either with my partner or alone.

I do know that it's quite common if I merely post some factual evidence on a Facebook page that is a pro-Trump page that points out a

Trump lie or hypocrisy a good percentage of the time someone will view my FB profile and respond with some ignorant attack involving my sexual orientation even though that has nothing to do with my post. Sometimes those border on direct physical violence. Their ignorance simply confirms the fact they are ignorant, desperate, and unable to counteract the evidence with contrary evidence of their own. – Paul Harris

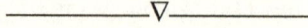

————————▽————————

(Australia)

No. Despite being what I consider an obviously gay man, I haven't encountered any – Tim Alderman

————————▽————————

St. Cloud, MN (USA)

I experience more microaggressions as a Jewish person than as an LGBTQ+ person in this part of the world. People say a lot of things that they think are funny that aren't, or do not realize why certain things they say or do are very offensive. People also assume that because I am a lesbian that I am a vegetarian or a vegan, which is hilarious. I am very aware that my civil rights are not guaranteed – civil rights for any minority is given and taken away on a whim by whoever is in power – so I serve on my local human rights commission and fight for civil rights for everyone where I live. No one should be discriminated against because of their race, religion, ethnicity, nationality, sexual orientation, gender identity, socioeconomic class, veteran status, disability, etc. – Rachel Wexelbaum

————————▽————————

Brunswick, ME (USA)

No, not knowingly. We are fortunate to live in New England, where acceptance of gay people is pretty good and we're very accepted and socially involved with our neighbors and their families here. I was born and raised in East Texas, but I have to say, when I go back to my hometown, my old friends and family there seem to readily accept me and my husband. They always ask about him, if I go alone. There have been a few "religious extremists" who severed old ties, when they discovered I was gay, but very few. So, I think I've been fortunate. – Michael Pickel

—————▽—————

Cork, Munster (Ireland)

I am living in retirement in an infinitely more tolerant Ireland. So, I don't experience overt prejudice but rather subtle and insidious forms of heteronormativity. I do my best to smash the patriarchy by throwing all the paint on the canvas. – David Clayton

—————▽—————

Palm Springs, CA (USA)

I'll take the risk here. I've worked as an educator for 18 years. And I have had to tell some of my bosses "I'm gay but I don't talk about it with the kids." Which is true since for the most part I show up to work to help kids and teach regular school subjects.

So, the prejudice is denial of my gay self, my long-term relationship, in my job and profession. Marginalized to earn a paycheck.

In the education world, heterosexism is the norm. And on one level, when I listen to the straight people talk about pregnancy, birth, families, child-rearing, and so forth, ad nauseum, I get it that they are the majority. My parents were heteros. Most gay folks have straight parents.

So, the form it takes is my silence. I honestly feel as a gay man working as a teacher that I am an at-risk employee. I have been fired before for being gay and under false accusations. So I very purposefully guard my speech and actions with my co-workers, clients, and families. – Tony Earl

—————▽—————

King, NC (USA)

My husband and I have recently moved from Denver Colorado (a very welcoming and inclusive city) to a small rural town in North Carolina. Before we arrived to North Carolina I was more than concerned that we would face prejudice and even hatred coming to this Bible Belt area with us living as an out, married, gay couple.

The exact opposite has happened. Our neighbors are wonderful – they are mostly older long-time residents of this area. We all look out for each other and help each other. I find that remarkable in the light of our current political climate with its hate and division on the rise. – Ron Cline

—————▽—————

Charlottetown, Prince Edward Island (Canada)

The only way I experience prejudice in my day-to-day life is though heteronormative assumptions that people make about me. I've experienced other more direct forms of prejudice – name-calling, threats of violence – but not on a daily basis. – Dave Stewart

———————▽———————

San Diego, CA (USA)

It's subtle. It's not blatant. You don't notice it until it's not there. Prior to transition I was valued for my ideas, I was valued for my contributions, I was included on emails, and I'm not anymore. I don't get invited to the meetings, they don't put me in the projects, my job prospects disappeared. I'm grateful to my employers for giving me a job when I was transitioning. They knew me before and they knew me afterwards. But where I'm at right now, there's very little growth. It's stable but there's very little growth. Prior to transition I was fast-tracking for a directorship. I'm an analyst. Do I think I'll go higher? Am I grateful to be employed now? It's a different world and there's a big recalibration." – Serafine Sawyer

———————▽———————

Des Moines, IA (USA)

Well even now in my HUD Section 202 senior residence, there are people who laugh at me behind my back and stuff, but I am very much NOT CLOSETED and scoff at their foolishness. – Sr. Freida Peoples aka DJ Chrysler Sheldon

———————▽———————

(Pakistan)
Worcester, MA (USA)

Societal prejudices continue to exist against LGBTQ+ people in Pakistan. I've faced the worst kind of workplace discrimination and death threats due to my activism. I have been forced to leave my country now. Seeking asylum is a very painful process, separating yourself from your loved ones, and family is even more painful. I hope this time will pass by and I will settle down in the US and continue the work from here that I'm passionate about. – Salman

———————∇———————

Fort Lauderdale, FL (USA)

No, not really, but I live in a very gay-friendly area and surround myself with like-minded people. – Rick Karlin

———————∇———————

WHAT MOVIES OR TV SHOWS BEST CAPTURE YOUR FUNNY AS WELL AS YOUR SERIOUS SIDE?

Lewiston, NY (USA)
Chicago, IL (USA)

My sense of humor being brought up on Canadian television is closer to *Monty Python's Flying Circus,* that influenced me and Martin Short and, of course, all the Chicago people. Serious, I love historical dramas. I'm a student of history. I don't like a lot of violence or action. I don't like that. – James Scalfani

—————▽—————

Chicago, IL (USA)

On the funny side, there's a couple of shows on that are horrible camp, absolutely the worst kind of television and they both make me laugh out loud. One of them is called *Riverdale* and the other one is the remake of *Dynasty,* which is just awful. It's badly acted, it's badly directed … everyone is over the top. I think that's the one line the director tells them every show is, "Go over the top." And serious, it depends on how serious I'm feeling on a particular day. I will watch things on PBS, *Call the Midwife, Sanditon* which was from an unfinished Jane Austen book. It's set in the mid-1700s so women are not allowed to be on the beach unless they are completely covered but the men just strip off and wander into the water. So there's an awful lot of male flesh going on and women pretending not to see. I love things like *Battlestar Galactica* which was simply a political think piece was what the entire series was about, was how do you handle differences and being a refugee and still trying to be assertive about who and what you are as a group. – Mike

—————▽—————

Oxford, MS (USA)

Movies: *What's Up, Doc?, Manhattan, Cries and Whispers, Fanny and Alexander, The Heart Is a Lonely Hunter, To Kill a Mockingbird, Bonnie and Clyde, Sleeper, Annie Hall, Love and Death, The Makioka Sisters, Hiroshima, Mon Amour, Black Rain* (1989 Japanese film), *Red Sorghum.*
　　　　Television: *CSI: Miami, I Love Lucy, Prime Suspect* (Helen Mirren), *Broadchurch, American Horror Story, The Dick Van Dyke Show, Twilight Zone* (original). – Oran Walker

—————▽—————

Nashville, TN (USA)
Chicago, IL (USA)

Nashville: When I was a young person, there were no movies or TV shows that explicitly reflected the gay experience. There were also no openly gay actors. As part of our oppression, society conspired to try to convince each of us that we were the only one who felt as we did, and that our feelings were bad and could not be expressed or reflected.
　　　　There is a hidden history of gay and lesbian performers. But knowledge of this had to be recovered, and then publicized. These tasks didn't really begin until the 1980s and are ongoing. Add to this situation the fact that there was no way to watch a movie or TV show whenever you wanted – Until video cassettes in the 1980s, and then DVDs and the Internet much later, you could only watch shows when they were broadcast or currently playing in theaters. That was it. So even if you heard about a gay performer, or a gay storyline, you were very lucky if you had a chance ever to see it.
　　　　The first TV show that really spoke to my experience as a gay person was the daytime drama *Dark Shadows*, broadcast Monday through Friday in the late '60s. Many of the actors in the show were gay, but I was not aware of that when I saw it broadcast. No, the significance of the show lay in the character of its leading man, Barnabas Collins.
　　　　Barnabas was a vampire. But unlike Dracula and all the other fictional and cinematic vampires before him, he was not a villain. He was a good man who always tried to do the right thing. Being a vampire was not his fault, and he didn't want to be a vampire. But that was his reality, and he

had to make the best of it. When I later began to understand myself as a gay person, I had no role models. But I was able to see meaningful parallels between my life and that of the character Barnabas Collins. Everyone around me let me know that as a gay man they considered me to be bad and evil, and they insisted that I must have chosen this way of life. But just like Barnabas, I knew that I was not inherently evil, but no better or worse than anyone else, and it was up to me to make good choices. I also knew that I had never chosen to be gay, and societies description of guilt to me on that basis was unjustified. I knew no other gay people, I had no sources of gay affirming information, I had to struggle with coming out completely alone. But the example of that show helped me find a path.

While there were gay performers in guest spots and even supporting roles in various TV shows of the '60s and '70s, few were positive portrayals and none of them were out. The first people who I figured out might be gay were celebrities on daytime game shows. In this context, they were not playing fictional characters, but versions of themselves. First Paul Lynde, on the *Hollywood Squares*, and then Charles Nelson Reilly on *Match Game* were the first public figures I saw in at least partly authentic roles who I guessed were gay, correctly as it turned out. They were comedians, but they were not clowns or figures of ridicule, or self-caricatures. They were popular with audiences and they were liked by the other performers around them. In the absence of any other possible role models, they were important.

Will and Grace changed the world. It didn't depict my life in specific terms. I never had a woman as a best friend or lived with one. But it was the first network broadcast show to have gay men in the lead roles, even if one was played by a straight guy and the other by someone in the closet. Yes, even at the end of the '90s. It showed the first kiss between two men on American television, even if it was a stunt. And it dealt with issues such as coming out to family, discovering yourself, and dating and relationships that American audiences have never seen before. And it was genuinely funny, winning over millions of people who might have thought they had nothing in common with gay men or even actively disliked them, but who welcomed these gay characters into their living rooms every week.

Queer as Folk slightly later, was more for the in group, more for us. It showed a wider variety of gay and lesbian characters and dealt with the full range of issues which the community was dealing with at that time. I not only saw every episode but watched many of them multiple times. The impact of this level of serious representation of gay people's lives was literally breathtaking. It deepened and enriched my own life experience.

I love movies, and watching them has been a big part of my life. But until recently, very few told gay stories and even fewer told positive ones. A rare earlier exception was *Rebel Without a Cause*, which was made in the '50s but I first saw in the early '80s. Sal Mineo's character Plato, although he was not explicitly labeled gay, clearly was. Sadly, he had to die at the end as almost all gay characters in American cinema until very recently. But he wasn't a killer and he wasn't a clown.

Things began to change very slowly. 1982s *Victor/Victoria* was mainly about gender portrayals and resolved its main plot in a reassuring heterosexual way. But two of the supporting characters were gay and wound up coupled and living happily ever after. Groundbreaking and revolutionary. And still funny. We had to wait until the '90s to see a positive gay character in the lead role of a mainstream comedy, in *Jeffrey*.

The first widely seen serious film to show a gay male romance, and give them a happy ending, was 1987's *Maurice*. I found it overwhelming. Very little has changed in the wider culture, since it was written in the 1920s and first published in the 1970s.

Other serious well-made positive gay films did not come until the new century. I identify strongly with the family issues of the title character in 2000s *Billy Elliot*, even though he was straight with a gay friend. I was mesmerized by the family and religious issues in *Latter Days* and *Dream Boy*, even with their sad endings.

The historical and biographical film *Milk* is exceptionally good. I had a strong emotional reaction to viewing it. I think it should be required viewing for everyone, especially for those who did not live through those years and do not know the story of Harvey Milk. Of course, just like the bad old stereotype, he too dies in the end. – Bert Thompson

————▽————

San Francisco, CA (USA)

The Daily Show with Trevor Noah, Real Time with Bill Maher, The Antiques Roadshow, and almost anything dealing with vintage automobiles. – Terence Smith (Joan Jett Blakk)

————▽————

Chicago, IL (USA)

I have a very dry sense of humor. I tend to be a fan of a lot of British comedy. The things that always make me laugh are the Rowan Atkinson *Black Adder* series. And serious, I'm a horrible sentimentalist, compelling dramas, things that remind me of people I've known or situations. – Steve

————▽————

Midwestern City (USA)

I loved *Queer as Folk* and currently enjoy *Grace and Frankie* and *Eastsiders*. *Call Me by Your Name* is one of my favorite movies. – Anonymous

——————▽——————

Chicago, IL (USA)

Funny side. I like a lot of the older Billy Wilder movies because they're so damn witty, like *The Apartment*. Serious side, there was a great foreign language film that was out about 1983 called *El Norte*, it was Guatemalan Indians coming up through Mexico into the United States. It was a very sad movie. I thought it was a masterpiece. I like tragic movies. I do like comedies, I think *Victor/Victoria* is hilarious. That's my favorite comedy movie. Serious again, *Chinatown*, *The Asphalt Jungle*. TV shows, I think *WKRP in Cincinnati* was a funny show. On of my favorite shows is *The Rockford Files* which is a drama but it has a lot of humor mixed up in it. – Xavier Bathsheba-Negron

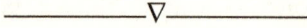

——————▽——————

Chicago, IL (USA)

The Munsters perfectly captures my funny side while *Sweeney Todd* captures a more serious side. They are different shades of black. Also, *The Mighty Boosh* will blow your mind! Eels! – Lars von Keitz

——————▽——————

Palm Springs, CA (USA)

Movies: *Some like it Hot* and *Sunset Boulevard*. TV: *Will and Grace* and *Six Feet Under*. – Gary Borgstedt

——————▽——————

Tulsa, OK (USA)

Several years ago, there was a short series on TV called *Come Fly with Me*. It's from the guys that did *Little Britain*. It is so funny. Or *Greater Tuna*. It's about these two guys who dress up as all the characters. It's about life in a small town called Tuna, Texas. It's really cute. I like documentaries, historical things like *The Crown*. I like things from across the pond. I was in England

and Scotland about a year and a half ago and I loved that. I also love *Call the Midwife*, it's such a sweet show. I like to cry. I like sentimental things. – Renny

—————▽—————

Chicago, IL (USA)

Any film from the general Book of Gay Iconic Films, but I most relate to are *The Women*. It was one that I had many of my mentors share with me over the years and I have shared it with them, as a must see. It helps to build your character in how to hold your own in a party/social situation, where the hens are everywhere, and one must be prepared for how to react and stand up for yourself. I think the other film that was meaningful to me, early on was *Boys in the Band*. This film and just seeing the similarities of some of the men I knew and related to helped me get in touch with how I felt, and get on with not being ashamed of that presentation. I did however recognize in later years the self-loathing in the film is something that is find hard to resolve. – Dean Ogren

—————▽—————

Waverly, IA (USA)

A couple of my favorite movies are: *Midnight Cowboy* because the hot hustler develops sincere feelings for a down and out ugly man. And where gay humor is concerned *The Ritz* by Terrence McNalley. – Robert Beck

—————▽—————

Chicago, IL (USA)

NOT a single one, TV is FAKE, its only job is to sell ideas and products that will never be enough. – Philip Bernal

—————▽—————

Chicago, IL (USA)

I love entertainment that is absurd and bizarre, things that make you go "what the fuck am I watching?" Where you have to just accept things as they happen because if you tried to make sense of them, you'd just get confused. This is why I love the new Netflix series *Midnight Gospel*. The animated show follows a guy named Clancy as he interviews people for his podcast on planets that are dying. The conversations they have are often deep and profound, discussing life and death, non-essentialism, mental health, and more. While they are having these conversations, we watch the characters traverse vibrant apocalyptic worlds. In one episode they're being chased by zombies, and in another they're pulverized and turned into sausage filling, while continuing their heavy discussions. This show is a lot to take in, and I enjoy every minute of it.

I have two favorite directors. The first is John Waters. How could I not love John Waters? His films are quintessential queer classics. Edith Massey and Divine are two of my biggest inspirations and I love all of the films they're in. Even the later films are quite good! My favorites are *Polyester*, *Serial Mom*, and *Cecil B Demented*. My other favorite director is Jean Pierre Jeunet. His French films are beautiful, bizarre, and hilarious. He's probably best known for *Amelie*, and I also love *Delicatessen*. One of my favorite parts of *Delicatessen* is the suicidal woman, who builds these elaborate schemes to off herself, but something always happens to thwart her attempts. It's morbid and fantastic!

One more film I'd like to mention is *Mary and Max*. This is one of my favorite movies of all time. It tells the story of a young, friendless girl from Australia who becomes penpals with an autistic New Yorker. The claymation style brings charm and humor to otherwise serious moments, and the film frequently dances along the edge of funny and serious. I get so invested in these two characters every time I watch it that I forget how sad it gets and wind up crying by the end. – C'est Kevvie (Wilhelmina)

———————∇———————

Rockford IL (USA)

One show that really captures me and aspects of my life is *The Real O'Neals*. I always found that it was funny and touching. The way that the characters interacted and grew over the two seasons of the show. I think also having been raised in a very Catholic house, I could relate to how the story flowed in and around the issues of the show. – Patrick J. Murphy III

———————∇———————

Seattle, WA (USA)

The TV show *This is Us* has some of the best writing I've ever come across on television. Although I don't directly identify with all of the characters, they still show the human range of emotion that are in all of our DNA. As for a comedy, it's difficult as my tastes change upon my mood. The problem with comedy (and gay characters) is that they eventually become too stupid (dumb-down for the general public) and aren't true to their form. While I have enjoyed many gay characters on TV, they tend to run the gamut pretty quickly. I'm not one to like a show just because it is "gay." I never got into *Queer as Folk* as none of the characters were likable. *The Real O'Neals* was good in premise, but there's no way you're going to tell me that everyone (including the Catholic school) was going to be supportive of an underage gay boy in OHIO! "Will" of *Will & Grace* got to the point of being almost unbelievable as a character – a good looking gay man in NYC can't find someone to date for more than three episodes? I don't buy it. "Cameron" and "Mitchell" from *Modern Family* I just want to slap so hard for being stupid and not communicating with each other. It gets old. – Eric Andrews-Katz

—————▽—————

Chicago, IL (USA)

Funny, *Strangers with Candy*, *Absolutely Fabulous*, *30 Rock*, the cartoon *Adventure Time*. Serious … that's a big question. I would say *Star Trek*, the recent two generations, *Star Trek: Picard* and *Star Trek: Discovery* very much in the vein of *Star Trek* but they're dramas, they are about our search for meaning, our search for place in the universe. Living in this complex world that they live in, but also dealing with a lot of drama and conflict that arises from living in a universe where there are people with competing ideas about how to live. It's very true to life. – Jeff Ramone

—————▽—————

Frinton-on-Sea, Essex (UK)

Being a Brit, my humour is campier and more "off the wall" than most American TV shows cater for, although I love some US shows like *Frasier*, *Cheers* and *Friends*. But my faves are British comedies, as that is what I am culturally attuned to. Many are popular with British LGBTQ people - AbFab, Victoria Wood, *Benidorm*, and the Carry On movies from the 1960s and '70s, but I also really enjoy a lot of "straight-man" humour, like *Only Fools and Horses*, Monty Python and Billy Connolly. For serious stuff – history, archeology, natural history, interesting documentaries and films, the BBC4 TV channel is brilliant. I admire HBO from the USA too. Loved *Six Feet Under*. – Diesel Balaam

—————▽—————

Bellport, NY (USA)

I am not sure I understand this question. I tend to read a lot of books, so I don't watch much TV. I do like certain shows though, such as *The Witcher*, *Grace and Frankie*, *American Horror Story*, and some animes. *Grace and Frankie* is hilarious. *The Witcher* has its funny moments but is serious too. – Erin Michelle Miller

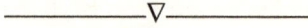

—————▽—————

Chicago, IL (USA)

Even though I'm a TV junkie, nothing stands out that would be important for this survey. Though I will say that some of my favorite Sci-Fi shows are doing me proud by having LGBT characters without having to make them HEY LOOKIE HERE! LGBT CHARACTERS!

On the topic of TV shows I will add this. The recent revival of *Queer Eye for the Straight Guy* and *Will & Grace* are fun and fantastic – but I don't enjoy them like the originals. Back then they were doing something. The word Queer was used on TV and people loved it and learned from it. *Will & Grace* made you like Will and Jack even if they were tame and sometimes the fool but both shows were groundbreaking and making change. Now that they've come back, Queer Eye is just another makeover show. Yes, it can appeal to a new age, but it's not the same (IMHO) – Chris Grace

—————▽—————

St. Louis, MO (USA)
Rancho Mirage, CA (USA)

I'll always cherish *The First Nudie Musical* (1975) as my favorite comedy. It's funny without being forced, lively, and most of all it was obvious the cast and creators were having a blast. I like to be funny while not TRYING too hard, just letting things reflect my being. Which is also why I like the material many people just don't get — the more absurd humor. While I can never get enough of Kristen Wiig doing "Ann Margret Trying To Throw A Wad Of Paper Into A Trash Can" and "Liza Minnelli Trying To Turn Off A Lamp," British humor the likes of Monty Python (as a kid in the early 1970s the humor just spoke to me) and projects by Matt Berry have me laughing with glee. This is also why I fell in love with the works of director Jim Hosking, from his features like *The Greasy Strangler*, *An Evening with Beverly Luff Linn* (which starred Matt Berry), and his TV series *Tropical Cop Tales*. While 80% of people might just sit there scratching their heads, I'm eating it up like ice cream and laughing my ass off. For my serious side, the movie that captures my feelings the most is the 1985 film *Static*, starring Keith Gordon and Amanda Plummer. That ending, oh man. For at least the last 10 minutes there is no dialogue, and the slowing changing on Amanda Plummer's face hits me hard every time, and I cry. I can't explain why it affects me like that, but you have to experience it and perhaps then you'll understand. Everyone I have introduced to that film said it truly affected them, and it irks me that director Mark Romanek basically disowned it, feeling it was a piece of juvenilia as his first film. I also deeply love the 1980 film *Resurrection* starring Ellen Burstyn. That one packs a punch and means a lot to me because while it deals with a woman who suddenly has the power to heal people, she refuses to be pushed into jumping on the religious bandwagon. She just does it because she cares. All these years later, giving Reiki sessions to cancer and stroke patients at a hospital (which is not "curing" people, by the way, basically helping them heal in many ways), I think back on Burstyn's character and her just caring about people. Then to veer off strictly serious yet not too fantastical, I love the films of Philip Ridley (*The Reflecting Skin, The Passion of Darkly Noon, Heartless*). Those have a serious tone yet pull you in with their dreamlike and surreal elements. Keeps life interesting and beautiful. – Todd Jaeger

—————▽—————

Cathedral City, CA (USA)

My funny side would have to be *Curb Your Enthusiasm,* I'm a big Larry David fan. I'm into that kind of humor, situationist humor, black humor as well. As far as the serious side, it's probably *Saturday Night Fever*, only because … sure, it's about dancing and growing up in Brooklyn …but to me it's more about having aspirations and drive, to want to do something better. Both of those characters did. They hit barrier after barrier and found it very difficult. I challenge myself through life to achieve a number of goals, I'm a goal-oriented person, and I achieved them all. So, I feel very good. No matter what life throws at you. – Andee

—————▽—————

Detroit, MI (USA)
Chicago, IL (USA)

To me, the best movie ever made is *Cabaret*. I've probably seen it 50 times. It's a love story, a political story, a comedy, and drama, it's everything. And the dialogue – oh my – how wonderful. Like this scene between Sally Bowles and Brian. Sally is talking at length about Maximillian:

Sally: He's suave, and he's rich, and he really knows how to please a woman.
Brian (exploding): Oh fuck Maximillian.
Sally, after a pause: I do.
Brian, after a pause: So do I.
Sally, suddenly putting it together: You two bastards!
Brian: Two?! TWO?! DON'T YOU MEAN THREE?!

    – Brian T

————————▽————————

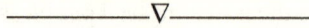

Chicago, IL (USA)

Now, see, this question makes me immediately ask myself, "What answer would be appropriate here? If I said "x" they'll roll their eyes and judge me. I might need years of counseling! Here goes: to me there is no show ever that is quite as perfect as *The Gilmore Girls*. Every freaking week it made me laugh out loud and also made me cry.

I don't really watch much in the way of drama anymore. I just can't handle it. When my mother died in 2015, I found that I couldn't focus for more than a few minutes on any media that was serious. I can appreciate and even love shows that have drama in them, but not if the whole show is serious and heavy. So give me a series like *Torchwood* where the dramatic moments can make me sit on the edge of my seat, and then the silly comedy of it will make me smile.

There are very few shows that I routinely watch anymore. I have deserted most network tv. I love *Grace and Frankie, Stranger Things*, and the *Bear City* movies. – andKevin

————————▽————————

Cathedral City, CA (USA)

I love all the John Waters movies, they're hilarious. *Pink Flamingos, Female Trouble, Polyester, Desperate Living*, all those. As far as TV show go, I like *Nurse Jackie*. There's so much stuff on youtube.com I can't keep up with it. I like *Pose*. I like documentaries about people struggling, homeless people … I think I prefer documentaries to anything else. Truth is more interesting than fiction. – Jim

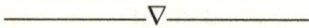

————————▽————————

Palm Springs, CA (USA)

As far as funny, the first movie that comes to mind is *Young Frankenstein*. That was one of those movies that has a weird sort of funniness … I like it a lot. Now, the movie we've just finished, which is *Cannibal Comedian*, I play two different characters in this film. Main character has a funny side and also a serious side. I'm constantly going back and forth. To bring forth that serious character and then in a second you have to change, from serious to twisted weird funny. I like playing characters like that. Offbeat and strange. – David Vega (Lucifers Axe)

———————∇———————

Palm Springs, CA (USA)

I've loved horror movies since I was a kid. I would get caught up with them on TV. All those B movies. I wanted to be one of those actresses in the film. I thought they were so cool. Being able to do this, to be cast in horror films *Big Top Evil* or the new one *Cannibal Comedian*. But the films that really would describe me were Fellini's *Satyricon* which is my life. I live that. Or Pasolini's *120 Days of Sodom*. I connected with it on a whole different level. It's a very bizarre film. It's one of my favorites but it was funny. Most people don't think that movie is funny. I thought it was hysterically funny. I thought it was hot. I thought it was twisted. I would like to star in a remake of it. I would like to redo the film myself. And Bette Davis' *Now Voyager* because I was the Aunt Charlotte character that transformed. I connected with that film at an early age. It made me the swan I am today – Keith Kollinicos (Missa Distic)

———————∇———————

Chicago, IL (USA)

Whenever I need to cheer myself up, I watch Rosalind Russel's *Auntie Mame*. Who cannot both laugh and cheer when Mame dismisses the Upsons and Mr. Babcock with this great line: "Patrick won't allow you to settle him down in some dry-veined, restricted community, make him an Aryan from Darien and marry him off to a girl with braces on her brains." There are quite a few people in my life that I wish I had told off like that. I was introduced to Auntie Mame as a teenager; I saw the touring company of the musical *Mame* with Janet Blair and Elaine Stritch (hoo-hah!) and afterwards fervently wished that I had an Auntie Mame in my life (All I had were Aryans from Marion – County, that is, in Indiana). Since then I've learned that it's much more fun to *be* Auntie Mame instead of *having* one. I'm tempted to walk into every new class and exclaim, "Darlings! I'm your Auntie Mame!" But that would scare off the few – the very few – who understood the reference.

The more serious film that reduces me to tears whenever I see it is John Houston's film version of James Joyce's *The Dead*. It's the flip side of Auntie Mame; Gabriel, an aging professor, realizes at a Christmas party that his life has been a hollow, passionless charade. "Better pass boldly into that other world, in the full glory of some passion," says Gabriel, "than fade and wither dismally with age." If life is a banquet, poor Gabriel has been starving to death.

I remember seeing *The Dead* on a Friday night at the Fine Arts Theater in Chicago and sobbing uncontrollably at the end. I'm sure other audience members found my behavior to be weird – fuck'em! Something shifted that night and pushed me off into a different direction. In retrospect I see that I was standing on the precipice of living a life as sterile as Gabriel's. Thank you, Mr. Joyce – and Gabriel. There but for the grace of God go I. – William Demaree

———————▽———————

Chicago, IL (USA)

I get a giggle out of every time I see *Clueless*. That's just super-silly fun, it's one of my guilty-pleasure movies. The last one that I watched that was kind of serious was *Das Boot*, you can't get more serious than that. The pathos is incredible, and it keeps me locked to the screen. – Drew

———————▽———————

Chicago, IL (USA)

Love *Will and Grace,* was mesmerized by *Queer As Folk,* and recently the movie *Sauvage*. I watch all the gay movies and other shows that I find. The resources for film, books and TV are unlimited. I have over 200 gay books on my kindle. Jay Bell is one of my favorite authors, as is T.J. Klune. – Dennis Hardenstein

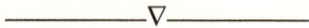

———————▽———————

Cleveland, OH (USA)

The Golden Girls and *Pose*. – Roger

———————▽———————

Louisiana (USA)

I love old movies/TV shows and movies of all kinds, comedy *Nothing Sacred*, *Bringing Up Baby*, *I Love Lucy*, *A Different World*, *Noah's Arc*, *Vida*. Drama *Mr. Skeffington*, *Anna Lucusta*, *Moonlight*, *Queen Sugar*, *David Makes Man*. – Katorri A.

—————▽—————

Chicago, IL (USA)

Probably the serious side would be the 1987 film *Maurice* based on the novel by gay British writer E.M. Forster; the novel was never published in his lifetime. But for its time followed a very open and profound relationship between two men. One of the closing lines always makes me cry, when the upper class Maurice tells his working class lover Alec when dedicating themselves to each other, promising never to "be parted," and *Cabaret* (1972) a musical comedy with dramatic elements, based on the *Berlin Stories* (1931) of gay writer Christopher Isherwood. Camp, comedy, singing and dancing of Liza (with a Z) and Joel Grey, and a chorus of mysterious and sexy Kit-Kat Dancers. A movie that haunts me still today is *The Living End* (1992) by Gregg Araki. A gay *Thelma and Louise*" plot about a HIV positive couple, who, after killing a homophobic cop, take off on a suicidal road trip in the desert. Surviving the plague era, while losing so many friends and lovers, haunt many, I think. – David Hatfield Sparks

—————▽—————

La Mesa, Tequendama Province (Colombia)

Mr. Bean and *The Big Bang Theory*. – Cristian

—————▽—————

Adelaide, South Australia (Australia)

I don't watch TV ... Well, the only TV I see is when I go around to the peoples' places I'm a carer for. One it's cricket/sport, another is just about every music channel on Foxtel scanned through so quickly I don't know why he bothers and the other just watches stuff I'm not interested in like *Sons of Anarchy*. I'll watch various things on YouTube. If I can catch one of the episodes of *Judge Judy*, I'll watch that before that gets taken down. My funny/serious/etc. side is more with the people I interact with.

Oh, I will watch some of the shows at 431 because the doorman will put on some good stuff. I got to see *Barbarella* there and that was the most bizarre experience. I do like a cartoon called *Archer*. That's so ridiculous. – Robert Verrall

—————▽—————

Palm Springs, CA (USA)

Movies and TV shows that best capture my serious side:
1) *The Haunting* (1963)
2) *Alien*
3) *Schindler's List*
4) *Valley of the Dolls*
5) *Buffy the Vampire Slayer*
6) *Dark Shadows*
7) *Orphan Black*

Movies and TV shows that best capture my funny side:
1) *Auntie Mame*
2) *Elvira: Mistress of the Dark*
3) *Steel Magnolias*
4) *Valley of the Dolls*
5) *The Golden Girls*
6) *The Carol Burnette Show*
7) *Absolutely Fabulous*

– D. Warner

—————▽—————

Cathedral City, CA (USA)

Seinfeld. I could watch *Seinfeld* re-runs over and over and over again. My serious side? *Blacklist*, I like that. I like spy thrillers, science fiction. I'm all gung-ho because BBC America on Mondays and Tuesdays are re-running *Star Trek: Deep Space Nine* which has never been in re-run. I like watching those because they deal more with the human aspect, relations with each other, rather than an adventure out in space because they're stuck on a space station. – Spike

—————▽—————

New Orleans, LA (USA)

My Life in Pink or *Team Zero* – Terry Gaskins

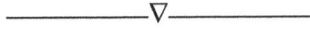

––––––––––––▽––––––––––

Grand Rapids, MI (USA)

I don't watch much of either. My favorite movie is *9 to 5* with Dolly Parton.
– Mark S

––––––––––––▽––––––––––

Palm Springs, CA (USA)

You know, my funny side would be *I Dream of Jeannie* and *Bewitched* because
both of those Jeannie and Samantha had an alter-ego that was their evil side
but fun and risqué. It kind of explained how life was growing up, you had a
double life. But it was funny, and Uncle Arthur and all these other goofy
people were an outlet. They were just great outlets for me. My serious side
… do I have a serious side? I'd have to say, *This Is Us* and that's because it
deals with growing up black in an all-white community. Being bullied at
school, beat up, assaulted, and raped. There are not many people you can talk
about those things with. There's not much of an outlet so you tend to be
mean. You want to get revenge on people that wrong you. But watching *This
is Us*, they tap on different things … what it's like to be black, what it's like
to be mixed, what it's like to not know where you came from, so for me I
end up crying a lot because it gives me an outlet for something I don't get an
outlet for very often. – Crusher

––––––––––––▽––––––––––

New York, NY (USA)
Palm Springs, CA (USA)

Saturday Night Live. I must say that back in the day the first *Saturday Night Live*
was fantastic, then it got mediocre, now, once again, it keeps me laughing.
On the movie side, I'm a big fan of John Waters. I know John Waters. I have
been a photographer of John Waters. Divine lived with my boyfriend in New
York, I spent a lot of time with Divine. The first time I saw *Pink Flamingoes*
was at the Rutgers Student Union in 1972 and I was terrified by it, because
the student audience rolled on the floor laughing. It was like a riot. I snuck
out the back door, fearing something terrible was going to happen there. That

stuck with me forever. Then I got to meet Divine after that. So the John Waters film series and also the film *I Am Divine* by Jeffrey Schwarz. I also have photographs in *I Am Divine* and a cameo appearance by myself. Those queer underground films, all types of underground films, are my inspiration. The Kuchar brothers are dear friends and still remain my inspiration. Their film *Sins of the Fleshapoids* is one of my favorite classics of all time. Serious side, PBS *Frontline*. I recently saw *Harriet,* about Harriet Tubman, and that is where my serious side remains. I thought it was brilliant and the story was unbelievable. Here's a working-class person who made it into the history books after the fact. Pure resistance against forces that were unbeatable, and she beat them. So this type of history film is my inspiration today and I'm an avid follower of documentary films. – Greg Day

—————▽—————

Chicago, IL (USA)

I was a *Will & Grace* fan. *The Mary Tyler Moore Show*. My favorite movie is *The Wizard of Oz*. I attended the 1993 March on Washington and wore a t-shirt that said, "I'm a friend of Dorothy." *Boys in the Band*. *The Crying Game*. *Moonlight*. The original French-language version of *La Cage aux Folles*. I'm sure I've forgotten some. – Steve Kmetko

—————▽—————

Chicago, IL (USA)

My funny side *The Women,* the 1939 film, and my serious, *Sparkle,* 1976 film. The first with all the different characters and how gay people took it as fun and funny. The latter, being a performer, it inspired me. – Mercury

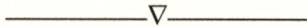

—————▽—————

Cathedral City, CA (USA)

Christmas shows capture my funny because it's something that I yearn to still have. I haven't had Christmas for most of my life. The excitement is not there anymore. But watching a Christmas show brings back the good memories I had. The serious side, movies that make me cry. Usually, it's either … a lot of times that I cry, it's almost like a Broadway show, a movie they've filmed. I have to force myself to cry. I haven't cried since 2001, when my mom passed away. So I have to force myself by watching a sad movie or something that brings out the emotion. It works for that moment. – David Hardy

—————▽—————

Chicago, IL (USA)

In terms of funny, when I was in high school I was a nerd before there was a name for that. My best friend and I would only speak to each other either in a phrase from *Star Trek* or *Monty Python's Flying Circus*. I would say that probably Monty Python and that whole ilk represented my funny side. And the serious side? I've always been attracted to things that make you think about the big picture of life. I would say the one thing from my childhood that encapsulates that was *2001: A Space Odyssey*, this mind-expanding drug trip kind of thing that talked about space and the universe and God, or the lack thereof, and talking computers. Movies like that capture my more serious side. – Thomas Stribling

—————▽—————

Cathedral City, CA (USA)

If you want to see the type of character I am, minus all the drugs, is *Mom*. The mother in that show is me completely. As far as gay shows go, I love Jack from *Will & Grace,* though he's too flamboyant for me. The role that I love is Beverley Leslie, the one that's always fighting with Karen. He's a shorter … as he likes to call himself … a homo. I love that show. – Marcous

—————▽—————

(Germany)

My Name is Earl, Tales of the City, Stonewall, The Green Planet, The Raspberry Reich, Otto or up with Dead People. – Cornelius Günther Körn

—————▽—————

Joplin, MO (USA)

When it comes to the one TV show that really captures my serious and comedic sides, I can only think of *The Big Bang Theory*. While it might be a show that some are not big fans of, I personally enjoyed it for the rather silly situations that occur as well as when the show goes serious for a bit. I was always a rather reserved nerd, but not in the sense of physics and science as the show portrays more of. I tended to be more into the pop culture topics and even when the show went into the science-type stuff, I still managed to get an enjoyment out of it. I think the reason why I thought of this show in particular is because I tend to be a huge nerd when it comes to certain subjects such as video games and foreign cultures such as that of Japan and the United Kingdom/Britain. As someone that is also a part of another minority group in society, I feel like this would be the only way to connect with other people. – Julie W

—————▽—————

Santa Fe, NM (USA)

TV doesn't do much for me. One of my favorite movies is *Harold and Maude* and we often watch different love stories, foreign films too, *Like Water for Chocolate*. The one that I saw not too long ago was *The Notebook*, about a woman who was diagnosed with Alzheimer's and her husband reads her, her diary. It was a wonderful story of getting older and being in love and walking back through the romance and their relationship and how it stayed with them through the years. And they actually died together. – Guy Selier

—————▽—————

Cathedral City, CA (USA)

They range from warped John Waters' films to *Borat*, *Bruno*, *Monty Python*, *Bad Education* (British TV show) or *Airplane* humor for the silly side. For the serious I love many documentaries such as *The Cove* and *The Family*. In terms of series I can binge on *The Good Doctor*, *This Is Us*, *Stranger Things* or *13 Reasons Why*. – Paul Harris

—————▽—————

(Australia)

I have a fairly perverse sense of humour, and enjoy sarcasm, clack humour, innuendo, and things on what many consider the sick side of life. British comedies like *Shameless* and *The Office* tickle my fancy – comedies that have a dig at people's lifestyles, the odd nuances that make us human. Pretty well anything that is British – be it a series or movie – will get my interest. The Brits gave a similar sense of humour to us Aussies, so we "get" each other as far as comedy goes. British movies like *Legend*, *Sexy Beast*, *Layer Cake* and *Lock, Stock and Two Smoking Barrels* are favourites. British gangsters are way more brutal than American ones. I love true crime, historical fiction and quality thrillers. Used to be a horror buff, but horror has gotten so cliched that it's just not scary anymore. Current series like *Taboo, Rillington Place, The Fall, Game of Thrones, Vikings, You, The Walking Dead* (which has now totally lost the plot), *The Affair* and *Homeland* give a fair indication of my diverse tastes. Gay series such as *Queer as Folk* (both the English, and American), *Looking, We Shall Rise, Riot* and *Tales of the City* are favourites. I also have diverse tastes in movies, though tend to ignore comedies. *The Color Purple* is right up there, *Shawshank Redemption, It, Hotel Mumbai, Out of Africa, Dolores Claiborne* are all favourites. – Tim Alderman

—————∇—————

Redwood Valley/Mendocino County, CA (USA)

Harold and Maude comes immediately to mind. I saw it in theaters more than 30 times soon after its release in 1971, when I was just out of high school. I totally related to the queerly intergenerational love the characters shared, and that move speaks directly to funny and serious.
We haven't had network TV for a couple of decades now, but I love catching up with RuPaul's escapades, which tackle serious social visibility with glee, and always makes me smile. – T. Lark Letchworth

—————∇—————

Brunswick, ME (USA)

I'm not a big TV watcher, but I used to like the (early years) of *Saturday Night Live*, and of course *The Golden Girls* and *Designing Women*. As for movies, I enjoy well-done fantasy, like *The Lord of the Rings* and *Avatar*. Comedy? Give me anything by Monty Python, especially *The Holy Grail*. British comedies, *Are You Being Served* and *Keeping Up Appearances* are favorites, too. I love the old films from the 1930's, Busby Berkeley musicals, Bette Davis films and *Gone with the Wind*. Oh, yes, *Tales of the City*. – Michael Pickel

—————∇—————

Chicago, IL (USA)

The serious one I love is *This is Us* on NBC. It just hits me to my core, it's about relationships in a family and how things have been, a lot of flashbacks. Because I struggle with my weight, I lost 80lbs in 2006/2007 so there's a girl in it that's really obese. They talk a little bit about her weight issue as she was growing up. One that hits my funny, I like to watch the reruns of *Kids in the*

Hall ... I have a bizarre sense of humor but some of the stuff on *Little Britain* ... I'll still go back and watch those two. – Greg R. Baird

—————▽—————

Chicago, IL (USA)

TV sitcoms like: *The Neighborhood, The Connors, Superstore, Mom* and *Will and Grace* are just some of the shows that tickle my funny bone and capture my funny.

My serious side leans more on movies. I rarely look to movies for comedy. *Ordinary People, Awakenings, Still Alice, A Single Man* and *Brokeback Mountain* are just some of my favorites.

When I need comedy and some silliness in my day I turn to television. When I need something serious which totally out-weighs my need for funny I turn to the movies. – Mark Contorno

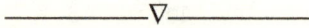

—————▽—————

Cork, Munster (Ireland)

I will always be a big fan of Roger DeBris and Carmen Ghia in Mel Brooks's *The Producers* (the original 1968 version).

And because I am a survivor of the plague years of AIDS, early depictions such as *Longtime Companion* and *An Early Frost*, though imperfect, still resonate for me. – David Clayton

—————▽—————

Palm Springs, CA (USA)

Funny side? I like the *America's Funniest Videos* clips with people doing nutty things. Serious side? I like *CBS Sunday Morning* for a thoughtful news show. – Tony Earl

—————▽—————

King, NC (USA)

My favorite movie and one that has helped me in my coming out journey is *Shirley Valentine*. It's a movie about the main character, Shirley, coming into her own and being her own person. She mounts difficult odds with her husband, children, and friends to become Shirley Valentine again after letting that person (herself) become lost in trying to please everyone else. The movie exposes many amusing foibles in the other supporting characters. I find myself revisiting this movie often – especially when I am facing a crossroads in my life. This movie gives me courage. – Ron Cline

—————▽—————

Charlottetown, Prince Edward Island (Canada)

At the same time? Movies: *Ghost World*, anything by John Waters (though the serious side of Waters work is in the way he turns fringe characters into heroes). TV: *Six Feet Under*, and most recently, *Fleabag*. – Dave Stewart

—————▽—————

San Diego, CA (USA)

As a titleholder [Ms. San Diego Leather 2019], my Mr. and my bootblack … Jody is my Mr. and Rowdy is my bootblack. We just got done with a photoshoot for Halloween, it was *Addams Family Values*. It's gorgeous because I play Morticia and Morticia's absolute irreverence and total dominance of the scene in the room, is internally what I want to become. She is amazing. Anjelica Huston does such a good job with that role. She nailed it. – Serafine Sawyer

—————▽—————

Fort Lauderdale, FL (USA)

Modern Family if I was 20 years younger. I have an Asian child, my husband's brother married a Colombian and, well there are so many other similarities it's scary. For my serious side I can't even imagine one. – Rick Karlin

—————▽—————

Milwaukee, WI (USA)
Scottsdale AZ (USA)

TV shows funny … *Soap* was the best ever. *Madame's Place* (Wayland Flowers), *Will and Grace*. Serious … Any show that made my brain think … *Law and Order*, *West Wing*, *Bones*, etc. *Grace and Frankie*, *Orange is the New Black*, and anything having anything to do with expanding consciousness (GAIA TV, CETV) and ways to teach others. I am awake and have been for several years

going back to my time in Milwaukee and am slowly waking up others. –
Sherrie Howe

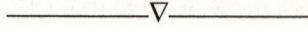

——————▽——————

Des Moines, IA (USA)

Who's Afraid of Virginia Woolf, The Lion in Winter, Boys in the Band, Paris is Burning, All About Eve. I'm such a fag! Lol. – Sr. Freida Peoples aka DJ Chrysler Sheldon

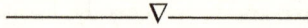

——————▽——————

Worcester, MA (USA)

POSH on FX has been an incredible TV show that showcases stories of Black and Latino queer and trans folks from New York. It is an interesting show that highlights the unique culture of a queer person of color (POC). I feel quite a connection as a queer person of color with the stories told in this TV show, they are also inspiring and beautifully depict the defiance of queer POC folks and their culture. – Salman

DID YOU HAVE A RELIGIOUS UPBRINGING AND HOW DID (OR DOES) THAT AFFECT YOUR LIFE AS AN LGBTQ PERSON?

Lewiston, NY (USA)

Very much Catholic. I wanted to be a priest. Then I was a part of the hippie Jesus movement back in the 1970s. Then I started studying all religions, Bhagavad Gita, the Koran, and Buddhism and the Native American spirituality, throughout my life. I began to see more of the similarities between them instead of the differences. I've seen a lot of horrible things in world history that's rooted in religion and religious beliefs and churches. So I tend to have a more free-flowing spirituality that's more about an energy and being interested in physics, it's more of a positive energy. Just living in an honest way with a positive energy for things. – James Scalfani

―――――∇―――――

Fulton, KY (USA)
Bardwell, KY (USA)
Martin, TN (USA)

I was born into the Methodist Church. Before I realized I was gay, it was a haven from the rough county-school world I spent most of my time in. Afterwards, in college I participated at the Wesley Foundation, the Methodist Church on campus. But theatre soon caught my imagination, and I abandoned the church for the Vanguard Theatre, on the campus of the University of Tennessee at Martin. After that, incidentally, the Methodist Church, formally, in conference, abandoned the LGBTQ population. I miss being able to commune on Sundays with like-minded people and to focus on the teachings of a wise man like Jesus Christ. Over the years I have added to my store of belief, if not faith, Taoism and Buddhism. I pretty much believe that all there is, is "The Way." – Oran Walker

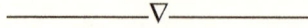

———————▽———————

South Bend, IN (USA)

At a young age I was raised Catholic. I don't mean today Catholic. I don't mean guitar-mass Catholic. I mean … Catholic! God did not speak English Catholic. How does it affect me? It doesn't anymore. One of the things I came to realize when I was coming out was the absurdity of it. How does it affect me nowadays? It gives me some perspective into people who continue to need that spiritual connection in their lives. But I am ambivalently agnostic now. – Steve

———————▽———————

Chicago, IL (USA)

My family was pretty religious but not in the traditional or conservative sense. Their core faith principles were grace, forgiveness, and unconditional love. My faith has gotten stronger as I've gotten older, although it has evolved from what I was taught at home. I believe in God, but I don't believe in hell. Because God is all powerful, it would be impossible to do something which He did not condone. He wouldn't punish us for what He willed us to do. One day I will die, and I will join my friends and queer ancestors in Heaven. – C'est Kevvie (Wilhelmina)

———————▽———————

Detroit, MI (USA)

I was raised Catholic, attending Catholic school and the whole shebang. I was an altar boy at one point and I remember doing the stations of the cross, the path Jesus took to the hill. This was in the evening of Good Friday and I had already been through the entire thing once that day because we had to go to mass that day during school, so I was over it. The thought crossed(!) my mind that perhaps we could hurry it up a bit and just nail the guy to whatever wall was nearby and go home. That was the beginning of my realizing that religion was a complete sham, some bullshit created to control people. The more I thought about it, the less sense it made. I don't remember any reading I did on the subject until much later, but by then I had come out of the closet as an atheist as well. I find that it is also something you have to bring up often because people automatically assume everyone to be a "believer" which I can't stand. I can even discuss it without calling people sheep, which I could not do a few years ago. – Terence Smith (Joan Jett Blakk)

—————▽—————

Texas (USA)

I had a religious upbringing in an evangelical fundamentalist family. While I was drawn to church for the socializing, the God I was presented with was an angry, vengeful God whose expectations would be impossible for me to live up to. As a young professional I would find a religious tradition which understood God who is loving and accepts us as we are. It was in this faith tradition that I was later able to come out and accept myself for who I am. My faith calls me to work for the inclusion and well-being of all persons in all aspects of life. – Anonymous

—————▽—————

Nashville, TN (USA)
Birmingham, AL (USA)
Chicago, IL (USA)

Nashville: My family was very strongly religious. My parents viewed the world through their strongly held religious faith. They worked for church related institutions. I was taken to church for long hours three times a week without fail. Church was the center of our social lives, the only place we ever went except for school and visits to the homes of relatives. The church was very sex negative and specifically homosexual negative.

When I first began to understand that I was gay, I was trapped in an anguish of horror and grief. I sincerely prayed for years daily through my teen years that God would change me. He never did.

Birmingham: I first met other gay people at a church related university. It took me a long time to come out because of the religious issues I had. I spent an entire winter in grief and depression, crying every night. I had no support. I had no role model. Except for my friends. We had no written sources of gay affirming information, none at all, and almost no gay positive images in the wider culture. It took a great deal of personal strength and courage for me to come out and form a positive gay identity in the face of all this negativity and oppression.

Chicago: I would be a happier, healthier, and a more successful adult if I had never had any kind of religious upbringing at all. – Bert Thompson

————————▽————————

Chicago, IL (USA)

My parents were raised Catholic, and their parents were Catholic, so my sister and I had to go to religious classes even though we went to public schools. So we had to make our communion and confirmation like any good Catholic did. Once we were done with that, it was … "If you want to go to church it's fine, if you don't it's whatever." My grandfather, my mom's father, was the one who set the tone, "It doesn't matter what church you go to or how many times you go to the church, when you drop dead and somebody puts fifty dollars into the priest's hand, he's going to pray and cry just as if you went every day." I have absolutely no use for religion whatsoever. Other than I would love to know where they get those fabulous embroidered gowns. – Mike

————————▽————————

Indianapolis, IN (USA)

I was raised Catholic on both sides. I would describe Catholicism as a toxin. It gave me an inferiority complex. The thing about Catholicism is that you're not good enough. The only time you're going to be worthy is in the afterlife. You're supposed to suck it up and put up with everything and not want anything, and not want to be happy or anything. That's something that I do, I endure, I endure any kind of bullshit, any kind of horrible crap, open heart surgery, being half blind, crap jobs … I endure. But I don't know why, I just do. I think that has something to do with it, but I don't think that is anything wonderful. It's the end. That's it. Basically, Catholicism gave me an inferior complex and I feel a tremendous sense of guilt about certain aspects of my sexuality. They say that most Catholic gay men are into BDSM and I'm very heavily into BDSM and I think a lot of that is that I didn't feel worthy and I felt guilty. That and all those pictures of people tied up and arrows in them and shit. It fucked me up, basically. When I was 18, I left the church. It caused a huge stir in the family, but I thought, "Fuck it, I'm not doing this anymore."– Xavier Bathsheba-Negron

————————▽————————

Fayetteville, AR (USA)

I was raised in the Church of Christ. This I not the United Church of Christ, which is pretty liberal. The United Church of Christ was the first gay-affirming mainstream church. The Church of Christ that I was raised in was very strict and I'm still dealing with that. Not because I think being gay is wrong but it was just shoved down my throat that it was. It's hard to shed some of that strictness and judgmental ... it affects me today that I sometimes have to watch it that I don't judge other people. But I find I'm much happier knowing that people don't need my approval. They really don't, to live their lives. I get a little angry sometimes about my upbringing because it was so restricted. – Renny

—————▽—————

Chicago, IL (USA)

I actually did have a fairly religious upbringing, as it goes. I went to Sunday School, I was confirmed in one church, converted to Catholic as an adult but in the scheme of things, I think I am religious, but do not think it really impacted my life as a gay man. I recognize that religion and being part of the LGBTQ community have many places of disconnect but I think it is in each of us to navigate religion to our own needs and use, and make it work for our own needs. – Dean Ogren

—————▽—————

Southern California, CA (USA)

I had to go to Sunday School and Church, but my parents weren't that religious. From about the age of 10 I thought the Bible was a crock of shit and I really didn't believe in any of it. I still don't. – Gary Borgstedt

—————▽—————

Northern Virginia (USA)

In the Catholic universe Gay people do not exist. All the way through Catholic grade school and high school there was no word for Gay people because they did not exist. So I grew up assuming I was like all the other guys who had girlfriends. I had girlfriends but it never went too far. In college I actually listened to the prayers we repeated in church and realized they were absurd. It wasn't until a few years later when I stumbled onto the Hardcore Punk underground of misfits that I started meeting some out gay people. So by the time I got to graduate school I had rejected the Catholic Church, rejected mainstream society, and met some well-adjusted out gay people. It was only a matter of time before I realized I too was gay. The odd thing about coming out is that one instantly goes into a minority status and is treated differently, yet one is still the same person inside. – Lars von Keitz

———————∇———————

Waverly, IA (USA)

I was quite religious as a young person but by the time I realized I was gay it was no longer an issue whether religion approved or not.

In fact, my first gay sex experience left me feeling liberated and I said to myself: "That's what I was supposed to fear, avoid???" – Robert Beck

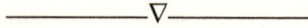

———————∇———————

Chicago, IL (USA)

Not at all. My grandmother ... her parents were immigrants from Lithuania. On my dad's side, all of my great grandparents came from Italy. People in my family are Catholic to varying degrees. I was baptized but I wasn't forced to go to Sunday school. My mom was not observant. It was never forced on me ... thank God! – Jeff Ramone

———————∇———————

North Carolina (USA)

In the rural area of North Carolina where I grew up it was sternly evangelical Christian. My family wasn't particularly religious but was happy if I went to church. They encouraged me to go to church, but my parents didn't go to church themselves. Go figure that one out. So when I was a child I went to church with some of my other relatives. I could sense right away that this whole Christian evangelical thing, there was something wrong with it. These people just seemed messed up to me. It was all about punishment and feeling ashamed. Basically, complaining about how terrible life was now and how wonderful it would be in heaven. And being judgmental about other people. At a very young age it felt so wrong to me. Before I came out, I did some exploration into my own beliefs and spirituality. I actually explored the Catholic church for a while. I think what appealed to me about the Catholic church was the pomp and circumstance of the ceremony. It was like being a part of a theatrical production every week. You get a nice little script and they tell you when to stand up and when to sit down, when to genuflect, when to say this line ... it was like being a part of a theatrical production. I also explored the Radical Faeries, some of that. I think what all of that taught me, along with my coming out, was really just a tolerance for others. A real desire to help other young people, who might be living in a pretty strict conservative religious upbringing, to come out. To be able to see a wider more interesting, more loving, world that is really out there. – Randy

---------▽---------

Seattle, WA (USA)

My family raised me Jewish. After my bar-mitzvah, it was extremely lackadaisical. I was introduced to Wicca by the time I was 15 and followed that path. I find that "Conventional" religion is far too limiting for my taste. Wicca's first rule is "All love and pleasure are rituals – Do as thou wilt, but HARM NONE." That's something I can get behind. LGBTQ people have always been represented if not celebrated – in Wiccan (and most Pagan) faiths. – Eric Andrews-Katz

---------▽---------

Rockford IL (USA)

I was raised Catholic/Christian. I think that I took to heart that I should care for others. I do try to continue to emulate the understandings of the Christian teachings. While I don't go to church anymore or really believe in a higher power. I do still try to live my life in a good way. – Patrick J. Murphy III

---------▽---------

Paris (France)
Menton, Côte d'Azur (France)
London (UK)
Luxor (Egypt)

My religious upbringing was split between two traditions: at home – whether in Paris, Menton, or London – we were very extravagant Catholics. But winters were spent at my great-aunt's villa in Luxor, where we completely abandoned Christianity and luxuriated in worshipping the gods of Egypt, including going to dawn rituals at Karnak. The Egyptian religion was always the one that we truly professed in our hearts, even though we maintained the façade of being Catholics in Europe. It put a great deal of strain on me until I finally rid myself of any respect for Christianity due to its shocking preaching of hatred, bigotry, intolerance, and its one spiritual supremacy. Now, I can look at the trappings of Christianity and see them for what they are: a vehicle of oppression that uplifts the ignorant and tries to destroy those who don't conform to its ridiculous morality. – Louis Richard de Bourbon de Parme et de Savoie, Prince de la Pau

―――――――∇―――――――

Chicago, IL (USA)

I was raised the only brown family in an all Swedish and German Southern Baptist convention church with very strong ties to Moody Bible Institute. I was first hand witness to the double standard. I was in junior high and two brothers had taken their own lives because they were gay. It was explained to the youth group this way! Sometimes suicide was God's way of bringing his lost children home to heaven. I stood there frozen with RAGE! and vowed I would reject the teachings of this hate filled faith. The conservatives are relentless. They believe they are solders of Christ. Never underestimate their hatred, wealth and influence. – Philip Bernal

―――――――∇―――――――

Rugby, Warwickshire (UK)

I had a regular Protestant free church upbringing, as my paternal grandfather was a minister in the Congregational Church (he baptised me) – the church is now known as the United Reformed Church.

I joined the church officially in 1979, but decided to leave shortly afterwards, after witnessing the Reverend Batt's 1980 New Year sermon, in which he started bellowing, red-faced, about the "sin" of homosexuality, slapping the sides of his pulpit. He worked himself up into a right old state! He berated society for "accepting the abomination of homosexuality" in the 1970s – which was news to me, as I was routinely insulted and picked on at school for being thought of as "queer." Even though I didn't identify as gay at that stage of my life (aged 17), I was shocked by this fiery sermon and knew that it was wrong. Thus began my long drift towards the adoption of secular Humanism. I see this, not so much as a rejection of my churchy past, but as building on and improving upon its legacy. Incidentally, the United Reformed Church, run along devolved lines, allows its church deacons to determine their own approach to things like gay marriage, so perhaps there has been some progress, however limited. Humanists, of course, have always judged any relationship by its quality, rather than the gender of those involved, which I'm much more comfortable with. – Diesel Balaam

———————▽———————

Bellport, NY (USA)

I almost died when I was first born. As a result my father had a Catholic Priest baptize me and read me the last rights. No one thought I would make it. Twelve years later, my Mom became a Born Again Christian. (My parents separated when I was nine years old.) Since I lived with my Mom she tried to raise me as a Born Again Christian. None of these religions stuck. I am of no religion now and refuse to affiliate with one. All religions have bloodshed in their history and even call for prejudice today, so why would I want to be a part of that? – Erin Michelle Miller

———————▽———————

St Louis, MO (USA)

Growing up in St. Louis (1960s, 1970s, 1980s), families were Christian, Republican, racist, and homophobic, all in varying degrees. I believe I was baptized as Lutheran, and when I was three my stepfather had us attend a Baptist church. Man, those were tedious because after going to Sunday school for an hour, then the church service itself was TWO HOURS and always included a sweaty rant from the pastor that went on for a very long time. My brother and I would bring Matchbox cars and Hotwheels to play with (which my mom would take away), or we'd pass the time by taking a pencil and filling in the letter O's and zeroes in the programs. Then we got the brilliant idea of misbehaving just enough to get sent out to the car where we'd listen to Casey Kasem's Top 40. Sure, we'd be yelled at by my stepfather when the service was over, but we felt it was worth the inconvenience. Once we were dragged along to a Billy Graham event at the St. Louis Arena (where hockey was played). I realized I was gay when I was 5, and hearing the mean things said about "those queers" by relatives, schoolmates, and people on TV scared me, particularly when they tried to say how those people were going to Hell. When a few times as kids there would be minor exploration with male cousins, I felt so guilty at first. Later, I'd intercept mailings in our mailbox from religious family values groups that claimed gays were out to recruit children, and I'd tear them up and put them in the bottom of the trash but didn't feel guilty about that. I realized I was a good kid and was starting to understand a lot of religion was about control, guilt, and power. I still allowed myself to be re-baptized at the Baptist church, only because I was pissed that I couldn't have the little wafer and cute tiny glass of grape juice. So a few years later I felt that that "baptism" didn't count for anything. Plus, my stepfather enjoyed beer like all the dads, and like many Catholics who don't go by what Catholicism dictates, none of the dads at that Baptist church ignored alcohol. That too had me realizing that religion was just not for me. Thankfully my parents realized being Baptist was just too much for us, so we switched to a United Church of Christ church. Stand up, sit down. Everyone reading passages in monotone unison. The "wherefore dost thou thee" language in the bible. I once asked a pastor why God kept appearing and talking to people at only one time in history, but then nothing except for the likes of televangelists claiming it. But most of all, I just didn't think I was evil for being gay (never told anyone I was back then, of course). Sometime in junior high school, I told my parents I would appreciate it if they didn't make me go to church anymore. They didn't like it, wanted to know who put these ideas into my head. I told them no one, I just didn't care for it. Thankfully they didn't push it after that. I felt free. I understand that for some people, including LGBTQ, that their religion is something they gain strength from. Fine. I respect that they can practice their religion, as long as they don't push it on me. When someone says, "I'll pray for you," I always tell them, "Please don't and respect my wish. I'll deal with a creator on my own terms." – Todd Jaeger

———————▽———————

South Carolina (USA)

My mom brought us up in a Southern Baptist church, but she always said, "this is what I believe, you find what speaks to you." I've often thought mom was more of a proper southern lady than she was a religious person. However, being in the south did have an impact. Luckily, because I didn't realize yet that being gay was how I was different, I didn't get the horrible hell fire and brimstone many gay kids got growing up. I did, however, learn early the hypocrisy of the "this is wrong because I say it is and I'm a proper Christian" thing. It wasn't until I was an adult and came out that I started realizing what had been said to me growing up and how there were people who used the Bible as a source of comfort and those that used it as a weapon. I will say, though, that although I grew up Baptist, later moved to being Lutheran it was always more to conform than belief. I'm now an unapologetic atheist but those I respect, I also respect their faith. – Chris Grace

———————▽———————

Detroit, MI (USA)

Yeah, we were Methodists. No drinking, no swearing, church three times a week. When I tell people I was Methodist, they say, "Well, at least you weren't a nutso Baptist." Well, I'm here to tell you, the Methodists are as nutso as the Baptists. I consider myself a "recovering Methodist." Make that an EX-Methodist. – Brian T

—————∇—————

Rome, NY (USA)

I did not. My father and mother were Episcopalian. The only time we went to church would be for a wedding … I think we went on Easter a few times. But I would say no, it wasn't a religious family. I grew up non-religious, then when I got to college, I became an agnostic, and have been ever since. – Andee

—————∇—————

Chicago, IL (USA)

My grandfather was a Southern Baptist Minister in Oklahoma City. When I was 18 months old, my parents left Oklahoma and moved to the Chicago area. We moved around a lot, but my parents were committed to us being a church-going family, and we attended fundamentalist Baptist Churches all my life – until I was out of graduate school. These were churches mostly characterized by the word "NO." You can't do this, you can't do that … no no. No. And we were in church for services twice every Sunday and every Wednesday night. Youth groups met on Fridays and many Saturdays as well.

I graduated from a more progressive (some would say liberal) Baptist graduate school shortly before I came out. This school taught me to jettison the negative and rules-based theology and helped me replace it with more life-giving and community building thought.

I was part of a core leadership group of a mega church in a suburb of Chicago from 1986 'til 1989. When I finally admitted to myself that I was gay and told this to one of the leaders of that church, and I was invited to leave. So I did.

But I had ALWAYS been part of a church, and I didn't know how to live without that community. So I asked around to find out which local churches had spearheaded and backed the local human rights ordinance that had recently been passed, and caused the city to include sexual orientation as a protected class. I began looking at those churches, and ended up settling in one, where I have been a member since 1990.

How does it affect my life? Well first, let me say that this church is open and affirming and very supportive of me in every way. They are happy to let me teach the teenagers, or to preach on a Sunday morning. I've laughed that if I ever decided that I wanted to wear a dress and makeup on a Sunday when I was preaching, no one would care. (That's not my scene, but it's nice to know I could).

Our church is a bit of an anomaly in the larger conference, however. Many other churches that are also members of this denomination condemn us and want us gone. This affects me deeply. Sometimes I have weeks and weeks where I just can't go to church because I know this. Other times I have to go because these people love me and I love them. If I ever moved out of Chicago, I doubt I would go to another church. – andKevin

————————∇————————

La Mesa, Tequendama Province (Colombia)

I was raised as a Catholic, but I no longer practice any cult or devotion for what it means and although I have some resentment towards the general public of churches it does not affect me as a gay being. – Cristian

————————∇————————

San Jose, CA (USA)

I was raised Bahai. For the most part they are very understanding and accepting. As a trans-person who is also lesbian, it was hard for me to understand. I didn't know what trans people were, nobody was really there out in the open to tell me I could be that way. I didn't start my transition until I was in my 20s. OK I'm straight but I still want to be a girl. I never had that experience with my religion, dating same-sex. At the time I was still identifying as a male. I was very closeted. I was one of the only Caucasian individuals in my community center ... they don't call them churches. That was difficult in a way because I could not resonate with the cultural aspects of things, most of them being Persian or from the Middle East. There was a lot of disconnect that way. I was also a very shy child, so I didn't have any friends growing up. But I do know that if I had come out back then there would have been a lot of reservation and backlash. A lot of the people in the community were not accepting of homosexuality, in a certain sense. It would have been frowned upon by a small minority of people there, but people with power within the organization. Although I did not face any individual struggles in that sense, there was an internal struggle that if I had come to the conclusion that I needed to come out at that time, it would have been really hard. – Kelsey Brookes

——————∇——————

Michigan (USA)

Yes, and I rejected it immediately. I've always felt that religion was my enemy at every level. Catechism … I told those bastards I was an atheist when I was six or seven. I did. I said, "I don't believe in any of it." Then I would hide up in the attic to get out of going to catechism on Saturday morning. It was bad enough we had to go to school five days a week, on the sixth day we had to go and put up with that bullshit. People don't believe in themselves, so they want someone else to believe in. – Jim

——————∇——————

Chicago, IL (USA)

I was raised a Catholic and fell away from the church the day I graduated from 8th grade. Always felt that religion should be a personal thing not a big business. I probably pray more than a priest. Most of my prayers and thoughts go to my friends that have passed. – Dennis Hardenstein

——————∇——————

Adelaide, South Australia (Australia)

No, I didn't. Mum sent me to Sunday School for five minutes but I had no idea why I needed to be there, so she pulled up stumps on that idea. Thankfully she did because it was one of those churches where kids were abused. Perhaps Mum had a gut feeling, I don't know. I did, however, get Immanuel College thrust upon me and that was religious like nothing else. Devotions every day, Scripture lessons and rubbish like that. Even the choir we had to do religious stuff which should come as no surprise. The Scripture lessons I didn't take seriously, much to the chagrin of the teachers, but they really couldn't do much about it. I was one who would question so it was best to keep me quiet rather than me asking about contradictions or stuff like that. I once did a cartoon style thing of a flame representing God and this OTT caricature of Jesus and they were talking. The flame boomed Jesus' name and Jesus responded with: "Yes, Dad." Well, Father, Son and Holy Ghost. So I'd do stuff like that. I generally ignored the religious aspect of things, even when they got a bit preachy with regards to sexuality and stuff like that. I'd have the latest song by Nik Kershaw or Wa Wa Nee or Pseudo Echo or whatever going through the head and that was a good distraction, lol.

The only good thing about Immanuel College with regard to religious stuff is at home where Mum would argue with my stepdad about stuff. Mum was Methodist and my Stepdad was Catholic. Mum would try to get me to back up her side of the story, but I'd always be able to come back with "you sent me to a Lutheran school and their teachings were different again." Thankfully that always set me free from that silly argument. – Robert Verrall

—————▽—————

Grand Rapids, MI (USA)

Yes. I would say, I tried to continue with my religion, but realized it was not a good fit for me. – Mark S

—————▽—————

Hollister, CA (USA)
Campbell, CA (USA)

It probably affects my life because I didn't come out until I was 30, so it affected my life that way. I thought when I was younger that I wanted to be a priest. I was an altar boy. I did the readings at the church when I was younger. I led the singing. I did it later too. I sang in the choir up until around 2008, or a little before that I quit going to church. I was donating money to the church and I came to find out that the diocese of Monterey – that's where the money went to because they built a new church at Hollister – were supporting the anti-gay marriage campaign. I was very upset, and I ran over the signs when I saw them on the road. Or I would slice them up when they were on public property because I owned that road too and I didn't say you could put that sign up. When the election was over, my partner and I went around and gathered up all those signs, knocked on the priest's door and said, "Here, you can have these back, you paid for them." He was very sympathetic, very pro-gay. He ended up leaving the priesthood. He married a woman, he wasn't gay. The priest in Campbell which is in San Jose when I was going to church when I was up there for a while, he was very sympathetic too. Because I went to confession one time when I first came out. He asked me, "Is this a sin against love." I said, "No," He said, "Then you're OK." So that settled me down a little bit. When I was a kid I wanted to be a priest, and then I used the excuse, "Well I want to get married and have kids." I wanted to have a big family because I was raised in a big family. Deep down I knew the reason I didn't become a priest ... I just didn't want to admit it. – Spike

———————▽———————

Indiana (USA)

While my immediate family was nominally religious, not attending church regularly, they were most serious about Spiritualism, believing in ghosts, spirits (our house was seriously haunted), and messages over the Quija board from ancestors. Growing up in a historically Quaker area, values from this religion permeated local ethical and political consciousness. Part of my family had been members of the Society of Friends, and while nominally Republican, some did share liberal values that the Quakers professed since the 1800s: being against war in general, aware of and against slavery, and were pro-union. This area of central-east Indiana was, due to their influence, a major center of abolitionists as well as free, or runaway, African Americans from before the Civil War. Both my mother (a basketball player) and grandmother (a suffragette and bread winner of the family) were feminists, if undeclared ones. When I came out in the middle seventies, their influence provided an entry into the Anti-Vietnam War movement, the 2nd Wave of Feminism, the continued Civil Rights struggle all of which influenced the growing LGBTQ movement. – David Hatfield Sparks

———————▽———————

Central Indiana (USA)
Indianapolis, IN (USA)
Chicago IL (USA)

To be blunt, I didn't have a religious "upbringing" because my family and friends in central Indiana were the kind of "Christians" who knew nothing about Christ, the Bible, theology, or church services. They adopted the label "Christian" as an ego trip, a label that allowed them to be judgmental, with religious power and approval, toward anyone they didn't like. They carried their religious beliefs like a concealed weapon. As a child I recall going to Sunday school exactly once and being occasionally subjected to those moronic Weekday Religion classes in elementary school: the instructor wrote "CH—CH" on the board and then crowed, "What's missing from church? U R!" Yeah, fuck you, lady!

However, as an adult (as a young college student) I began to explore religion – ALL religions – on my own and forming my own opinions. I recognized the beautiful poetry and painful ambiguity to be found in religious texts. I remember seeing an awesome production of MacLeish's *J.B.* at the Christian Theological Seminary in Indianapolis as a college student and being inspired to go off and study the original Book of Job. It remains one of my favorite most troubling works of literature. At about the same time, I was introduced to Hinduism through the *Bhagavad Gita*, which also remains one of my favorite works of world literature. I wish I could go back in time to tell my family and friends – futilely, I am sure – that most religions are about doubt, kindness, and love rather than narcissism and judgment and hate. I would love to confront any of my relatives who believed that the story of Lot in Sodom – which they most certainly never read – establishes that homosexuality is a sin. If we accept that, I would say, is it then morally acceptable to throw your daughters into a crowd of rapists as a way of avoiding a homosexual gangbang? I would do that just to see their heads explode. – William Demaree

———————∇———————

Cleveland, OH (USA)

Yes. Being raised as a Christian taught me a lot about how religion can be used to control and shame. No thanks. I can't imagine that if there is a higher power that it would be as petty and closed–minded as all that. -Roger

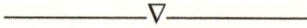

———————∇———————

Louisiana (USA)

I had a slight to moderate religious upbringing. I was raised by my mom and two grandmothers who wanted me to do right by people as a reflection of them and if part of that meant loving and respecting GOD, that's what it was. To the credit of the people I congregated with references were made to my lack of rambunctiousness, if you will, but there was never talk of sexuality or how that might relate to it, masculinity was more important, not what I did with my body, thank goodness. – Katorri A.

———————∇———————

Wisconsin Rapids, WI (USA)

My religious upbringing was more incidental than a serious part of my life. While I was raised Catholic, I don't think anyone in my immediate family really embraced the creed of the Church, let alone lived by its dogma. It was more happenstance and family tradition than it was anything resembling faith. I was taught by my parents to read widely and to question everything which, in hindsight, was pretty revolutionary given the whole Catholic gestalt, so it was only natural that I was at odds with the church from childhood until the day I decided it was all bunk and walked away from it, never looking back. There was never any kind of crisis of conscience or deep pondering about the fate of my soul. The only impact at all that Catholicism had on my life as a gay man was in the way that relatives have responded to me and to any significant relationship I had in my life. I adopted a "fuck you" attitude to any judgments that came my way and eventually most of them came around. And those that couldn't or wouldn't ... well ... fuck them until they do. – D. Warner

————▽————

Oxnard, CA (USA)

I grew up Episcopalian, Church of England, so we could sin and have divorces. We went to church every Sunday through most of my high school years, but the interesting thing was when one of my dear friends came out. He was sent to the church to discuss coming out. The father of the church said, "That's OK this religion doesn't care" ... which set off my friends' parents but allowed me to understand that I was accepted. As I got older, I don't really identify with Episcopalian unless someone asks me. I haven't been to a church in a hundred years. I'm much more spiritual. Live and let live. I'm not feeling guilty, I'm just being me and having a good time. – Crusher

————▽————

Cleveland, OH (USA)

I was raised in a strict Baptist home, the youngest of five children. My dad was a Baptist minister. We went to church a lot. My brother is 14 years older than I am. He's gay, too. Neither one of us had the opportunity to discuss it with Mom and Dad. We were discouraged from discussing any "problems." "Put it in God's hands" my mom would say of problems. Once, when I was going to tell my parents, my father stopped me mid-sentence. He put his hand up like a traffic cop. "Steve, there was a time and place when people's private lives were private. Let's keep it that way." My brother and I have grown very close over the years. And that's very nice. – Steve Kmetko

————▽————

Huntsville, AL (USA)

My parents were not religious but in rebellion against them, I became religious. I was a very contrary child. I had a lot of issues with my father about what I liked to do and my appearance etc. As a youth I joined the Methodist Youth Group, this is in Huntsville, Alabama. I became the vice president of it. This is where I had a penchant for being a community organizer. I became an officer in this group. After the meetings at the church we would go to the drive-in and make out and drink beer. Then I became a Christian Witness missionary for the Methodist Youth Fellowship for Northern Alabama. I went out door to door with the Bible. I went to a conference in Birmingham, Alabama, and I went door to door speaking to young Methodists about being involved in the church. I thought being involved in the church meant having a good social time and going to the drive-in afterwards. This was not exactly appropriate. That was my first activist move, then I went away to Sumatanga in the Appalachian Mountains, and we did a lot of praying in the woods. I really got into this for a short period of time. My parents were terrified, and I don't blame them a bit. Then when my parents moved to Washington DC, I was still in the church and I was an actor in a church play at the Methodist church. I was baptized, but then as I came out as a gay person, and as a worker in the civil rights movement, the church was both a blessing and a problem. Very quickly I thought, "Oh no, no, no." By the time of Anita Bryant, I realized that Christianity was the big problem that was in my way. I abandoned that. I still believe that some aspects of every religion are positive. But the way it's used in our culture to isolate and control people, I find very offensive. It has nothing to do with the original teachings. They've just become a moral police. At the same time, I never gave up spirituality, the mysticism and magic of being in the moment. – Greg Day

————————∇————————

Chicago, IL (USA)
Milwaukee, WI (USA)

Oddly, I did not have any hardcore religious upbringing. My parents were part of a very liberal Protestant kind of thing where it was more of a community activity, where you went to church on Sundays. It was a nice community, not particularly oppressive. It wasn't conservative by any means. When I was in junior high school, I figured I was different from the other little boys and I had this issue to deal with. I was told that religion would take care of this. This problem with homosexuality would go away. At the time there was a very conservative Pentecostal movement that was sweeping through a lot of the more liberal Protestant and the Catholic Churches, called the Charismatic Movement. They were what we think of as the modern Pentecostal mega churches. That was the start of all that. I got involved with that. I was 14 at the time, when most kids were sneaking off to go drinking or drugging or clubbing, I was trying to get out and go to these all-night Bible studies. Prayer meetings where you'd speak in tongues and dance around. In terms of my religious upbringing, that was something I did to myself as a way to deal with the whole gay issue. I could spend hours telling you about that but let's fast forward to the end. After I was 29, I thought, "I've given this since I was 14 years old and I've done everything that everybody asked me to do. I've been a good little soldier. I haven't done anything to violate the rules that I was given." I confronted the elders in my church about that and they didn't know what to do, so they finally said, "We're going to ship you off to a place that is an ex-gay ministry. So I had to drive up to Milwaukee for this, I couldn't be seen in Chicago. There I would go to my homosexual anonymous meetings ... HA. Which was styled after AA obviously. I would do all this stuff to try to pray the gay away. They became very upset with me because the way those organizations work is that they pray on someone doing something outside of their little system. So either you had sex with a guy, or you did drugs, or anything they could latch onto. They said, "Well that's the problem. That's why this is not working for you, because you're not following our plan." They would come to me and say, "Are you doing drugs, having sex with men." ... "No, I'm 100%, I'm praying when you're telling me to pray. I'm going to all the meetings. I'm doing everything to the letter." Finally, they got very mad and said, "You're not cooperating" and threw me out. It was at that point that I realized there was nothing wrong with me but there was something terribly wrong with my theology. I'm the kind of person where it takes me forever to make a decision about something, but once I do, I go out the door like gangbusters. So when I came out of the closet, I came out with all guns blazing. I came out in June 1987, by October of '87 I was on the March on Washington leading chants against the Reagan White House and dating a guy that started a chapter of Queer Nation in Los Angeles. – Thomas Stribling

———————∇———————

Cathedral City, CA (USA)

Some people think it was a religious upbringing but to me it was more of an acting job. My parents acted like the good Christians. My parents were in the front row of the church every single Sunday. But once you got home it was totally a different world. There was a lot of abuse, so they were not the good Christians that they portrayed in public. We started out Lutheran, my brother wanted to become a monk, which threw the family until turmoil. Then he became a Southern Baptist. Then my mother became a Southern Baptist. So they went off to be Southern Baptists. My father and mother divorced, so my father became nothing and I continued being Lutheran for a while. Then my brother went from Southern Baptist to being Mormon. Then he would pop back and forth from Catholic church to Mormon, to whoever could do the best for him. This is what I mean by acting. – David Hardy

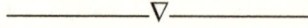

—————▽—————

Fontana, CA (USA)

I was raised very strict old-school Catholic and I didn't believe anything they were teaching me as a child, even today as an adult, I don't believe in it. I consider myself more Wiccan today, than I ever would be a Catholic. A lot of my family, except for my cousin who lives here, is either Catholic, or my mom's side of the family, they married Mormons. They shrug me because of all the tattoos I've had on my body. And they consider me to be a devil worshipper. I'm like, "Ok, whatever." – Marcous

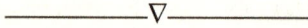

—————▽—————

Chicago, IL (USA)

I was raised Catholic but ditched it when I was old enough to know better. Spiritual and believe the good in all people unless they try to cut me off on LSD [Lake Shore Drive]. – MrZor

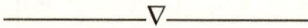

—————▽—————

Joplin, MO (USA)

My mother and I were never into going to church until I was at least in late middle school into early freshman year of high school. Most of the time, I would go for a while before mom and I would stop and then go to another church a few years later. Even now, I still go to church with mom – even if I refuse to admit it. To me, the church we go to sort of portrays that being LGBTQ was still considered a sin and while I can't say they're wrong – it's not exactly a valid reason to deny them from being welcomed into a community when the religion preaches to love your neighbor as yourself. I feel like Christians as a group could be doing a lot better aside from pushing beliefs that being LGBTQ and Christian is impossible – let alone teach those out of the Bible when you take into consideration that not a lot of people would be willing to accept that religion. It feels like that while I can attend like a regular individual, I feel restricted on showing my LGBTQ affirmations whether it's in the form of a button or a t-shirt. To me, I feel like a church should be more inclusive of people and not just wearing a fake mask of being such in real life and online they would turn around and do something that feels like the complete opposite. I've only been able to relate to the Christian religion since I live in an area of what is called the "Bible Belt" in the states, but I've noticed that some religions can get pretty brutal on the treatment of LGBTQ individuals. But going back to Christianity for the question, I tend to have mixed feelings as an asexual individual. I can understand the celibacy before marriage – but when it comes to specific people that are aces but are sex repulsive (whereas I feel like someone that favors safe sex between two individuals), they just want to be loved and are capable of showing affection to their partner that isn't sex. I'm someone that has been through a rather rocky childhood and other than just being naive into doing such a thing, I can't rule out trying it again with someone that I deeply care for and trust. It gets rocky when we're given the speech on make more babies when some of us, like myself, are on the fence on having kids. I was one of those people that didn't like kids and even as a kid myself, I rather avoid contact with other kids. Sure, it would be nice to find someone that loves me for being a unique individual and such – but the breaking point would be if he's not willing to go without having offspring of any sort. I've considered adoption as there are some kids that are in need of a loving set of parents, but at the same time, I think that should be a decision that my significant other and I would make together as a couple. I just don't think that a church that excludes people based on their sins or that they are LGBTQ is really a church that welcomes everyone. – Julie W

————————▽————————

Wichita, KS (USA)

I was raised Catholic, in a German Catholic community in Kansas. Everybody was Catholic, we even had nuns in the school. I went to public school and the nuns taught there. My first grade teacher was Sr. Bernard, the second year was Sr. Patrick, and the third grade was Sr. Christine. At that time there was three hours of fasting before going into communion. So we had to take our breakfast with us in little lunch pails. I remember helping my mom making the breakfast and putting it in the lunch pail before we went to school. Then we had a hot lunch program at the school.

I didn't have any pedophile priests. Actually, the priest was seeing the housekeeper, so that wasn't an issue. We had the same Catholic priest all the way through high school, college. The man never left. I think he may have told the diocese, "If you move me, I'll quit." The nuns weren't mean. I think because I had a priest friend who was gay and a mentor ... the Catholic Church at one point was starting to get a little more liberal with their views, then of course John Paul II came in and everything became more conservative again. I remember when I was a kid, all the nuns had habits, then they did away it's the habits. They were wearing regular dresses and you wouldn't know a nun from a lay person. How it affected me as being a gay person? I started working away from some of the beliefs. As far as confession was concerned, I didn't do confession. After all those years it was ridiculous, I thought. Did I delve into the beliefs of the Catholic Church? No, I live by what allowed my life to function normally and allowed myself to express my feelings. – Guy Seliers

——————▽——————

Santa Fe, NM (USA)

I used to go to church with my sister because she was not allowed to go if I didn't go. I was older. My mother figured I talked a lot so if anything happened, I would say so. My sister and her girlfriends realized that by bribing me with candy and ice scream or gum I would stay quiet. That was the only time I had anything to do with the church. I don't believe in organized religions because – it is only my feeling and point of view and nothing to do with anyone else – I believe it's all about control and there's no need to control anything or anybody. – Juan-manuel Alonso

——————▽——————

Imlay City, MI (USA)

It depends on who my mother pissed off. I grew up Episcopalian for a while and then we went to Lutheran, Wisconsin Cynic, that was another form of Lutheran. I remember they were so strict they didn't even believe in the Girl Scouts. We went to church every Sunday. I hated going to church. I found it boring. I didn't like to dress up. I was a little fat kid, so I didn't like to dress up, wear anything tight fitting. I would rather stay home and watch old Abbott and Costello reruns, old movies, *Frankenstein* or whatever. When I was a teen my parents joined a church where they didn't really have a church yet and we were meeting in a Christian school gymnasium, metal seats, and it was freezing. I hated it. So there were a lot of religious undertones ... did we sit and pray before each meal? No, that happened at Easter, Thanksgiving and Christmas. We prayed then, but not any other time. My parents got divorced in 1979. My mother would tell me how my father would have sores on his body because he committed adultery with another woman and pus would come out of his skin. She was all about that.

But I heard a lot of anti-gay jokes. I came from a very bigoted family. The anti-gay was, "Oh it's all in the Bible." There was my brother and I in the family. I didn't understand what I was, but at 14 I was fooling around with my first guy. Well, being an adopted kid, I thought they were going to send me back. It was often spoken of if we got in trouble. "The lord's going to tell me to send you back." Then my brother, who was adopted from a different family, is also gay. My parents won the Homo Lotto, as I say. So when we came out it was not a good situation. I came out first and my stepfather was extremely homophobic and caused a lot of problems in voicing a lot of things my mother never let on about. I didn't find out until later on. So much so that when my mom died, he didn't put us in her obituary. I had to call the funeral home after it was brought to my attention. I phoned and said, is there a reason my brother and I are not in the obituary? The funeral home director, who I've known for years, said, "Well, you know how your stepfather is and how he feels about you two boys." I said, "I'm appalled. Jesus tells me you need to put my brother and I in the obituary and this is what it's going to say." I dealt with a lot of that from my mother. During the AIDS crisis, I came home briefly for a while before going to broadcasting school. I lived at home and my mother would not allow me to wash my clothes in her washer and dryer. I'm negative but she thought everybody was contaminated. So I look back at that and a lot of it was religious based. I would try to educate her. After I came out, she talked to the minister. The minister would say, "Oh he's wrong, tell your son this." He was a really big influence on my mother in a negative way. It really screwed my mother up. – Greg R. Baird

———————▽———————

Chicago, IL (USA)

I had a very serious religious upbringing. I went to Catholic grade school where I was taught by the Felician Nuns followed by going to an all boy's Catholic high school taught by the Christian Brothers of Ireland. Those Christian Brothers really took pleasure using a leather strap to discipline their student boys. I ended my education years going to a Catholic College.
Given all of my early years embroiled in catechism I ended up flirting with being a Christian Brother in both the Franciscan and Jesuit religious orders.

Today I am no longer a Catholic, practicing or otherwise: however, I continue to be a spiritual person adhering to the teachings of Jesus and Buddha. – Mark Contorno

———————▽———————

Lawton, OK (USA)

I was brought up Southern Baptist. I was brain washed. It has affected me because when I went to visit my mom, she introduced me to the new pastor. She had talked to him prior to me coming in. I left home because my parents found out I was gay. I felt that if I wasn't accepted at the Southern Baptist churches, then why should I go. I started going to the Metropolitan Community Church founded by Troy Perry. Those churches, rather than the Baptist churches. – David Hayes

———————▽———————

Tallahassee, FL (USA)
Redwood Valley, CA (USA)

This is a big question in my continuing journey. Both my father and maternal great-grandfather were Southern Baptist preachers in North Florida's Bible Belt from the 1880s into the 1990s. My blood family continues to follow that religion, and others. When I was 18, after coming out and getting busted for drug charges, my father confronted me with the question, "I want to know something, are you queer?" and soon later told me how he had prayed for a son before I was born, and if his god gave him a son, he would raise his son to be a Southern Baptist preacher.

I was the best church son growing up. I excelled at the Bible drills, "walked the aisle" as a preteen to be "born again," even taught Sunday school. I had started leaving the church as a teen, when our junior high schools in Tallahassee were first integrated racially, and I began to look my fellow black classmates in the eyes, and finally see the hypocrisy of my family's Baptist church, while my dad and other church deacons were standing guard at the front door of the church to make sure black families wouldn't enter. (As if any black families wanted to come inside). The juxtaposition and hypocrisy opened my eyes and heart to the harm organized religion does when it veers from the messages of love proclaimed by Jesus Christ in their Bible.

I continue to deal with the religious hypocrisy to this day, with some cousins, and other relatives who are religious or political zealots. They pray for me and "hate" my "lifestyle." I show them what love really means, and remind them that the messages of Jesus that I learned about include the outcasts, the refugees, and even the prostitutes, and that Jesus never mentioned homosexuality (or abortion), only love.

I can clearly see that my social and political activism throughout the past several decades, and continuing today, are rooted in what I learned from the Baptist teachings about "love one another" and "do unto others as you would that they would do," and about rejecting and speaking out against the harm organized religion does in the political arena in our country. – T. Lark Letchworth

———————▽———————

Sacramento, CA (USA)
Davis, CA (USA)
San Diego CA (USA)
Cathedral City, CA (USA)
Eureka Springs, AR (USA)

My Dad was raised Jewish but was an atheist from Brooklyn. My Mom was a Christian from Florida. They told us three boys we were welcome to attend Church or Temple if we wanted to. None of us took up the offer. I think in spite of not having that formal religious upbringing imposed on me I considered myself a Christian as a kid simply because we are inundated with Christianity in America from a young age. As a child starting to deal with the concept of being gay and not being able to change, and feeling that most religions viewed me as lower than pond scum, it no doubt had a huge impact on my self-worth and self-confidence as a child. I imagine it also contributed to me almost committing suicide at age 20.

Since I came out at 21, I chose to learn from how I had dealt with religion and had let it impact me. I took a much more critical look at questioning all authority. It made me examine the power of Groupthink, cults and the emotions of fear and guilt.

The only "miracle" I've observed is that I somehow managed to be born in spite of my Dad having the audacity to question my Mom on their honeymoon as to how she could believe in God. – Paul Harris

———————▽———————

Sylvania, New South Wales (Australia)
Campbelltown, New South Wales (Australia)
Leura, City of Blue Mountains (Australia)
Melbourne, Victoria (Australia)

My father was a (non-practising) Catholic, and my mother a (non-practising) Methodist. I was born in Sylvania, a very WASP (White, Anglo-Saxon, Protestant) area to the south of Sydney. The prominent religion there was the Congregational church (which became absorbed into the Uniting church). As a way of fitting into this newly developing area in the 1950s, my parents started attending the Congregational church at Sylvania Heights, so when I was born I was christened into that church, with our husband and wife neighbours ... who lived opposite us ... and were stalwarts of that church, as my Godparents. However, religion and church attendance were never forced on me, and I was left to make my own decisions regarding it all. In 1967 we moved from the area, and I was sent to a Catholic boarding school in Campbelltown (Marist Brothers St. Gregory's Agricultural College). Having only encountered the simplicity of Protestantism up until this time, the Catholic religion left me awe-struck with its rituals, colour and richness. In 1967 I converted, with no resistance from my father (my mother was out of the picture at this stage). I started having some contact with the Discalced Carmelite Fathers in Minto, and started thinking I may have a vocation to the religious life. In 1976 I joined a newly founded contemplative religious order called The Community of St Thomas More, who had a monastery in Leura. They had a lot of contact with the St. John of God Brothers in Richmond, and through this contact I came to realise just how many gay people there were in religious orders. By this stage I was questioning where I was with my own sexuality, and started asking myself if perhaps my religious "calling" was perhaps more a way of having to deal with it by hiding myself away in a remote monastery, where an active sex life was something I didn't have to confront. I also found that the monastic life robbed me of my independence, and my free-thinking ways, so now having doubts about why I was actually doing this ... I left. It was also a time when I was starting to dissect and evaluate a lot of what I'd been taught about belief and doctrine. I mean ... virgin births? Someone arising from the dead? Someone floating up to heaven? Holy Spirits? Indulgences? A white, Western Christ? Our looking at a book ... and using to base our beliefs, ethics and morality ... whose origins couldn't be firmly established, and was written for a Jewish community living in the Middle East, and who every Pope, king, and new evangelist edited, added-to, and subtracted from, to suit their own ends? Priestly celibacy, not established until the 12th century, and only then because priests were passing on their money to their wives and children instead of the church? Angels ... who never appeared until the 5th century? I looked at the poor around me, and the wealth of the Church and it's hierarchy; the Crusades; the Inquisitions; decadent Popes; sexual abuse ... witnessed personally at boarding school; the hypocrisy; the double standards; the prejudice and stigma; the inability of the church to move forward; people depriving themselves and leading lives of miserable austerity in the name of religion; and a lot, lot more. And I thought ... this is a crock of shit, one of the world's great con jobs ... and tossed it. As covered in one of the above questions, I did use Catholicism to assist with my coming out by joining Acceptance in Melbourne ... I won't go into it again for your sake. Funnily enough, I managed retail stores for one of Australia's leading Catholic retailers

(Pellegrini & Co Pty Ltd) for around seven years, but one didn't have to be religious to do that job. I've seen so much hate, prejudice, discrimination, stigma and violence and murder committed by so-called religions (especially fundamentalist sects) churches and organisations against the LGBT community, that I couldn't … in all conscience … follow any of the world's major mainstream religions. The hate and vitriol aimed squarely at the gay community during the HIV/AIDS pandemic was so vile, so divisive, so unforgiving that one could never believe in the concept of all-loving, all-forgiving God … because all this was done in his name! It's like believing in fairy tales … you get to an age where you have to assess these concepts of God and the hateful following that belief has generated … and you would have to find it wanting! Ever since my teen years I have had a love of Asian cultures, and have studied it extensively over the years. This included a more-than-passing interest in Buddhism, how it is not a "religion" in the true sense of the word, but a lifestyle ideology. It was not started by someone who claimed to be a god, or a messenger of god, or the son of god … but by someone who was just a person seeking to better their life through simple concepts, and practises. I am slowly making my way down the Buddhist road, and my life is the better for it. – Tim Alderman

―――――∇―――――

St. Cloud, MN (USA)

I am Jewish, and while I did not get a religious education as a child, I definitely learned a great deal about Jewish history and culture. I saw how many Jewish celebrities were LGBTQ+ even back in the 1970s-'80s, so I knew it was not a strange thing and not even a terrible thing for non-religious Jewish people. When I was growing up was when women and LGBTQ+ people were starting to become rabbis in the more liberal congregations, and when LGBTQ+ Jewish folx were establishing their own synagogues, religious study groups, and community organizations.

I knew that there was a place for me. I remember my parents taking me to see *Yentl* when I was a kid and how much that movie impacted me. I read the original Isaac Bashevis Singer story after that, and learned that Yentl was indeed either lesbian or a transman at that time – Singer had no words to describe her – but unlike in the movie, Yentl actually *wanted* to be a man. And she wanted that regardless of her interest in religious study.

The worst thing, really, for a Jewish person to do is to give up one's Jewish identity or be ashamed of being Jewish. We take great pride in all that we have accomplished over millennia of oppression, systemic discrimination, genocide, and so on. We are still here. And it is the same for LGBTQ+ people. I am both. We always existed. The cranky cishet folx in Biblical times wanted to label us as sinful and unnatural, but with the exception of the ultra-religious communities, LGBTQ+ folx are accepted in the Jewish community and often are the most beloved. So often the LGBTQ+ folx are the ones who care the most about the religion and traditions, and they are often the ones who teach Hebrew school and keep the traditions alive. Our religion, history, and community building helps us to endure, and steels us for what is to come. – Rachel Wexelbaum

―――――∇―――――

Palestine, TX (USA)

I was raised in the Methodist Church in a small East Texas town, attending Sunday School and church most Sundays. Around my junior year of high school, I started attending the Roman Catholic Church with my best friend and his family, as had begun taking catechism instruction for conversion, but something didn't seem quite right and another friend suggested I attend the Episcopal Church with him. I found my "home" at least for a while. Once I went away to college, I stopped attending church and it was only later when I turned thirty, that I returned to regular church attendance. It was also the time I pursued "a call" went to seminary and was eventually ordained an Episcopal priest. That was the loneliest time of my life. In the 80's, even the Episcopal Church was not ready to openly accept gay clergy. So, again, I was in the closet, alone, longing for a relationship and it didn't help that the cute young parish sexton (custodian) had made a pass at me and got me into bed (once), but then went back to his partner, leaving me not just alone but freshly reminded of what I was missing. So, I left the parish ministry and moved on. My "spiritual odyssey" continues, but that's enough for now. – Michael Pickel

―――――∇―――――

Chicago, IL (USA)

Irish, Catholic, alcoholic and dysfunctional. My family of origin covered all the bases. I can still recall the Latin Mass from the 1950s and I think that is where I began my lifelong love affair with the Broadway musical.

When I finally gave up on the USA and expatriated in 2015, my sister gave me a rosary that belonged to our dear, sainted mother. I put it in my backpack which I stowed as carry-on for my trans-Atlantic trip. About midway across the pond, we encountered some serious turbulence. I whipped out that rosary and began a frantic decade. I may have been a long-lapsed Catholic, but I still remembered all the words. Hail Mary! - David Clayton

———————∇———————

Glenview, IL (USA)

My religious upbringing was Roman Catholic. Its essential teaching was that being gay was a sin and I was not allowed to be myself. When I confronted myself and told my confessor, he told me I would lead a miserable life. I was suicidal for a number of years. I walked away from the Church and pursued more liberal spiritual philosophies, such as Taoism which does not pass judgment on the nature of a person's being. Some religions have evolved to acceptance of LGBTQ individuals. I have since embraced Reform Judaism and am content, even challenged with that choice. However, I still study all traditions to see the commonalities in philosophy. I walk away from those that cannot accept the LGBTQ community and will not invest my energy in them. And I did prove my confessor wrong. – Yehuda Jacobi

———————∇———————

Delavan, WI (USA)
Denver, CO (USA)

I was raised Catholic. Mom was so proud my brother and I were altar boys. And I grooved on the Jesus vibe, which I still love.
But like most queers, I felt condemned by the Church. Kind of a "wink-wink nod-nod" relationship where I saw queer organists and yet knew they were only allowed in the Church for their talent and service.
These days I talk about my awakening to Wicca when I lived in Denver in the 1980's. And my expansion of male Jesus love to encompass the awesome depth and power of Goddess love.
The "harm none" philosophy of Wicca continues to guide me. I am a solitary witch, as I have given up cloak flapping and following orders and rules. I enjoy my personal communion and connection with the Goddess and God. – Tony Earl

———————∇———————

King, NC (USA)

I grew up in a conservative church in the '50s and '60s. I met my wife when we were both eight years old in a Sunday School classroom. We were married at age eighteen.
     The church certainly taught that being LGBTQ was wrong, even worse – an abomination. So, it goes without saying that I remained closeted.

I thought by getting married and starting a family that my gay feelings would simply go away. They actually did for a time – especially when my wife and I had three children right away. Our busy lives left little room to think about much else.

But after a few years, I crossed the line and I had my first same-sex encounter. I began to live a double life. This craziness and self-loathing brought on by the church's teachings led me to attempt suicide. That event brought everything crashing down and I finally had to begin dealing with who I actually was. I made the decision to come out of the closet despite all of the ramifications of doing such a thing would involve.

The church initiated a court trial by the elders and ultimately a public excommunication of me from the congregation. – Ron Cline

―――――――∇――――――

Charlottetown, Prince Edward Island (Canada)

I was brought up in a Presbyterian household, although only my mother and I attended church on a regular basis (I'm an only child). That upbringing emphasized my feeling of not belonging, and though the church has attempted to make positive strides towards queer acceptance in recent years, my personal belief is that it's too late. We've moved on and the church is irrelevant to me now. – Dave Stewart

―――――――∇――――――

San Diego, CA (USA)

I was brought up Episcopal, but I didn't care. In high school, shortly after I started struggling with coming to terms with the fact that I was trans, it became more difficult. I ended up in a youth group, a Baptist, conservative youth group. They told me that God said I couldn't do this. That sounded great because nobody else was doing this … if God says I can't do it then I won't. As I went to church, I was ready to just dive in. Some of my best friends are still … They aren't all Christian anymore. It was very much about keeping the dysphoria and misery of not being who I was, not liking who it was I liked, under wraps. I could do it in patches at a time. But the moment I stopped, it was right back. It never went away. It never got easier. It never subsided. I can remember one night – and this haunts me because it was one of the first times that I saw someone who was trans – on a religious program. Late night. And they had de-transitioned. They said how horrible it was and how God hated it. I saw this person as me because I didn't want to have to de-transition. At the same time, it was just misery inside. – Serafine Sawyer

248

—————————∇—————————

Des Moines, IA (USA)

I was a "cradle Catholic" but was unaffected by dogma. I was immune to guilt and shame, I think. Later in life I became a monk but my abbot knew I wasn't there for sexual activity. I was very open about being queer and his attitude was that in those matters, it was better not to come between someone's soul and "god." I am not an atheist, but I reject reward/punishment spirituality and the notion of a cosmic meter maid. I know some about other religions, but I see religion as a commercial enterprise and various notions of "god" as more human than divine. – Sr. Freida Peoples aka DJ Chrysler Sheldon

—————————∇—————————

Watseka, IL (USA)
Minocqua, WI (USA)

No. My parents dropped my sisters and I off to church for a couple years when we were 10 and 7, but being in small towns, I believe it was a hassle driving us into town, so it just stopped. I am SO THANKFUL for that. I'm not easily persuaded by something that's not right (for me anyway) according to my intuition which has been very strong all my life, and happy that my siblings were not brainwashed. I do believe that it at least had a positive influence because that was just one more organization that could NOT say it was wrong to me! – Sherrie Howe

—————————∇—————————

Fort Lauderdale, FL (USA)

I grew up in a mixed faith household (Jewish and Lutheran) We were brought up Lutheran (at least I was, by the time the others were old enough to attend Sunday school, my parents had five kids and had given up on any kind of parenting, including religious training). We were kind of self-sustaining. – Rick Karlin

—————————∇—————————

Karachi, Sindh (Pakistan)

I never grew up in a very religious conservative Muslim family, my parents were moderate and middle-class folks. I was born in Abu Dhabi, UAE, I was 10 years old when I'd to come to Karachi, Pakistan just after 9/11 and much of my life I was raised there. I wasn't happy at first, I'd to leave my school and friends to a country that was quite new to me.

I was raised in a tough neighborhood; I witnessed a lot of violence and was bullied a lot. I remember in a span of five years alone, there must have been 10 suicide attacks and some happened quite close to my home. Our home once got attacked by rival political factions, the front of the house was smeared with bullets and me & my family had to take shelter inside to be safe for the entire day.

In all the ethnic and sectarian violence I witnessed and the homophobic bullying I'd gone through, I started questioning religion. I questioned the scriptures (Quran/Hadiths) and did a lot of research of my own on comparative religions. I've always felt a spiritual connection to nature, for me the conventional organized religions with all its homophobia, misogyny, and racism didn't attract much love and I was able to abandon religion and be an atheist at a very young age. Still though, I feel a spiritual connection to the natural world, the teachings of the great Sufis, and gurus of South Asia who have influenced a more progressive outlook of the world around me. – Salman

WERE YOU BULLIED IN SCHOOL AND IF SO, WHAT FORM DID IT TAKE?

Lewiston, NY (USA)

Yes, I was bullied for being short. At one point I was extremely short, I didn't have a growth spurt. And I couldn't swim. I remember it was a turning point, they took me in the pool and they made fun of me because I was so skinny and I had negative buoyancy. They threw me off the diving board, everybody laughed. It was one of those "Carrie" moments. It could have changed my life in a very bad way. Then they laughed at me and said, "Try it again." So they did it again and they laughed. Then they said, "OK that's enough." I went to the end of the diving board and put my hands up into the air like I was doing a performance. I threw myself off. They had to rescue me again. Then when I came out of the water, I did a big bow. I made the joke on me. Then everybody took me into the locker room on their shoulders. All of a sudden everything changed. I thought, "Wow! Shit happens, it's how you do it. It has to be funny." Then I ran for student office and I got it. I made fun of my shortness and then I grew. – James Scalfani

———————∇———————

Chicago, IL (USA)

I was bullied mercilessly in middle school, in ways that were so bad a bully even got suspended. In high school I was mostly ignored, except for one significant event. When I was a junior in high school, one of my class assignments was to devote 40 hours to a new creative endeavor. I decided to start making lipsync videos. One of the first ones I decided to do was for

Lady Gaga's *Christmas Tree*. I bought a sexy elf costume and a pair of heels, and hung festive decorations around my house. This was my first time "crossdressing" and I was euphoric making this campy, suggestive video.

When I uploaded *Christmas Tree* it spontaneously went viral. In the 12 days it was initially online it got over two-thousand views! Everybody in my school watched it, some even interrupting classes to play it on the projector. Overnight I went from peaceful anonymity to public figure, with all the harassment that comes with it. Everyday people shouted at me in the halls. The most frightening experience was after PE one day when we were in the locker room changing, all the other guys began chanting, a mix of "Lady Gaga" and "faggot." After that the school gave me a personal security guard escort in the locker room for the rest of the semester. I would have been fine with all of this, because it meant my video was a success, but the people close to me grew concerned. Apparently, I had begun to receive death threats; they weren't said directly to me, but a teacher overheard a student say he wanted to kill me. I haven't a clue if he was reprimanded for that, but I certainly was. My parents and teachers freaked out, forcing me to delete the video. Then my mother made me promise to never dress that way again. My brief shining moment of gender exploration was squashed, and I was shoved back into the closet for several more years. Honestly, I'm far more hurt by my family's reaction than any of the bullying from this time. They may have called me names, but I was finally getting to be myself, and was on my way to becoming the next viral sensation. All that was taken away from me. If I were allowed to keep dressing up maybe I would have learned sooner that I was trans. I don't know if I can ever forgive them for that. – C'est Kevvie (Wilhelmina)

—————▽—————

Detroit, MI (USA)

I never had any problems in St. Luke's (1st-6th grade), or at St. Aloysius (7th – 8th grade), which was kind of odd, seeing as I was one of the less than five black kids in the entire school at St. Luke, and one of the handful at Aloysius. However, I ended up going to St. Martin de Porres, a highly accredited all black school in Detroit. At first, I was really excited to go to this school, but my excitement turned into fear very quickly. Almost immediately, the other black kids took notice of the way I spoke and decided I was an Uncle Tom, (a black man who wants to be white) and they taunted me constantly, and then the taunts became threats and I did get beat up a few times. My locker had Oreo written on it more than once, and even in class, kids called me Uncle Tom. I was never really injured and for a couple of months I kept all of it from my parents, but at one point I got so mad at the constant torture I was enduring that I stood up and turned my school desk over on the kid next to me, who was having a good time razzing me about my white boy shoes. Needless to say, we both wound up in the principal's office where I spilled the beans about what I had been going through, crying the whole time. Mr. Dulin, the lay principal, called my parents and they both had to come down to school. By the time they got there, I had decided my life was in danger and that I had to leave that school if I were to survive. Well my grades were good enough (something else I was teased about) to get me into Cass Technical High School, a college prep high school where I majored in Performing Arts (*quel surprise!*) and it was there I began blossoming into the creature I am now. – Terence Smith (Joan Jett Blakk)

——————▽——————

Texas (USA)

In my rural small-town school, I was not bullied, but saw peers who were gay being bullied. Popular jocks in my high school would bait these young men to perform oral sex on them and then another jock would come in and urinate on them, leaving them with wet, smelly clothes – so they would have to leave school. These same young men were talked about and ostracized. As a result, I totally repressed my same-sex attraction for years because I didn't want this to happen to me. – Anonymous

——————▽——————

Kentucky (USA)
Tennessee (USA)

Oh, yes, I was bullied. It took the form of ridicule, which, over time, becomes emotional abuse. Only one time was I assaulted, and it was a single slap in the face from a boy jealous of my having fun with his girlfriend. – Oran Walker

——————▽——————

South Bend, IN (USA)

A little bit. When I was around the 6th grade, because I had more of an interest in young men, I displayed more flamboyant gesturing for a few years there. There was an assumption that I was girly, though I'm a pretty big guy. I always thought that was odd, but it's interesting what kids pick up on. They taunt you with names. One of the things about that, in some ways it was a really bad experience and, in some ways, it made me question who I was. All these kids were saying things about me and … when you're young, you say, "I'm going to be the opposite of what kids are saying about me." But at some level, you think, "Well, is that true? Am I like this? And what does that mean?" As I got older, I thought about that a lot more. I thought about that as the relationship between "What does that mean?" to who I was as a man. "What does that mean, what does being a man mean? – Steve

—————▽—————

Chicago, IL (USA)

It was in high school and it was jealousy is what it was. Being gay, I've always known that I was gay, even though I wasn't out in 1980 at high school, I had a lot of female friends. They were all very attractive. This one boy in particular was infuriated by the fact that girls wouldn't talk to him but would spend time with me. But I think even at the age of 14 girls know who's threatening and who's non-threatening. Even though they don't have a word for it yet, they understand that you're not going to jump on them or grab their breasts or try to put your tongue down their throat. That's why I had the friends I had. But he was terribly jealous of me. The whole four years he just could not get over the fact that he couldn't attract anyone and there I was … and I was not interested in a single one of them beyond friendship. – Mike

—————▽—————

Nashville, TN (USA)
Birmingham, AL (USA)

I was bullied in junior high school and again in college.

Nashville: When I was a young teen, it took primarily physical form, being shoved, being punched, having my books knocked out of my arms, being spit on, having the metal door of a locker slammed into my head. Of course, I was always chosen last for teams. I also had my pocket picked and other things stolen. This had a racial component, as almost everyone who attacked me was a different race from mine.

This went on for an entire school year. No one helped me. No teachers took a stand against it. No one was ever punished or held accountable for bullying me.

Birmingham: In college I was bullied by the Baptist boys in my dorm. At first there were pranks like turning out the light on me or pouring cold water on me when I was in the shower. This escalated to having my room trashed and vandalized on several occasions. I complained to the adult residence hall staff, and was told that I deserved it, it was my fault, and I should stop provoking them. Needless to say, I had done nothing to provoke anyone. Except be myself.

One night a crowd of them threw a blanket over my head, picked me up, and carried me over to the edge of the second-floor balcony, swinging me and saying they were going to throw me over. I was terrified. This was only stopped by a resident assistant from another wing who saw the commotion, came over, and broke up the crowd. I left the dorm that night, a week before exams, stayed with a friend, and only returned after everyone else had moved out to pick up what was left of my things.

I managed to move to an apartment off campus for my senior year. No one ever admitted to me that they had been the ones carrying out the campaign of bullying and terror. I graduated with honors. – Bert Thompson

———————▽———————

Fayetteville, AR USA)

No, not at all and I think that's amazing, simply because not only was I gay but being a person with a disability, sometimes people who are physically challenged are bullied. I seriously had wonderful parents who instilled self-worth that I was really a confident person. The funny thing when I was in 3rd grade teachers used to write on your last report card a little summary of your year. My 3rd grade teacher summed it really well. She wrote, "Renny is such a happy child, he always seems to be so pleased with himself." I just love that, so no I was never bullied. I could always make people laugh. Maybe because I bullied myself a little bit, before someone else had the chance to do it. I made light of my physical challenges before anyone else. It's like the fat kid … the fat kid becomes the class clown. I was the class clown. – Renny

———————▽———————

Wauconda, IL (USA)

Of course, I was bullied in school. It took the form of name calling, and some physical contact but not much in that way. I think what was most obvious to me throughout my entire school life up to high school my senior year was, not fitting in. I never felt like I was included with others, I was always kind of the outsider. I was not the healthiest of kids. Allergies/Asthma made participation in sports, or activities of that nature. But my senior year in high school, my family hosted the first foreign exchange student that had come to Wauconda, and all of a sudden, I went from zero to hero, because everyone wanted Wolfram to be a part of their circle. I still am in touch with him and he came back to Wauconda for our 40th reunion in 2016. It was fun to catch up and that was really an awesome time to go to my reunion with my boyfriend Steve … who the girls I went to school with were like … Wow … and Wolfram … yeah it was very satisfying after all those bully years and I think that the folks from high school finally realized that maybe it was them that missed the party, as a majority of them are still in Wauconda, and have not ventured far from that life. – Dean Ogren

———————∇———————

Virginia (USA)

In Catholic grade school the other boys would pull me away from the urinal, exposing my dick, and laugh. I was also picked on for being a nerdy kid. Funny thing is that it never occurred to me that it was odd that I was the only male in the Art Club in Catholic High School. – Lars von Keitz

———————∇———————

Southern California, (USA)

Several times, but it wasn't because they thought I might be gay. They were just mean. One was an older girl in grade school and another time it was a small group of older boys in ninth grade who stole my wrist watch and tried to dunk my head into a toilet in the locker room. I never told anyone because I suspected the boys were gang members. I also felt embarrassed. – Gary Borgstedt

———————∇———————

Roselle, IL (USA)

I went to St. Walter's Catholic School in Illinois. Looking back at it, I was bullied with the tacit approval of the nuns and priests. They saw what was going on. One tried to stomp it down a little bit, but it didn't happen, it made me a total depressive underachiever. By the time of my sophomore year of high school, my mother said, "You can fail at the public schools just as well as you can fail at a private school and it's a lot cheaper." Again, I was bullied incredibly in grade school and high school. I'm not an atheist, I'm more of a hopeful agnostic. And that's from the Greek literal translation "unable to know." – Drew

———————∇———————

Chicago, IL (USA)

I was never bullied for being gay because I was not out. It was the 1980s, I graduated high school in 1991. I was not a popular kid. I was not a jock, wasn't a super-smart kid. I didn't fall into any of the stereotypes. I was just a regular kid. I wouldn't say there was bullying per se but there always … you're an adolescent male, there's always going to be someone who tries to up with you. Other than the occasional schoolyard fight … no bullying really. – Jeff Ramone

————————∇————————

Waverly, IA (USA)

I wasn't bullied at school except for my late changing, high pitched voice. My anti-intellectual classmates couldn't afford to alienate me if they wanted help with their homework. – Robert Beck

————————∇————————

Rome, NY (USA)

No, I wasn't bullied in school because I thought I was a little different and I tried to keep a low profile. I actually did very boyish masculine things. I played baseball, I hung out with guys, I did the guy thing. Nobody knew my other life, how I felt inside. I tried to blend in with the boys, so growing up, I can't say I was ever bullied. The only time I was bullied was when I was in my 50s and 60s when I was out. That was more homophobic bullying than anything else. Not growing up, I tried to keep that part of my life a secret because growing up in the '50s and '60s, it wasn't something you were proud of or could share. – Andee

————————∇————————

North Carolina (USA)

Just the usual kind of stuff. I've got red hair, so people were always rubbing by hair and stuff like that. I was always the awkward, unathletic kid. I never felt bullied because I was gay. I felt bullied because I was a nerdish, bookish, guy. – Randy

————————∇————————

London (UK)

laughing out loud No, I wasn't bullied. I was the school Social Director – the most powerful post for pupils at the school. – Louis Richard de Bourbon de Parme et de Savoie, Prince de la Pau

————————▽————————

Chicago, IL (USA)

I was not bullied in school, for this reason ONLY! My older brother, a leader in our church youth group, was a gang member and a savage bully. Everyone in school was terrified of him. Once a guy picked on me in fun, my brother found out and beat him bloody. In school I did not even have a name. I was only known as Tony's little brother. – Philip Bernal

————————▽————————

Rockford, IL (USA)

When I was a kid I was bullied. Not for being gay, but for being a bigger kid and having braces. I was called "Fat Pat" or "Metalmouth Murphy," among other things. At the time it was very hurtful, but I was able to learn to grow my thick skin, and let things slide away. I still carry this mentality to this day, which sometimes makes me standoffish but once you get through the tough outer shell, I am warm and loving. – Patrick J. Murphy III

————————▽————————

Springfield, OH (USA)

I was bullied through junior high and the first two years of high school. Pretty much every time we passed from class to class, the same three upper class men would find me and knock my books to the ground and then knock me down as well, calling me "sissy" and "retard" or saying really horrible things to me. Once I was in high school, they also came to my gym class (how the teacher allowed them to be there, I don't know), and would repeat the name calling and hitting/pushing me. Once they pushed me down a whole flight of bleachers during the class. I felt alone and so very, very abandoned by all my friends. – andKevin

————————▽————————

South Carolina (USA)

I was never beat up nor got into fights. I never started anything, and I think being 6'7" and wasn't slight of build, no one really ever pressed the issue. One football player used to call me Band Fag, but I knew he was an idiot and just let him be. God love Facebook because all these years later I can see that he is a run of the mill pig and being gay kept me young and happy. – Chris Grace

————————∇————————

San Jose, CA (USA)

I was severely bullied for not sticking up for myself. When I did, I received punishment from my school and authority figures. I was in a class of 20 kids, so I was the outcast, I didn't resonate with the boys and the girls didn't accept me after a certain age. Boys are icky and I was more effeminate at the time. So, I was an easy target. There was no openly gay or trans individuals in my school. There was probably about 800 kids in the entire school. And there weren't any teachers I could turn to with that. At the same time my family was not wealthy, so the school thought, "OK 'he's' getting bullied but the people bullying 'him' donate a lot of money, so we'll be lenient." I was beat up every day in elementary school, I was drawn on, poked with sticks, kicked, bit, punched … I had my skull cracked open by one kid who stole my lunch. The two times I did stick up for myself and fought back, I was severely punished, suspended for many weeks, put on probation. Whereas the other person who instigated the incident was not as severely punished. In high school that changed a little bit, but it didn't get much better. I wasn't bullied as much physically. I was still an easy target. Teasing, being picked on a lot. For instance, I had one kid who relentlessly tormented me every day. He called me fag and gay and used the "F" word. One day he drew a Nazi sign on a piece of paper. He put the Nazi sign on my table and told the teacher I did it. So I had to go to the principal's office and explain it. I had no idea what was going on. Luckily the principal understood what was going on, because we got a new principal. He's African-American so I feel like he understood, at least from some aspect of his own childhood, being of mixed race. I wasn't so lucky when it came to other teachers.

A lot of teachers would not stick up for me, a lot of teachers would put me down. A lot of teachers did not want to deal with me because they didn't understand my struggles. They tried to help but it was too overwhelming for some of them. They put me in a corner, "OK we're not going to deal with this person, because we don't know how to deal with them."

They're going through a lot being bullied, but there's nothing we can do about it." Even today it still happens. I've just heard about a trans boy that got beat up outside a school and the teachers and administration didn't do anything about it because it happened outside of the school. I was beat up outside the school and the teachers and administration did the same thing. "Oh we're not going to do anything about it, we're going to look the other way because if we do something about it, we'll have an opinion on the matter." It's even worse now because if this person identifies as trans and a man then it becomes an LGBT issue, instead of just a bullying issue. It's opening up a whole new can of worms for them to take a stance on it, which limits their donor possibilities. It also puts them in the limelight of being seen as trans-friendly or LGBT friendly which should be a good thing, but a lot of people don't want to associate with it. A lot of people want to say, "OK over here we want to be supportive but at the same time we don't want to say that we are, because we'll be attacked as well." We're an incredibly marginalized group. That all happened in San Jose, California, in the Bay Area, which generally is pretty liberal but there's a lot of conservatives there. It's more conservative now after the whole Silicon Valley.com boom. All these businesses are building there, Amazon, ebay, Apple. So there are a lot of people who are rich and have those conservative values. I'm not saying all conservatives are this way but I'm saying it seems to be the general thing where they look down upon people who are not like them. They turn off to hearing other people's stories and struggles. They come from an entirely privileged mindset because they have financial security. – Kelsey Brookes

————————∇————————

Chicago, IL (USA)

This is, in my case and probably for many others, complicated, as at five years old I started training as a dancer, followed with music, singing, and acting lessons throughout childhood and adolescence. So being bullied for me was just as much about this as being a too ridiculous "soft" boy, "pranced around" on stage, played with girls, didn't play sports, and was too touchy-feely with boys. My one experience with the local boy's Little League baseball was an unmitigated disaster – I was not asked back after that summer. While much of this was kept from me, only heard in town gossip, my parents and others I danced and sang with, were, of course, supportive, even if overbearing like most "stage mothers."

     Three incidents stand out, two as an adolescent, and the other as a young adult after joining the Navy during the Vietnam War in 1966. The two earlier bullying episodes were in iconic places, on the playground and in the gym locker room. On the elementary school playground, I was pushed down and hit by a gang of bullies, infamous in the town, as a roving band that caused trouble – this was two brothers and friends who were models of the 1950s juvenile street gangs made up of the most notorious boys, known even in this small place for their violence and cruelty. I was pushed off a swing, punched, and called a sissy (the first time I'd actually hear this word) until stopped by a teacher. I was brushed off and sent to the school nurse – a friend of my mother, oops! Later, after being scolded for getting into trouble, she (no, not my father) tried to teach me how to defend myself. From a poor family with two older brothers, and a local girl's basketball star, she knew more than my father, how to react to bullying.

The second was later as a freshman in high school, when P.E. (Physical Education) classes were mandatory. After a sweaty work out in the old gym, we were sent to shower, dress, and return to classes. After stripping down, I was confronted by about a dozen boys in various states of undress. The locker room in this old building was actually built underneath the bleachers and was very small, mildewy, and cramped. They tore off my towel, and proceeded to ridicule me in general, and have a big laugh over my small penis. I was especially shocked as my cousin was one of these taunters. I then hear all the insults that I had never heard before, but had voiceless nightmares about, "queer, sissy, pansy, faggot," with other descriptives added like "mincing, dancing, lipstick wearing," they were especially enraged knowing about my Fred Astaire top hat, white tie, and cane act, in which on stage, "shuffling off to Buffalo," I wore makeup. By that time, I was actually very expert in applying my makeup, and was, I must admit, fascinated with lipstick and rouge. I did sometimes secretly, I thought, wear a little in everyday life, or would forget to completely wipe it off after a gig. How did they know this? By some bully boy means of mental reading – or had my cousin shared all the incriminating evidence that he knew from family gossip.

The last experience was more seriously violent, being beaten up and raped by a group of sailors, Seabees, actually, from the U.S. Navy's Construction Battalion, along with random Marines and Green Berets, who were housed in the same barracks as the Navy musicians. Not the smartest or safest of ideas to put these very different groups together. Having more concentrated on my music skills in high school, I auditioned in boot camp for the Navy School of Music in Norfolk, Virginia, in an effort to avoid deployment to the Vietnam "killing grounds." There was still a chance I would be assigned to a battleship and trained to load high explosive shells onto the automatic launchers in the Pacific. Until then, I was learning jazz piano to be used to entertain in Officer's Clubs and play drums when marching in formation for special events. The musicians' barracks were on an upper floor, the others below stairs and an elevator (when working) between.

While there were more positive experiences with fellow sailors in that barracks, in both bunk beds (called racks) and in the massive and mysterious dark showers, several times the above-mentioned Seabees and others would raid the musician's "deck" in the middle of the night. The purpose was to terrorize us, and it worked. It was also a homophobic attack to "get those faggot musicians," and make them pay for their crimes against nature, by forcing us to perform various sexual acts. We were awoken by screams and marching chants by men in groups who would pull down their pants while others held me and others down either for a blow job, or a quick fuck – often ending up as being pissed on by the horny drunks.

Of course, the duty Master-At-Arms and barracks chief were called, but the Seabees and others were long gone. We were blamed for the event, ironically sent to the showers, or back to sleep, after standing at attention for what seemed hours. This was traumatizing enough, but another incident scarred me more, which I actually blocked from memory until much later. After returning from a weekend's leave, late on a Sunday night, I was entering the elevator on the ground floor when I was pulled out by three Seabees and a Marine. "What's a pussy musician like you returning so late? Been out getting fucked?" When I said no, the grim laughter came with, "Well, now you are goin'a be." They proceeded to each rape me in the stair well. Mostly I was in shock, and all I remember thinking was that I and a couple others had just painted (in a horrible Navy grey color) that very stairs. As a punishment, for some infraction, we were ordered to repaint it multiple times until exhausted and had to appear for nightly roll call.

I had tried to run up the stairs from my attackers to the musician's floor where I knew someone was on watch, but was stopped and held against the wall (that awful grey again) and forced to perform oral and anal sex. After each finished there was applause and taunts, they then drug me up the final flight and threw me onto middle of the barracks office near the public telephone booth. A young musician on night watch, came out of the Chief's office to see what the commotion was, but my rapists said only they found me drunk on the stairs. Not wanting trouble, or to wake the Chief (not a smart thing to do), he grunted and returned to his T.V. show. I laid there for a long time. It was the middle of the night, and finally managed to crawl, stand, and wobble back to my bunk. My upper bunk mate had disappeared early on, so no one noticed me coming in. – David Hatfield Sparks

———————∇———————

Bellport, NY (USA)

In 7th grade before I came out (again, I didn't officially "come out" until I was 17), I was called a bunch of different nicknames such as "dyke," "bulldyke," "lesbian," and then some. I was in the closet most of my high school career but when I was 17 and in 12th grade, I came out. Some of my friends at the time knew I was gay already and was waiting for me to accept myself. Other classmates refused to believe that I was gay. I didn't bother with them afterwards. – Erin Michelle Miller

—————▽—————

Lansing, Michigan, (USA)
Denver, CO (USA)

Absolutely. People punched me. Every so often I'd punch back, and they'd stop. My brother bullied me. I was bullied a lot. But people who are different always are. I was bullied for being a little queer. It just slipped out and it made people nervous. When you're a little odd or different, they can't handle it. I couldn't wait to get out of there, to live a different life. Then you go to a small town, Lansing, a city of 130,000 and yeah there's one or two gay bars but talk about the dregs of society. You really have to go to a big city like Chicago or Denver to feel like you have a sense of community. You're not going to find it in a small city. You're just not. I ran off to Denver when I was 21 and stayed. – Jim

—————▽—————

Chicago, IL (USA)

I had a medical condition in grammar school and the first year of high school; eczema on my chin. There were a few people that would chide me about it. I ran with a gay group in high school and I think most of the guys that I had classes with were scared of us. Never really had a problem. – Dennis Hardenstein

—————▽—————

Wisconsin Rapids, WI (USA)

I wasn't bullied in school as much as those young men who acted more effeminate than I, but there were still incidents that I recall vividly that changed the way I interacted with the world completely. In high school, I remember once being called a faggot and getting punched in the side by one of the biggest bullies in my class, just because he could. The summer before my sophomore year I allowed my hair to grow a little too long and another bully – who sat directly behind me in my sophomore biology class – told everyone that I must have a vagina and suck cocks because I looked like a girl. And soon after that, when I declined to go to a high school dance with a girl from my class, my biology teacher, who commonly made homophobic remarks while teaching, asked me, in front of the class, if I was just afraid of girls or if I was "one of *those* types" as he feigned limp wrists. Despite these early incidents, I think I got off much easier than others in my school because I learned quickly how to pass – I grew a full beard at the age of 15, I cropped my hair short in military style, I was careful not to be flamboyant or stand out in any way, and I kept to myself as much as possible, focusing almost exclusively on getting into college. To avoid things like high school dances, I got a part-time job after school and on weekends so that I always had a ready excuse not to go. – D. Warner

———————∇———————

Louisiana (USA)

Yes, more mental or verbal than physical. The physical I remember distinctly on a school bus, mostly because of the physical contact without consent, that sticks with me more than the actual result of the contact. His name or nickname was Duke. He was older, bigger, stronger, and probably in need of a serious hug. In retrospect he was abused himself, probably at home, maybe by a man, but it was clear that it was him against the world, and for the few minutes of that bus ride I was the world. – Katorri A.

———————∇———————

Indianapolis IN (USA)
West Lafayette IN (USA)

I avoided bullying as a teen by staying invisible most of the time – of course, there were drawbacks to that survival tactic, to be sure. I had a small circle of nerd friends in high school and was essentially ignored by the obnoxious popular kids. There was an occasional scornful remark about the fact that I was unlike other kids (unathletic, smart, well-read), but mostly I was ignored – nothing physical or threatening like bullying. In college, I began to feel threatened by society at large. One day, a group of moronic Purdue frat brothers with toy rifles and fake army helmets pushed themselves around campus in a green garbage dumpster – clearly oblivious to the irony! – with a hand painted sign reading "Shoot a Queer." I watched them go by from the safety of my office window. But it did send a chill. – William Demaree

———————∇———————

Cleveland, OH (USA)

All the time. It was ignorant pack mentality. Names and general meanness, but looking back, those kids treated me that way because it was seen as okay. Other kids got it worse. It was only years later that I realized conformity was a crock of shit. – Roger

———————∇———————

Adelaide, South Australia (Australia)

I wore glasses so there we go right there with the whole "four eyes" stuff. That's where I got the "that means I can see four of you" disdain from. However, that tapered off the older I got. I was also the fat kid, so I got teased in that regard. Even when I lost the weight I was still referred to as Big Bob due to my Year Eight House Master nicknaming me that and it just stuck. There was a caricature of me drawn in the back of the end of year book as a bloated overly fat kid with all these chins and stuff. I just took it in my stride. Whether or not I said something smart arse in response to that one, I don't know. All through school I was teased as a fat kid even though for the last three or so years I was fairly slender.

But I was seen as an easy target but I would always respond to that. I once got so pissed off I threw a chair at the people, told them to get fucked and stormed out. I was criticised for using the word fuck more than anything else. It was because of that they decided that the lesser of the two evils was to give me permission to walk out of class if I was given too hard a time, so I used that as a great way of just pulling myself from a situation. I had bits of paper thrown at me, so I calmly walked out. Next day he tried it again only to have me turn around and say, "I know what you're trying to do and it's not going to work." I had bubblegum put in my hair that Mum had to cut out. I think she rang the headmaster over that one and blasted shit out of him. Can't remember but she was livid.

The good thing about learning piano is I could seek refuge in one of the music rooms because I knew that at least one of them would be open. If I was sprung, I'd just say I was waiting for my piano teacher. I knew it would never be double checked.

I was accused of being gay because of one of the friends I hung around with. One of the main bullies came up to me and told me that by associating with this guy people will think I'm gay. I got him to confirm this school of thought of "gay by association." Okay. I then responded with: "So because you THINK he's gay therefore you THINK I'm gay so, going by your logic, doesn't that make YOU gay???" He raised his fist as if to deck me one and I stood firm and said: "Well???" He realised he had nowhere to go with that and backed down. I know I was lucky I was able to do things like that whereas other kids weren't. I'd stand up for them where I could, unless they themselves were pieces of shit then I wouldn't want to know. – Robert Verrall

―――――▽―――――

Santa Cruz, CA (USA)
Salinas, CA (USA)

I wasn't called names too much, but in grade school I was the last one picked on the team. I had one or two friends, but I hung around more or less with my middle brother's friends, rather than make my own friends. I went to a Catholic high school in Salinas and I was bullied there. I remember sitting in an assembly at the Catholic boys' high school and people behind me were spitting down. When I left there the back of my jacket was just covered in phlegm and crap. That was pretty bad. At the Catholic boys' school your parents were either rich and had money to send you there, or you were incorrigible, and they thought the brothers would straighten you out. By the way, a brother hit on me when I was a freshman there. He called me out of a class and asked me if I'd been masturbating. I thought, "How did he know?" because I'd just barely discovered it on my own. He said, "When I was your age, a brother called me out like this too. The brother told me to masturbate in front of him and I did, and I never masturbated again after that." Hint hint wink wink. I was naïve but I wasn't that naïve. Unfortunately, I saw another guy get called out later to the same priest. He seemed kind of messed up after that. I figure he might have fell for it. – Spike

―――――▽―――――

Portland, OR (USA)

The first bullying experience I can remember was when I was in kindergarten. I didn't know I was being bullied at the time. I went to school and I came home, and my mom said, "So, how was your day at school?" I said, "It was great, I got to play kickball with the second graders." She said, "How did you do that?" I said, "I let them call me nigger." So she went on this diatribe about, "You don't let anyone do that. A nigger means a stupid person." She drilled it into my head that you never let this happen. To which my response was, "If sticks and stones can break your bones but words will never hurt you, what's the big deal." Her reply was, "You should probably go to your room and read a book right now." From then on out, walking down the halls, I noticed all the kids were calling me nigger. It made me feel bad. My mom always said that being black you had to work harder than everyone else. So I had to do homework before I went to bed, before dinner. Then go to bed at nine o'clock at night. Then she would check my homework. I had to get up an extra hour before school, to make any corrections, and I had to erase in such a way that people wouldn't know that I made a mistake. Needless to say, when I was finally in a school with students who had the same skin color as me, I was beat up repeatedly for taking care of my books, for not being like other people. I've been asked to leave dance clubs that were predominantly black because I wasn't black enough. I didn't speak, I didn't look, I didn't dress like I was from the inner city. I've been out in bars and had black men confront me because they didn't want me talking to their white boyfriend. I've been out and people have said to me, "You know, you're really hot, I'd date you if you weren't black." I've had people say, "Your tattoos are great, too bad you're black." … "Oh, you're a black nurse, I didn't know they had black nurses." To which my reply was, "In case you don't know, we have a black President." I've not been served in restaurants. That happened in Boston at an English pub. They did not serve me. But it happens. I think I'm in a better place now because when those things would happen, I would make a big stink about it. But I think with all the inclusion that's happening on TV, that it's given me a chance to step back and not take it so personal. It's hard and there are times I cry about it. Another time I was in a Mr. Leather contest. It was a really bad period for me. I entered this contest and I walked out there and gave it my all. There were four contestants and two of us were black. They allowed us to walk through the crowd while they tallied up the score and I knew most of the crowd. They called us back to the stage. I was walking back to the stage and for once in my life I was proud of myself. Someone stopped me before I climbed onto the stage and said, "I want to commend you on a fabulous job. It's a pity you can't win because you're black." I wanted to cry, I wanted to punch him, I wanted to do so many things, but I said to myself, "Instead of focusing on the chance that you could win, you're not going to win. Practice your pageant smile, so you don't appear to be a bitter queen." Well, they announced the winner and it was me. I was prepared to not hear my name, but someone else's name. When they announced my name, I almost fell off the stage. At that moment I learned how to deal with all my own demons. – Crusher

———————▽———————

Raytown, MO (USA)

I wasn't bullied in school and I'll tell you why. Because I knew at such an early age that I was different, I made it my priority that no-one is going to find this out. And I was going to fit in as best I can. So what I did was …

there was a girl in 6th grade who was interested in me. She came from an incredibly conservative family. Of course, I was religious, so the two of us worked out really well together. She needed a boyfriend because she wanted to do all the things that girls do in Junior High and High School, so she could say she had a boyfriend. There was no way her parents would let her date anyone except me. I was the only one that they trusted. On the other hand, I needed some sort of cover so that I made it through OK. We dated from 6th grade up until senior prom. I knew I had to make it through senior prom. So in 6th grade, I thought, "I've got to make this work until the end of high school." And I did. Then I broke up with her after I went to college and there were lots of tears and I was relieved that I could finally get away from all that. So no, I wasn't bullied but part of that was because of the fact that I carefully planned out ways of getting around it. – Thomas Stribling

—————▽—————

La Mesa, Tequendama Province (Colombia)

Yes, mostly with nicknames. Something I now find quite funny is that when I was in 6th grade guys were demanding I stay away from pretty girls, 'cause they were taken. Also, my math teacher on that year was a monster. After that I became stronger and didn't care so much about bullying. Just minding my own business. – Cristian

—————▽—————

Grand Rapids, MI (USA)

In elementary school, I bullied others, but I wasn't bullied. In junior high it was about equal the bullying I gave and the bulling I received. In high school and after, it did not continue. – Mark S

—————▽—————

Wichita, KS (USA)

I wasn't. I was kidded as a kid because there was a local chip company in Wichita called Guy's potato chips, and that's my name. That was the only kidding thing around. In high school I was student body president, so I was a popular kid. Most of my friends were more female than male. I did the male things, I played on the football teams. I went out for sports, decent athlete, but not great. I preferred to swim, which I did when I could. I played athletics. So, I wasn't bullied. But most of my friends were female. In high school I had a group of girls, we all got together at lunchtime. Did the boys make fun of me? No, I was a tall kid, I was 6' 1" in 8th grade so I had the height. I was probably a little more effeminate than your usual run of the mill person. It was a rural community high school and people didn't make fun of me. I was lucky. – Guy Seliers

———————∇———————

Cathedral City, CA (USA)

Yes. It probably started out with teachers because we were not wealthy or have a good income. They bullied you into thinking you were stupid. Then in high school my cousins would bully me because they had money. People would bully you because you weren't the pretty one or in the clique, but it didn't really bother me because there were other things that I was doing that kept me grounded. – David Hardy

———————∇———————

Spokane, CA (USA)

Constantly. I graduated at 117lbs and I didn't hide that I was gay. I was called a faggot every single day. But it made me a tougher person. I didn't do what they do today, with the kids getting depressed and suicidal. No, it made me a tougher person. I would always stand up to anybody who confronted me. They respected me that. Even in the Army, I had a 6' 5" black guy from South Carolina came after me and called me a fucking faggot. I didn't care how big he was, I still grabbed him by the neck. He still lifted me off the ground by my neck, but I still stood up to him. He respected me for that. – Marcous

———————∇———————

Tallahassee, FL (USA)

One of my earliest memories takes me back to the playground in the first six months of the first grade, before we were moved to the new school. One of the boys was picking on skinny, little ole me, and another boy stood up and said, "Leave him alone!"

I still have a scar on my Achilles tendon from 5th grade, when Paul R. stomped on me with his combat boots during PE, because he could. I think that was the same year I filled a sock with rocks and fought back against Fred ____'s harassment on that same baseball diamond. I got in trouble, but knew I was right, even though I was the runt. Fred continued to bully me through junior/high school. He wanted me to fight him, but like with my older, taller, evil sister, I took the higher road. I was active in student council, class officer, honor roll, and didn't have time for bullies. Both Fred and my older sister are single today, and Paul died homeless a few years ago. – T. Lark Letchworth

—————▽—————

Cleveland, OH (USA)

Mostly name calling and nasty remarks. "Hey Femme … " "You sit like a girl." "You're too pretty to be a boy." That kinda stuff. – Steve Kmetko

—————▽—————

Chicago, IL (USA)

I was, but don't like to write or think about it. It seemed cliché – I was very girly and beaten up for it – or threatened to get beaten up. Once, in the lunchroom, a bully grabbed my sandwich shoved it into my face and made me wear the plastic it came in on my head like a bonnet. He kept calling me a fag. I never fought back. I'm ashamed about it to this day. Why didn't I push him away, punch the fucker in the nuts, anything? Because I felt I deserved it. I knew I was a girly little fag and felt I got what I deserved. I was also in the school play that year, and on the photo of me, posted in the lobby, someone has written "FAG" across my forehead. – MrZor

—————▽—————

Sylvania, New South Wales, (Australia)
Gymea, New South Wales, (Australia)
Campbelltown, New South Wales, (Australia)

Not at school, no. I got a bit of a ribbing off the boys in primary school because I often played with the girls, but not what I would have called bullying. In fact, I was always fairly popular at school, including being voted in as Class Captain. There was one incident at boarding school … I can't even remember what it was over now … but a rough tough country boy, who was a mate of mine, stepped in. There were never any other incidents after that.

I have been bullied in the workplace. I worked for a company called "Liquorland" (under the then Coles/Myer umbrella) from 1990-1993. I managed their store in Darlinghurst, which made me a gay manager of their store in the gay ghetto. One would think there'd be no problems. However, in mid-1992, a new Area Manager started. A really nasty, sneaky piece-of-work! Not only was I openly gay, but openly HIV+, due to the fact that I worked all day with glass, and if I had any serious accidents, I wanted my staff to take all safety precautions when looking after my injuries. My staff had no issues with either gay, or HIV. However, the Area Manager did. He went out of his way to make my life a misery, always out of sight and earshot of staff, so that if I complained, there was no one to back me up. I didn't dare make any mistakes, because if I did, I'd pay for it for months. Anyway, with working long hours, drinking and smoking heavily, and not eating properly my health started going downhill (leading to my encounter with AIDS in 1996), and I took a demotion to try to ease my workload. I was planning to leave the company and take some advantage of the HIV services then available to me, but didn't want to do it in a way that made it appear that the Area Manager had got his way, and got rid of me. It's a longish, complicated story so won't go into it here … and it's off subject … but I requested a transfer to another store in my area, and went on annual leave while awaiting the transfer to be approved by him. He thought that if he dragged out the approval, I'd get fed up and just quit. However, I hung out, ringing and leaving messages with him daily requesting his approval of my move. He eventually approved the transfer the day before I was due to go back to work. I turned up at my new workplace the next day … and gave my notice. I believe he was livid. It was the only smile I gave during the whole traumatic 18-months I'd had with him. He never spoke to me again … a relief and blessing for me … not even on the day I finished up. He totally ignored me whenever he was in the store. I found out shortly after this that he was using the same tactics on another gay manager in another store. – Tim Alderman

—————▽—————

Sacramento, CA (USA)
Davis, CA (USA)
San Diego, CA (USA)
Cathedral City, CA (USA)
Eureka Springs, AR (USA)

I was one of the shortest, skinniest kids in school till my Sophomore year of high school. I was not viewed as traditionally "nellie" and I participated in Scouts, had a girlfriend in 6th grade, was okay at basketball and tennis and got along well with a variety of kids. Still there were a few times that were fleeting throughout grade school where I was bullied a tiny bit but I truly think I was well-liked so I was not so big of a target.

My biggest fear was Junior year in high school when a guy I knew called me "Hair Ass." Utter panic went through my mind as I thought it was so clever and I feared it might catch on. I ignored him and he never called me that again. Funny but today he is an actor who has appeared in major motion films. – Paul Harris

—————————∇—————————

(Germany)

I was coming out to my whole school of 1500 pupils and almost half were Muslim when I was 16. I was not really physically assaulted heavily or often, but insulted a lot, all the time, always everywhere. – Cornelius Günther Körn

—————————∇—————————

Lawton, OK (USA)

Definitely yes, they'd spit on my clothes, chase me after school, beat me up, throw balls and rocks at me. Public humiliation. Ostracizing. The girls wouldn't talk to me and the boys I wanted to talk to would beat me up instead of kiss me. I had the hots for this one guy who was in the band. He was a bodybuilder from age 18 and I couldn't keep my eyes off him. He figured it out and ostracized me. – David Hayes

—————————∇—————————

Mequon, WI (USA)

I was in 4th grade. It was winter. Mark Ravenscraft taunted me – "Nooey Nooey blank blank" he said as he pushed me into a snowbank. I was so shocked that I wet my pants. He laughed and as my other classmates went inside after recess. In the warm classroom the pee in my underwear and pants got warmer and it smelled. It was embarrassing. – Tony Earl

—————————∇—————————

King, NC (USA)

I was bullied in school at around the age of ten to twelve. I thought, in those days, before I became aware of my true nature, that it was because I was a fat kid, clumsy, and not into sports. Looking back, it was more likely because I was sissy-esk in my demeanor and very shy.

When I turned thirteen, my parents bought an organ and I began to study music. Music was my salvation and I no longer thought about the meanness of the bullies at school. During those days, little was done to address being bullied. You just had to "man up" and take it or suffer the consequences – which many of us did, suffer.

I became the musical star of all the other organ students. It wasn't long before I was selected to have the coveted last spot at all the organ recitals held only for the best talent. It was truly my escape – not only from being bullied, but also from having to think about and deal with my budding gay feelings. – Ron Cline

———————▽———————

St. Cloud, MN (USA)

I was bullied nearly every day of my K-12 experience. I was bullied in every way you could imagine, for things I could not help. I survived because I could escape into my art, books, movies, and music. I survived because I had a goal – to get into college and be the best I could be. I survived because I had some good teachers who helped me through it. I was not a nice person after that experience, though … from college onward I had an uphill struggle relearning how to be a human being. I am still learning. – Rachel Wexelbaum

———————▽———————

Palestine, TX (USA)

Not like you see and read about today. I wasn't all that "gay" and I was respected by most. There were a few nasty bullying types of guys, but I could hold my own with them and they never gave me much trouble. I put forward a pretty good façade. – Michael Pickel

———————▽———————

Des Moines, IA (USA)

I got called names, but I was always a big guy and handled my own shit. I did not always "win," but I got respect for having heart. Plus, I had a boyfriend and, in a pinch, could give dynamite head. – Sr. Freida Peoples aka DJ Chrysler Sheldon

———————▽———————

Charlottetown, Prince Edward Island (Canada)

Yeah, I was bullied in school, usually verbally, though sometimes with treats of violence and occasionally with physical confrontation, though I don't consider that violence (headlocks, etc.). The taunting and threats scared me, but it was the lack of action on the part of teachers (and sometimes their participation) that disturbed me on a deeper, more long-lasting level. Gym class and having to change with other boys for gym class, were absolute nightmares for me. – Dave Stewart

—————————▽—————————

San Diego, CA (USA)

I was 5'2", 119 lbs., in my junior year of high school. I was the smallest boy. My body had not started puberty, probably on purpose. I was called "faggot," I was horribly taunted, I was pushed around. It wasn't until I started in a church group that I could fall in with that cluster of protection that I got any relief whatsoever. I didn't get to be friends with other queer folk. The bullying was … you just couldn't be yourself. It was ok not to be you. That was the underlying rule. – Serafine Sawyer

—————————▽—————————

(Pakistan)

Yes, I was bullied a lot in my school and especially more in my neighborhood for being an effeminate gay. I was called "Larki, larki" (girly, girly) a lot because I was quite effeminate. My style of walking was joked about, my soft tone in voice was also ridiculed. At times, it was so bad that I started skipping school and also stopped going out in my neighborhood.

    The bullying I went through continued to affect me and for years I'd very low self-esteem. My education was impacted due to it too. I campaign for the rights of LGBTQ+ youth now and I wish to see a world where homophobic and transphobic bullying at our schools and at our neighborhoods cease to exist. – Salman

HAVE YOU EVER LIVED WITH AN LGBTQ LOVER/PARTNER/SPOUSE? IF SO, WHAT ADVICE WOULD YOU GIVE TO SOMEONE ABOUT MAKING A LIVE-IN RELATIONSHIP WORK?

Chicago, IL (USA)

I lived with a partner for many years who passed. I would tell people patience and distance are good. You're still people and you can't be on top of each other all the time. You have to allow the other person to be who they are. Then come together. The patience part is something it took me a long time to learn. – Steve

————————▽————————

Midwestern City (USA)

Strong and lasting relationships are built on honesty and caring. These are the hallmarks, which have kept my husband and I together for almost 23 years. – Anonymous

————————▽————————

Oxford, MS (USA)

Above all, let the other person be free to be him/herself without trying to change or mold him/her. Communicate, communicate, communicate, even

if it's frightening and painful. It's the festering of locked-up emotion that splits a relationship, sometimes never to be repaired. Don't be pressured by contemporary gay culture either. You don't have to get married and have children. At my age that is tantamount to aping one's captor. Emotionally it's appealing (I follow a young married male couple in Texas on YouTube and find it oddly comforting.), but intellectually it just seems mistaken. Social roles can become crystallized into invisible prisons that stymie personal growth and creativity. (I realize that there are at least two sides to this issue.)
– Oran Walker

—————▽—————

Chicago, IL (USA)

I'm not so sure I should be giving advice on that topic. I've been in two live-in relationships in my life. The first, Leonard, had grown up in a wealthy family in Lake Forest, Illinois. We'd met at Man's Country, a huge and popular bathhouse in Chicago in 1979, when he walked right up to me and said, "I don't want to be rude, but I would love to suck your dick." He was a skinny white boy with long hair. My cup of tea. I followed him to his room where we smoked a joint, did a line or five of coke and he did what he said he was going to do. Exceptionally good at it, he was. He invited me over to his house, an apartment on the 34th floor of a Lake Shore Drive building. Addison and LSD [Lake Shore Drive]. I stayed for five years. We had a wonderful time together. Sometimes we'd go to Man's Country, where we'd met. I'd find hot colored guys for him and skinny rockers, skaters, and the occasional skinhead for me. Our trust was deep. Toward the end of our 5th year, I felt it was time for me to live alone. Not at all a reflection on us, we were by then more friends who played rather than lovers the way we had been. We evolved and our relationship did as well. Then he died. A cerebral hemorrhage. He died so fast he most likely had no idea what was happening. I miss him all the time. Then I met Milton. Very tall. Very long hair. When our mutual friend introduced us, I was thrilled to discover he studied the harpsichord. The week before I purchased a Wanda Landowska album because I'd heard some music of hers on WFMT, the classical station in Chicago. He was stunned that this Black feller had just dropped the name of an obscure and forgotten musician. We kinda fell in love right then and there. I know I remember feeling a contained rush, sort of like that first really good line of coke, which of course, is artificial but dopamine was flooding my Mississippi. We were together for three years. I'd found us a great place on East Lake Terrace, the street as far north and far east as you can go in that huge city, and we were tucked in a corner with Lake Michigan right outside the back door. I helped Milton buy his first harpsichord. He was a very good musician, if a bit timid. I took him to see a conductor he truly admired, a man named Gustav Lionheart. After Mr. Lionheart's performance, he went to have a smoke and we would have to walk right past him to leave the church where the concert was held. Milton refused. I was baffled, but unfortunately he never felt he was any good, which was a lie. He got so twisted that he eventually sold Harpsy the Harpsichord and moved back to Red Wing, Minnesota. He left me with treasures, though. I still listen to and love early music. So, like I said, I'm not sure I know how to make a relationship work. I haven't been in one in 30+ years. However, I can say one thing, a lover is your confidante, your comrade ... the one person that you don't get cross with. Oh, you'll disagree but that can be a learning experience for you both. Or the three of you. At this point in my life, my friends fill a place that would maybe be a place for a love. That way I'm not living everyday thinking there is a huge hole in my life. I know where the huge hole is, but that's for me to know, unless you happen to find out. – Terence Smith (Joan Jett Blakk)

————————∇————————

Chicago, IL (USA)

The glib answer is, "Make sure they have a job." Actually, I've had a couple that turned out to be, "Oh I'm supposed to pay for everything, right?" – Xavier Bathsheba-Negron

————————∇————————

Tulsa, OK (USA)

Determine what is important between the two of you and go from there. Don't try to fit someone else's mold because every person is unique, and every couple is unique. Do that and never take them for granted. – Renny

————————∇————————

Chicago, IL (USA)

Yes, I had a live-in relationship for 21 years. And quite honestly most of my life I had either a boyfriend or lover, or roommate/mates that either lived with me in a relationship or some that were just platonic. And now, although I am in a relationship, we live apart at the moment and for the last five months it's the first time that I have lived completely alone. But again, I have a six-year relationship that means the world to me. I think the key to a live-in relationship, or really any love interest relationship is that there is clear communication, and trust and honest conversation. I think that is where in my past relationships the rubber really hit the road or did not. When the communication stops or fails to be open, then I think that is where the troubles begin. – Dean Ogren

—————∇—————

San Francisco, CA (USA)
West Hollywood, CA (USA)
Palm Springs (USA)

I'm currently in my third long-term relationship and we are married. We recently went through a complicated kitchen remodel that required excellent listening skills for both of us. The project also reminded us how important it is for both parties in a relationship to be able to compromise. He won some battles and I won some.

Don't try to change your partner. You need to respect them for who they are. Trust and honesty are really important. – Gary Borgstedt

—————∇—————

Waverly, IA (USA)

I've never lived with any of my lovers. This was partly because of living and working in different towns. But I think that may have contributed to the survival of feelings between us. Studies have shown that lust lasts for about two years average. Possibly because lust needs some distance/difference: age, profession, education, etc. Too much familiarity kills lust. One's "perfect lover becomes a perfect fool" – The Eagles. – Robert Beck

—————∇—————

Chicago, IL (USA)

I've had 2 ½ long term relationships, actually three … and I lived with all of them. The first one was right after I got out of university with a gentleman I met while I was still in school. We were together for about 4 ½ years before he passed with complications from HIV. The one after that was for 10 years with a wonderful man who passed to cancer. I don't break up, I bury them. The third was a square-dancer and I moved out to California for him and moved back last year because the relationship exploded. What I'd recommend is call yourself out when you see yourself being passive aggressive. And don't be afraid to call somebody else out and say, "Look, we need the reality here." Yet, at the same time, you have to understand that there are things you are not going to be able to change about them. You have to take them as they are because you love them. Just be honest. – 'Drew

————————▽————————

Chicago, IL (USA)

First thing I would say is date the person for at least two years. Not one year, two, because after that first year that's when the honeymoon phase is over. That next year is when you're going to see who the person is and who they're going to be to you. Who they are to their core? One year is not enough. After two years if it makes sense, do it. But I've had so many relationships, my longest was four and a half years and we lived together for three and a half years. The advice I would give would be you gotta be real with each other, you have to be able to be vulnerable and you have to let the other person be vulnerable. You have to be truthful, especially if you're going to be engaged in an open relationship, which a lot of people do. My biggest advice for that is you have to have your expectations aligned. If you can't do that then you can't live together, and you can't have an open relationship. It's a cliché but communication is everything. You have to be on the same page. You have to be on board. I feel like my one long-term live-in relationship … I look back and think, "What the hell were we even doing together?" We're not friends now, but we're not enemies. We're connected on social media and that's about it. I look at his life and the things he's interested in and I look at the things I'm interested in, and I think, "Why did we even do this?" The core advice I would give is be honest, be real, have aligned expectations, but sometimes you have to take a leap of faith. If it doesn't work out, it doesn't work out. It's not the end of the world. You'll move on. – Jeff Ramone

————————▽————————

(Bulgaria)

Yes, I've lived with two – one for fifteen years, who is still my business partner and closest friend, and my "husband," with whom I've been for ten years. We usually spend three days per week together as he works in another city 100 km away. Due to the coronavirus shutdown, we've been living together fulltime for three weeks. It's going even better than expected.

A live-in relationship only works through a vast, complex web of compromises, mutual understanding and respect, and sharing the burden of domestic chores. I cook, I arrange meal plans, compile the shopping lists, clean the bathroom, and do the laundry. My partner does the rest of the cleaning, the ironing, helps with the shopping, runs errands, and does the washing up.

There's a large age difference between us – 16 years. That should make me the dominant partner, but I don't believe in that kind of patriarchal setup: even though we come from vastly different backgrounds (he's working class and I am a member of one of Europe's oldest families), I treat him as a full equal.

Another thing that has helped our "marriage" is that our relationship is technically an open one. We're both free to have sex with other people if we want to, or to have threesomes with fuck buddies. But that freedom has actually meant that neither of us is looking for sex outside our relationship more than about once or twice a year. – Louis Richard de Bourbon de Parme et de Savoie, Prince de la Pau

———————▽———————

Bellport, NY (USA)

My longest relationship was 2 1/2 years on and off. We never did live with each other although I wanted to at the time. As such, I don't think I'm qualified to answer the second question but I would think teamwork, patience, and communication are three key things to keep in mind. – Erin Michelle Miller

———————▽———————

Rockford, IL (USA)

While I have never lived with a partner, I do believe that the most important thing in a relationship is listening to each other, giving your partner the space they need when they ask, hold them when they need to be held. It is important to talk with them when you are both upset. It is important to turn off the distractions and be present with your partner. Sit down to dinner and talk about your day. Share activities with each other. These things will help you connect. – Patrick J. Murphy III

———————▽———————

Frinton-on-Sea, Essex (UK)

All relationships require tolerance and may sometimes require forgiveness too. Don't expect your partner to be a saint, but don't put up with repeated abuse of the relationship either. Sexual infidelity isn't necessarily the end of the world, but you must insist on fidelity of the heart and being treated with kindness, understanding, consideration, and respect. That's what love is and it's a two-way street. Never put up with physical violence, or devious manipulation. And accept that some relationships have a shelf-life. When it's really over, have the courage to move on and decide if your ex is still worth having as a friend. It can work. – Diesel Balaam

———————∇———————

Seattle, WA (USA)

I was with the love-of-my-life for 20+years and we lived together for 17+ of them before he died. Communication is the key. Talk to one another. Share happiness. Don't go to bed angry (the issue may not be resolved, but at least have a potential solution discussed before turning out the light), make each other laugh. Respect differences and celebrate the commonalities. – Eric Andrews-Katz

———————∇———————

St Louis, MO (USA)
Rancho Mirage, CA (USA)

I was only in one relationship, between 1982 and 1985. I thought I had nothing to worry about. I wasn't a jealous person, but when my partner was out playing around and I found out about it, my trust was destroyed. If I gave in, it never got better. Everything else about him I loved, but I couldn't trust him. After he became ill in Spring of 1986, I felt compassion and helped look after him, getting him an apartment in my building. He died from complications of AIDS in December 1987. I've not been in another relationship since, but not because I don't want to nor because I'm scared. It just never happened, but I turned out just fine. I honestly can't give any advice since I've not had much experience in relationships, but I feel much of the success of being together is by trial and maybe even lucking out on finding the right one. About five years ago three intuitives (and I never gave them info to go on) told me that someone is coming down the road (how long is that?!) and that it would be very mutual, equal energy, very natural. So, I don't go hunting and have expectations. If it happens, then great. Otherwise, continuing with my life and enjoying the things I do is good enough for me. – Todd Jaeger

———————∇———————

South Carolina (USA)

Now that marriage equality is law of the land advice for us is probably the same as with anyone. If you get married, you're set. If you're not going to make it legal, do your due diligence and over-protect yourself especially if either family is not accepting. Cover your ass. The rest is all just regular relationship crap. – Chris Grace

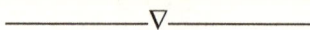

———————∇———————

Chicago, IL (USA)

Always fill up the ice cube tray when you put it back in the freezer. – Brian T

———————∇———————

Chicago, IL (USA)

I had a live-in relationship for 2 ½ years. I don't think I should be giving relationship advice to anyone. I will say this, however: stand by a strict rule that you will not move in together for at least six months after meeting, and until after you have had one really large argument. When two people argue, you learn a lot about each other. My ex and I did not argue until a month after he had moved in. We had a horrible argument over a very tiny thing. But from that I learned that he was mean and did not argue fairly. I learned that this relationship was going to be all about what he wanted and thought, and nothing at all about what I wanted. If we had argued before he moved in, we would never have lived together. – andKevin

———————∇———————

Palm Springs, CA (USA)

I've only had one other person I've actually lived with. A former boyfriend, we lived together for six months. That was my first experience with sharing a space with someone. That was a big learning experience for me. It taught me that with my current relationship the most important thing is honesty and communication. I didn't have that the first time around. That was a mistake that I made. I assumed certain things were happening that weren't happening. And the things that were happening shocked me when I found out. With my current relationship it's communication and honesty. One thing that's important to me is that when we go to bed at night, I have to say "I love you" and a kiss. It washes away the bad of the day. That's how I feel about it. This is the person you're with, you're relying on. This is the person that completes you. At least for me, it completes me. That's what I have in this relationship that I didn't have before. – David Vega (Lucifers Axe).

—————∇—————

Cathedral City, CA (USA)

I would say don't settle down until after you're 40. There's way too much wild oats you need to work out in your 20s and 30s. I know when you're young you have a tendency to be idealistic about things, but as a gay man the testosterone is so overwhelming. I mean, you're going to fuck around on each other, so wait until you're after 40. I see these young gay guys getting together in their 20s and 30s and wanting kids. That's fine but I just don't think it's realistic. They're going to end up getting divorced just like straight people. Sow your wild oats and wait until after you're 40. – Jim

—————∇—————

Palm Springs, CA (USA)

I can only tell you about my relationship now. I'm with my partner 17 years. Loyalty is No 1 for me. You have to love every speck and accept completely and respect the person you're with. Flaws and all you have to love everything, even the worst part of the flaws, the highest highs of greatness that you see in them, you have to love the entire package to make it work. You have to be there through the great times, have fun with them, and make them the best great times ever. And the lowest of the low times, you can laugh through. You'll find a way. Just use it like connective tissue to all the great times. And never go to bed angry. – Keith Kollinicos (Missa Distic)

—————∇—————

Palm Springs, CA (USA)

I have lived with two lovers/partners/spouses. The first relationship lasted 10 years, from the time I was 19 years old until I was 29. The second, and current relationship, is with my husband. We met in 1993 when we were both 30, and we're still together 27 years later. We're asked all the time for advice on making a live-in relationship work and we always tell people who ask that the number one issue is communication – as cliché as it might sound – and absolute honesty, even when it's hard. Talking to your partner openly about everything, even the difficult things, is critical, because if you can't talk it out honestly and with compassion, it's not going to last. Second, compromise – you can't be rigid. Stand up for what you need, but don't get caught up by unimportant details that won't matter in the end. We have a rule – when one of us gets upset about something the other has said or done, we ask ourselves, "Will I care about this issue five years from now." If the answer is no, let it go. If the answer is yes, talk it out and find your common ground. In our experience with other LGBTQ friends, the two things that break up most relationships are sex and money. If you can commit yourself to finding common ground on those issues, everything else usually takes care of itself short of things one cannot anticipate. If you can't find common ground, there will undoubtedly be problems down the road. For instance, do you both have the same philosophies about spending, saving, investing, and managing what money you have? Who makes the most and who pays which bills? Do you prorate expenses based on income or split everything down the middle? The answers to these questions might impact your decision to commingle your funds or keep them separate. Do you have the same philosophies about sex – absolute monogamy, open relationships, or somewhere in between? Do you have any secret fantasies and is your partner willing to try acting on them with you? You have to work to keep things exciting or invariably the bedroom will get a little stale. Try planning a sex vacation. It works for us. – D. Warner

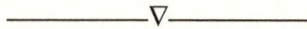

—————∇—————

Chicago, IL (USA)

Don't settle. There are a million men out there. The right one will find you and you him. All it takes is a smile. And after you have found the one, communicate and listen. – Dennis Hardenstein

—————∇—————

Los Angeles, CA (USA)

For a while yes. In order to make it work, honesty, transparency, conversation, if I'm living with you, in love or lust, let's talk, all night, ask questions. The deeper the understanding of who you're living with the better the accommodations, the 50/50,80/20,20/80, and hopefully the greater chance at something lasting. – Katorri A.

—————∇—————

Cleveland, OH (USA)

Friendship needs to be the foundation of it all, at least for me. I could have saved myself a lot of headaches if I realized that sooner. – Roger.

———————▽———————

New Orleans, LA (USA)

I have been with my partner Therese for 25 years. It's a give and take. Sometimes it tilts more on one side than the other. We have been through a lot. She was hurt and became disabled. We went through Hurricane Katrina, which was incredibly hard and Therese had a heart attack a few months ago. Life throws a curve ball, and it is better to have it with your best friend to help catch it. – Terry Gaskins

———————▽———————

Cathedral City, CA (USA)

It's been 36 years. I moved in with him soon after I met him. About three months afterwards I started dating him exclusively. People always say this, but it's true, don't go to bed angry. Try to talk about your feelings … that doesn't always work. Talk about what's upsetting you, rather than hold it in … that doesn't always work. Another thing is to have outside interests, separate. – Spike

———————▽———————

Adelaide, South Australia (Australia)

Oh geez, how much time have you got??? I have had two partners and they couldn't be more opposite if you tried. The first guy I met I actually befriended while using the Topham Mall beat. We had a few goes at each other, so to speak, and, me being me, would talk to him afterward. We got to know each other that way. After a couple of weeks or so I went back to his place at Norwood. I think that was the first time. Anyway, he said he wasn't feeling very well so I thought I would stay with him to make sure things were okay. Again, that's just the way I am. I'd rather stick around to make sure things were okay instead of pissing off and leaving someone in the lurch.

Soooo …

I rang up Mum and told her what was going on and I can't really remember how I worded it but it was kind of blurted out. Well, she went totally nuts and accused me of being on drugs and all sorts of garbage like that. I can clearly remember saying to her that "I'm still the same person, it's just this new thing you know about me." Oh no. She wanted me to come home and all that kind of stuff. Oh yeah, I was 25 at the time and was just living at home. Well, the conversation was cut short. The other guy thought it would be funny to record a message saying something like "we're off playing with our whips and chains and we'll get back to you when we can." Mum's message was "hooley dooley ... go back to your whips and chains ..." At that point I realised I couldn't go home because she would make it horrible. Well, that wasn't the end of it. She sent the police around because she thought I was being manipulated and/or had no control or whatever. Can't remember that modus operandi but I know the cop told me to go home to my mother. I could tell he didn't want to do it though. Mum and Stepdad knew the Publican at the Duke of Brunswick was an ex-cop and it seems they called in a favour. So with that I felt I needed to stay with him because home would be awful.

What also didn't help was my brother was also gay and he came out first. He was safe though because he lived with Dad so didn't have to put up with Mum's sniping. That was the other problem in that I would hear some terrible things behind Matthew's back. My Stepdad would refer to it as "a lifestyle" apparently they got their hopes up when told by some idiot it was a phase he was going through in order to get drugs. Matthew was quite drug fucked which is why Mum associated me with that and why my response was the way it was. I'm not Matthew, I'm me. You know I don't do that shit. But it was heard on deaf ears.

Didn't take me long to learn he was one for Domestic Violence. There was some argument and I got slapped across the face. He was a total fuckwit but there was nowhere for me to go so I was kind of trapped in there. I had a cracked bone in my wrist, there was something else that sent me to hospital. He would get on gear and be up for hours and I'd be too scared to go to sleep so I'd be running on empty. Or he would drink, and the booze would make him nasty as well. Money was wasted like crazy. He could get whatever he wanted but I had to go without. He manipulated the doctors so much he made me look like a loony to the point I was thrown into Woodleigh House thinking I was this crazy person. I kept a diary in there, too, and still have it. All this is diarised. Reading it back is like a different person. This was late '90s by this stage. He then decided sex work was a way to go so guess who got roped into that. If I didn't do that the hair would be pulled or I'd get whacked. Most people were okay actually. We moved to a unit in St Peters and, at that point, I decided enough was enough. I learned a lady had gotten away from an abusive partner by sequestering money into a bank account the partner did not know about. I was looking at doing that, but something happened which put a halt to that.

I work as a carer. He tried to sabotage everything along the way, though, like he did with my job at Tea Tree Gully library. How the hell I completed my studies I will never know. There was one day I was out all day with a lad I was taking to the Royal Show. I had a gap of an hour or two before going on to another I had to do a shower for. I decided not to go back home and have tea at Hungry Jack's at Firle. I got on well with the guy I showered so I'd often stay behind and chat. By the time I got home it was about 9:30. The place was quiet which was bliss, so I'd just get on the computer and do stuff. ' By this stage he was doping himself up on pills so it wasn't unusual for him to get wasted and fall asleep. At least he wasn't punching me or spitting in my face. It seemed to be a bit too quiet, so I went in to check on what was going on and I found him dead. Called the ambos and all that and he was carted off. For a while I kept in contact with his sister and brother in law but in the end, I just wanted to cut ties. So the best thing he did for me was cark it. Oh, he also did introduce me to 431 so there was something useful.

After he went off, I had an MRI done and there was scarring on the brain. Fortunately, that's all healed now.

This was 2005 so we flash forward to 2008 and I was at 431. So speaking of 431 ... I met this guy who I was unusually persistent with. Normally I won't be as persistent but this guy I was. Anyway, we went upstairs, as you do, did our bit and then went downstairs and started to talk. We got along really well so we swapped numbers. The next day I contacted him and his initial response was to ask "who are you." When reminded, though, he was pleased to hear from me so that was good. We met up a couple of times and he got the courage to ask me out on a date. I was so nervous that he wouldn't show and when he showed up he was nervous I wouldn't show. Our first date was Pancake Kitchen. It was all I could think of.

Anyway, we started to blossom something from there. He was the who made the first moves with everything, though. That first date was his idea. We would meet up at 431 because I couldn't go back to his place and I wasn't sure about him coming back to mine. He was from the country and would stay with his grandma when in the city. We got to know each other more and his grandma was lovely. She kind of knew about him and was really supportive. His Dad, while a typical country gruff farmer guy, was also quite good about the whole thing, much to Daniel's surprise. I said later on it probably did help I wasn't a screaming Queen tizzying around everywhere and was more "g'day" and firmly shake the hand. Daniel tended to agree with that.

Things blossomed and he was the total opposite to the first one. He was a really lovely guy, very kind and all sorts of stuff like that. His family were quite supportive. By that stage mine were all gone so they never got a chance to meet him. I always feel that's a shame as Dad, especially, would have gotten along with him.

In fact, prior to meeting him, I had a dream where Dad and I were at a cafe or somewhere like that and a guy was trying to get my attention. Dad told me to go after him but when I did the guy had gone. Dad said: "Don't worry, you'll get another chance." Well, that was the week I met Daniel. He said he went to 431 the previous week, hated it but something compelled him to go back the next week which is when we met.

We finally moved in together in 2010. We had a commitment ceremony in 2011. Again, he had to be the one to pop the question. We appeared together at the Mass Illegal Wedding and as soon as Sue Wickham pronounced us illegally wed, I burst into tears and all the cameras zoomed in one me. I was interviewed by the ABC and all sorts. I still believe it affected a care work job I had but that can never be proved, even though my work spat out the biggest load of bullshit about it. They said the decision was made prior to the march and I called that out by saying the timeline was I was told after the march. Oh no no no, it was made the Friday before. Protesteth too much there.

We did split in 2014 but we have remained very good friends and always have each others' backs. Heck, it's just as well we do get along because we're the backbone of the tenor section in the Qwire. We also are the most animated ones in concert. We were the ones doing the Dancing Queen moves at last years' concert while everyone else just stood there looking bored. On more than one occasion I've had great feedback from people saying without us, the thing would look boring.

What advice would I give? There are more support systems out there for Domestic Violence so use them if that happens. That idea of sequestering the money worked for that lady, too. Do the dishes, too. That's a bone of contention with many, I'm sure. Enjoy each other's company but don't get jealous with their friends as that can drive a wedge and be the basis for an argument. The good one and I never did that but the bad one did. Trust is definitely the key, too. If you're not sure of something and you know you can talk to the person then calmly do it. I always have a thing where if you're trying to have a discussion and/or argument about something you have immediately lost it if you swear. To me you've gone the low route that way. A discussion is more likely to stay that way if you let it stay that way.

When Daniel and I talked about splitting, it was a four hour conversation where no voices were raised and it was calmly discussed. He was worried I'd boot him back up to living with his grandma or whoever but there was no need to do that. It was decided to still remain friends. I do realise that's rare but it did help we had separate rooms. He was a starfish so a double bed was going to have me whacked but by accident, he would have felt bad knowing my history, etc. so it was decided to sleep in separate beds in separate rooms. When we needed to make whoopie it was always in his bed because mine was backed up against the wall. Don't want an arm or leg to fly out the window. – Robert Verrall

———————▽———————

Palm Springs, CA (USA)

I currently live with my partner. We've been together for five or six years. Let me tell you, it's hard work. Don't think it's going to be easy. Every day is not a parade. A lot of days it rains on your parade. Be honest, be truthful, and never set out to intentionally hurt someone. Think about their feelings. Choose your words and choose your words carefully. – Crusher

———————▽———————

Chicago, IL (USA)

I lived with one spouse for 17 years. The advice I would offer is the same advice I've heard given to straight couples: You may be one-half of a couple, but that doesn't mean you can give the relationship just 50% of your attention. You need to give 100% all the time. – Steve Kmetko

———————▽———————

Palm Springs, CA (USA)

I've lived with my current partner for ten years. I have looked at other couples as role models in this and I was married to a woman for five years. When we got married it ruined our relationship because we were then institutionalized, treated like real estate and one couldn't do anything without the other one. When I got a gay partner there was no role model for this. I would say the best advice to give … to keep the love going, you have to make exceptions for the details. I don't want to say compromise … of course, we all have to compromise. Maybe a better way to think about it is, to grow together and stay together as a couple, you have to be very supportive of each other. Especially of where you have things in common and where you don't. You have to give space and support to your partner. There is no formula to achieve that, except for to be present. I think communication, verbal constant communication, is the key to making it work. – Greg Day

———————▽———————

Chicago, IL (USA)

The short answer is yes. I have a pattern of being in long term relationships and jumping into them, trying to make them work, holding onto them way too long and then having some sort of disastrous ending. I've had three long term relationship, Andre is No 4, and they've all ended with a lawyer involved. So I guess my first advice would be to get a good lawyer. If I had to give any advice, it would be don't jump into anything, really get to know the person … you have to wait until you get behind the façade of that person when they're not on their best behavior. Sometimes that takes a long time, sometimes it takes years. Certainly, don't take all your assets and sign them over to your lover, [laughs] as someone might have done in their early years. I'd be living in a much nicer home. – Thomas Stribling

—————▽—————

Cathedral City, CA (USA)

I find the biggest key in a gay relationship is that you have to have communication daily, no matter if it's positive or negative. If you don't have that communication, then you don't have the basis of a relationship. Most couples I've seen over the years of being in the gay community, they lack the communication. They'd rather cheat on each other than talk to each other. They'd rather lie. They'd tell their friends, but they can't tell their partner. How can you be in a relationship if you can't communicate with each other? To me it's just two guys or two women living together. – Marcous

—————▽—————

Cathedral City, CA (USA)

Well, I'm 67 years old and I had one lover for 3 ½ years which was abusive, so I don't give people advice. Especially people who are in relationships already. – David Hardy

—————▽—————

Santa Fe, NM (USA)

I had a partner for 13 years and he died 6 1/2 years ago. I think what made the relationship work there was the communication. We talked about a lot of different things. If we disagreed on something – there weren't too many disagreements – it was more that we talked through things. He was retired at the time and I was still working as an educator, but he was very supportive of what I did, and he actually learned about education from me. After I retired I started a consulting company where I would do training for schools and he would put all the power point presentations together for me. – Guy Seliers

—————▽—————

(Germany)

I did twice. I'd say that communication is the key, and checking in with your own needs, ideals, hopes, and to be able to communicate them and to see for both if those comfort zones match or can merge. – Cornelius Günther Körn

—————▽—————

Norfolk, VA (USA)

Make sure you're compatible. If you're willing to give in to certain lifestyles, like a vegan versus a meat eater, a Buddhist versus a Baptist, or atheist versus Christian. I remember this cartoon, two masculine men, one blond, one dark hair, they were both crying. The caption was, "I'm sorry dear it's not going to work, our furniture won't even match." You can't jump into a relationship with someone until you really know them. – David Hayes

—————▽—————

The Berkeshires, CT (USA)
Niagara Falls, Ontario (Canada)

When I was in college, I lived with my first boyfriend, James. We lived a short time together. I met him in April 1990. We worked together in summer camp in Connecticut, in the Berkshire's. Then he moved in with me when I started the next semester at school, which would have been my last year on campus before I did my student teachings. He lived with me from September until right before the holidays. We got along great and everything. It's just that I was in school working on my life goals and future, and he didn't know what he wanted to do, so he did a telemarketing thing, he worked at KFC. I told people I had pans of coleslaw and cold chicken in the refrigerator all the time, so in winter I had a boyfriend and chicken dinner. But to really make it work you need to sit down before you live together and talk about finances and make sure the communication is good, above anything. And what are your goals, what do you want to do together? Not everything is set in stone, but you really need to have that communication and run over what your likes and dislikes are. I always say don't move in right away. You've got to know their smallest quirks because anything can set a blaze under you. James and I got along great and we didn't fight or anything. He enjoyed cooking so he would find crafty ways to make the great American casserole ... I say that with a smirk on my face. They were ok. You've got to have good communication. If you don't have that communication and openness ... I think that's what happened with James and I. He moved in very quickly. Just don't do it really fast. Don't get that wedding dress out before you do the courtship. James passed away from complications of AIDS in 1998. I learned a lot from him. When we first dated in Connecticut, he gave up a job at Perry drug store, where he was a pharmaceutical tech, to come and work with me for the summer. I was very honored by that ... that my man was going to be with me in the summer.

This was before I knew that leather was a thing. I don't know how I found this place; I think I had one of those Damron guides. We were in Niagara Falls, Canada and we found this gay B&B. So we pulled up ... it was a long way from Connecticut through upstate New York, a boring ass drive and James was enamored laying on the bed with all these Agatha Christie novels around the headboard. We went out to dinner at this Italian restaurant. We didn't have a lot of money. It was one of those touristy places, shit but we didn't care. We were just having a good time. We were walking out and this big leather guy walks out front. It was all touristy and this guy stood out. He had everything, chains dangling and everything. I had not been around that. Now, I'd be "Oh well, big deal." The guy walked by and James looks at him and goes, "Honey, how do you think I would look like that?" Without missing a beat, I said, "Lonely." Even when he was on his death bed and he could still hear me. He was at his mother's house. I used to whisper in his ear, "James, remember that time ... " and I'd tell the whole story about the leather guy. James would laugh with all he could muster. Our sense of humor was really screwed up and I loved it. We would do this thing we called Kiss Me. We would be out in public and I'd say, "James if you love me, you'll kiss me right now." And he'd go, "goddarnit." So then it was his turn. We would be somewhere totally inappropriate. It was that stupid little couple thing, but I loved it. – Greg R. Baird

————————∇————————

Tallahassee, FL (USA)
Santa Cruz, CA (USA)
Redwood Valley, CA) (USA)

My first two live-in relationships with guys, at ages 19 and 20, were short-lived. Both guys were compulsive liars. Twenty-five years later, I decided to settle in. That lasted only a few years, mostly because I was unable to commit to a long-term relationship. I'm now in a 22 years long "marriage" that is based on strong and reconfirmed devotion, commitment, compatibility, communication (emphasis on listening), and negotiation. Those qualities are what it took, and what continue to sustain our relationship, even beyond the waning sexual connection. – T. Lark Letchworth

—————∇—————

San Diego, CA (USA)
Cathedral City, CA (USA)

I lived with one partner for seven years and currently another for 10 years. Hell if I know! – Paul Harris

—————∇—————

Darlinghurst, New South Wales (Australia)

Jeez – where do I start lol. From my first boyfriend Fred ... this was a couple of months after coming out ... I learnt that if you are a bottom ... don't try to have a sexual relationship with another bottom!! And educate yourself more fully about aspects of gay life that you weren't aware of ... like beats ... which he was addicted to! Doomed from Day 1!

From Frank, my first partner after moving back to Sydney (a relationship that happened after I went home with him on the night I met his group of friends outside the Albury Hotel ... and was trying to pick up his housemate) I learnt not to make sex a Sunday morning habit ... and not to lie about him (a) dyeing his hair, and (b) having dentures, which I found out about when he came home totally shit-faced one night, and lost them when he threw up in the loo. He was another beat addict ... seems I learnt nothing from Fred! Our relationship lasted about 12 months. He died from AIDS in the late '80s. We remained friends even after our break-up. Never hold grudges if relationships don't work out. It takes two to start it ... and two to finish it.

From Damian, my partner for about two years after Frank and I split, I learnt not to get into relationships with someone in their early 20s ... nor someone you met when they worked in a gay male brothel. And don't be too blasé when they flaunt another guy they are getting off with to your friends ... behind your back ... and think they are not going to tell you! When this relationship ... not surprisingly ... headed towards the rocks, he decided that the best way to find out just how much I cared about him was to fake a suicide attempt ... staged with empty pill bottles. This is not a good thing to do if you are desperate to save a relationship. It was the final straw, but again we remained friends after the break-up. He died from AIDS in the early '90s. He was followed by Tony, who was visiting Sydney from Queensland, and I met in my local pub. Tony was very naive, and very dependent in the couple of years we were together. Due to this, I found it difficult to extricate myself from yet another relationship that just wasn't working. Sexually, it was a disaster, and I truly dislike being totally depended on in a relationship, the one that has to initiate everything. Tony also had issues with alcohol abuse at that time, and told me several lies when we first met, which eventually came to light. Never a good thing to do. We didn't so much split up ... we continued to flat together ... as me moving myself into the spare bedroom. We not only remained friends ... he is currently my housemate.

A_____ was yet another short-lived, disastrous relationship. We got along well, but we had an erratic sex life due to him having a low libido ... driven by his addiction to prescription drugs ... which he stole from deceased patients in the aged-care health facility he worked in. This led to us having a huge fight in a pub one night, and he left and went home. I stayed at the pub and fumed until I finally snapped, stormed down the road to home, almost ripped a screen door off his hinges, stormed up the stairs ... our other housemate took one look at me and fled ... and dragged him down the stairs. I was tempted to hit him ... I was so furious ... but it's really not in my nature to be violent ... so kicked his fish tank instead, breaking it. That was pretty well the end of it. The moral here was ... if you are having issues, talk it out. Don't let friction build up, as it will reach an explosive point, which is bad for both of you. A_____ and I are still friends.

John ... we met at a very bad time for me. He is someone I could gave settled with for ... who knows ... a long time. I treated him badly ... something I have recently apologised to him for, an admission of guilt that was, for me, cathartic. I had just finished up at Liquorland after all the shit that had gone on there. My health was deteriorating, and I sort of gave myself maybe another two years before AIDS got the better of me. I had beaten the odds as it was. I didn't want to intentionally get a partner tied into all the shit that AIDS involved ... the slow, inevitable decline of one's health, the hospitalisations, the shortening periods between high and low times. I had seen too many other couples go through it. I knew it really wasn't my decision to make within a relationship, but I thought it was very unfair, knowing what was coming, to drag someone into it. So just as John thought things were travelling well ... I pulled the plug on it. Don't get involved with someone if you are not in the right headspace. It's unfair, and unhealthy for both of you.

Then there was David! 16 years this one lasted for ... the longest for both of us. On the surface, it appeared to be almost a perfect relationship. For the first few years, the sex was wild. But that passes. We almost never argued, but that is not always a good thing. I like to keep the peace and will compromise my own beliefs and opinions if it means the peace is maintained. There was a lot of this over those 16 years. We had a pretty good life. Nice homes, never went without anything, had regular holidays. I got along well with his parents and relatives. David was an extrovert, and I'm a bit of an introvert ... so that balanced out. I turned a blind eye to a lot that went on over those years. David pretty well played up behind my back from the word go. I'm monogamous inside a relationship, and even though it crossed my mind occasionally to play up ... I could never bring myself to do it. I was angry and upset about it in the early days ... he thought I didn't know, but I'm not an idiot. I never confronted him about it. Ever! As time went on, I just accepted it. That adage of "well, they might be fucking around, but they always come home" was the attitude I adopted. But as the years rolled by, it eventually became the elephant-in-the-room. David would never talk about any issues we had in our relationship, be it financial, emotional, sexual or anything else. So when the issue of the elephant-in-the-room had to be raised ... and there is only so long you can leave it for, as it grows and grows ... it had to be me who raised it. It was a good thing, as we both then realised that our relationship had run its course. There was genuine love there, of that there was no doubt, but it wasn't enough to hold it together. There was a 14 year age gap ... I'm the older ... which had become more obvious as we both aged. David wanted to be open about his sex life ... and I just wanted one, having gone without for some years. So, we called it a day, though again we are still close friends. So, out of all if this, what advise could I give anyone in a relationship? Firstly ... talk to each other! Be honest, and don't keep secrets! If David had been willing to talk about our sex life, it could probably have been resolved. I would not have been averse to third parties being brought into the relationship ... nor to the possibility of an open relationship. Not talking about it just turned it poisonous. Be clear about what you both bring to the relationship ... and what you expect from it. Don't push for a serious relationship if you are not in the right headspace ... there are other alternatives, such as just being fuck buddies for some time. Don't live together if you don't have a lot in common. It just causes conflict. A relationship can work just as well from two separate residences. The old-fashioned attitude to relationships is that you both have to make sacrifices for it to work ... but I don't necessarily agree. I think both parties can run separate finances ... as long as household costs are shared ... that both parties can retain a good bit of their independence, without compromising it. Use common sense. Have mutual respect for each other. Be practical. Be romantic. And most importantly ... if it ends, don't play the blame game ... don't hate each other, or denigrate each other. Even after you break up, the love can still be there. It is not fair to try to demean or destroy it. If you fight, don't demean each other ... and ALWAYS be willing to say "I'm sorry" ... whether you think you are right ... or wrong. Holding onto anger is

poisonous, and destructive! As is always thinking you are right!
Every year, I have a pretty-Christmas party at home. Three ex's attend it …
Tony, John and David. There is still love between all of us, and I am so glad
to have their friendship. Because, after all, who knows more about each other!
– Tim Alderman

—————▽—————

St. Cloud, MN (USA)

I have a wonderful partner and we have been together for almost twenty-five
years. Communication, cooperation, and compromise are the "secrets" to a
committed relationship if you both truly love each other. – Rachel
Wexelbaum

—————▽—————

Arlington, Texas (USA)

I met J.P. Jackson at a summer theatre camp in Denton, Texas in 1975. I was
still a virgin and he gave me my first kiss. We were on again/off again lovers
for 10 years. And in the mid-80s, J.P. suggested we buy a house and settle
down. I said yes, but I predicated it on one condition. We had always had an
"open" relationship, but we never brought our partners home. I told J.P. that
I could take the big leap as long as we continued the "no tricks at home" rule.
So, we found a lovely tract house in Arlington, Texas, and we moved in,
determined to queer up redneck suburbia. And we were happy, for a time.

I think it was during Pride Week of 1986 that I went to an all-night
rave at the Starck Club, a Bauhaus-style pleasure palace. When I returned
home at dawn, I opened the door to our bedroom and someone was sleeping
in my bed and it wasn't Goldilocks. I was heartbroken. I went into our guest
bedroom and locked the door. I stayed there all day on Sunday and waited
until I heard J.P. leave for work on Monday.

I went to the bank and withdrew my half of the money from our
joint bank account. And I stopped at a hardware store and bought a can of
red spray paint. When I got home, I went into our bedroom, took down the
large print of Moira Shearer in *The Red Shoes* that hung over our bed. And in
big, red letters I painted ASSASSIN! I packed up all my clothes, kissed the
Maltese dog goodbye, and got onto Interstate Highway 20 and headed west.

I don't think I was cut out for cottage small by the waterfall. – David
Clayton

—————▽—————

Brunswick, ME (USA)

Oh, Lord! Where to start? As I said previously, I am in a long-term relationship with a man twelve years my senior. We met through a classified ad in *The Dallas Observer* in 1989 when I was 40 and he was 52. I knew he was the one for me, but it took him a long time to see that, due to his own self-esteem issues. Prior to meeting Doug, I'd only had one other long-term relationship, in my early twenties, when I lived in a somewhat unhealthy, immature relationship with a man my own age. I threw away a good job and moved from Dallas to Atlanta in 1973 to make a life with him. He was narcissistic and irresponsible, but extremely jealous. We eventually broke up on friendly terms and I discovered that he had been unfaithful to me with one of our best friends. I was lucky to get out of that relationship with only a bankruptcy to deal with.

It may sound trite, but "love and maturity" go a long way in keeping a relationship going. If you really love someone, you'll accept them as they are, not as you wish they were. When arguments arise, don't always try to win. When your partner feels threatened or hurt, just don't rub the wound, stand your ground, grab him and give him a big hug. If he pulls away, don't let him. Show him you mean business, that your love is unconditional. While not trying to be "the martyr," giving and sacrifice are important from both sides of a relationship. In time, sex becomes less important, so don't press it, if your partner loses interest. It's not necessarily about you. There are many ways of showing affection and intimacy. The two most important things loves can say to each other are "I love you" and "I'm sorry" (when wrong). Never be too proud to say either. – Michael Pickel

———————∇———————

Chicago, IL (USA)
Glenview, IL (USA)

I lived with my late partner, Arthur, starting in 1976. We moved in together several weeks after we met. Looking back, I thought it was too soon to do that. Yet, in spite of that statement, I don't regret it. We got along fine and our values were very similar. We had to compromise on very little. There was an easy flow of give-and-take between us.

I have been with my current husband for the last 27 years. Unlike Arthur, we did not move in together until six months later. This was due to the difficulty in finding a place agreeable to both of us. I was living in Chicago at the time and he was living in Des Plaines. I found there was more of an adjustment this time around. He was more of an extrovert and I, an introvert.

So I wasn't used to the social calendar he kept. It didn't take long to adjust because I valued my alone time which I obtained when he went out for evening dinners with his friends. So it did work out well.

What advice would I give? Well, intuition helps. What does your heart tell you when you see his residence? Is it clean or dirty? Does it conflict with your values of how you would like to see a home? If he has an animal, how does he treat it? What does your heart tell you when you see him interact with his friends (or your friends, for that matter). Learn about his values (which can but doesn't have to include religion). Do they have a common ground with your values? What is the nature of your chemistry outside of the bedroom? While disagreements can occur, if you end up arguing too often, it can be a danger signal that there might be an issue that needs to be resolved. I consider myself lucky that I moved in so quickly with both of my husbands. That may not work for everyone else. So, contradicting my own experience, take time to get to know the other person. Is he jealous or possessive? Better to see that or any other problem while you are dating so it can be addressed beforehand. – Yehuda Jacobi

—————▽—————

Palm Springs, CA (USA)

I had one 15-year relationship – I ended that one after domestic violence in the early 1990's. Now I am enjoying my husband who I have known and loved for 25 years.

Advice? Honesty. Commitment. Compromise. Shared goals. Flexibility. Humor. – Tony Earl

—————▽—————

King, NC (USA)

After my thirteen-year traditional marriage to a woman ended (and three children), my first LGBTQ partner had also been married for eighteen years who had four children about the same age as my own kids. We were together for fourteen years. I used to kid that we were the gay version of *The Brady Bunch* in those early days. My second long-term LGBTQ relationship was with a severe, abusive alcoholic that lasted for seven years. My third LGBTQ relationship lasted twelve years and ended suddenly when I realized that he was (and had been) involved with someone else for over two years. I blamed myself for not being aware enough to realize this. That realization said a lot about the state of our relationship in the first place.

I am now in my fourth LGBTQ relationship and we've been

together for eight years and married for five.

Looking back, I smile when I think that I've probably been single only twenty-seven minutes total my entire life after I left home as a teenager – and that's really saying something being that I'm nearly seventy years old, now.

What advice would I give someone who is considering a live-in situation? Well, being in my fifth long-term relationship now, I offer up to the gods each morning a prayer to give me more patience, understanding, kindness, and to be more loving. By keeping those things in the forefront of my desire, they really do begin to take place in my life.

My success in a relationship and obtaining peace and less drama are important things to me. They have to begin with me proactively taking responsibility for that happening – not blaming anyone else if it doesn't happen.

And also, NEVER let more than an hour go by without addressing a disagreement or argument. And one other thing, NEVER storm off in the night. That never did anything for me but to escalate things. The pleasure and drama of doing such a thing is short-lived. – Ron Cline

———————∇———————

Charlottetown, Prince Edward Island (Canada)

I'm married, and not surprisingly, my husband and I live together. I'd lived, off and on, with one former lover. The best advice I can give about making a live-in relationship work is to make sure the communication is open, allow each other to have your own space when needed, and that you both have some interests separate from each other that you actively participate it. Also having some friends that are yours exclusively is a solid idea. The big one, though, is to keep communication open, from talking about monogamy vs. an open relationship, to having an understanding of who's responsible (financially or otherwise) for what at any given time. – Dave Stewart

———————∇———————

San Diego, CA (USA)

I transitioned with a beautiful trans girl in San Diego. We both transitioned together, which was phenomenal. I'm an extrovert, they're an introvert, they were a sub for me. It was a great experience, but it didn't work out in the end because after the primary transition, the first couple of years of hormones, the crazies happen … you get through all that and you start finding your way, find your sea legs … and you realize that it's not really about falling in love, it's about surviving the storm. That's what I was doing. Did I fall in love with them, their personality? No. I care very much about them but we were so incompatible on so many things. I put those aside to just be with someone. My suggestion is, find your strength, find who you are, bring to the table the best you, you can. And the relationship will be stronger. – Serafine Sawyer

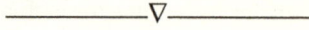

—————∇—————

Milwaukee, WI (USA)

Yes, a partner. Only one for 33+ years. My advice for ALL couples. Respect each other's beliefs, way of thinking, their likes, dislikes … and so on. You don't have to like everything a partner does or is, as long as it's not hurting you or someone else. But if you respect them and are honest with them, as they should be with you, you will have a lifetime of love and hopefully laughter. – Sherrie Howe

—————∇—————

Des Moines, IA (USA)

Yes. Say "yes" more than "no." Like the song says, "It's hard out there for a pimp" so create an environment that is a real refuge free of bullshit. Fighting doesn't serve anyone. Breathe and be patient. Learn to compromise. Being right isn't worth anything. Be fair. Be real. Always temper truth with tact. Seek peace. Learn what love really is by loving yourself. Learn to step up, step back and step aside. Accentuate the positive. Say thank you. Act your age not your shoe size. Jealousy is like drinking poison and hoping someone else will die. – Sr. Freida Peoples aka DJ Chrysler Sheldon

—————∇—————

Fort Lauderdale, FL (USA)

My husband and I have been together 27 years. The first thing I'd say to anyone is lower your expectations. No one person is going to be the be-all and end-all for you. Next, be forgiving and learn to compromise. Finally buy property together it makes splitting up harder. – Rick Karlin

—————∇—————

HOW DID YOUR PARENTS REACT WHEN YOU CAME OUT TO THEM?

Lewiston, NY (USA)

I ended up not coming out to them. Even when they got older and I thought they could handle it. I lived with a guy for 17 years in the same house, we had a camper, we did everything together, we were in a band, in a business, traveled together, both without girlfriends. I don't know how they didn't figure it out but I thought it would hurt them more than anything. It was the big pink elephant in the room. It was very palpable when I was there and then when I came back once I was recording a CD and I had this lock of fuchsia hair in the front and I went to visit. I hadn't seen my parents for two years and they looked at me and said, "You look terrible, what is that?" Everybody shunned me just because my hair was like that. I said, "Don't you get it, I have an agent and I just put out a CD and it's got my hair like this and he said, 'Leave it like that for performances.' It's business. I'm in show business." It was odd to me, that type of thing … that's why I left that little town. It was too small for me. You do anything there and it's just outrageous. When I went to the city, I realized that's where I belonged. It was too small of a pond for me. – James Scalfani

───────▽───────

(USA)

Silence, emotional hatefulness, astonishing in adults I had always held to be liberal. They were active in the civil rights movement in the 1960s, but that discourse didn't carry into the gay lives of their two sons (yes, my brother was gay, too). I divorced myself from them for about a decade, right after my brother died of AIDS-related disease. Finally, we three survivors made a sort of peace until my father died. After that, I once again divorced myself from my mother. It seemed to be, and still does, even after her death, that it was my father who grew into understanding and acceptance. My mother on the other hand never changed from the first memory I have of her. – Oran Walker

—————▽—————

South Bend, IN (USA)

My father had died. My mother was not very happy, in fact she threw me out of the house. I was homeless for about a year. Like a lot of parents, she thought this was somehow her fault or somebody else's fault. Regardless, it was a bad thing. After about a year I was desperate to be in shelter again. She did love me very much, but it was an aspect of me she couldn't accept. "I'll accept you back but this is a subject that can't be discussed." I went back for a couple of years and finally moved to Chicago. – Steve

—————▽—————

Chicago, IL (USA)

When I came out as trans to my mother, she had a really hard time with it. She had a lot of gay friends, but her only experience with gender nonconformity was her friend Simon. Simon was an older gay with a two-story house. The entire second floor was full of gowns and tiaras for him to play dress up. His number one rule though was that this stuff was never to come downstairs. It was a dirty secret, never supposed to see the light of day. So, when I came out as trans, it made no sense to my mother. She didn't understand why I couldn't do like Simon. That she could have supported, dressing like a woman in private but still presenting male in public. That couldn't work for me though. It took her a long time to come to terms with it. – C'est Kevvie (Wilhelmina)

—————▽—————

Detroit, MI (USA)

Well, I didn't tiptoe out of the closet, I kicked the doors down with my silver platform boots. One day I was the meek geek they knew as Terry, the next I was a creature of indeterminate sex (*You've got your mother in a whirl, she's not sure if you're a boy or a girl)* was my LIFE. Minds were blown. They just were not ready for the budding pansy that was their son(?). We had a couple of enormous fights, one was about how much I adored, no loved David Bowie. Then, as soon as I turned eighteen, I moved out of the house. Since the drinking age had been dropped from twenty-one to eighteen, I was an adult, even though I was still in high school. I moved into a house for gay youth run by the Gay Liberation Front in Detroit. I stayed in school but my mind and heart were not in it anymore. Before I graduated, I was working as a drag queen in the bars as Terri Stuart. My theatre training at Cass had given me a seamed stocking covered leg up in many ways in that respect. One thing I did was perform opera arias, something none of the queens were doing back then, in Detroit anyway, and those old white queens ATE IT UP! My parents and I have come full circle since then with them being Proud that their boy made somewhat of a name for himself by running for President of the United States. In drag. – Terence Smith (Joan Jett Blakk)

———————∇———————

Lawton, OK (USA)

I was at work, I was doing retail, a cash runner for the cashiers. My mom brought me the keys to her car which I gave her. I gave her my car because I'd got a new '78 Pontiac LeMans. She took my keys from my Pontiac LeMans and gave me the '69 Ford Fairlane and said, "There's not much gas in it, give me all your money you've got in your wallet and come straight home and don't go anywhere." So I get there and she starts asking me all these off the wall questions. All of a sudden, she said, "I found the books under your bed and threw them all away." It was my muscleman magazines. Basically, they said you're going to get fixed, get shock therapy.

I left and went to Atomic Annie's and I was crying. My parents found out about me and I'm blackballed in the house and I had nowhere else to go. Around the corner comes this cute redhead guy from Pennsylvania. His name was Bill _____. Biggest mistake of my life. He said you need to come and live with me for a little bit. He was visiting from Pennsylvania and was visiting somebody in the army, a girlfriend of his and her husband. I stayed with them for about a week and the girlfriend got tired of us making giggling and kissing sounds coming from Bill's bedroom. She called the police. Her neighbor was very anti-gay and convinced the girl to call the police on us, so we gathered up our stuff and left. We went to another person's house and stayed with them. Then he said, "Let's move to Pennsylvania." So we went from Oklahoma to Pennsylvania.

When my mom got sick and I visited her, I visited her twice. The third time was her funeral. She softened but she was still prejudiced. She did not like ... she used the "N" word a lot. My sister was the same way. She was talking about how the boyfriend of her granddaughter was Black. She would badmouth the blacks up and down. My mouthed dropped open and I said, "Mom, my Cliff, that I'm living with, is Black." She turned white. I walked out of the room. This was when she was sick. – David Hayes

—————▽—————

Texas (USA)

HORRIBLY! My religiously fundamentalist parents in our rural community berated me and verbally abused me for months after I had told them. I had been married and told them after my marriage ended. My father would literally scream at me on the phone during this time, telling me a real man would not have abandoned his family and have repressed his orientation and stayed with his family. Later when I was in relationship with my life partner, my parents attempted to be more accepting, but remained homophobic. – Anonymous

—————▽—————

Chicago, IL (USA)

I never really came out. We never had that discussion. If you saw my bedroom as a teenager, posters of Boy George, Frankenfurter and Greg Louganis, it was pretty obvious but we never really talked about it. – Mike

—————▽—————

North Carolina (USA)

I never have. It's something that we never discuss. – Randy

—————▽—————

Springdale, AR (USA)

It was pretty rough with my mom. My mom found out before I came out. When she did find out she went ballistic, she got out the Bible. We looked at the Bible together, we prayed, she yelled at me, she screamed. She said, "We cannot tell your father because he will castrate you." So for three years she did not tell my father but when we had discussions, she would threaten to tell him. Finally, I said, "OK I'm going to tell him myself." So I called my dad at work and he wasn't there and about five minutes later there was a knock at my door … I was living in an apartment … and it was him. My mother had told him. I answered the door and wanted to know if he could come in. He said, "Your mother told me that you are gay and I just want you to be happy. I don't want anyone to hurt you." This was what I was so afraid of for three years. My dad was very loving and understanding about it. – Renny

———————▽———————

Northern Virginia (USA)

I was going to graduate school in Columbus, Ohio. I had been living with my African-American boyfriend for a couple years. My parents told me they were coming up to see me graduate. Oh shit! So I wrote them a letter, "Before you come up here there is something you need to know … It is not your fault …" They said, "We love you but we think you should see a counselor." (I already had) They came up to Ohio, watched me graduate and never met my boyfriend. – Lars von Keitz

———————▽———————

San Francisco, CA (USA)

I wrote a letter to father when I was 38. (My mother had already died, and I suspect she probably would have disowned me if I had come out to her.) My father wrote me back and admitted that he had sort of known this for a long time. We had been estranged for about five years … my doing, and I wanted to reconnect. His letter was supportive and gentle. – Gary Borgstedt

———————▽———————

Bloomingdale, IL (USA)

Oh boy that was fun. My mother was the first one and she flipped her lid. The funniest thing about that is, when this whole thing was happening, she said to me, "It's taken me almost 20 years to get used to living in the United States, and you pull this on me now." OK … I have no idea what that means about being an immigrant. But she came around. And ended up – through Horizons – I introduced her to people from PFLAG and she's absolutely in my corner and that's wonderful. My father, on the other hand, we barely had a relationship to begin with because I was a nelly little boy and my father was an Iowa hillbilly. The only thing he ever said to me was – I remember this vividly, as I was in the basement when I was home from university – he's walking out the door and he's like, "Boy, straighten up your act." That was the only thing that was said by him. However, it got so bad that after my freshman year at university I was home for the summer. I was working a graveyard shift – sleeping during the day – and I get up and my mom is sitting on the step glaring at my father. What happened is she kept him at knifepoint from beating the shit out of me and kicking me out of the house. I shed not one tear when that man passed. We barely had a relationship. But again, he was a first-class bigot. – Drew

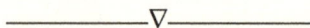

—————▽—————

Waverly, IA (USA)

I never formally came out to my parents. I didn't expect them to talk about their sex lives so didn't feel the need to tell them about mine. My mother probably figured it out, however, since I came home one day and found her swatting flies with a copy of a gay newspaper. – Robert Beck

—————▽—————

Rockford, IL (USA)

I came out three times. The first time was when I was sixteen and came out as Bi to my mom and stepdad. They did not take the news well. Between my Stepdad trying to shove the Bible down my throat and my mother worried I would end up like her brother, this was not a good experience. When I came out to my dad at nineteen, it was much easier. He confronted me about the rumors that he had heard around campus. When I told him that yes it was true, he simply told me that he wanted me to be happy and safe. This still sticks with me that I had his support. Six years after I had first come out, I told my mom and stepdad again. This time it allowed me to be better prepared for their responses. And while I don't think we would sit down and talk about me dating I do think they accept me. So for that I am thankful. – Patrick J. Murphy III

—————▽—————

Chicago, IL (USA)

I came out when I was 19. I'd been living in the city for maybe six months. I read a book, a "how to" book about coming out. At the end of the book you were supposed to write a letter to whoever, in this case it was my mom. I know this is shocking but, "Gay man has close relationship with his mom."

When the letter arrived, before she even opened it, she knew what it was. It was like, "Why is he sending me a letter?" She was cool, my mom was the black sheep of her family, so she was always very supportive. I always brought my boyfriends around. At the time I came out I didn't have a relationship with my dad. That ebbed and flowed throughout my adulthood. When I did finally start talking to him again, I told him and he was fine with it too. It was what it was. The parents always know, especially the moms. We think, "Oh my God, I don't want my parents to know." It's such nonsense, they almost always know. – Jeff Ramone

——————▽——————

Paris (France)

My father was dead by the time I came out. My mother reacted oddly: we had never been close, and I barely knew her. Even though she had many gay friends, she didn't really approve of me, and in the end, we parted in acrimony. I didn't speak to her again or have contact with her before she died 13 years ago. – Louis Richard de Bourbon de Parme et de Savoie, Prince de la Pau

——————▽——————

Bellport, NY (USA)

My Mom didn't accept it at first. But ever since she befriended her neighbor who happens to be gay, she has calmed down a lot.

When I came out to my Dad as bisexual, he proceeded to tell me that I'm actually a lesbian. In my case he was right but he believes bisexuality doesn't exist. That's terrible. A year later I came out to him again as a lesbian. His words, "Yes, no babies!" I was stunned. – Erin Michelle Miller

——————▽——————

South Carolina (USA)

My father passed when I was little so I never got to know what he would have thought. Oddly it was Dr. Phil who helped me come out to my mom. I had been petrified of telling her. She was the only person in my life (even counting my siblings) that it would have killed me if she'd rejected me. Many times I'd go to tell her and my mouth would dry up, my throat would close and the moment would pass.

One day I was visiting and she was watching TV (Dr. Phil) and I was reading a magazine. Dr. Phil's topic was something completely off topic but as he came back from commercial he said he wanted to take a phone call that had come in. A mother was calling to ask how she could get her daughter to realize she should change colleges because the "girls" she hung around with at school had made her a lesbian. I heard lesbian and froze. My mouth went dry and I tried to look at mom's reaction without seeming to be looking at mom's reaction. Dr. Phil went on to say having the daughter change schools wouldn't help because the girls hadn't made her a lesbian, since being homosexual was biological and not a choice. (I am, by the way, puckering up my butthole so tight I could create a diamond). The mother counters Dr. Phil and he holds strong to his point and then goes back to the topic of the day. I don't know where the strength came from for me to ask, but I turned to mom and said, "What do you think of that?" She said Dr. Phil was right. It didn't matter who someone loved they were still "the same sweet person" they always had been. My mother always referred to me and my siblings as the same sweet people so I knew she was making a reference to me. That opened the topic and she was fine. – Chris Grace

------------▽------------

Detroit, MI (USA)

Remember Bea Arthur? *Maude* and Dorothy on *Golden Girls?* My mother, Jewell, looked, talked, and acted just like her. Except my mother was meaner. The whole world revolved around Jewell. She expected everyone – me, my sisters, my dad, really everyone – to do what she told them. She was loud, crass, demanding, and simply a Methodist terror. Oh, and she was homophobic. She never got over my being gay. She's the main reason I left Detroit and moved to Chicago. You didn't cross Jewell, and if you did, you better get the hell out. – Brian T

------------▽------------

Rome, NY (USA)

They didn't because I didn't. Interestingly, my father was a doctor and I can remember this vividly, I was watching a TV series called *The Untouchables.* In this show they said "homosexuals" … I had no idea what that meant, so I turned to my father in his recliner and said, "Dad, what's a homosexual?" Dad said, "That's a person with a mental illness." In those days, it was considered a mental illness. So, in his defense, that was his training. It was an ICD-9 medical code, being homosexual was some kind of mental deficiency. From that point on, I had a tremendous amount of guilt on my back because

I didn't want to be mentally ill. So, when I had these attractions to men, my father's words rang through to me, so I wouldn't want to go there. That really affected me. The second was, I'm a pleaser when it comes to the people I love and my parents. There's no way I would ever disappoint my parents. My parents said very negative things about gay people, because we had an uncle … I suppose everybody did … they would say he was a little weird, or light in the loafers. When he wasn't there, people in my family would talk negative about him. My feeling was that I didn't want to disappoint my parents, so I never really did that. Then when I got older and I knew I had to come out, I said, "They don't really need to know." I didn't tell them, then they passed and I came out to everybody else in my family. Then I felt really bad because I was very apprehensive of my brother and my sister. They took it fine. They both said to me, "Mom and dad would have been fine with you." I'm sad that I missed that opportunity, but it was a decision I made. – Andee

———————∇———————

Michigan (USA)

I never came out to my mother, she just figured it out. My dad had died when I was eight years old. I thought that being gay was much better than being straight because I saw what happened in my parents' relationship. "This is what straight is all about? I want nothing to do with it." My mother was depressed all the time, she had six kids on her own. It just seemed like the straight world was really fucked up. "Puleaze! I'd rather suck dick than go through all this. It's much more fun." – Jim

———————∇———————

Chicago, IL (USA)

I did not ever officially have that discussion with my folks. By the time I admitted the truth to myself, I was 33 years old, and had been out of their house for 15 years. They weren't living locally to me, and I didn't see why I should put them through the struggle they would have by my truth.
It became clear to me that they knew within a year or two of my coming out. But it was also very clear that this was not a topic we were ever going to discuss.

Sexuality was never an approved topic in our family. Commercials or TV shows that were "body related" or even remotely sexual in nature were turned off, and sex was seemingly never a reality to my parents. When I turned 13, my mother gave me a book about sex and told me to read it. By the way, it was a book written to parents about how to tell your kids about sex, and the first chapter said very clearly, "Never give your kids a book to teach them about sex."

Any time I was with my parents for the last decades of their lives, my mother would – within 15 minutes of my arrival – tell me a story that was purposely designed to let me know that this subject was closed and that they didn't want to know anything. – andKevin

———————∇———————

La Mesa, Tequendama Province (Colombia)

My mom told me that with time, it was going to go away. Never spoke with my father about it, for my mother was raising us by herself without any support from him. – Cristian

———————∇———————

Chicago IL (USA)

I once tried coming out to my father as a bisexual. His only reaction was "Can't you fight it?" He then told me not to tell my mother because she wouldn't handle it as well as he did. My parents died many years later; for the rest of their lives, my sexuality remained a rather large elephant in a rather tiny room. – William Demaree

———————∇———————

Hollister, CA (USA)
San Jose, CA (USA)

They were OK pretty much. I had a twin bed. I was living next door to my parents in a mobile home for quite a few years. It belonged to my grandmother before I moved up to San Jose for work. I had blown through all the jobs in Hollister, quit 'em all, there wasn't much left. I was working at 7/11 16 hours a week and it just wasn't cutting it, so I moved to San Jose. I stayed with my aunt for a few months first, that was in 1980. Then in 1983 I was in my own apartment and I was moving in with my partner, husband to be, and I didn't need the twin bed anymore. So, I told my parents, "I'm moving, and I don't need the twin bed anymore, do you want it back." That's when I came out to them. I had come out to my youngest brother a little bit before that. He was staying with me for a short time when he was looking for work in San Jose after graduating from UC Davis.

My parents were OK, they didn't say much. They weren't too

surprised. They didn't *seem* surprised. I always talked more to my mom than my dad. My dad wasn't a big talker, even though we did things together. We worked on cars and worked the farm … we had a farm with lots of chores to do. I went hunting and fishing with my dad. The whole family would go camping too. When my partner came down to family gatherings, he was another in-law. It really went pretty good, all things considered. – Spike

————————∇————————

Milwaukee, WI (USA)
Madison, WI (USA)

I never had a chance to come out to my parents. Shortly after my 18th birthday, I went with my college housemate to my first gay club – The Factory – in the old 3rd Ward of Milwaukee, Wisconsin, which was about 170 miles from my hometown. Literally, moments after I paid my cover charge and walked through the entrance to the bar, I ran into someone I knew from high school, and by morning, my parents had been told that I'd been seen in a gay bar in Milwaukee. They never confronted me about it, but my sister and a family friend both confirmed that they knew about it. Their reaction was typically Midwestern – we didn't talk directly about it, but they always were very courteous and welcoming to anyone that I was seeing. The first absolutely open conversation I ever had with my father on the issue was just before he died in 2014, and he let me know in no uncertain terms how much he loved me and that he was always proud of me. When I married my husband, he asked if it would be okay to introduce him to people as his son-in-law. – D. Warner

————————∇————————

Grand Rapids, MI (USA)

They were supportive, kinda surprised, and started learning about gays. – Mark S

————————∇————————

Oxnard, CA (USA)

My mom asked me if I was gay when I was 27. I told her yes and she said, "OK I just want to keep the communication lines open." A few years later at the height of the AIDS epidemic, she decides that she's against it. I told her that, "This was your choice to know. I didn't tell you, you asked me." We didn't talk for quite some time, several months at least. She didn't accept my boyfriends or my life. If I was having a difficult time in a relationship, she would say, "Then just leave it" but later on she would say, "You jump from one guy to another." She and my father have been married for 56 years. She's more accepting now but I don't really trust her. – Crusher

————————∇————————

Chicago, IL (USA)

They knew and we never talked about it. I didn't ask about their sex life and I expected the same from them. I always introduced my partner of the moment to my family and they were always accepted readily. – Dennis Hardenstein

————————∇————————

Los Angeles, CA (USA)

Never was a conversation with my dad, and my mom was confused because it wasn't something I openly expressed as a child. She questioned if I had been sexually abused as the cause. – Katorri A.

————————∇————————

Cleveland, OH (USA)

They made it about them and how could I do this. No surprises. I figured they might, so I only told them after I left home. – Roger.

————————∇————————

Chicago, IL (USA)

I'm the kind of guy who plans everything, maps it out. Part of the story in my family is that at a very young age, probably all of five, I came to my mother and asked, "Mom, would you describe me as a cautious child?" To this day, if I do something, my mother will say, "Well, you always were a cautious child." So I had everything mapped out for the whole coming out story. I was about to be 30. I was living in a house in Chicago. I had my own place, so I knew that I needed to tell them at some point. They were coming back from California. They went to a financial planning guru in Santa Barbara. His name was Richard Mercer, I remember that. It was a kind of Tony Robbins thing, that's a big ra-ra ... you know, we'll figure out your finances and here's our great philosophy of life. My parents had never been exposed to anything like that before. They were very much middle-class, mid-west people. They flew directly from California to my place in Chicago to see me. They were all excited ... the line this guru used is, "You need to do things that add meaning to your life. Whatever adds meaning to your life." I sat them down and fixed them dinner, right before they had to leave. I thought that if things go horribly wrong, then I'll push them out the door. They realized something was up when I told them I'd make dinner, because they didn't know I could cook. We're sitting around having dinner and they're talking about how they can add meaning to their life. So, I said, "I did something recently that added meaning to my life." They said, "What?" I said, "I've decided that I really need to date men." My parents just froze. My mom's face, she went stoic, you could tell that the wheels were turning. You could tell that she was like, "What do I do? What do I say? What would Oprah do?" Suddenly she blurts out, "We love and accept you, but don't tell your grandmother." That was pretty much it, they were really good. Then a year later with my first husband, we were raising two kids and we had full custody of the kids. My mother always said she wanted grandchildren and a year later I said, "Mom, here you go." They were really good about it all, they really love the kids and have always been supportive. – Thomas Stribling

———————∇———————

Chicago, IL (USA)

My stepfather told me when I came out that he wanted nothing to do with me and that he would be dead the next time we saw each other again. He had passed two years before I knew. Funny thing, it is the only promise he kept. – Mercury

———————∇———————

Cathedral City, CA (USA)

I never came out to my parents because they were very strict old-school Catholics. Rick, when we broke up, wanted to get so evil toward me that he called my parents and told them I was gay. He outed me. That caused a family feud. My sister hates any homosexuals, she despises us and wishes we were all dead from AIDS. (AGAIN??? THIS IS BEING PUBLISHED???). She'll tell you that to your face. But my dad, he literally threw the Bible at me down the phone. They didn't talk to me for two years after that happened. My mother got hold of me two years after that to let me know somebody has passed away. She started a relationship with me until she passed away. But my dad ... we've never been close. He just despises any type of homosexuality. – Marcous

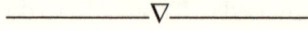

———▽———

Huntsville, AL (USA)

I never came out to my father, although he certainly thought I was gay and was very upset about that. I had many funny incidents with him over the years. My mother, who I was much closer to, when I came out to her, she said, "I've known that since you were a small child." I said, "Why didn't you say anything?" She said, "I didn't want to influence you." I said, "So I'm the last person to figure this out, right?" She knew when I was a small child, but I didn't really accept it until I was an adult. She said to me, "I don't care if you're gay just as long as the neighbors don't know." I thought, "What?" So my mother still had this built-in homophobia that she was a victim of as well. A fear of other people knowing. – Greg Day

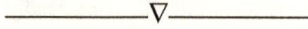

———▽———

Chicago, IL (USA)

I never formally came out to my parents. They lived in a state of denial and when I attempted to tell them, they made it clear they didn't want to hear what I had to say. – Steve Kmetko

———▽———

Wichita, KS (USA)

It was interesting, my mother always knew, and she said, "You're my gay son and that's OK." My father said, "I'll pray for you like I pray for the other eight children in the family." He was cool. – Guy Seiler

———▽———

Cathedral City, CA (USA)

My mother was Southern Baptist so it was difficult. She loved me and I knew that. She didn't kick me out of the house. She didn't stop showing me affection. But then years later my brother came out as gay. She said, "It's your fault because your brother envies you." Because he was married and had children. She blamed me for that but then, eventually, she got over that. Never talked to my father because my father was estranged from us by then. Discussing with my brother was like talking to a complete stranger. He just wasn't open to talking. We had very different tastes. He liked young boys and he was slimy. (AGAIN?? SLANDEROUS??) He would go to the adult movie theaters and watch the movies, or performances, then he would go down into the shower room and give them a dollar and he would play with their cock. It was just very bizarre. Most of my relationships have been with older men because they were people I could talk to on an intelligent basis. – David Hardy

—————▽—————

Tallahassee, FL (USA)
Houston, TX (USA)

I believe I began my coming out process as a toddler, when I demanded a teddy bear for Christmas. As the story goes, my dad responded with an empirical, "No son of mine is going to have a doll!" My understanding is that both my grandmas intervened in my defense, and we won. I even got a baby boy doll a few years later, with wardrobe made by Grandma Essie.

During my early years, I loved playing with my sister's and our neighbor best friend's Barbie, Midge, and Ken dolls, as well as putting on the dresses, robes, and high heels in the drag box in the spare room. My parents were clearly perplexed about how to deal with me. One of my most frightening memories is when the two of them confronted me in the corner of the kitchen one day in my childhood to ask if all this dressing up meant that I wanted to have my penis cut off. It wasn't anything I had considered up to that point, and it shook my world.

I hid my personality and sexuality inside, and in the neighborhood woods, until my late teens. Although I had begun coming out to myself as early as age 14, I hid my self and my sexuality until the day after I graduated high school. (Christmas break before I graduated high school, I needed to know for sure about my desire, and had pursued an encounter at a roadside stop. Though I climaxed, I remained closeted in my identity.

Immediately after high school in 1970, I began coming out to the world, although, being more circumspect and gentle, with my parents. I joined the Gay Liberation Front at Florida State, flamed a "natural" bouffant, swished widely, and brought some of my sissy friends home to meet my parents.

In the mid-eighties, some fifteen years after my official "coming out" (though not so much with family) I found myself seated around a family dinner during a favorite niece's high school graduation celebration, with parents and all present. My sister's six and nine-ish year old sons were asking important questions. "Why do you have only one earring, uncle?" "What does the pink triangle on your sweater mean?" I took the opportunity to come out to my whole family, explaining the importance of identity and the horrors of the Holocaust. My father was stone silent, but I heard the angels sing.

Months before my father died of a suddenly diagnosed terminal cancer, he mailed me a card, one of the few throughout our relationship, celebrating the bridges of love that connect us. I was able to be there for his final month, and three more with my mom. It confirmed for me that love is not about how we are taught to think, but how we learn to feel and experience life. – T. Lark Letchworth

---------------▽---------------

Sacramento, CA (USA)

At 24 I sat them down. My Mom turned pale and didn't say a word for several minutes. My Dad who was a clinical psychologist immediately spoke up and said, "Paul, you're the same person today as you were yesterday and I love you! There's nothing you could say that would shock me and you know I lived in Greenwich Village and had some experiences myself."

My Mom finally spoke up and said, "I love you."
In spite of tears shed, it actually went as great as I could have anticipated. I then was a selfish arsehole and said I was going to spend the night at my boyfriend's. – Paul Harris

---------------▽---------------

Sylvania, New South Wales (Australia)

There was never any real "coming out" with either of my parents. I would never have come out to my father! NEVER! The repercussions could have been deadly. If he ever suspected … and there must have been a time he did … it was never mentioned. His suicide in 1978 was a blessing for me, as I could then lead my life as I saw fit, without having to hide this side of me.
My mother left home when I was 11. I reconnected with her after my father's death in 1978. I still wasn't out myself at that stage … that wasn't to happen until 1980. However, in early 1978 my stepbrother's wife … they lived in Campbelltown … had a stroke at 33 years of age. My stepbrother wasn't very good at looking after her, so I moved there for a while to help out. After my father's death, I moved back there again as there was a lot to be arranged, and asked my housemates in Granville if they could pack a bag for me and

deliver it to Campbelltown. After making the call ... I realised I had some gay porn magazines hidden in my underwear drawer. Too late to do anything about that. Anyway, they delivered the bag ... and said nothing. A year later I was sent to Melbourne, where I came out in 1980. I wrote a letter to my housemates informing them of the great event. Received a letter back informing me that they already knew ... thanks to some porn magazines. And ... oh ... we have accidentally outed you to your mother ... we thought she knew! She didn't! Anyway, I returned to Sydney, and it was never really discussed with her. I guess I was waiting for her to raise the issue. All she said about it at the time ... this was during a chat about my childhood ... was that she always knew I was "different." The closest we got to talking about it was over lunch in Sydney one day ... around 1984 ... where she told me she blamed herself for my being gay. I gather she thought she had "mothered" me too much. I said it wasn't her fault, and that I had no regrets about being gay. I had a good life, and a lot of good supportive friends. That was the end of it, though evidently she did discuss my being gay with her sister ... who also supported me. I would have loved to be a fly on the wall for that discussion! – Tim Alderman

———————▽———————

St. Cloud, MN (USA)

My mom never really expressed her feelings about it. I know that it took her a long time to accept it, and she still might not completely accept it, but she chose not to say anything that could possibly upset me. My dad, on the other hand, continues to process and vacillate over whether it is right or wrong, whether it is due to something they had done to me as a child, etc. I know they wanted me to marry a man and have kids, and for a while my dad was so beside himself with me being lesbian, he said "I can see why women like black men – they are very masculine – I would be OK if you were with a black guy, I would understand that. I don't understand this." He is not the type of person who can just accept something that can't be explained. – Rachel Wexelbaum

———————▽———————

Palestine, TX (USA)

My parents were forty years old when I was born, the first of two sons, my younger brother having Downs Syndrome. So, I was their last great hope for grandchildren. My parents were separated when I was about ten or eleven and I lived with my mother and brother through high school, but kept good relations with my father. In my mid-twenties, when I lived in Chicago, I came out to my mother, by sending her the book, popular at that time, *The Best Little Boy in the World*. On my next visit home, she was quiet and finally asked, "why did you send me that book?" Well that got the conversation going and it went mildly OK. She was adamant that I would never bring any of my boyfriends into her house. Well, time passes and by the time I met my current husband and my father had died, he and I would go down to Palestine from Dallas and sleep in the same bed "in her house!" She later came to live with us in Dallas for radiation treatments before she died in 1995. As for my father, I suspect he may have known, but I never discussed it with him. He was a conservative Texas cattleman and I just don't know if he could get his mind around his son being gay (as he would have understood what that meant). – Michael Pickel

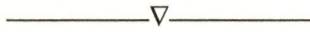

———————▽———————

Charlottetown, Prince Edward Island (Canada)

I was outed to them by a jealous lover. It didn't go so well (understatement), but when the dust settled, and over time, they grew to accept my sexuality. Luckily, I was an adult by then, but I was still living in their home. I didn't push them, though I would certainly stand my ground on certain social issues regarding the LGBTQ community. By the time my husband and I were getting married, my mother got so into the whole thing that she was offering all kinds of wedding suggestions. Not overstepping any boundaries, mind you; she'd just grown to be excited about the whole thing. – Dave Stewart

———————▽———————

Milwaukee, WI (USA)

My father died not too long after I came out, but he didn't mind. My mother was a little bothered by it at first, but she soon grew to love my partner … a lot! – Sherrie Howe

———————▽———————

Denver, CO (USA)

My parents ostracized me from the family at age 21. I only saw them together one time in the late 1980's when they drove from Milwaukee to Denver. They parked the van in the parking lot of the apartment building I lived in on Capitol Hill. They did not want to go into my apartment or meet my partner.

So I shared a 45 minute dinner with them at a nearby restaurant called New China.

After dinner they drove away. I saw my mother about 12 years later when my father died. That was the last I saw of her since she died a year later. I gave the eulogy at her service. – Tony Earl

———————∇———————

San Diego, CA (USA)

My mother died a few months back before I came out. My father, it's been over two years. He doesn't fully understand it. Same questions over and over again. When he first found out, he went straight to the lawyers and had me removed from the trust. Right away. I was not invited to Thanksgiving. I wasn't invited to Christmas. We talked, but about every three or four months it would be the same questions. "Maybe you could just pretend to be a girl and then go out as a boy." ... "Let me know when this is done." "Why do I have to call you by your name that I didn't give you?" He'd use the same hello every time with my dead name. I communicate with him because he's my father. I like to know he's alive. It's irrational, understanding our relationship with our parents is beyond me. I continue to talk to him even though almost every other conversation I'm either in tears or I'm just angry. – Serafine Sawyer

———————∇———————

(Pakistan)

When it comes to my family acceptance, I have an interesting story. My father passed away in 2015, that time was the hardest in my life. I was 25-years old and this is the time I have seen him take his last breath in front of me, I was quite attached to him. He passed away due to liver cirrhosis, he never knew that I was gay. I didn't want to torture him because he was old and sick too.

At this time I was in my celibate/closet phase too because I was outed by elder brother to my mother and for years I had to struggle with my sexuality. I later knew it was my uncle from Saudi Arabia that had gone through my mobile phone and read my test messages and outed me to my brother, that I'm meeting men and having sex with them.

For days I was scared and lived in fear, my mother covered it up ... she's always able to brush all the tensions in the family so that it does not fall apart but for years till my father's death I had to hide myself and I struggle to come to terms with my sexuality too.

Finally, when I did come to terms with my sexuality, I had to be brave and self-aware too. It wasn't easy but took me more time to come out to my mother and she was fine with it. My younger sibling is a transwoman and she's an activist, even for her it wasn't easy to come out but by the time my family had grown tolerant of our existence and in fact love us. – Salman

—————————▽—————————

King, NC (USA)

I didn't come out until I had been married to my wife for thirteen years. By that time, I was thirty years old. My father had committed suicide when I was eighteen years old. My mother and I never discussed my being gay. It was just understood. For years, with her, I often changed my pronouns from 'we' to 'I, or me' just to not make our interaction uncomfortable. That is a very tiring thing to keep going. That all changed when I came out at the end of my marriage to my wife and the church excommunicated me. I became an activist and over time, fearless in my true self. We all had to be fearless in one way or another. It was the beginning of the AIDS crises and being a gay man – we were being vilified, despised, and feared on all fronts. – Ron Cline

—————————▽—————————

DID YOU HAVE A FAMOUS LGBTQ ROLE MODEL
WHO INSPIRED YOU TO COME OUT?

New York, NY (USA)
Seattle, WA (USA)

No. Still, I was always glad when prominent people came out publicly. It was encouraging and heartening. I was greatly inspired by Split Britches and the WOW Cafe Theatre in New York and value my good fortune to have had a beer with Peggy Shaw, one of the group members. Also, my doctoral work with Dr. Sue-Ellen Case, as I said above, changed my life. I became more aware of the world around me and its impact philosophically on the lives of LGBTQ. Dr. Case is a brilliant champion for lesbian and gay people and has devoted her life as a scholar to delineating our lives in the world. – Oran Walker

——————▽——————

San Francisco, CA (USA)

David Bowie – Terence Smith (Joan Jett Blakk)

——————▽——————

Chicago, IL (USA)

I first realized I was transgender when I was 19. The trans person I was most familiar with at the time was Chaz Bono, so one of the first things I did was buy the *Becoming Chaz* documentary. When I watched it, the thing that stood out to me the most was Cher. She described her experience with Chaz coming out; she really struggled with it at first, but over time she grew to better understand and support it. This was pivotal to my coming out, because it prepared me for what could happen. Cher showed me that my parents may not get it right away but if I'm patient with them they'll come around. After I finally came out, my parents said some things verbatim to what Cher said in the documentary. – C'est Kevvie (Wilhelmina)

———————▽———————

Indianapolis, IN (USA)

When I was a kid/teenager back in the 1970s, Truman Capote was on all the talk shows. He was usually pretty witty and to me he was the first representation of homosexuality that I had ever seen. I didn't know what a gay person was until I started seeing him on TV. I can remember my dad said, "Oh that faggot." And I said, "What's a faggot?" I don't think he was a role model exactly but he was someone who tuned me in on what I was about. There was also a comedian called Paul Lynde. One of his big things was a game show called *Hollywood Squares* ... he was in one of the squares. He was really funny. I thought he was hilarious. He did a couple of TV shows, he was in *Bewitched* and he had his own show briefly. I just thought he was hilarious. He was witty and I got the wit. – Xavier Bathsheba-Negron

———————▽———————

Tulsa, OK (USA)

No, in fact the people who were out and about, were really out there, made me want to stay in the closet. The people who were overtly gay when I came out, to me they were too stereotypical. There was no Ellen back then. I'm older than Ellen. – Renny

———————▽———————

Columbus, OH (USA)

When I came out in graduate school, we were doing a theoretical project for our gay Architecture professor designing a shelter for the 'other' inside ourselves. I knew my 'other' was my attraction to men as a straight (ha, ha) guy. I wrote poetry and did some found object sculpture. I sat in studio one day and was imagining what it would be like to be attracted to a guy. Suddenly I realized I already knew what that was like as I remembered kissing the male singer of one of my favorite bands on the lips at a band festival in DuPont Circle in Washington, DC a few years earlier. We each thought nothing of it at the time. But now I realized I had a crush on him and all my best guy friends I used to hang around with. Later my studio class all took a field trip to New York City where we saw *Paris is Burning* in a theater on Houston Street in the West Village. My classmates all thought the movie was like prying into strangers' lives. But for me these were my people. They became my heroes throughout my coming out process. – Lars von Keitz

─────────▽─────────

Southern California, CA (USA)

Not really, but I recall hearing that Cary Grant was gay, and that gave me hope that I might have the courage to come out to myself. I had to move to San Francisco to make that happen. – Gary Borgstedt

─────────▽─────────

Waverly, IA (USA)

I didn't have or feel the need for a famous gay role model. – Robert Beck

─────────▽─────────

North Carolina (USA)

Not to come out but I think to really start exploring my identity as a queer person. I would say two people. One would be Randy Shilts, the famous author. His books inspired me and showed me that you could be a really good reporter, a really good writer focusing on gay history. That was a real inspiration to me. The other person was John Waters because he demonstrated to me that you could be gay and out and queer and in-your-face and still get things done. You could still make art even if you didn't have anything and you were really determined, you'll do it. – Randy

─────────▽─────────

Seattle, WA (USA)

I always admired Truman Capote. There were so many things stacked against the man and yet he prevailed to become one of American's greatest authors. He never tried to hide who he was (as if he could) and learned to embrace his own personality.

Another person (living) is Felice Picano. His writing has spanned across five decades, showing the changes of LGBTQ lifestyles. I've observed him in public, taking notes on how he presents himself and his work, how he interacts with others (including some crazed fans) and the selflessness of wanting to help other LGBTQ authors find their place. – Eric Andrews-Katz

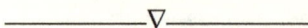

—————▽—————

Chicago, IL (USA)

When I was young the only role models were often celebs and they were the object of ridicule and scorn. –Philip Bernal

—————▽—————

Chicago, IL (USA)

Not specifically. Again my '80s upbringing. I was listening to Bronski Beat and other LGBTQ singers. That was part of the "building up your self-esteem" kind of thing. – Drew

—————▽—————

Rockford, IL (USA)

I didn't have a LGBTQ role model that helped me come out. But one of my favorite LGBTQ celebrities is Sir Ian McKellen. And this is because I love the work that he has done both as an actor and member of our community. – Patrick J. Murphy III

—————▽—————

Frinton-on-Sea, Essex (UK)

No. I don't believe in gay role models, as they can sometimes let you down. For a while, in the UK, the entertainer, Michael Barrymore, was held up as an example of a wonderful gay man who was talented, popular, not effeminate (that's important to some people), and a regular working-class hero. This ignored the shabby way he treated his poor wife, who only found out he was gay after he'd come out on stage at an East End gay bar (throwing his wedding ring away). Then a while later, a young man drowned in his swimming pool during a cocaine-fueled party and was found to have sustained rectal injuries. While Barrymore was proved innocent, he handled the whole business incredibly badly and his reputation fell through the floor, along with his career. So, the lesson seems to be – be your own man, or woman. Stuff role models! – Diesel Balaam

—————▽—————

Menton, Côte d'Azur (France)
Paris (France)

Yves Saint-Laurent. He was a regular visitor to our homes in Paris and Menton, and he was very supportive of me. It was he who told me to come out to my great-aunt when I was 13 and she threw a small coming-out party for me. She was a lovely woman and a huge LGBTQ ally. – Louis Richard de Bourbon de Parme et de Savoie, Prince de la Pau

—————▽—————

Bellport, NY (USA)

I never really paid much attention to celebrities so no I did not. I came out on my own because I wanted to live my truth. It wasn't until later on I started paying attention somewhat and learning about celebrities. Having more positive visibility in the LGBTQ community is a good thing. – Erin Michelle Miller

—————▽—————

St Louis, MO (USA)

While in high school and reading an article in *Time* about successful LGBTQ people, I was fascinated by an attractive, bearded exec at Casablanca Records, shown pictured with his partner and felt that IT'S POSSIBLE one day for me. But what helped me finally accept myself and feel hope was reading the young adult novel *Trying Hard to Hear You* by Sandra Scoppettone. I had read about it and asked my high school librarian (who was super cool, she introduced me to the band Martha and the Muffins) about the book – it was listed as being in stock at our library but wasn't to be found. She later handed me a copy when they got another in. Though the book had situations that were sad (a death occurred in it), I felt this power wave come over me one night and everything felt different. It was the kind of feeling I've seen happen when I've done a Reiki session on someone who has never experienced Reiki and had no expectations, but then at some point would just feel a wave of something and even get emotional. I asked the librarian how I could get a copy of that hardback book and she was glad to. I still have that book, kept nice and safe in a box. I read it a few more times over the years and will always keep it as it was part of a major enlightenment in my life. – Todd Jaeger

—————▽—————

Palm Springs, CA (USA)

I don't know why this was the first person to pop into my head, but when Greg Louganis first came out, that was a wake-up call to me. Only because I saw someone who was in the spotlight for what was happening at the time. I thought, "If this person can do that and be ok with it, then I can." That was one of the things that inspired me to come out of the closet, to accept myself for being gay and being who I am. – David Vega (Lucifers Axe)

—————▽—————

Palm Springs, CA (USA)

No, I came out so young there weren't really "out" role models back then. – Keith Kollinicos (Missa Distic)

—————▽—————

Cleveland, OH (USA)

No one inspired me to come out, but once I was out, I looked to role models for how I wanted to live my life. They were friends, no-one famous or anything, just good people living very exciting lives, not taking any shit. – Roger.

—————▽—————

Chicago, IL (USA)

I was in a position in my work life where I meet a lot of famous people, one stands out Billie Jean King, a truly down to earth nice person. – Dennis Hardenstein

—————▽—————

Chicago, IL (USA)

Me. Life was very hard when I first came to the realization that I was gay. A square peg in a round hole. I realized over time that I had to be my own self. I had to find a way to be authentic. It's taken many years of therapy. My parents like to say, "What will the neighbors think?" Not about my being gay, but about every other familial infraction. Who cares what the neighbors think? It's what I think that's important. – Steve Kmetko

——————∇——————

New Orleans, LA (USA)

I watched *Purple Rain* and thought yep Wendy and Lisa is it. – Terry Gaskins

——————∇——————

Milwaukee, WI (USA)

For me, the greatest LGBTQ role models were former San Francisco City Supervisor Harvey Milk – who literally died for the cause – and former Executive Director of the National Gay Task Force (Now the National LGBTQ Task Force), Virginia Apuzzo, who was one of the most powerful LGBTQ rights leaders of the early 1980s. – D. Warner

——————∇——————

Baton Rouge, LA (USA)

Not sure I've ever officially come out but now in the 21st century and current digital age there are annals of records of people I look to for motivation for myself and to advance the progress of LGBTQ people. Darryl Stephens, Maurice Jamal, Deondrey Gossett, Quincy Linear, Patrick Ian-Polk. – Katorri A.

——————∇——————

Chicago, IL (USA)

I won't say it's a role model but it's a movie. There was a movie that came out around '85-'86 called *Parting Glances*. That was the first movie that I saw that normalized a gay relationship. There was all sorts of drama in the story and all that, but the crux of the movie is these two guys who were in a relationship that were trying to work things out in the relationship. I'd never seen anything like that before. At the time I was really into journaling because I was very introspective. I remember writing this long journal article about the movie, that it was so incredible to see two guys in a loving relationship. I had been told that all gay relationships were crazy drug-filled, party-fueled, things that never lasted. That there wasn't any love involved, it was all about sex. To see that as a model, if it was only in a movie, was so life changing. That was one of the main catalysts that kicked me out of the closet. – Thomas Stribling

—————▽—————

Cathedral City, CA (USA)

No, I've been with famous people, but they weren't the cause of me coming out. – David Hardy.

—————▽—————

Chicago, IL (USA)

There were no role models when I would have liked to come out. I didn't come out until 23. By then, I had heard about Larry Kramer and Harvey Milk who both had a great influence over me. I performed Ned in *The Normal Heart* many years ago and contacted Larry about it. We shared email during the rehearsals and the run of the show. He was amazing – honest, encouraging and fierce. – MrZor

—————▽—————

(Germany)

Some I had. I guess Hella von Sinnen. I remember some German TV celebrities ... nothing too special. – Cornelius Günther Körn

—————▽—————

New York, NY (USA)

I remember the Marlboro man who lived next door to me. It was thrilling to see him jump from his terrace to mine, 30 something floors up while I was naked holding the guard rail. And we would have sex. It was amazing the first time. I lived in a penthouse and I was watering the plants naked. I was holding the hose and all of a sudden, this person came out. He said, "That's a nice hose." I said, "You should see it closer." He jumped from his terrace to mine. – Juan-manuel Alonso

————————▽————————

Cathedral City, CA (USA)

I met Troy Perry and he was very well spoken. He said all the right things. He had a lot of good things to say. I grew up in Oklahoma, so I wasn't exposed to much. When I got out most of my exposure to gay life was in gay bars. I didn't have any gay culture to attach to. Now I'm older, I'm seeing that there is so much that I missed. So regretful I don't know more. I don't know too much about Stonewall. I just hear there was a riot and people were thrown into into jail and it changed the course of history. Other than that, I don't know much. – David Hayes

————————▽————————

Davis, CA (USA)
Sacramento, CA (USA)

Not really but without a doubt Harvey Milk was a huge inspiration and emotional support for me shortly after I came out. After his assassination, I got to know his replacement, Harry Britt, who encouraged my political activism and wanted to date me.

Ironically it was the homophobic Minute Maid orange juice spokeswoman and singer, Anita Bryant who was a major impetus for me coming out to my parents. My Mom was from Florida like Anita, and would say, "She has a right to her opinion." I knew once I told her the truth it would put it all in perspective for Mom. – Paul Harris

————————▽————————

Interlochen, MI (USA)

I remember watching *Soap* with Billy Crystal. I was the only one in the house who watched it. We had a little TV room that used to be a breezeway. It was my secret thing that my mom didn't know I was watching because there was a gay character in it. I don't consider that a role model. I watched, of all things, *The Real World* on MTV and the young man from Cuba ... Pedro Zamora. He was an advocate for LGBT rights and they really focused on him one season in San Francisco. He was very handsome. He was also HIV-positive and they showed the progression of his health decreasing on the show. When I worked at the Interlochen Center for the Arts in Northern Michigan, I remember watching his funeral and they did his life story. I was really inspired by him speaking to others. Not only as an HIV-positive man but also as a gay man. He was a person of color who inspired other people. In my eyes he's famous for a lot of reasons. There's been actors that come and go and you think, "Well, OK." But I want to hear more about people who are coming out and working in their community. Those for me inspire more than an actor would. – Greg R. Baird

——————∇——————

Tallahassee, FL (USA)

Oh, gee. The media didn't offer us baby gay/bi/lesbians much in the fifties and sixties. TV personalities like Rex Reed, Paul Lynde, Liberace informed my gay sensibilities, but also left me less than inspired. I thank the goddess for Snagglepuss, the Hanna-Barbera cartoon character created in 1959 and voiced by Daws Butler. "Heavens to Murgatroyd!"

Documented by Wikipedia as "a pink anthropomorphic cougar sporting an upturned collar, shirt cuffs, and string tie, Snagglepuss enjoys the fine things in life and shows particular affinity for the theatre."

In my early teen years, I went toward authors like James Baldwin, Jean Genet, Gore Vidal, and Bernard Malamud, although most of them were way over my 14 year old head.

Then, the Stonewall Rebellion happened during my senior year in high school. Can we say "inspired!" – T. Lark Letchworth

——————∇——————

Brunswick, ME (USA)

I wish I could say I did, but no. I was late in coming to gay literature and activism. I admire the works of Oscar Wilde, the Spanish writer Frederica Garcia Lorca and the French philosopher and essayist Montaigne, but can't call them "role models." I enjoy listening to music by gay composers, reading books and poetry by gay writers and art by gay artists. I seek some bits of "gayness" in their expressions. Many led tragic lives and I'd like to try and "hear" the cries or their expressions within their works, if indeed they put anything of the sort into these works. Maybe it's all a bit of romanticism, but I like to think that gay men (I can't speak for gay women) share something that, if we allow ourselves to get in touch with, can deepen our lives and perspectives as gay men. We're gay for a reason, I'm not sure why, but through art, literature and music we might come to terms with who we are. – Michael Pickel

————————∇————————

St. Cloud, MN (USA)

I was never in the closet … but there were plenty of people out there who showed me that it was possible for someone like me to exist and be strong. The Village People. Pete Burns from Dead or Alive and Freddie Mercury, Harvey Fierstein, Ani Di Franco, Barry Manilow. Barbra Streisand isn't a lesbian but she was Yentl. Those were the folx I had when I was young as role models. *Xena Warrior Princess*, *Wonder Woman*. There were a lot of fictional characters in books and movies as well, I can't remember them all. – Rachel Wexelbaum

————————∇————————

Milwaukee, WI (USA)

Not really. It was the late 1970's. I remember Paul Lynde on *Hollywood Squares*. That was about it. My parents were convinced Tiny Tim was homosexual – until he married Miss Vickie. I also remember Lance Loud, from the PBS documentary. He seemed like a lovely creature from another planet to the poor queer person of color I was back in conservative Milwaukee, WI. – Tony Earl

————————∇————————

Chicago, IL (USA)
New York City, NY (USA)

My dear friend, Michael Pakis, dated the Chicago columnist and raconteur Dominic Hamilton-Little. We were having breakfast at the Melrose Diner on Broadway and the owners were very proud of their newly-laminated menus. But Dominic noticed a typo and began shouting, "It's not Belgium Waffles, it's BELGIAN WAFFLES!!!!" I think we were escorted out before the police arrived.

Danny Sotomayor was a fierce and fabulous ACT-UP activist and cartoonist. And I had a major crush on him. I remember meeting him at a "tent city" that ACT-UP erected in front of Cook County Hospital in the early '90s, to force the city to open up more beds for HIV treatment. Another time, Danny climbed to the roof of Chicago's City Hall and unfurled a banner that read "We Demand Equal Healthcare Now." A true warrior.

I was always a fan of the work of Fran Liebowitz, Judy Grahn, Audre Lorde, Jon Reich, Allen Ginsburg. And others. – David Clayton

———————▽———————

King, NC (USA)

My role model when I came out wasn't an LGBTQ individual. It was Barbara Streisand in her role of *Yentl*. That character was someone who was definitely suppressed by being a woman who wanted to just be herself and learn and read books but wasn't allowed to do those things. She took things into her own hands and made it happen for herself. In the end, she finally revealed who she really was at tremendous risk and cost. The song, *No Matter What Happens It Can't Be the Same Anymore* gave me the courage to see my coming out through to its conclusion. I felt a great kinship in this movie, and it helped me a great deal. – Ron Cline

———————▽———————

Charlottetown, Prince Edward Island (Canada)

To be honest, there weren't many clearly gay role models when I was a kid, let alone many openly gay ones. This has always been a pet peeve of mine, an absence that I hope is long dead and gone. It's so, so damaging. I had Liberace, Rip Taylor, Waylon from Waylon and Madame and Paul Lynde to choose from. Lynde was the one I could most relate to, but I have to say that Village People, the way I was drawn to the construction worker and the leather man, they became role models in a sense for me. Later, John Waters inspired me, both as a gay man and as someone involved in the arts community. Truth is, I've always wanted to be Debbie Harry. – Dave Stewart

———————▽———————

San Diego, CA (USA)

Yes and no. Everyone knows Caitlin Jenner. She started a verbal conversation. Fucked it up 100 percent, so painfully. But the words were there in everyday society now so that when I said, "I have dysphoria" or "I am transgender" I didn't have to sit there and educate people, I wasn't the only one out there. There was this great wave of trans-folks that exploded after that. Between that and the marriage equality from 2008 and 2012 was an amazing time for us. The strides and the joys that happened were incredible. Not role model, but I'm grateful she tripped open the door. We all, unfortunately, stepped over her on the way in. Somehow, someway, it was in the public's eye that trans-folks were any one of us. And we weren't monsters. We weren't killers or murderers or depraved, we could just be. – Serafine Sawyer

—————▽—————

Milwaukee, WI (USA)

No, but I enjoyed the whole Ellen and Rosie dialogues that made it easier for others to open up. – Sherrie Howe

—————▽—————

(Pakistan)
Worcester, MA (USA)

I would never say Harvey Milk inspired me to come out but when I saw *Milk* (2008) and got to know about Harvey Milk's life, his work in San Francisco with the gay community there and how he was the first openly gay elected official in the history of California but was tragically shot dead. I'd tear in my eyes, his work and activism had inspired me a lot.

In addition to Harvey Milk, the life and work of Sylvia Rivera and Marsha P Johnson was also quite inspirational too. Since I have been to the US, I learned a lot of its queer history and activism in the USA from Pre and Post-Stonewall. If it wasn't for these heroes, their courage and their sacrifices … there would've been no LGBTQ+ rights in the US, we owe our freedom and rights to all our queer and trans heroes of the past. – Salman

—————▽—————

Fort Lauderdale, FL (USA)

I always admired Noel Coward, but I didn't know he was gay. He always seemed so suave and such a witty person. – Rick Karlin

—————▽—————

WHEN DID YOU FIRST HEAR ABOUT AIDS?

Waterloo, IA (USA)

In 1983, I was living in an old upstairs apartment with my second lover, Ken. This was just at the beginning of cable television and Ken and I would stay up late to watch Nick at Night (we loved *I Married Joan*) and then later we would turn the channel to watch *the PTL Club* and a couple of wackadoos by the name of Jim and Tammy Faye Bakker. We were watching the late news one night before our regular habit and the newscaster mentioned the strange deaths of several gay men in San Francisco. I remember the story stating the men had contracted some odd cancer that was usually only seen in elderly Jewish men. I distinctly remember saying something to my lover about how weird that was. – Timothy Juhl

—————▽—————

Downey, CA (USA)

I can't remember. I certainly became aware of it back then. I mostly hung out with straight friends of mine at the time. I really didn't have that many gay friends. I don't think I was out of the closet at that point. I was religious, I would go to church, and I was very involved with an evangelical protestant church that I belonged to. The attitudes about gay people that some of the pastors had were repulsive. I had a friend who was on the staff, he was a pastor, but he was a little man on the totem pole. There was some guy apparently who was freaking out, he wanted to talk to somebody – he knew he was gay – he was religious – and he wanted to talk to somebody at this church, and nobody would talk to him. They kept handing it off to the next person down the rung on the ladder, then the next person down. Then this friend of mine, bottom man on the totem pole, he was the only one who would talk to this guy. I thought that was disgusting. It was experiences like that that pushed me further out of the closet at the time. – Tim Barela

—————▽—————

Indianapolis, IN (USA)

Living off Post Road in Indianapolis in the '80s, the story of Ryan White, the Indiana kid with HIV was a big local and national story. I think his treatment brought a lot of attention to the issue. – Thomas Bottoms

—————▽—————

Chicago, IL (USA)

Early 1980's ... fell over a sign at DePaul University ... a medical expert speaking about a new virus ... not called AIDs yet ... was one of six people in a big lecture hall. – Don Strzepek

—————▽—————

Chicago, IL (USA)

While I know I heard about it multiple times before Rock Hudson's death, being announced over the speakers in the gym during gym class has stayed with me over 35 years like it was yesterday. – Jim

—————▽—————

San Francisco, CA (USA)

I turned twenty in 1982 when the crisis was at its peak, and I first heard about it in the *Advocate* news magazine. It was hitting SF, LA, and NY pretty hard, and I recall reading so many stories about what it was doing in the big cities, it did make me wary about meeting guys when I got to SF, and men would strike up a conversation with me. It was also the AIDS crisis that gave birth to my first novel, *The Saint of San Francisco*. A friend gave me a porn magazine he wanted to get rid of, and there was a story about the crisis and its effects. It painted grim reality of straight friends casting off long-time gay friends. It went on further to picture major cities around the country building ghettos and walling gay men/lesbians inside its walls with no proper sanitation/food/utilities/and medicine. It made me cry, but at the same time I wondered if love could flourish inside the walls of such a place.

I started writing, and when I finished it was a work 110,000 words. It ended with the two men living happily ever after, because everyone deserves such an ending. I let a friend at the time read the completed work. They thought it was good, but they believed that such a thing could *never* happen here in America. I destroyed the whole manuscript, even the drafts.

The work I finally went on to publish bore the same title but is an entirely different story. I do think about resurrecting it sometimes, a different title. Who knows? – Jerry S

—————▽—————

Montivideo (Uruguay)

I was in a bar with a group of friends of mine and in low voice, one of them told us the news, that a friend of ours was infected during a trip. Without the proper information it was scary news. – Dr. Eduardo Levaggi Mendoza

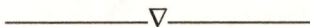

—————▽—————

Chicago, IL (USA)

After moving back to the Chicago area in the early '80's after my very promiscuous times in Fort Lauderdale, thankful to this day I was so fortunate, many I had been with weren't. – Robert Hansen

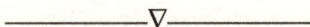

—————▽—————

Indianapolis, IN (USA)

That's an easy one, 1984. Right around the time it was named. My friend Derrick was trying to fuck me, but seeing as we were both young and not complete (shall we say) he didn't know what he was doing. I told him he better not give me AIDS. That was the day after our local news reported the story. I don't doubt for one second we didn't get the latest reports or information, seeing as Indianapolis didn't care about queers. At the time the virus was starting to be called AIDS, a serial killer was murdering gay guys, his call sign was their pants would be down. Indy news, cops and government blamed the victims.

In central Indiana though, the virus was still called the gay cancer, or god's punishment. Funny thing is my mom was experimenting with these diet chews named Ayds they disappeared off the store shelves after the local news reported the term. According to my nurse practitioner who has worked fighting and treating HIV for the last 30 years or so, the stigma didn't abate until well after 2000. By then I was in Philly and already a part of ACT-UP. I moved back to Indy in 2010, and by then the opioid epidemic hit the Midwest pretty hard so even Mike Pence had to stuff his AIDS-phobia, considering his policies helped cause the crisis. – Daniel Fisher (Raid)

———————▽———————

Chicago, IL (USA)

In the seventies, I was very active in drawing attention to the STD issues in the Gay men's community. In 1981, Harley McMillian was CEO of Howard Brown Clinic. Harley called a meeting with a group of us who might be interested in the possibility of raising funds and attention for this new discovered disease. Out of that meeting came the first AIDS benefit in Chicago, Cornucopia at the Park West. As we discovered it, Cornucopia was the first of many of these events. – Gary Chichester

———————▽———————

Denver, CO (USA)

1984. The man I was dating discovered a man he had been dating had AIDS. Up till then, neither of us had been using condoms. We did from then on. – Louis Flint Ceci

———————▽———————

Greenwich, CT (USA)

I was in middle school, the music teacher, who everybody knew was gay, died and all the kids said it was from AIDS and that I gave it to him. – Thomas Autumn

———————▽———————

Modesto, CA (USA)

Now this is going to fly in the face of what some of the public think about the timing of AIDS. It wasn't 1980. This was early 1978. I was in Modesto, but we would drive over to San Francisco which was about 90 miles away. Guys just started to get sick and were dying. This was even in Modesto, they started to come down with it. We thought it was a strain of flu. That's all we thought it was. There was something going on. Then friends in San Francisco started to get sick. So we knew in 1978 that something was going on. – Dave

———————▽———————

Bloomfield Hills, MI (USA)

An acquaintance of mine, he and his partner, obviously gay … he had *Time* magazine and he asked me if I had seen it. I said, "No." He gave it to me. It was the late '80s. I'm an engineer and I love medicine, so immediately the thing goes through my mind … What? How? When? Why? Where? I just had to know everything about it. So that was my reaction to it. – Dan Brazill

———————▽———————

San Francisco, CA (USA)

I was living in San Francisco and people started talking about this mysterious disease that supposedly only the gays contracted. It was a little nerve-wracking. I didn't really go to the baths that much, maybe once a year, but it was scary hearing about it and seeing the people in the hospital dying. – Rory

———————▽———————

Hollywood, CA (USA)

I was living in Hollywood in '78, '79. I worked for a film production company. I went to the baths. I was very sexually active and there was this scuttlebutt by about 1980 that something was happening. This was in LA, the epicenter, so everyone was scared. I was scared. It was Labor Day of 1980 that I lost my job and decided to move home to San Diego. It was about that time I was hearing this scuttlebutt among friends, about the gay cancer, "What's happening?" It was all word of mouth. This wasn't in the newspapers. It just coincided with me withdrawing from an active sex life, so it was coincidental then that my sexual behavior changed considerably. Not because of what was going on but because I went back to a more conservative life in San Diego. I wasn't nearly as active after that. Then, of course, the news came out little by little in '81, '82. So, to answer your question, I heard about it from friends. Everyone was scared. – Bill

———————▽———————

Trinidad (West Indies)

1984/1985. One of my cousins got the "cold" and passed away shortly thereafter. So many theories were told, a few months later while speaking to someone I knew, he told me about this virus and there was no cure, he suspected that was how my cousin passed away. Many years later when my family became more comfortable it was revealed. – Dale

—————▽—————

Laguna Beach, CA (USA)
San Francisco, CA (USA)

I guess it was at different cocktail parties, individuals were talking about it. One or two people had been ill. They didn't know what the matter with them was. I had a very dear friend, loved him, his name was Skylar. He was five or six shades lighter than myself. He had this sparkling smile. He had freckles, one or two years younger than myself. The reason he was important was because we would go to bars and things. This was when I lived in Laguna Beach, so there weren't that many black people who were there, but surely someone as slim as this young man and as vivacious, more masculine acting, than myself to have people as I walked into the bar say, "Thank you for last night." I'm thinking, "Last Night! I thought I was home in bed all night." Or they would come up to me and use his name. It was just amazing. And it happened to him all the time, people would just confuse us. Anyway, he had got this gorgeous, strapping, handsome man. Skylar was new in the hi-tech businesses that were going on. So he and his lover moved to San Francisco. At some point in our communications – I wasn't paying much attention – Skylar said something about his lover being sick. Then later something about him being deathly sick. At one point I was asked if I would go to San Francisco to relieve Skylar for one day so he could take a break. He was saying that trying to work and take care of his lover had just depleted him. So I said, "Yes." So I go up to San Francisco. I'm not prepared, I know that the individual is sick. From this strapping muscular man, he had wasted away. I wasn't ready for the shock. I was told what I could do and what I couldn't do. What I couldn't do was to … there were one or two chores the lover had to do every day and one of those was to wash the dishes. I had to stand back and wait until he could do that task, so that at least he felt vital and that he was contributing to the household. That was very heart-wrenching, that whole experience was. But when I came back was when it really got ugly. I get back to my community and individuals are going, "Well, you went to San Francisco." I said, "Yes." … "We know you don't like San Francisco because it's too cold. What were you doing up there?" I said, "I went up to visit

Skylar." So the conversation got around to that Skylar's lover wasn't well and I'd gone up to help with that. All of a sudden somebody said, "Don't you know that Skylar's lover has AIDS?" I said, "No." The concept hadn't sunk in at that point. He goes, "You weren't around him too much." I said, "Yes, I was there, we kissed, and he hugged me." You could hear a pin drop in the room. There had to have been 30 or 40 people there. I don't remember if it was a bar or a party, or whatever. It became deathly quiet. Then people regained their composure. I knew something had happened. Individuals started leaving the room. From that moment on I was never invited to another party. Individuals would say hi to me but hugging never occurred again until they finally realized you didn't get it through hugging or being in the same room with someone. So, for me, that whole thing was devastating.
– Kalvin

—————▽—————

East Hampton, NY (USA)

1983. I had just moved out to East Hampton and a couple of friends were talking about it. Then a year later, a friend of mine started to get sick and I moved him in with me. I took care of him until he died. I found out about me being HIV positive, having AIDS actually – I wasn't just positive – in 1986. – Ron

—————▽—————

Central Michigan University, Mt. Pleasant, MI (USA)

In the mid-eighties while I was in college. Being just out in college it scared me even more about coming out and living my truth. – Greg R. Baird

—————▽—————

New York, NY (USA)
London (UK)

1972. I was living and working in New York. My boyfriend, who was still living in London, called me and said, "VJ has been put into a seniors' crazy house." I said, "What's he doing there?" He said, "Well there's something wrong with him, they think his mind has snapped. Or his brain is gone. I think he's going to die." I flew over to London to see VJ and he was in what-you-call a nuthouse. Nobody knew what was wrong with him. He died a few weeks later. Then the second one in 1973 was a friend of ours called David

Peel and he was taken ill. Same thing, they didn't know what was wrong with him. That was in the '70s. I moved to Los Angeles in 1974. We knew that AIDS was in England. In fact, a friend of ours who was living with Bob Robinson at the time had joined a group of people and they were being tested – this was at Paddington Hospital in London. These doctors got together and were thinking it was something in the gay community and they were checking people and doing blood work and testing on gay guys who were having a lot of sex. They were hoping to find something out about it. – Bob Brown

—————∇—————

Washington DC (USA)
San Diego, CA (USA)

I was somewhat detached from the gay world because I was still living in the marital household. I had a wife who had been suspicious our entire marriage of less than 10 years. When I finished grad school, I graduated with honors and I had orders to the Pentagon. That was my last Navy tour. By then my wife found a counsellor that was good and that counselor was able to get her to draw herself out from all these self-fulfilling prophecies she had all these years. One day out of the blue, she said, "Are you gay?" Well, you cannot not tell the truth. So then all hell breaks loose. "Oh how can you say you're a God-loving person and be gay?" I said, "Look, it's not whether I decide to wear my uniform or my three-piece suit to work, it is what it is" … "Well, you're going to have to move out." Meanwhile, I met another Navy guy at the Pentagon and neither of us could afford to live alone. He was in a horrific situation, sharing rent with a real jerk. So we got an apartment together. But initially, when she said, "You've got to move out," I ended up in a cul-de-sac with a card table, a folding chair, and service for one. But life goes on. Anytime there was an emergency at home, I got a call to drive 30 miles out to pick one of them up to take them to a dispensary, I took them to all their soccer games and everything else, but I was persona non grata. That's the background story. I'd seen articles about AIDS, read articles, then there was a popular thing that was going around in the print media about "Patient No 1." I was always curious about that. I'm not sure if that got me to thinking, but once the divorce was final in 1980, and the settlement was complete in 1981, I moved to San Diego where I grew up. There it became apparent what was going on. Even in San Diego guys were dying like flies. Essentially, nobody knew what it was per se or how it was being spread, it was just being spread. I was under Navy healthcare at the Navy Hospital in San Diego. A great HIV infectious disease clinic, the best in Southern California, second only to San Francisco. My Navy doctor had me tested and I knew what kind of a life I'd been living, it was very freewheeling, sexually. It came back HIV positive. This was in 1981. My doctor asked me if I was going to need counselling. I said, "No, the results are no surprise to me, because I'd already had my ear open to what was going on. I know what kind of life I've led. It's no surprise and I don't need counselling." – Hal

———————▽———————

Chicago, IL (USA)

The early '80s from my doctor who said, "There's a gay epidemic going around." That's all he said. I was in a relationship then. That was it, then you started hearing about it on the news. Then in '82 it had a name. – Laurie Cowall

———————▽———————

West Hollywood, CA (USA)

After I had it; before it had a name. My boss had already died of "gay cancer." I believed myself to have Epstein-Barr Syndrome [curiously relevant name]. The first batch of us in WeHo had all been addicted to a drug called TT1 – we thusly believed that the drug was killing us. That was, what, 40 years ago? Jeesh! – Gavin Geoffrey Dillard

———————▽———————

Fire Island, NY (USA)

Fire Island was my favorite hangout, but we only had eight weeks in the summer there. You had your eight weekends and I would go every weekend, even if it rained. It was really all we had, then it tapered off, the season ended. '79 was great, then '80 came and there were rumors, people were getting sick, but I didn't think much of it. By '81 people were really getting sick. At the beginning we didn't even have a name for it. They had a bunch of initials. You saw gorgeous people that everybody pined after, that turned in one season, you couldn't recognize them. I remember getting off the boat in Cherry Grove and you saw walking death. People were afraid to go near people who had it. People were dying so fast. It was awful. – Keith Kollinicos (Missa Distic)

———————▽———————

New York, NY (USA)

Before coming-out, not only to myself but to my family, I used to watch PBS a lot. They used to do a lot of documentaries. Whenever Gay Pride came along, they would always put gay documentaries on between 12 and 2 in the morning, so I used to sneak out of my room and watch these shows. So I knew a lot about the history of AIDS. You would hear about it on the news and they called it gay cancer, people didn't know what was going on. Even though they really did. Being the youngest in a family of six, raised by myself with my mom, my dad wasn't in the picture. She would talk to her friends about how there was something out there. But she never wanted to talk about in front of me because I was too young. But then one of my cousins got sick and the rumors started, and we thought, "Maybe he has this new sickness." Although it wasn't talked about in front of me, I knew something was happening. Over time I realized the magnitude of it. And the seriousness of it. – David Vega (Lucifers Axe)

———————▽———————

Cambridge, MA (USA)

Sometime in the early 1980's, the papers were reporting a mysterious gay cancer or pneumonia or something that some guys speculated might come from doing poppers or other drugs. Soon it was called ARC, then AIDS. People we used to see at the bars began to disappear, one by one. Because of this weird disease? Gradually, we suspected it was communicable, but how? We didn't want to believe there was a serial killer picking us off, seemingly at random. – Daniel M. Jaffe

———————▽———————

Honolulu, Hawaii (USA)
New York, NY (USA)

In 1983 a friend of mine, who I used to do Broadway shows with, he got sick and he was in the hospital. Maybe it was 1982 and it wasn't identified as AIDS or HIV yet. He died, then his lover, who was a well-known Broadway musical writer, he died to. This is the guy who wrote *Fame*. He wrote the screenplay for *Fame*. He did a lot of shows before that. The first time was because of Patrick, who died before it was called AIDS. Later he was diagnosed as having died from AIDS. He died in New York, but I was back in Hawaii at the point. – Simeon Den.

—————————▽—————————

Sydney, New South Wales (Australia)

It would have been in the later part of 1982. I was very promiscuous at the time and was having regular check-ups with my doctor. My doctor was aware of how I was making a living (prostitution) and we had a very open conversation about this new disease [that was] spreading worldwide. He showed me the information he had, which was only a pamphlet size piece of paper. It scared the crap out of me and I decided at that moment that no money was worth dying for. I told everyone I knew about it and made a decision that when the first case is diagnosed in Australia, that I would no longer work the streets.

This wasn't an easy decision because at the time the money was excellent and there was a lot of fun to be had. When the first patient was diagnosed in Melbourne, I quit the streets that day. Everyone thought I was over reacting and joked about it, within six months everyone I knew had been diagnosed with AIDS and life suddenly changed big time. That doctor saved my life. – Ian Davies

—————————▽—————————

Los Angeles, CA (USA)

I first heard about AIDS when my best friend, Bob, who I met standing in line at a Liza Minelli concert in Las Vegas – he wasn't really out then – it seems I have a lot of men friends who I took to their first bar. We just bonded. We even slept together at one time because he was trying to do this, "I can sleep with a woman, I can sleep with a man." He got AIDS and I didn't know it. I had just gotten together with my new girlfriend in Los Angeles. He was in San Francisco. Everybody was calling, "Bob has AIDS, Bob has AIDS." I had to go through that. Then my mother had died, and he said my mother had come to visit him at the hospital. Then all my friends like dominoes started going, so I was put in the middle of it. Then he gave me as a sexual partner. They flew down to LA and took my blood for a book that they were doing about, "What if? What do you feel now that you may be exposed?" I had to do a similar interview about it. It was scary, like do you have it? What are your blood tests going to be? So it was that kind of experience. – Siouxzan Perry

—————————▽—————————

Newcastle upon Tyne, Tyne and Wear (UK)

It was the beginning of the 1980s, maybe 1981. I was starting at university and it was talked about, but it really started hitting home when my mother, a nurse in the north east of England, they were treating patients and they hadn't been told that they had AIDS. She was quite an Amazonian no-nonsense person. She came home very upset because they'd found out they were treating AIDS patients and hadn't been told and given the right protection. I always remember her words, "I would treat any fucking patient if they'd just fucking tell us what they've got." It didn't matter but they knew it was something infectious. She was so upset. She even wrote a letter to the Queen about this. She said, "I'm writing to the Queen." And she did. – Helen Macfarlane

—————▽—————

Tallahassee, FL (USA)

I would say mid-'80s, I was in graduate school in Florida. Probably '82 or '83. That was probably when I started becoming aware that there was something going on, specifically in the gay community. Probably through the news, the media, the newspapers, or the evening news. I didn't have any personal exposure to anybody with HIV or AIDS for a very long time. I was very closeted in grad school. I'd made some good friends and I just kept everything to myself. That was probably when I became aware that something was happening health wise. – Cody

—————▽—————

San Francisco, CA (USA)
Napier, North Island (New Zealand)

When I moved to California in 1984. I just heard about all the nasty things were happening with gay people, for the most part. I really wasn't concerned about it because I'm old enough to have lived through polio and TB and that stuff. It got bad. *The Bay Area Reporter,* in San Francisco, used to print obituaries at the end. Some of my friends had gotten AIDS and I decided to do something. There was a group called Shanti and most of the clients I worked with were partners of someone who had gotten AIDS. They were dealing with all this trauma. It never bothered me. I became HIV positive in the mid-'90s, late '90s, I have no idea. But it didn't show-up until about 2002. We were living in New Zealand at the time, 2002 or 2003, when the virus really hit. My doctor was an AIDS specialist. They don't refer to them as

AIDS specialists there, they're infectious disease specialists. He put me on two pills twice a day and one pill at night. Since then I've been on one tablet a day. – Marc

—————————▽—————————

Sydney, New South Wales (Australia)
Auckland, North Island (New Zealand)

1983. I must have been 20 and living in Sydney, Australia. I heard about it then but because I was 20, it was "Ah yeah, whatever!" I really didn't absorb it much, or take much in, because A) I was 20, I was too busy out and about as a young gay man. Then later I remember in the late '80s, living in Auckland, New Zealand, it was Wow! These men were dropping off like flies. I remember people were panicking. It was panic in the air amongst the gay community. That would have been 1988. I was working at KAOS … KAOS was a high-end boutique, hair and make-up salon. Only five staff, extremely high end. – Gib Maudey

—————————▽—————————

New York, NY (USA)

My first lover worked for Lufthansa, so a lot of people from the crews from all the different airlines came to visit us. That's when we really started hearing about it. It was called the Gay Plague or the Gay Cancer, there was something happening. All I remember was suddenly everything became empty, there was no-one out and that was the beginning of the '80s. – Juan-manuel Alonso

—————————▽—————————

Baton Rouge, LA (USA)

I was building some scenery for LSU [Louisiana State University] theater department. I was taking classes there, getting my degree. I overheard the set designer mention to somebody, "Hey, did you hear … (so-and-so in Chicago) … just died of AIDS." This was probably around 1984. I was still living with my parents. And when he said, "He died of AIDS," my first thought was they can't be talking about the diet candy. I didn't say anything. This was before the Internet and nobody had any information about it at all. I heard about it, but I didn't really know what it was. – Michael Wayne

—————————▽—————————

Chicago, IL (USA)

I first heard about it before it had a name. There was that strange, liminal period when GRID (Gay Related Immune Deficiency) was the name ... even though heroin users and Haitians also fell prey in prodigious numbers early on. This was in 1984, or thereabouts. I was in high school and needless to say, my first sexual experience was substantially delayed. My formative sexual experience was feeling a fear of contracting AIDS if I so much as masturbated while thinking of an HIV-Infected individual. Virology became something of an obsession of mine. (This was 1984: HIV education didn't exist at the time and the only known "cause" of AIDS, according to the media, was homosexuality, heroin, and Haiti, the "unholy triune.") – Chip H

—————∇—————

Santa Monica, CA (USA)

I was in elementary school and it was the disease fags got. I was 10 years old and that was from my peers. That's who got it because what happened was that gay men had sex with monkeys. Obviously now, that's ridiculous – now I do HIV/AIDS/Hep C testing and counselling, as a 25 years-old adult queer. I'm totally in the know, but 10-15 years ago I didn't know. Up until I was in school that's how I thought AIDS started, gay men in Africa had sex with monkeys and brought it back to the States. It only killed gay people because of what happened with the monkey disease. – Bambi

—————∇—————

Victorville, CA (USA)

I was 14 and when I came out my parents gave me the talk. I did have very supportive parents when it came to coming out, which I did in stages. That was their biggest thing, "Protect yourself." They explained it all to me, so I was prepared when that time came. – Hayley

—————∇—————

Riverside, CA (USA)

I think I heard the term AIDS when I was around 11 or 12 but I didn't really connect with what it really was until I was 18 or 19 when I started talking to a lot more friends that I was hanging around with who were gay and out in our community. Some had it, some didn't, and that's when I really learned about what it was. Like I said, I was very sheltered. In the secluded area where I lived there was not a lot of information or anyone talking about it either. – Chloe DeCamp

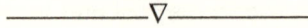

——————▽——————

Vicksburg, MS (USA)

I was in the 10th grade in high school and there was a *Time* magazine cover talking about AIDS. I don't remember what the cover looked like, I just remember the word AIDS on it. There was a boy in my class, I used to mess around with him a lot. I remember him and I getting into a discussion about it but not really understanding what it was. But I had this feeling inside me that these were my brothers. It was really hard to decipher at that age, at 15, still not knowing a whole lot about the world. Yet being told it was gay men, not feeling hatred or disgust, I felt like I needed to help but I didn't know how because I was 15, in the 10th grade. But I was so aware of it. – Jade

——————▽——————

Provincetown, MA (USA)
Oakland, CA (USA)
San Francisco, CA (USA)

I think the epidemic started when I was in Provincetown in the summer of 1979. I had a girlfriend at that time whose brother was also gay and lived and worked in Provincetown. I think it really came to the forefront of my attention because she found out that Glen had AIDS, or AIDS Complex, or whatever they were calling it at the time. Shortly thereafter, not too long later I got sober and we started losing the guys in the program, like often. I got sober in Oakland. My friends in the program were in Oakland and San Francisco, and AIDS just decimated the guys in the program. It was quite something to have to stay sober through something like that, I have to say. It was a different kind of … I've always thought that male and female were pretty separate in most of the places that I've been. In separate worlds, communities, friendship groups. It became that women started taking care of the guys, there was a different kind of connection and love there. I think it was related to Glen in 1979. He's still around, by the way. – Leslie Tisdale.

——————▽——————

Dallas, TX (USA)

In the '80s. I was still closeted. I was married. Had I not been married, I'd probably be dead. Being married limited my opportunity to get out. I had two fairly good friends, who I knew casually – one was the organist at church, and another was the man who brought me out – they both passed of AIDS. There was a huge amount of fear of the unknown, so it seemed best not to get out. We didn't know if this was air-born or what its source was. I knew it would really mess up my life to be diagnosed, being married and having a kid. – Don Rockwell Coffee

———————▽———————

Santa Cruz, Colchagua Valley (Chile)

I was probably around 10 or 12 years old. It may have been a bit later. It was in this show that we have in Chile called *Sábado Gigante,* a silly show that went all day long. Out of nowhere they say, "Hey, there's .this new disease that is killing people." It was portrayed in this horrible ad. It was a bowling alley, then somebody throws the ball and there was a family on the other end. And the ball was hitting them. It was like the monster from the Black Lagoon, or whatever. After that we have a talk for a bit, the show host talks about having a unique partner and all that. I remember they even had a priest on the show. – Ives

———————▽———————

Melbourne, Victoria (Australia)

It's 2000. I'm in sex ed class, we've done the reproductive system. We're talking failure rates of contraceptives and STDs. – Anita Morris

———————▽———————

Hartford, CT (USA)

I heard on the news that there was some weird gay disease. I was very hygienic so wouldn't do anything … even now, I wouldn't do anything where I might catch something. But I was nervous about it. – Paul

———————▽———————

Portland, ME (USA)

I was probably in my 30s. I just had this conversation with Leslie yesterday. I said, "Can you remember when people were saying it was contracted from a guy who came from Africa and he got it from a monkey?" I was thinking recently, and then, "How preposterous. How does a human being get it from a monkey?" I want to say I heard it on the news. I think of where I lived. It wasn't like Palm Springs where people are openly out about everything, about their medical conditions, about their sexuality. I think that if I knew someone who had it, I wasn't aware of it. – Cathy Melton

—————▽—————

Canton Township, Ohio (USA)

I heard about AIDS in 1992 when one of my father's best friends from his childhood group died from it. It was the second time I had ever witnessed my father crying. In that moment I knew in my child mind that I could never be gay, or I'd die and hurt my parents. – Mike

—————▽—————

New York City, NY (USA)

1981. I actually saw and read the original July 1981 *New York Times* article "Rare Cancer Seen in 41 Homosexuals." I remember thinking that, for some, having cancer might be a metaphor for being gay. Wouldn't this just happen, I thought. But I didn't think seriously about it for several more months. I remember suggesting to a friend that fall that it wouldn't happen to guys like us. A few years later, he was dead. – David Pratt

—————▽—————

Milwaukee, WI (USA)

I heard about it on the news. I was terrified. I was closeted and promiscuous and I thought it was God's special wrath for me. Then people started talking about it and all the time they were judging about it. Saying those people got what was coming. Calling it karma. Telling jokes. I wanted to say something but was too afraid to speak. No matter what I did I could not escape the feeling that I was doomed. I kept silent and suffered for two years before I got up the nerve to take the test. It took years to undo the Catholic in me. – Anonymous

———————▽———————

Baghdad (Iraq)

I was working in Baghdad and I was there 1981 thru '86. I first read some news reports in papers. We didn't have TV and radio, but people would bring back papers from their trips back to the UK. That was when I heard about it. It was probably '82 that I first saw an article about the Gay Plague. – Tess Tickles

———————▽———————

Bath, Somerset (UK)

About a week after I came out, in early 1982. It was in *Gay News*, I think, and some of the more serious newspapers. It was scary and was like knowing there was an escaped panther stalking us, waiting to strike. I was in a monogamous relationship with my older partner at the time, which shielded me from the risk, but a few local men did contract the virus shortly afterwards and died. – Diesel Balaam

———————▽———————

Seattle, WA (USA)

It would have been 1982 and it was on the news. I dismissed it. I was concerned but I hadn't done anything, so I wouldn't have been exposed to it. But some of my gay friends in Seattle had it. In fact, there was a threesome in Seattle and all three of them had it. I watched as they slowly debilitated. – OT

———————▽———————

Chicago, IL (USA)

I remember seeing a television program, perhaps either *Nightline* or *20/20*, on AIDS when I was in high school in the mid-late '80s. The program had an impact on me, and I even did a presentation on AIDS for my chemistry class at Clemente H.S. Back then the groups most at risk according to reports were homosexuals, Haitian refugees and drug addicts. There was quite a bit of misinformation and hysteria at the time. – Robert Castillo

————————▽————————

La Puente, CA (USA)

We thought one of my best friends had it. He was younger than I was, we became good friends in high school and then he started getting sick for no reason and it was one thing after another, recoup then get sick again, recoup then get sick again. Everybody started to think he had AIDS because he was dating an older man who was Asian and at that time, they were saying it was coming from Asia. So, my friends and I put two and two together and said, "Maybe he has this disease." So that was the first time I heard about it. So that must have been about 1980. – Felix

————————▽————————

New York, NY (USA)

I was living in New York, in Chelsea, in an apartment on 22nd Street. I remember that a guy I worked with, who I used to buy amyl from got sick. He was older than I was, but not that much older. He was out of work, and then I heard he was in the hospital with some kind of strange pneumonia and died. I think that was about 1979 or 1980. I then, sometime later, read in the *New York Native* about guys getting sick and at the time it was called GRID (Gay Related Immune Disease). It was maybe a couple of months after that that they started calling it AIDS. – Ian H

————————▽————————

HAVE YOU ATTENDED A SCHOOL REUNION AS AN OUT LGBTQ PERSON AND IF SO, DESCRIBE THE EVENING?

Rural Iowa, (USA)

This summer, I attended my 40th class reunion and I am completely out to my classmates, as I was also out for my 20th reunion. I went to a small, rural school and my class numbered only 99, so we all know one another. This reunion was especially memorable attending as a gay man. Since I'm friends with many on Facebook, they were aware of my recent dating status. I was sitting with the former jocks, and one of them commented on my new friend and I jokingly referred to our 22-year age difference and one of the jocks high-fived me for having a younger date and said he wished he could find a girlfriend who was 36! – Timothy Juhl

—————▽—————

Newport Beach, CA (USA)

I attended my 10-year high school reunion. I even did the artwork for the memory book. I was really, really, into it and I wanted to go. It was at the Newporter Inn and Newport Beach and all the guys I went to high school with looked great. Everybody had grown a beard or mustache, they were all so hot looking. But being there, around all those people, all the bad memories started coming back and I couldn't go through with it. I just walked out. I threw my meal ticket away in the trash and I left. I went to have dinner at McDonald's. The tickets for the reunion was my payment for doing the artwork. I was told later that they called my name, asking me to stand up so that everybody could give me a round of applause for the beautiful artwork I did. I wasn't there. I just couldn't stand it. Too many bad memories. That was the only reunion I've ever been to. In two or three years, it will be my 50th high school reunion, but even if I bothered to go, I don't know those people and they don't know me. Why bother? – Tim Barela

——————▽——————

Chicago, IL (USA)

The evening was pleasant ... Lane Tech Class of 1979 ... everyone encouraging and supportive. – Don Strzepek

——————▽——————

Parker, CO (USA)

Oddly, it wasn't my high school reunion, or even my year, but I attended the high school reunion in Parker Colorado in 2012. It was a friend's reunion. She was a year ahead of me. I transferred high schools my senior year, and my high school has since closed with no reunions. (On a cool note, I did graduate with the oldest high school graduate in Colorado. He was in his 60s and got his diploma to set an example for his grandchildren.)

I think the universe was telling me NOT to go to the reunion. I had to leave the dinner/bar gathering early because I got booked to headline a comedy show. I couldn't go to another event because I had been booked for another comedy show. I did attend the afternoon tour of the high school, Ponderosa. Never trust a high school named after a steak house. Walking the halls, I was reminded that I never belonged there and I was right to leave. – Thomas Bottoms

——————▽——————

Murphysboro, IL (USA)

I attended my 35th and my 40th high school reunion. At the 35th, I mentioned to a male high school friend of mine, "I'm gay." "I'm not," he replied, and that's all that was said. At my 40th, another high school chum asked, "So, are you married?" I replied, "I've been married twice, once to a woman and once to a man." "Well, that's different," he said. Again, nothing further came of it. – Louis Flint Ceci

——————▽——————

Chicago, IL (USA)

Yes, both 10 and 20 year reunions as an out gay man. It was great. I was thrilled and very surprised to see how nice and kind my former classmates were. We danced, drank, and enjoyed ourselves tremendously. – Jim

———————▽———————

Gainesville, FL (USA)

No way in Hell! I spent a LOT of money on drugs and therapy to block out those years. But ... I did go onto Classmates and signed in as "Ben Dover" to look at how physically unpleasant most of my tormentors now looked. Slight comfort for deep wounds. – Eric Andrews-Katz

———————▽———————

Chicago, IL (USA)

Yes, at both mine and my husband's reunions. It was an amazing feeling to attend as a couple and you could see some "looks" and whispers about us, but basically all went great, some we didn't know very well in school went out of their way to come talk to us too, thinking it was pretty cool. – Robert Hansen

———————▽———————

St. Louis, MO (USA)

I graduated high school in 1981 in St. Louis, Missouri. I had moved to California in 1995, so I flew back to St. Louis in 2001 for my 20th reunion. There were two people, a gal and a guy, who knew I was gay and that I had even starred in a porn film called *Rural Erections* that had been released on VHS and DVD that year. At my reunion, I figured word had spread around more about my "involvement in porn" than whether I was gay or not. Sure enough, I didn't have to walk around to say hi to people. Not even once. All I had to do was stand in one spot and throughout the evening they all approached me, in an actual state of awe. Now this was just as the internet was booming and not EVERYONE was posting sex videos of themselves on websites yet. One gal boasted to me that she has bought all-male porn and loves it, and one guy said he was so impressed that I was being free and enjoying myself "with your long hair and beard, it's so awesome," while he was just a guy in a suit working in an office. Of course, the entire evening wasn't spent on this specific topic about me, but people were so friendly to me and a couple of them wanted to apologize for being jerks back in high school. They said they wish they had just been more sensible while growing up. I didn't want the evening to end, it was a blast and getting to see a few teachers I had admired. Those even told me they knew I was unique back in high school and were so happy for me that I got to do what I want and love. – Todd Jaeger

---------∇---------

North Kingstown, RI (USA)

I went to my 10-year class reunion. It was strange. Firstly, I didn't take a boyfriend because I wasn't with anybody at that time. My friend who went with me – she's an architect in Boston – I said, "I don't want to go to this thing alone, I know it's going to be boring. I promise we'll cut out early, we'll go to the picnic in the afternoon and the dinner, and when dinner is over, we'll go." Well, during dinner, it turned out that my friend Karen knew two of the guys from high school. She goes, "Well, you know they're a couple." No, I didn't know anybody was gay in high school. Think about it, this was the late 1960s, early 1970s. I graduated 1970. It wasn't talked about so when I went up to them with Karen, the looks on their faces … the color drained away. Karen says, "I think you should know something about Art." Rick goes, "What?" She says, in a voice a third of the room heard, "He likes boys like you do." Come to find out, they'd been together since high school. Never saw it, and they were co-captains of the football team. Interesting, when it came time for a 20-year reunion, neither of them, nor I, got an invitation. The girl who ran the 20-year reunion, her husband is the pastor in a huge evangelical church in Rhode Island. – Art Healey

---------∇---------

Chicago, IL (USA)

Just the opposite! When my twentieth-year high school reunion rolled around, my wife was about nine months pregnant with our third child and didn't want to leave the house, so I took my eight-year-old daughter as my date. People were shocked: "I thought he was queer?!?!" Sat at the dinner table with four of my old boy-friends. People kept asking if my partner and I had adopted the girl; loved getting indignant and saying, "I'm married, I have a wife, this is our little girl." So proud of my little girl who had no problem with my kissing and holding hands with my high-school boy-friends and girl-friends. Also, very sad that my real boy-friend, Wally, and so many others, had died of AIDS and could not be there. — R.M. Schultz

————————∇————————

Chicago, IL (USA)

It was my 20th reunion and there was a whole table of us. I went to school in the city and several of my schoolmates are heavily involved in LGBTQ issues now. It was a wonderful night. – Kbro

————————∇————————

Washington DC (USA)
Chicago, IL (USA)

I ignored my earlier reunions thinking I would not have much in common with my classmates. That changed in 1995 when the reunion was being planned to take place in DC with President and First Lady of the United States. I went and had the best time with my classmates. I haven't missed one since. – Gary Chichester

————————∇————————

(USA)

I was really a nerdy kid, coke-bottle glasses, I was skinny. I just didn't fit in with the rest of them. I had one friend in high school and then when I left high school my whole look changed. I went back to the 20th high school reunion, and all these people that were really mean to me, they were all fat and had six kids. I walked in and they said, "Oh my God, who's this guy?" Then they tried to be all friendly with me and it was like, "Oh yeah, really, remember that time ... " I threw it up in their face. I didn't stay very long. Long enough for me to make sure everybody knew who I was and that I was successful. – Rory

————————∇————————

(USA)

I've never attended a class reunion in my life and have no desire to. As you may have surmised high school was less than fun, my graduating class was entirely white. When I graduated in 1990, only two people of color had made it through that school. In my class we had one woman, who left after she was threatened with a knife in the bathroom by the cheerleaders. They taught creationism as a viable option to evolution and spread lies that every "homosexual" will get AIDS and die, because god wanted it so. The only Jewish people in my school were the Jews for Jesus and mind you this was a public school. So, the only people I would have ever cared to stay in contact with were the stoners, and they either sold out or died from overdoses. The rest of the class can crash and burn. – Daniel Fisher (Raid)

—————▽—————

(USA)

I have attended my 30th HS reunion. I went as myself and everyone treated me great. However, they totally needed a homo to put that party together. Can we say straightsville? I hope that my 40th will be more fun. – Tripp

—————▽—————

Trinidad (West Indies)

What an interesting event, over the years I spoke with several people so getting together was not very awkward with those who were in class. After a few glasses, I did speak to some people who were quite mean, most were very apologetic and tried to make amends. A few of those young men indicated they were unaware at the time they were hurting someone and hope that their current actions and respect toward the LGBTQ helps future generations. It was quite refreshing. – Dale

—————▽—————

New York, NY (USA)

I have never gone back to any of my reunions. I didn't have a lot of friends in school. In junior high school I had one friend, maybe two. Same thing at high school, one maybe two. When I graduated from high school, I was more shocked that people wanted to sign my year book, to say, "Oh you were a great guy, David." And I'm thinking, "We weren't fucking friends at school. You never talked to me and now you want to write in my yearbook." So they all wrote in my book but I didn't know them. Because of Facebook I'm connected to one or two from high school, but that's because they were people who were actually my friends back then. The rest of them I didn't stay in contact with. I don't remember their names. I barely remember their faces.

I pushed them out of my head, out of my space of existence. They were nobody's to me, just not important. – David Vega (Lucifers Axe)

————————▽————————

Yankton, SD (USA)

Yes. It was actually a whole weekend. I rode my motorcycle to South Dakota from San Diego. I had a great time. My first roommate from college was there, we corresponded for a couple of years. I'm still on a Facebook page with the college, so they can all see my profile. – Ron

————————▽————————

Imlay City, MI (USA)

(Class of 1979) – I just attended my 40th reunion a week ago (Aug 2-3, 2019) It went over great. I also encouraged a school friend that is gay to attend who was not going to go. He thanked me over and over saying how healing it was. I went to the reunion at the country club with the notion I was not discussing politics as many of my former classmates are Republicans and Trump supporters. I was treated with respect and had a great time. My friend that I encouraged to go, and I, were the stars of the reunion. The following day was a picnic and that was wonderful with no feeling of homophobia but friendship and respect. – Greg R. Baird

————————▽————————

Honolulu, Hawaii (USA)

I was very popular in high school, student government, so I was a leader. The top of my class. So I had the respect of my friends. My class, we were the wrong side of the tracks, but there were 1100 kids in my class. Only 800 graduated. In that class there were only two white people and three blacks. The rest were Polynesian. It's a different fish bowl. When I went to my reunion, I had already appeared in Broadway shows, so I was a celebrity when I went. People knew and it was no big deal. My friend from high school, who I grew up with him from the 4th grade, we happened to be in New York at the same time. He was gay too. We were sisters in college, then we lived together in New York, then we went to the reunion together. He was an artist. So we went home to Honolulu to the reunion. I think they just assumed that we were colorful. – Simeon Den.

———————▽———————

Amersham, Buckinghamshire (UK)

Not a reunion, no. In England in the late-'80s a girlfriend of mine, a gay girl, she and her girlfriend gave a party at their house. This is someone I used to go dancing with. In fact, if I was ever going to marry a woman, I'd marry this woman. We're still friends. We met when we were 18 years of age and we're still friends all these years. She gave a party in their house and she got all the kids we'd been to school with during World War II. I flew over for that. The embarrassing thing was that I'm meeting all these guys with their wives and children and four of them I'd fucked at school. It was wonderful. I was seeing kids with who I was dodging bombs with during the war. – Bob Brown

———————▽———————

North Carolina (USA)

No, never. My high school was NC School of the Arts — I had already slept with most of my professors; college was California Institute of the Arts – where everyone slept with everyone. Either would be a non-issue. – Gavin Geoffrey Dillard

———————▽———————

Chicago, IL (USA)

No. I don't think I would enjoy it. And I went to a pretty rough high school on Chicago's south side. Most of my classmates are either dead or on parole. – David Cee

———————▽———————

La Mesa, CA (USA)

I'm not one to blurt it out to the masses. It was obvious because I made reference to my partner and may have dropped his first name, Ron, but nobody seemed to care about that. The high school beauty was there. She had been a Miss California. She was my age, we were in the same class. Her parents were close friends with mine. She was there, still had real style. She went around and introduced herself to everyone, reintroduced herself … everybody knew who she was. She asked them about their personal lives. When she saw me, she said, "Oh my, this is just amazing." She was married to a motion picture writer and producer of Western films. I went to my 50th, 52nd, and 62nd class reunions. Rode my motorcycle from out the back country. – Hal

——————∇——————

Sydney, New South Wales (Australia)

I almost attended a school reunion a few years ago, with an ex-girlfriend and her current partner that I reconnected with a few years ago. My school friends found out about me being gay after I left school and the gossip was incredible, none of my friends wanted anything to do with me anymore.
We thought it would be amusing to go as a trio and let everyone guess who was with who, but several people got abusive when they heard I was coming. I assumed people would have grown up over the years, but abuse turned to threats of bashings and we ended up not going at all. – Ian Davies

——————∇——————

Palm Springs, CA (USA)

Hell, no! I have no desire to look at those people again. – Siouxzan Perry

——————∇——————

West Allis, WI (USA)

I went to my high school reunion in 2016. I'd seen profiles of my classmates on a website prior to the reunion, and many seemed to be pretty conservative, so I was nervous. But the folks I talked to there couldn't have been more supportive. I'm now Facebook friends with many of them and they continue to be supportive. It was a nice surprise. – Yvonne Zipter

——————∇——————

(UK)

That was when I was 35 and I hadn't seen these schoolfriends since I was 14. I remember going in – and I wasn't really out – but some of my friends knew, even though I hadn't seen any of them for twenty years. I remember going around and catching up with my core group from school – and I hadn't kept in touch with them – they were just normal and lovely and we were having a chat and there was another person who was gay and so-on. But the rest of them, when it came to "Are you married?" and "Have you got kids?" I kind of thought, "Should I say something now to these people?" I always remember this one girl saying, "What's a nice-looking girl like you, not even married with kids." I thought, "I don't think I'll be telling her." They were the bullies at school. But I was not openly gay then. – Helen Macfarlane

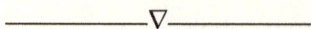

————▽————

South Bend, IN (USA)

I did attend the 35th high school reunion. I was so pleased because at high school I wore glasses. I don't wear anything now because I had cataract surgery, implanted lenses. Everyone was saying, "Whose husband are you?" It pleased me so much to see all the jocks that were fat and bald. I told them, "I have an alternative lifestyle." – Marc

————▽————

Chicago, IL (USA)

Beginning with my 10-year high school reunion, I made the decision to be out at the events. Since that time, the subsequent reunions I have attended, I have brought my husband Rick with me. My former classmates love him! – Gregg Shapiro

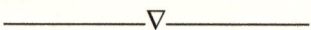

————▽————

Indianapolis, IN (USA)

No. I've never attended a school reunion. I didn't like my fellow students when I was in school with them. I have even less desire to see them now. – Xavier Bathsheba-Negron

————▽————

Mississippi (USA)

No. My classes never had a reunion. We hated each other. I'm not kidding. I went to a private Catholic school, 42 was our graduating class. We were the highest number in the school ever. There were 32 girls and 10 boys in my class. When it came time for senior pickings of names, flowers and mascots … our class motto was, "Let's just say we're testing the bounds of reality." Our class flower was the black rose. Our class song was *If Looks Could Kill.*

Our class bird was Opus from *Bloom County*. We weren't a kind bunch in that school. We never had a class reunion. Ever. They all know I'm gay now, though. – Jade

————————∇————————

Southern California (USA)

I'm a little too young, but I do plan on going just to shock everyone. The person I was back then, both physically and emotionally, is not the person I am today. I want to go to one of them and say, "Huh! You didn't drag me down." I look forward to one. – Hayley

————————∇————————

Riverside, CA (USA)

I missed my 10-year reunion. I never got an invitation to it. If I had done it, I would have gone as myself now. I've connected with a lot of people in school and a lot of the girls I dated, or knew me, were either, "It makes sense now," or "We kind of knew but we were waiting for you to figure it out." Some of the guys were very confused about it. The hardest one was my best friend. I came out to him and I didn't hear from him for a year. I've known him since he was born. I came out to everyone officially when I was 28 years old. I think he had to wrap his head around 28 years of one person, then all of a sudden here's a completely different person. Then finally he said, "I support you, I'm here for you, sorry it's been so crazy, I just want you to know that I'm proud that you're living who you are." It meant a lot to me. I guess that would be the only kind of reunion I've had. – Chloe DeCamp

————————∇————————

Gloucester, MA (USA)

I have never attended a reunion. Now I'm living in Palm Springs, openly out, and it's funny because friends of mine from the time I was 16 to 20, who I'm still friends with on Facebook. People say now, "Oh I always knew you were gay." And I was thinking to myself, "How did you know, I didn't know?" When I went back for a visit one time, I hoped to reconnect with a lot of those friends, and everybody said yes but when I went back home nobody hung out with me. Gloucester is a very small town and you're either Portuguese or your Sicilian. If you're Irish, Polish, if you're African-American, you are a minority, the town is split in half. It is narrow-minded, a town of bigots. So, looking back, it doesn't surprise me that nobody met up with me for dinner. Hurtful, yes, but surprised me no. I saw the way they treated black people driving down the street, so why would I being openly out … why would they be any different? – Cathy Melton

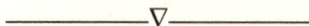

—————▽—————

Weymouth, MA (USA)

Never. I ran away from home and never went back. – Leslie Tisdale

—————▽—————

White Deer, TX (USA)

I've attended many of my school reunions. Going back, I learn about some in school who were gay. One was a drum major on the band. He's still in the community. I did not go back, as some do, and take a boyfriend with me. I would join a friend of mine from – we knew each other from the first grade, that's 70 years. I would join him and go to the high school reunion together. We were always friends even in high school. He's gay and has never been married, no kids, or any of that baggage. I attended with him but there was never any discussion of people being gay. – Don Rockwell Coffee

—————▽—————

Chicago, IL (USA)

At both my 10 year and 40 year reunion, I was out. At the 10 year it seemed like a big deal to some folks, by the 40th no one cared. – Rick Karlin

—————▽—————

Albuquerque, NM (USA)

Yes, I attended my 40th high school reunion summer of 2017 and I was, at that time, on the verge of getting my coming-out and coming-of-age story "PUBLISHED" so I was very much out and trying to drum up interest in the book, in which many of my classmates appear (with names changed) as characters. Book publication went sour and I was realizing that was the case by the night of the reunion. People came up to me and asked some questions, asked me to clarify about being gender-inverted, or apologized for how I had been treated in junior high and high school. One person sat at our table for a while and told an anecdote of his role in one of the harassment events, which he dismissed as childhood antics like silly fun. – Allan Hunter

———————▽———————

Chicago, IL (USA)

Yes, I went to my 20-year high school reunion many years ago with a lesbian friend and was greeted very warmly by all. I was nervous as hell about going but decided that it was more important for me to continue living my truth no matter what. I believe that conviction to truth is stronger than hatred and my experience has born that out. The haters wilt in the face of honesty once they see that they are outnumbered by those who practice acceptance. – Paul Mikos

———————▽———————

Wauconda High School, Wauconda, IL (USA)

40th Reunion October 2016. I went with Steve my boyfriend. I decided to go because we had gotten ahold of the foreign exchange student that had lived with us in my senior year, Wolfram. My family had not heard from him in many years but through others that I went to school with, that had contact with him, they convinced him to come. Well if he was coming then I surely needed to go. Which was kind of my senior year in school, and why I had never really gone to any of the other reunions. My thought was if I did not want to see most of them then why would I go see them now. But in my senior year of high school I went from infamous to famous cause the foreign exchange student lived with me. I got invited to parties and things that I never had before. So, I guess part of it was to see, did any of these people change or would they be accepting. It turned out to be a very good evening, people were nice and friendly, and accepting, for the most part. There were still those that really had no loss of friendship to me, and you know, it was ok. I will say that the girls were envious of the hot guy I had with me. So that was a huge score for me. I enjoyed it. – Dean Ogren

———————▽———————

Seattle, WA (USA)

I've never attended a high school reunion and I have never attended a college reunion, but I have attended a reunion for a school that I worked at. I was very well-received, it was not a problem at all. Because they knew me as a person. The fact that I was gay was secondary to my reputation, and my career, and how these people thought of me. It was kind of like, "Oh, that's interesting." In fact, some of them said, "We thought you were gay." They knew I was married but still thought that I was gay. – OT

—————▽—————

Chicago, IL (USA)

I organize an annual reunion for the former Goethe Playground in Logan Square, which still technically exists but not in the same capacity as it did when me and my friends hung out there in the '70s thru '90s. The event I organize is called the Goethe Playground Reunion Picnic and I am out to all my friends from the playground days and the current principal, who was my 6th grade teacher back in the late '70s. There were a lot of Chicago Public Schools in Logan Square that had playgrounds with field houses, but the field houses were shuttered and athletic directors let go as part of cost cutting measures taken in the '90s. The best part is that the friendships begun there have endured and I have lost ZERO friends for being my true authentic OUT, PROUD self! – Robert Castillo

—————▽—————

WHAT FAMOUS PERSON FANNED YOUR DESIRE AS A YOUNG LGBTQ PERSON AND WHY?

Madison, WI (USA)

Maybe Adam West as *Batman* when his nipples would pop up. And Burt Ward too, just because he was so cute in that outfit. – Vincent Rideout

———————▽———————

St. Louis, MO (USA)

I could go on about how someone important inspired me to be proud and help the cause, but that's just not what happened. Growing up in St. Louis in the 1960s, 1970s, and 1980s, the U.S. Midwest was very Republican and religious. Not exactly open-minded. I knew I was gay and kept it quiet because there were no youth groups, organizations, nor help from school guidance counselors like there are today. The only "known" gay people were basically stereotyped gay male characters and flamboyant actors on TV and in movies, like Paul Lynde, Liberace, and Alan Sues. They were to be laughed at, tolerated for being perceived as weaker and non-threatening because of their outward personalities. So, all I could do is look at men that I felt attracted to like Dan Haggerty. Mr. Grizzly Adams himself. The beard, the hairy chest ... I wanted to be hugged by him. As a child I didn't think so much of it being sexual, more of that's a look that made me melt and wanted to touch that. It was a little later I realized I wanted that but NAKED as well! Even though he had starred in a bit of homophobic cinema called *The Pink Angels* in 1971 (about a gay biker gang, Dan was in a rival heterosexual gang), I just tried to put that aside and tried to find any magazine shots of him shirtless. I told myself one day I'LL look like that, and have someone like him to be with. Well, I did turn out to look like him minus the full build and I'm still single, but hey I can still hope! – Todd Jaeger

—————▽—————

Gainesville, FL (USA)
New York, NY (USA)

Frank Langella. I first saw him in the play *Dracula* (1977) and literally had my first homoerotic experience. When I saw the movie with him reprising that role, I stopped eating garlic and got into trouble for leaving my bedroom window open on full moons – we lived in New York at the time, and I was ten years old.

The first famous "image" that fanned my desire was the Greek God Pan! I started having visions and dreams of Pan when I was three years old. When I was seven years old, he appeared to me and invited me to follow him for the rest of my life. I immediately agreed. – Eric Andrews-Katz

—————▽—————

Chicago, IL (USA)

Patrick Duffy from *Dallas*. I couldn't figure out what it was about him, but I just couldn't stop staring at him every time he came on TV. It was only later that I determined the qualities I found attractive were called rugged, handsome, and masculine. I just knew I felt happy when I saw him. – Jim

—————▽—————

Chicago, IL (USA)

Jack Carson! When I saw him in *Mildred Pierce,* I became a huge fan; he was SO manly! Sexy as all hell in *Cat on a Hot Tin Roof,* where he plays the straight brother-in-law to queer Paul Newman. He wasn't in a whole lot of good movies, but he has one fuck of a scene in *A Star Is Born!* A drunken James Mason punches him effetely, and Jack just picks him up and tosses him across the room. Shit, did I want to be Jack Carson! There's a guy in my parish that I see every Sunday that's handsome in the same way; straight, five kids, patent lawyer – he has no idea of the crush I have on him! – R.M. Schultz

—————▽—————

What famous person fanned your desire as an LGBTQ person?

(USA)

Younger years, probably Richard Chamberlain. He was athletic and self-assured. Then, in college years, one who I actually got to know, Roddy McDowell. Always thought, "He can't be gay" ... until I met him at a party, and he was. – Art Healey

———————▽———————

Chicago, IL (USA)

I had several crushes on hairy boys and men of the '70s and '80s. Matthew Laborteaux, Albert on *Little House on the Prairie*, Dick Gaultier on *Match Game*, Tom Selleck on *Magnum PI*. – Martin Mulcahy

———————▽———————

Chicago, IL (USA)

Bobby Sherman. He was so sexy! – Kbro

———————▽———————

Long Island, NY (USA)

Hugh O'Brian and Tab Hunter. I used to cut out pictures of the both of them and jack off to them. – Ron

———————▽———————

New York, NY (USA)

There were a lot over the years. Michael Landon, the father from *Little House on the Prairie*. I don't know what it was about him. I was very young back then. But there was something about him that I thought was cute. Even his younger self, in *Bonanza*. That's where I first saw him. I thought, "Wow, this is a good-looking dude." He gave me the hots. There were a lot of different guys over the years in movies and television. He's the first that came into my head. I had a hard crush on him at a young age. – David Vega (Lucifers Axe)

———————▽———————

(USA)

Roddy McDowall. I used to see him at auditions because he used to go to the same auditions I went to. And he always got the fucking part. I always played second fiddle to Roddy McDowall, but I loved him. He was so pretty. – Bob Brown

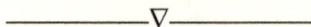

——————▽——————

(USA)

This is going to sound weird, but Dan Rowan from *Laugh-In* was one of them and I always felt Gregory Peck was hot too. – Rory

——————▽——————

Chicago, IL (USA)

Lou Reed. – Martin Mulcahy

——————▽——————

(USA)

Julian Sands. He was so hot in *Naked Lunch*, even though, maybe because of, he became a giant bug creature who impaled his lover in the butt. Hated him in *Warlock*, such an awful movie. I did have a moist spot for Patrick Stewart in *I Claudius*. That skirt and hair … Yum. – Daniel Fisher (Raid)

——————▽——————

New York, NY (USA)

Yul Brynner. The first time I saw him, he was so unique. He had beautiful features. He was the embodiment of hot, hot, hot, to me. As young as I was, he was just "Ahh!" I'm still like that with Yul Brynner. It didn't matter what age or era because as he went from *The King and I* to *Westworld*, it didn't matter to me, how old he was. I thought he was the most gorgeous man. I still feel that way. –Keith Kollinicos (Missa Distic)

——————▽——————

Los Angeles, CA (USA)

Dr. Kildare, Richard Chamberlain. The movie *Ben Hur* ... Charlton Heston. – Kalvin

———————▽———————

New York, NY (USA)

I was just thinking about this the other night. I had to Google it because I couldn't remember his name. There was a western cowboy character in a movie. It was a Disney movie. Traditional square jaw, American, burly. When I was in New York I met him at a bar, and he came home with me and he fucked me. My only reality was seeing him on a wide screen, and all of a sudden, I'm lying there and he's walking toward me. Later I had a thing with him, but he wanted to get fisted all the time, so that was an end to it. – Simeon Den

———————▽———————

North Carolina (USA)

I adored reluctant heroes, especially when they took their shirts off, and especially when they were capable of whisking me away from childhood bourgeois hell. Any version of *Robin Hood*, *Tarzan*, even *Star Trek* worked quite well. I was also passionately obsessed with John Astin as Gomez Addams (my perfect family). – Gavin Geoffrey Dillard

———————▽———————

East Randolph, NY (USA)

I think it would have to be this actor named Paul Kratka who played Rick, the male lead in *Friday the 13th, Part III*. He seemed to have a very chill, confident energy as a performer and, naturally, he had a very beautiful body. The fact that one of his major appearances in the film was a long scene that featured him, sweaty and shirtless, was a huge plus for me, as well! The character of Rick would also, generously, probably be described as a kind of a goofy bro type, an attitude that I still, for whatever reason, find incredibly sexy. So, I think that film and Kratka kind of paved the way for many of my unrequited crushes for years to come. Interestingly, there is a secondary character in the film named Andy, played by an actor named Jeffrey Rogers. Physically, Rogers is much more of my type than Kratka – wavy dark hair, an athletic masculinity – but I never paid any attention to him at the time. It has only been upon reexamining the film in recent years later that I've realized what I've been missing out on! So, all apologies, Jeffrey! It's definitely Andy all the way now!! – Brian Kirst

——————▽——————

Sydney, New South Wales (Australia)

As an adolescent I had a huge crush on Tom Selleck when he was in *Magnum PI,* I had never been with a guy, but I knew that this was the kind of man I wanted. I'm not sure I paid much attention to the program itself, I would just fantasize about what I wanted to do with him. I was always trying to hide my "interest" during that show and had to make some lame excuses a few times. – Ian Davies

——————▽——————

Chicago, IL (USA)

I used to swipe my sister's copy of *Tiger Beat* magazine in the 1960s and these were some of the heartthrobs who made my budding homo flame flicker: Davy Jones of The Monkees, Bobby Sherman, David Cassidy and Donny Osmond. This was also around the time that my family started banging on the bathroom door, asking how long I was going to be ... – David Cee

——————▽——————

Racine, WI (USA)
Riverside, CA (USA)

Who turned me on? Baseball players in general. Actor – Steve McQueen, rugged, masculine, and beautiful. – Mark Zubro

——————▽——————

Cherry Hill, NJ (USA)

Rock Hudson (long before we all found out he was gay) – he was so romantic in those movies with Doris Day, a real "dreamboat." And macho John Wayne (long before we all found out he was a rabid homophobe). And Johnny Weissmuller and the other various loincloth-wearing incarnations of Tarzan. And all those ancient Greek and Roman gladiator movie heroes. And amateur wrestlers back in the late 1960's – muscular and bulky and rolling around with one another all sweaty and sooo masculine. – Daniel M. Jaffe

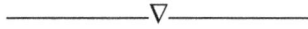

—————————∇—————————

(UK)

I adored Annie Lennox as a teenager, as a musician and a person. – Helen Macfarlane

—————————∇—————————

Los Angeles, CA (USA)

Kim Novak, look at her. I didn't want to be her, I wanted to be with her. I finally did get to meet her and interview her at one point, and it was ... I couldn't even breathe. It was great. By then I was a photographer and doing an event, where she was out for *Vertigo* at the Egyptian. I was the only female paparazzi there and the guys were pushing me around. Some guy pushed me into a tree. She got really indignant. She spread the crowd and I got up there and she posed only for me. – Siouxzan Perry

—————————∇—————————

(USA)

There were a lot of different ones. I liked musicals, so I liked Gene Kelly, I thought he was really hot. Then when I was about 15 I saw *My Beautiful Launderette*, so I fell for Daniel Day Lewis. I love that movie. When I discovered that movie as a teenager on TV, I thought, "I've got to tape this." I watched it over and over and over again. I loved it. That's what I wanted, I wanted someone like that. Somebody unpredictable. – Bart

—————————∇—————————

Indianapolis, IN (USA)

A toss-up between William Shatner on all those *Star Trek* reruns, and Randolph Mantooth from *Emergency*! I'm leaning more toward Randy Mantooth. I can remember the first time I saw his face on my parents' TV at our home in Indianapolis in 1972, I blurted: "Oooooh, he's pretty!" As a nine-year-old, I didn't actually comprehend that the feeling was sexual, all I knew was that I *really* liked him, and couldn't wait to see him every week. He was my special TV friend, and I was ecstatic when I got an *Emergency!* lunchbox with his picture on it for my tenth birthday. I would clutch the lunchbox to my chest and feel this incredible sense of happiness and contentment. I wish I still had that lunch box. – Xavier Bathsheba-Negron

—————▽—————

Baton Rouge, LA (USA)

Robert Redford. During the years he was doing *The Sting*. I fell in love with Robert Redford and Paul Newman, and that's what made me want to become an actor. They were so cool. – Michael Wayne

—————▽—————

Chicago, IL (USA)

Walter Koenig's portrayal of Pavel Chekov in the original *Star Trek* series. He bore a vague resemblance to Davy Jones of *The Monkees*. I was attracted to both, though Walter Koenig's portrayal of Ensign Pavel Chekov was particularly appealing to me as I was intrigued by the idea of a "Soviet" on a spaceship with a black person, even though the black person was a woman in a red miniskirt. My desire as an LGBTQ+ person was fueled by most of *Star Trek* as it was the only aspect of reality that came anywhere close to matching my own aspirations in life. – Chip H.

—————▽—————

Milwaukee, WI (USA)

Nancy Sinatra. Those pouty lips. Those boots. Need I say more? – Yvonne Zipter

—————▽—————

Albuquerque, NM (USA)

No one. Nothing like that. When I was young, I found people my own age fascinating and attractive and had zero sexual or romantic interest in any adults. I assume that's what you mean by "desire." Now, after I came out, I did sort of get a crush on Bette Midler, because of *The Rose*, but I wasn't so young at that point. I wasn't much tuned into popular culture as a kid. Didn't go to movies, listened to classical music not pop (and hence no interest in pop stars), didn't watch much TV and didn't give a rat's ass about the actors. Famous, schmamous, who cares? – Allan Hunter

—————▽—————

Southern California (USA)

The remake of *Peter Pan*. I used to masturbate to the thought of the live action Peter Pan, like kissing and having sex, I wanted him so bad, for some godforsaken reason. I thought he was hot. I wanted him so bad, he's got that curly blond hair, he's this fey type of person, covered in glitter. It was a mixture of, "Do I want to be this boy, or fuck this boy?" Probably both. – Bambi

—————▽—————

(New Zealand)

Burt Reynolds. Oh fuck, I used to masturbate over him. Patrick Swayze, Donny Osmond, of all people. Tom Selleck in *Magnum P.I.*, George Michael, Michael Jackson even. – Gib Maudey

—————▽—————

Chicago, IL (USA)

Gene Kelly, that ass, that smile! – Rick Karlin

—————▽—————

Central Illinois (USA)

Jessica Lange. I still love her. For all the right reasons. – Terry Gaskins

—————▽—————

New York, NY (USA)

That's an easy one, Cat Stevens. I lusted after Cat Stevens. Aside from the fact that he was and is an incredibly talented songwriter and performer, I thought he was one of the sexiest men alive. In high school, I hung a poster of him over my bed. Now, I hadn't come out yet, so what my parent's or friends thought, I don't know. I used to have many fantasies about him. I think a highlight for me was when I got to see him perform live in November 1972 in Philharmonic Hall in New York. THAT fueled my fantasies for quite a while until I came out in 1973. – Ian H

—————————∇—————————

Mississippi (USA)

Drew Barrymore. Not LGBT but friendly. I grew up with her, I read her books, I followed her as much as I could on TV. I read everything she wrote. I still follow her. I still have a crush on her. – Jade

—————————∇—————————

New York. NY (USA)

Elliott Gould was so masculine. Back in high school I would go and see every single movie he was in. It's not that I wanted to have sex with him, I just thought he was very masculine. – Juan-manuel Alonso

—————————∇—————————

Southern California (USA)

In high school I was obsessed with Channing Tatum and the whole *Magic Mike* thing. That's what I want for a husband, so he was my first everything. – Hayley

—————————∇—————————

Seattle, WA (USA)

Tab Hunter and the bodybuilders in the bodybuilding magazines. – OT

—————————∇—————————

Chicago, IL (USA)

I remember being infatuated with Dutch from the groundbreaking ABC sitcom *Soap*. As a budding queerling, I loved that the show contained a gay character who was in love with a football player. I played football at Goethe playground and on Logan Boulevard as a teen, so I identified with the show, but Dutch was the one on the show that I found myself crushing on. Later on, it was Erik Estrada from the NBC cop show *C.H.I.P.S.* that made my young queer heart skip a beat! – Robert Castillo

—————▽—————

Cathedral City, CA (USA)

Hayley Williams from *Paramore*. Definitely, hands down. I loved her '80s style. I loved how she was just like, "I don't care what people think of me, I'm just gonna be me." That was very attractive to me. I'm very attracted to powerful dominant women who aren't afraid to take charge. – Chloe DeCamp

—————▽—————

Weymouth, MA (USA)

I would say Cher. I wanted her to be my girlfriend. I didn't want to be her at all. But she was pretty hot, she still is. Also, Ann Wilson of Heart, and she's still hot too. – Leslie Tisdale.

—————▽—————

London (UK)

I suppose this is uncharacteristic, but I didn't have heroes when I was a kid. Not human heroes. I was a great fan of Superman, the comic, as he appeared to wear his underwear on the outside. That was an attraction. – Tess Tickles

—————▽—————

Northlake, IL (USA)

If you are referring to sexual desire, I would have to say the young Marlon Brando, and Sal Mineo who still drives me wild to this day! It was their sheer beauty and raw magnetism that attracted me as a young boy and still does. – Paul Mikos

—————▽—————

Rugby, Warwickshire (UK)

Captain Kirk of the Starship Enterprise. It took a while to work out if I wanted to be like him, or be with him. Lots of my contemporaries had a crush on the young William Shatner – the singer Jimmy Somerville, included, by his own admission. He was our Marlon Brando, I think. So damn sexy. – Diesel Balaam

————————∇————————

(USA)

I was fascinated by the physique photographs of Richard Harrison & Bob Hover posing together. & the photo of George Nader kneeling in the water. But it was the photo of Sal Mineo showering that gave me tingles. – Alex Gildzen

————————∇————————

AS A YOUTH OR YOUNG ADULT, WAS THERE A PLACE, OTHER THAN A BAR, WHERE YOU CONGREGATED WITH FELLOW LGBTQ PEOPLE?

Los Angeles, CA (USA)

Because I was a religious person, I was involved in churches for a long time. I started getting involved with gay-friendly churches and bible-study groups. There was a bible-study group that I used to go to at Mike and Andy's house, that's all I can remember of their names. They were up in Los Feliz in LA and I used to go there. There was a bunch of other guys, it was a large group of people. There were other groups like that. But that's the fondest memories I have, of getting together with those guys every week. They were just nice people. The interesting thing is that Andy had been – I think, I am not sure – really involved for Campus Crusade for Christ before he came out of the closet. He was a very religious person. There were some interesting people there. – Tim Barela

———————∇———————

Denver, CO (USA)

In Denver Colorado in 1992, a friend gave me some information about Outright, a teen gay support group. She got the information from East High School where she attended. (Oddly, I met her through an ex-girlfriend who outed me to the entire high school I attended. A quick google search shows she never left her parents' house. I chuckle about it now, looking at my life of travel and adventure. I guess its karma.)

Outright met on Sundays, 2-5pm. I had a girlfriend at the time but attended the group on the down low. It was the first time I was around out, open gay people. The facilitators gave lessons and helped foster a sense of community. My natural stand-offish nature prevented me from getting passed around in the hormone drenched after gatherings, but the lessons I learned from others mistakes still help me today. I attended the group for 2 ½ years before aging out in college. Through the group, I was able to make many lifelong friends. – Thomas Bottoms

————————∇————————

Chicago, IL (USA)

THE BELMONT ROCKS!!!!! – Don Strzepek

————————∇————————

Milwaukee, WI (USA)

No. When I was a youth, there were no fellow LGBTQ people. I was the only one in the world. I was well into my 20s before I began to suspect this was not the case. – Louis Flint Ceci

————————∇————————

San Francisco, CA (USA)

That was one of the biggest reasons for wanting to move/travel to San Francisco, I was very sheltered as a youth and as I probably said before, I didn't know Chicago had any venues for gay youth/young adults. I used to subscribe to the *Advocate* and saw dozens of listings for activities in LA and San Francisco, and New York. – Jerry S

————————∇————————

Chicago, IL (USA)

I was on a gay bowling league at the Marigold Bowling alley in the mid '80s. My team was three black gay men and me, we called ourselves "3 nights and a day!" – Robert Hansen

————————∇————————

San Diego, CA (USA)

Balboa Park. Not only was it a cruising park but it was also a park in the daytime where a lot of us hung out because it was safe in the daylight. It wasn't so safe at night, but it was safe in the daylight. We could be almost overt there, not completely, but almost. It's interesting that Pride in San Diego is held in that park. – Art Healey

———————▽———————

Chicago, IL (USA)

Belmont Rocks! This was a gathering place along Lake Michigan just north of Diversey Harbor for queer men in the seventies and early eighties where guys would cruise, sunbathe, listen to tunes on the AM radio, drink, hang-out. I was too young for the bars and being able to go there was great! Even if I wasn't cruising for a pick-up it was nice to be able to talk to guys, find out what the life was like. It was there that someone called me a "leatherman" for the first time and, suddenly, it all became clear to me.
My dad lived in the Lincoln Park neighborhood at the time and would often go for bike rides along the Lakefront Trail. He would often stop in sight of the Rocks and ask rhetorically, "Why do so many young men go to that beach? There are never any women there." – R.M. Schultz

———————▽———————

Chicago, IL (USA)

Lincoln Park and various bath houses – Gary Chichester

———————▽———————

Indianapolis, IN (USA)
Minneapolis, MN (USA)
Chicago, IL (USA)

From 16 until I left the state after high school, me and my friends would hang out at either the Waffle House or Future Shock head shop in Indianapolis. Future Shock was in Broad Ripple, a neighborhood in Indianapolis. When I moved, there was the Emma Goldman Community Center in Minneapolis, we had queer space there. The 404 in Chicago, also had a queer only space for meetings. In 1993 when I moved to Philadelphia there was the A-Space. We had queer café and cabarets there. Then Penguin Place opened and that was another venue. After '98 pretty much both places faded, and we were everywhere. At least we treated the city as if we were. Later on, in the early 2000's, there were the fairy circles and the gatherings, but those were more family gatherings in my mind than a place away from the "real world" and it's idiots. – Daniel Fisher (Raid)

—————▽—————

Chicago, IL (USA)

Never. It did not exist on the south side of Chicago in the '80s. – Martin Mulcahy

—————▽—————

Central Michigan University, Mt. Pleasant, MI (USA)

Yes, in college we had our meeting on campus in our LGBT group. Afterwards, many came to my place for coffee, drinks, food and often watching movies on VHS. It was a great sense of community. We also had potlucks in different apartments as well. – Greg R. Baird

—————▽—————

Amersham, Buckinghamshire (UK)

I used to hang out at the public toilet in Amersham high street. A lot of gay men lived in Amersham. This was in the '40s into the '50s. Not that anything happened necessarily, but you see them masturbating and looking at each other's dick. I used to go there quite often. – Bob Brown

—————▽—————

Newark, NJ (USA)

The only other place I hung out was when I found out that gay guys hung out in parks. I was living in a basement apartment and a guy who lived across from me was also gay. We started talking one day, and hung out together, just as friends. On my keychain I had a thing from the Monster in New York City, when he saw that he said, "You go to the Monster?" I said, "You know what the Monster is!" So we started hanging out together and he went to the parks. So he invited me a couple of times. He said, "Let's go hang out because a lot of gay guys hang out in the park." … I said, "The park! That's dangerous in Jersey, in Newark, New Jersey at night." The park was walking distance from the apartment. Six blocks or so. But I never did anything or met anyone. Once or twice I talked to people. If they didn't know you, you were a stranger in their space. And I wasn't someone who was going to hang out in the park every weekend for them to get to know my face. I was more interested in going to New York. I would take the train into the city to go to the gay bars because that's where I knew other gay people are at, close enough to talk to and meet. You couldn't do that in a park. You see shadows in the distance and I'm not into shadows in the distance. I don't know what's over there. – David Vega (Lucifers Axe)

—————▽—————

Seattle, WA (USA)

Seattle Gay Community Center was paramount. Once I moved to Hollywood the gay community center seemed redundant. I lived at the disco, and the streets of WeHo were already on fire (and I was sleeping with our first mayor). – Gavin Geoffrey Dillard

—————▽—————

Chicago, IL (USA)

My first lover was an alcoholic. I started going to ALANON meetings and there were other gay people in the group. We all looked at each other, because there was quite a number of us, and we formed our own gay ALANON group. – Marc

—————▽—————

Dolton, IL (USA)

When I was a freshman in high school my friend Mike announced that he was auditioning for the school play. That year, the school play was G.B. Shaw's *Androcles and the Lion*. I think we both auditioned and neither of us got a part. But I fell in love with the theatre and discovered that was where all the sissies were! So, it became my home away from home. The teachers were very supportive and I could be as gender-variant in the works of Shakespeare and Williams and Albee.

Years later, when I was participating in one of those HUGE Marches on Washington (1993), I was marching along Pennsylvania Avenue and looking into the faces of the large, cheering crowd and I saw someone that I recognized from Thornridge 20 years earlier: my friend, Brian, and I ran up to him and said, "I knew you were gay way back then!" We hugged and kissed and the crowd around us burst into applause. – David Cee

————————▽————————

Sydney, New South Wales (Australia)

When I first found the gay scene, the bars were the only contact I had with other gays. There were no clubs or groups at that time, only saunas and beats if you knew where to go. Other than that, we used to have a lot of parties at friends' homes. Anything that did happen had to be kept private, because being gay was still illegal in Australia. To be honest, I think the secrecy made it more fun and exciting. – Ian Davies

————————▽————————

Cherry Hill, NJ (USA)

No. No place. Nowhere. Maybe some such place existed across the Delaware River in Philadelphia, but that might as well have been on the moon for all of my ability to get there on my own. Until: one Sunday, the local newspaper did an exposé, replete with photos, on a shocking locale – a homosexual bath house in nearby Camden. The exposé was in the paper's entertainment section where the TV listings were, so I came across it by complete accident and read it and re-read it and imagined it and couldn't believe such a place existed and re-read it … until finally Dad asked where the TV listings were. Once he got hold of the paper, somehow that week's entertainment section disappeared for good … I couldn't even find it later in the trash. But now I had acquired an actual place where my fantasies could run riot … although I'd never actually go there. – Daniel M. Jaffe

————————▽————————

Leesburg, FL (USA)

When I lived in Florida, we didn't live in Orlando or Miami, we had to drive to go to a gay bar. So my town had the typical rest stop. It was nice, really secluded, off the road, there was a boat dock. We would all congregate on the dock. That's where things would go on. – Bart

————————▽————————

Milwaukee, WI (USA)

Not until I was in college. Then Sister Moon Feminist Bookstore and Art Gallery opened, and I would often go there to hear women's music in the early 1970s. – Yvonne Zipter

——————▽——————

Southend-on-Sea, Essex (UK)

There were about four of us at school who hung out together a lot. I knew one of them was quite out at school. Since leaving school I've found out the other two are gay as well. So, without mentioning it, or even knowing it, the four of us were all gay without ever mentioning that word, or that concept. – Martin

——————▽——————

Chicago, IL (USA)

After I finally came out, in mid-1980s Chicago, I developed two types of friends: those who liked to go to gay bars – specifically dance clubs; and those who didn't. For the crowd who didn't, our main destination was usually the Belmont Rocks. Before we went there, though, we would almost always meet up at the McDonald's that used to be on Broadway south of Belmont. We called it the "Boy Hooker McDonald's" because of all the young male hustlers who hung out there. They didn't actually work out of the place but would congregate in a particular area – usually near the windows – eat their Big Macs, and dish about their weirdest tricks until their beepers went off. My friends and I would sit nearby and listen to them as we ate. For a sheltered Catholic boy, it was very educational. Like most of Newtown/Lakeview at the time, the place was incredibly gay – including most of the staff – and there was a party atmosphere with all the young queens trying to outdo each other for general outrageousness. It was a blast, and then we would move the party over to the Rocks and claim an area. We'd hang out, partake of controlled substances, sunbathe, boy watch, cruise, and commune with Lincoln Park and Lake Michigan. Boys would frequently wander by and join in the fun. There were a lot of hook ups. The Rocks where a special gay zone where heterosexuals weren't welcome. I recall several spray-painted signs saying just that – HETEROSEXUALS NOT WELCOME – mixed in with the rest of the gay graffiti the Rocks were covered in. There was a lot of history in that graffiti: men pledging undying love for each other; some of the messages going back to the 1930s. The Rocks were pure magic, and they were *ours*. That is until the city destroyed everything back in the early 2000s when they yanked them out and replaced them with that hideous revetment shelf. – Xavier Bathsheba-Negron

———————▽———————

Riverside, CA (USA)
Los Angeles, CA (USA)

Lots of events. There was Pride Prom at UC Riverside. I went to Models of Pride almost every year at USC in Los Angeles. I went to tons of conferences. I was the president of GSA, I was on the GSA network youth council. So I was at a lot of LGBTQ events. Back to the Grind Coffee in Riverside is where a lot of people go, trans folks would meet there. – Bambi

———————▽———————

Victorville, CA (USA)

I met my friend Mike about 12 years ago and it became a thing where we all got together at his house to hang out, socialize, have parties, because it was a safe place for people. He happened to be gay and blind. He knew I was trans and a lesbian. We hit it off very well because of how we connected intellectually and how our viewpoints were, so we had get-togethers every weekend at his place for people in the community who had nowhere else to go. There wasn't places where I was living. – Chloe DeCamp

———————▽———————

New York City, NY (USA)

I have "never," in my entire "life," been in a whole roomful of people like me. I meet other gender inverts face to face at a rate of 3-4 per decade. (More interaction online, of course). I first became interested in meeting gay and lesbian people to discuss our politics-in-common starting in 1980 but didn't actually do so until I hitched/emigrated to New York City in 1984 and began hanging out at Identity House intermittently. – Allan Hunter

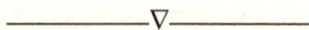

———————▽———————

Melbourne, Victoria (Australia)

2004-2008: There was a corner of one canteen at uni where my friends hung

out. There was a high number of bisexuals in that group. I met Klaire, my ex-girlfriend, through them. At uni there was also the Queer Room. It was mostly empty when there weren't meetings on. I sometimes sat in there for the quiet. I stayed away from the Queer Room lesbians because they had a reputation as separatist feminists. The boys were sweet. – Anita Morris

———————▽———————

London (UK)

Well, there wasn't. Nothing like that existed. I became aware of pedophiles fairly early on. I was sexually abused as a child. I was about 13, so I was aware of sexual attraction between men as I saw it existed. But that was all I had to work from, so this was all force and control and not about good natural sex. So I didn't become aware of anybody in the LGBT community until I went to college where I met a guy who very out, a member of the Campaign for Homosexual Equality (CHE) and initially I was terrified when I met him and he and I went out for drinks and almost got to the point of kissing and I ran away. I was scared to death of my own feelings. He saw me the next day and he said, "You know, it's alright, eventually you'll get to where you're comfortable, so there's no pressure. I knew him at college, and he convinced me to join him on marches, where I was a "straight supporter." – Tess Tickles

———————▽———————

Chicago, IL (USA)

I bowled Thursday nights during winter and played softball in the summer for many years. Also, at 18 I joined gay youth group (Horizons on Sheffield). And during the AIDS crisis I did volunteer work at Saint Joe's on the AIDS ward. – David Plambeck

———————▽———————

Bath, Somerset (UK)

I wish. It wasn't until I joined Gay West in Bath that I began to meet other young gay people (even then, most members of Gay West were 40 or even 50+). However, more younger people began to join in the late 1980s and several, including me, even became active committee members. There was no gay club in the city and even nearby Bristol only had a couple of gay venues. With little money and a rubbish train and bus service, a night out in Bristol was not practical unless you knew someone with a car who wasn't going to drink alcohol. Like that was going to happen! – Diesel Balaam

———————∇———————

Chicago, IL (USA)

I don't recall anyplace that wasn't a bar or adult book store. And so, I guess I was hanging out with my fellow horny men that I enjoyed. My favorite bookstore was Peeping Tom's on Wells Street. It was set back in sort of an alley, south of the Bijou and Over 21 Bookstore, and just north of The Glory Hole bar. It was the first bookstore I had gone to with a friend who was showing me the ropes, and the guys that worked the front door took a shine to me, so I loved to hang out there, so much I even worked there for a bit. – Dean Ogren

———————∇———————

(USA)

I never congregated much. When I became single at the age of 34, I joined an LGBT writing workshop and an LGBT outdoors group. The outdoors group had been founded in the early '80s, specifically as an alternative to the bars. Also, in my 30s, I was in recovery for sexual compulsion, so there was a lot of what the 12-steppers call "fellowship." And that was definitely not in bars! – David Pratt

———————∇———————

New York, NY (USA)

I was lucky to have grown up in New York, because I had lots of opportunities. I was very involved in gay student associations at both Brooklyn College and Boston University. While there was going out to bars there was a lot of hanging out, either on the quad or in dorm rooms. I also used to go to a youth center called The Door in New York, where I met other young Gay people. I was lucky because it gave me the opportunity to learn from them and have a fairly normal gay adolescence. I think I became very socially connected to the gay community and my peers which was a very nice and healthy balance to the sexual connection I had on the streets of the Village. – Ian H

———————∇———————

Chicago, IL (USA)

The neighborhood bowling alley, Fireside Bowl, was where I would meet a friend who would become a confidante, and eased me gently out of the closet. His name is Steve and he and I would hang out at the bowling alley and we also hung out at Humboldt Park, where we soon found a whole other community of LGBTQ folks, mainly gay and bisexual men but a few trans folks and lesbians. – Robert Castillo

———————▽———————

Chicago, IL (USA)

The Belmont Rocks. That was my favorite place to spend summer days. I fell in and out of love (and lust) there many times. It seems a lifetime ago. – Anonymous

———————▽———————

Chicago, IL (USA)

During the mid '70s through the '80s I spent as much time as possible at the Belmont Rocks, weather permitting. The freedom we felt as young LGBTQ people to be outside, nearly naked, luxuriating in our youthful exuberance and beauty was beyond description. That all seemed to change abruptly once the AIDS epidemic struck. – Paul Mikos

———————▽———————

NAME THREE THINGS THAT ARE ON YOUR LGBTQ BUCKET-LIST?

Chicago, IL (USA)

I want to have a hit record. I'm open to being in a relationship. And just being able to live life and have fun because years ago I was paralyzed, had cancer, couldn't move, I didn't ever think I could dance or walk again. It's been a tough road and I'm back. I really think a lot of it is attitude, "OK this is my path … OK next chapter." I'm lucky enough now that I'm working physically, I can still do it. I'm still not out of the game. – James Scalfani

————————▽————————

Chicago, IL (USA)

As someone who is not just queer but fat, trans, and disabled, I have had a difficult time finding romance. Some people could handle maybe one or two of those things, but it's hard to find anyone who's comfortable with all of them. I've never been in a serious, loving relationship. The closest I've gotten was someone who was ashamed to admit he was spending time with me, making up lies if someone called while we were together. I'm lonely. Some days it hurts more than others, but it *always* hurts to some degree. I dream that someday I can have a beautiful, real, queer relationship.

As a queer artist, my mission has always been to make people like me feel seen and represented. I do this with my drag, modeling, and photoshoots, but I also want to do this with music. My goal is to release an EP by the end of the year, celebrating intersectional, marginalized folks.

My biggest lifetime goal is to open a drag museum. Drag has such a rich history that so few people know anything about. It isn't taught in schools. Unless you actively seek it out, you probably won't be exposed to it. The world *needs* a drag museum so that the history of our community can be preserved and made accessible to the public. – C'est Kevvie (Wilhelmina)

———————▽———————

Oxford, MS (USA)

I'd like to go back to Provincetown with my husband. I'd like to go to Eureka Springs, AR with him. And I'd like to attend a March on Washington to protest what the hell is going on in our government (Trump presidency, Democratic House, Republican Senate). Our government has become deadly and totally cut off from the needs of the United States citizenry. That third item would include concern for the LGBTQ population. – Oran Walker

———————▽———————

Chicago, IL (USA)

Finally finding a partner who won't die on me. Going to the gayest city in America and doing the gayest things I can think of. So eventually I'm going to Palm Springs. I'd love to be someplace where people are very uncomfortable because they're straight. Go to an East European gay dinner and have some prime minister from some backwards backwoods pseudo-Slavic country have to sit next to me and watch me be gay all evening long. – Mike

———————▽———————

Midwestern City (USA)

The most significant thing on me and my husband's bucket-list is to travel in Europe, and we are eager to visit the "gay" districts of cities such as La Marais in Paris. – Anonymous

———————▽———————

San Francisco, CA (USA)

You know, that is something I just don't think about at all. I'm pretty flexible and curious and the things I want to do before I shed this mortal coil I've done or find a way to do through some hokus poke-us. Like for instance, I will most likely never be able to afford a Bugatti fast enough to do the autobahn, but people do it and take cameras. That's plenty for me. Longboard down winding hills in Switzerland? I can enjoy it without getting up from my desk. Hmm. I would love to see the end of race being considered any difference in humans. I long ago grew weary of that conversation, the ways I have and do manipulate the trajectory of it all, the bullshit game I run just to be able to stand other people and their games. That is my bucket (B00-kay) list. – Terence Smith (Joan Jett Blakk)

———————▽———————

Chicago, IL (USA)

I would love to travel to Japan and Asia, because I've never been to that part of the world. I want participate in a "horse market" ... the horse market is an event for gay men who are then divided up into stallions and mares. It originated in Berlin at the Kit Kat. I have a friend who was a wrangler who helped originate it and they now do it in Berlin, Frankfurt, Amsterdam and San Francisco. At some point I would like to live outside the United States. – Steve

———————▽———————

Chicago, IL (USA)

I'd like to go to the most famous of the gay pride parades. I always go to Chicago's and I made it to San Francisco once. But I would like to see the parades in New York, Los Angeles, and Toronto.

I would like to get published. I've done a lot of research and had a lot of education and know a lot of things. I'd like to write it up and share it.

I'd like to have a boyfriend. I never have.
–   Bert Thompson

———————▽———————

Tulsa, OK (USA)

I want to have sex in a sleeping bag and not be by myself. I want to go on a romantic trip with somebody. And I would like to live long enough to see a gay person in the White House or close to it. – Renny

———————▽———————

Name three things that are on your LGBTQ bucket-list?

Chicago, IL (USA)

I suppose that San Francisco has turned into an over-priced shithole. But I always wanted to go to San Francisco, to the Castro, and have sex with a beautiful black man with a British accent. I think black men with British accents are really hot. I would like to go back to the gay hedonism of the 1970s and have a wild time. I feel like I missed something by being too young … not by much, but just enough to be annoying. I want to be the next greatest literary lion. – Xavier Bathsheba-Negron

—————∇—————

Chicago, IL (USA)

Connecting with the European gay community. Visiting the Holocaust Museum to learn exactly what we went thru. Being recognized as the gay songwriter I am. – Lars von Keitz

—————∇—————

San Francisco, CA (USA)
Palm Springs, CA (USA)

I don't have a LGBTQ bucket list. I lived in San Francisco for 38 years and had the opportunities and support to do anything LGBTQ that I wanted. I've lived in Palm Springs for seven years now, and the opportunities and support continue to nourish me. – Gary Borgstedt

—————∇—————

Seattle, WA (USA)

1: One or two sexual positions I won't detail here.
2: A gay cruise
3: See Barbra Streisand in concert – it don't get much gayer than that
   –   Eric Andrews-Katz

—————∇—————

Chicago, IL (USA)

I don't know. I've never had any desire to go on a cruise or any of that stuff. I've never done any of the marches on Washington or Springfield. I've always wanted to do that because … I'm not a super-politically active person. I mean, I pay attention, I know what's going on. It's hard to drop everything and go to a march in another state. That's one thing. Does this count? I'm dying to go to Berlin. It's like the county seat of queerness in Europe. That's two … this is a hard question. – Jeff Ramone

—————▽—————

(Bulgaria)

I would like to attend a Pride march in Bulgaria without fearing for my life.
I would like to marry my partner legally and have that marriage recognised as equal to any other, with all the rights and obligations thereto.
I would like to be reinstated as a senior member of my family, instead of suffering "damnatio memoriae" as has been the case since 1985. – Louis Richard de Bourbon de Parme et de Savoie, Prince de la Pau

—————▽—————

North Carolina (USA)

Finding out what gay life is like in Berlin. Paying my respects to Matthew Shepard at the National Cathedral. Going to Los Angeles to research and go to the places where Ray Bourbon lived and worked. Ray Bourbon being the nightclub performer I've been researching for 25 years. – Randy

—————▽—————

Rancho Mirage, CA (USA)

Two have already happened for me: I wanted, through my creativity, to make funny and performance art videos of all kinds and have them reach people. There are ones that are obviously LGBTQ-oriented, particularly in humorous ways. For years I was doing fine with them on YouTube, even making sure they were listed as age-restricted in some cases. Apparently, there were trolls who will just flag anything if they just don't like it, not because the videos are offensive (which mine weren't). But dealing with YouTube over that was too much drama, so I am slowly but surely putting them all on Vimeo. By checking the right boxes for mature content, I'm safe. This has been my happiest endeavor, and hearing from indie directors (whose films I had already seen), being complimented by my favorite singer Krister Linder (who is very Zen, and him saying I made him laugh out loud is my proudest moment), and by others I feel I've reached people and entertained them. Not seeking attention, mind you ... just having a fun way of being able to utilize my creativity. The second happened 20 years ago but was on my list: Doing an adult film/video. This was just before the internet became the main way to get new porn creations and older vintage flicks, with anyone able to shoot their own home-made video and post it somewhere. But before that wave, I was fortunate to be contacted by the guy behind Altomar Productions and got my chance. It WAS fun, and when a year later *Rural Erections* was released on VHS and DVD I was proud, it was a legitimate "studio" release! On the DVD's initial release I was even pictured on the back cover along with other guys. For a while I got plenty of e-mails forwarded to me from viewers that appreciated me being in it and am surprised that all these years later I will get occasionally get recognized and told that title is still a fave of theirs. I wanted to do something bold and fun, and that opportunity was perfect for me. Another on the list would be to have someone to travel to Scotland with to explore my heritage and see how LGBTQ life is there amongst my kilted brethren. One day, perhaps! – Todd Jaeger

—————∇—————

Chicago, IL (USA)

My main bucket-list is to find a life partner who will love me for who I am. Without condition. I have never known unconditional love. Second, buy a restored 1985 Buick Riviera convertible red with white leather interior. Third, go back and forth to the UK on the QE2. – Philip Bernal

—————∇—————

Frinton-on-Sea, Essex (UK)

Get a dog, visit San Francisco, become an openly gay councilor in the town where I live. – Diesel Balaam

—————∇—————

Chicago, IL (USA)

Well, let's see. My first visit to the BDSM clubhouse checked off a couple of those items on my bucket-list. There are a couple of other sexual things I would like to do (or have done to me) at some point. Do I need to be specific? Will you line someone up to help me with those?
Otherwise, I'm afraid I don't know what an LGBTQ bucket list would look like. I've seen Liza in concert. I've marched in a Pride Parade.

Here's the only one I can think of, but I think it is a great one: I would like to live until I am 100 years old, just so I can say to those bigots from the churches I grew up in, that gay men are not doomed to die young and miserably, and to let them see that life can be fabulous even for cocksuckers like me! – andKevin

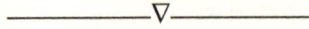

———————▽———————

South Carolina (USA)

One of my bucket list items already happened. I never thought I'd actually see marriage equality happen. Being able to watch it happen was something I'll be able to claim part of making happen.
I'd like to go to Provincetown just once during the high season to see what it's like.
I'd love to be at one of the final episodes of *RuPaul's Drag Race*.
 –   Chris Grace

———————▽———————

Rockford, IL (USA)

First off, I would love to be a part of New York City Pride Parade and see the Stonewall Inn. Second, I want to write a book featuring a LGBT young adult character, that makes my name a household name. Third, I would like to be in *Out* magazine top 100 list. Ideally, I would love to be on the cover. – Patrick J. Murphy III

———————▽———————

Palm Springs, CA (USA)

One thing on my bucket-list is to get married. I think it would be interesting if we had kids. Only because I've helped to raise nieces and nephews. I'm good with children. It would be interesting to see our mindset being put into someone else's head. Children are sponges. I would also like to do more music together with my partner. The fact that we can act in films together, that's a dream that's happened. I still cannot believe to this day that this has happened. And to do something musically would be cool. – David Vega (Lucifers Axe)

———————▽———————

Name three things that are on your LGBTQ bucket-list?

Bellport, NY (USA)

I don't have a bucket-list. If I want to do something I just go out and do it. I have even written an article about bucket-lists that was accepted in *Lesbian Connection Magazine*. – Erin Michelle Miller

———————▽———————

Cathedral City, CA (USA)

I would love to go to Mykonos. It would be fun to go to Israel … I'd like to see Tel Aviv. A third place is Barcelona. – Jim

———————▽———————

Palm Springs, CA (USA)

I want to star in the leading role in a horror flick with my partner as the leading man. I always get cast as female. I want it to be such a groundbreaking film that it paves the way for any other little kid that's looking at films, "I wanna be that. I wanna do that." They can walk in through a door and not have to kick the door open and knock it off its hinges. I would love to let myself go, completely go, without a thought in my head, at an orgy. And just be consumed into the middle of the entire orgy. That would be so cool. And I don't want kids. I've just got down to a 27-inch waist and I'm not ruining my figure. – Keith Kollinicos (Missa Distic)

———————▽———————

Chicago, IL

Ten years of letters that I want to donate to the Gerber-Hart Library. To meet a younger gay person. To be thought of as a good, kind person after I'm gone. – Dennis Hardenstein

———————▽———————

Cathedral City, CA (USA)

Mardi Gras in Sydney, but my husband doesn't like big crowds, so that isn't going to happen. A gay cruise, but I'm not into the whole circuit party thing or dress-up stuff. I've been on a cruise a couple of times. Maybe being done up in drag professionally, where someone else does it to you. I'd like to see what it looks like. I've done it myself a few times for Halloween but it's not the same. I looked ok but you could see a five o'clock shadow. – Spike

—————∇—————

New Orleans, LA (USA)

Australia, Paris and London Pride events. – Terry Gaskins

—————∇—————

Palm Springs, CA (USA)

Selfishly, about me, I want to go to Sitges for Bear Week, so I can experience the Bear and leather culture somewhere other than my own back yard. And I speak Spanish, so it gives me a chance to use that. To participate in the International Mr. Leather Contest. Those are superficial because they're about me. The one thing that I really want to do is make a difference … I want to work to prevent suicide amongst LGBTQ, the younger generation that's coming up, because it's happening. They often don't know how to express themselves and it breaks my heart. I see it every day at work and I see what a little bit of love and a little bit of attention can do. So I hope to be involved on a more regular basis through outreach. I'd like to push that and see where that can go. – Crusher

—————∇—————

Cleveland, OH (USA)

To keep making friends, hopefully ones that lead different lives than me – generational, cultural, etc. I still have a fantasy about living in a gay commune sort of like *The Golden Girls* with benefits. Also, I'd like to pass on a little of the queer wisdom I learned along the way. – Roger.

—————∇—————

Chicago IL (USA)

1) I've been working on a series of memoirs/essays about talking to strangers as a necessary part of coming out as a gay man and of becoming a fully functioning human being. I want to at least finish them; publishing them would be icing on the cake. Or maybe the last few drops of the bucket.
2) Having enjoyed several gay communities, like Boystown and the Castro, I

would love to visit Key West one day before I get so old that some young, bored gay hotel attendant has to push me along the shore in a wooden wheelchair with a blanket across my lap. "Ricardo! Ricardo! I'm hot. Take me back to the bar for another Mai Tai."

3) A few months ago, meeting John Waters would have been on this bucket list. Too late! I met him, briefly, at a book signing a few months ago. I got to sit next to him while he autographed his book for me. The experience was – ahem – Divine. – William Demaree

———————▽———————

Louisiana (USA)

1) Launch a Production Studio with LGBTQ projects.
2) A national Fund or Program to support abandoned LGBTQ youth.
3) See vacation destinations that are strongly LGBTQ friendly.
– Katorri A.

———————▽———————

Palm Springs, CA (USA)

I've already had many of the most popular gay experiences since I came out, but the top three things remaining on my LGBTQ bucket-list are: Visit the final three of Europe's "Big Four" gay summer destinations – Sitges and Gran Canaria, Spain, and Mykonos, Greece (I've already been to Ibiza); Attend Southern Decadence in New Orleans; and attend the Burning Man festival. – D. Warner

———————▽———————

Palm Springs, CA (USA)

I want to tell my story. I have documented many of the stories in my life, but I feel I have a responsibility to make sure that the stories of all the friends I've lost to AIDS and other things ... all the struggles and great times we've had. I want to get my archives permanently placed somewhere. To return stories I've collected to their place of origin. That's a concept that has come to me in the last three years. I have 50 years of storytelling and archiving in my photography and ephemera. It's from various places, it's the Rainbow Migration. An excellent example of the rainbow migration of gays and lesbians in the United States in the 1970 and 1980s. Rural to urban, south to north, east to west, that was the migratory route. On my bucket list is to go back on that trail and to return the memories of that to those different locations. So far, I've done New York, Los Angeles, and the next is Charleston, South Carolina, San Francisco, Washington DC, Atlanta. All the places where I've lived and worked. The third thing on my bucket list is to return to Berlin to show my early work. – Greg Day.

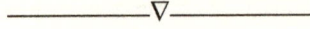

—————▽—————

Chicago, IL (USA)

In no particular order: Falling in love again – I'm currently single and seeing no one, go to Europe with my partner, to once again have a partner I can be intimate with. – Steve Kmetko

—————▽—————

Palm Springs, CA (USA)

To finally get a long-term relationship right. I've told Andre, "If this doesn't work, I'm just getting a lot of cats. I'm gonna be the cat guy. And I'm going to live out the rest of my life with a bunch of cats, as a recluse." The other thing that's on my bucket list is that I want to get involved in an LGBTQ organization that's really making a difference internationally. And somehow contributing to that, other than in a monetary way. Actually getting involved. To somehow make a difference in the LGBTQ community, especially on an international level. As much as things are screwed up here in the US, they're a hundred times worse everywhere else. We live in this bubble and we don't think about that … how horrible it is outside our little bubble. Let me make No 3 more frivolous. I really want to go to the Big Bear event in Sitges in Spain. I think we're actually going to pull that off in September, that's our goal. – Thomas Stribling

—————▽—————

Chicago, IL (USA)

#1. Not necessarily nominated for The Chicago Lesbian and Gay Hall of Fame but for the people who are in charge of it to recognize the role (go-go boys, male dancers, etc.) played in the history of bars. Other types of gay performers have been. And being honest it would be nice to be nominated. #2. To complete my book I started. Being a dancer for over 25 years, I got a chance to meet many celebrities, porn stars and an array of other important people.

#3. To have an article written about THE LIFE OF A GAY DANCER, the pros, cons, misconception of dancers. With most bars now having straight boys A PART IS LOST. – Mercury

———————∇———————

Cathedral City, CA (USA)

Believe it or not I've always wanted to be on one of the floats in the Gay Pride Parade. I want to do that stupid wave for a couple of miles. The other thing I've wanted to do in the LGBTQ community is to run for a title, which I actually did last year. To me the whole thing is really stupid, but I wanted to do it just to say I did it. That's why I did it. I'd like to change some of the bars. To me they're just generic. Everyone wants to be the same. Everyone wants to ... it's kind of like shopping at the Gap, same white, same khaki, same thing. You see everyone wearing old Levis, old jeans, old shirts ... people just don't care. – Marcous

———————∇———————

Santa Fe, NM (USA)

Traveling is one. I have achieved all the craziness I wanted to, now I just want to settle down ... and the other one, I always wanted to go zipline but we did that in Alaska ... get my butt worked up and open so I can get fucked again. I had it reconstructed when I had rectal cancer and now it's too small. It's on the bucket list. – Juan-manuel Alonso

———————∇———————

Chicago, IL (USA)
Palm Springs, CA (USA)

I used to do stage and film makeup. I want to do Halloween dressed in drag, but I really want to ... there's a guy here in Palm Springs called Clay and he looks gorgeous dressed in drag and he often dresses up other people in the community for a before and after shot. I want to dress in drag and do a number, but I don't want to look like a housewife that's been thrown to the curb. Because when I dressed up before and I looked like a cross between Rosanne Barr and Oprah. I have those pictures. But I want someone to do my makeup ... I mean, I'll shave my goatee ... I would love to do a number in complete drag, stunning. That's one for my bucket list. I've never been to Key West. I know it's changed a lot over the years. I've spent an overnight in

Provincetown and I'd like to go there for a week. If I had more money, I'd like to do more philanthropy. For LGBT youth or homeless youth. – Greg R. Baird

Cathedral City, CA (USA)

Travel some more. I would love to go out of this world by being multiple fucked by many people at one time. It seems like a wonderful fantasy, just being gang-banged to death. One of my sayings used to be, "Fuck me into a coma." And then I would like to be acknowledged for the person I am. Artistically, as I've turned out exactly the way I wanted. – David Hardy

Chicago, IL (USA)

Name three things that are on your LGBTQ bucket-list?
1) To fall in love again with a man who deserves me.
2) To have a three way with Dean Flynn and Colby Keller.
3) To age gracefully and with little regret.
    – MrZor

(Germany)

A Canaan faerie gathering. Being a sub in a bukkakke fuck fist gangbang. Participating in a high-end arthouse queer porn movie. – Cornelius Günther Körn

Redwood Valley/Mendocino County, CA (USA)

1. To live to see the world become one. One love, one blood, one skin, one sun, one in spirit, one shared existence, no matter our DNA, appearance, heritage, being, or place of belonging.
2. To live to see my religiously right wing, politically driven blood and in-law relatives learn from my 90 year old Mama about love, Christianity, open heart, open mind, support, hugs, and that they each do their part to help change our shared world for the better.

3. Keep on volunteering and pushing forward with the agenda of love, openness, justice, equality, environmental health, and human growth. – T. Lark Letchworth

—————▽—————

Cathedral City, CA (USA)

Get involved with the community more. Make an impression of myself in the community and be proud. – David Hayes

—————▽—————

Cathedral City, CA (USA)

Hmmm, no specific LGBTQ bucket-list unless you're talking about sleeping with Robbie Benson. On my bucket-list though are marrying my partner, Tony, seeing Stevie Wonder in concert, seeing Donald Trump and many of his associates brought to justice and for once, a democratic socialist as President. – Paul Harris

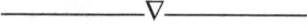

—————▽—————

(Australia)

It's very short.
(A) Visit San Francisco ... I suspect that's on every gay man's bucket list.
(B) Visit London to explore the gay scene there. This is driven by me getting hot over English boys ... the accents drive me wild!
(C) Ditto for Ireland ... and more so for those sexy accents!
(D) I was a DJ in Sydney back in the '90s, where I had two residencies, and played House and Handbag dance music. I have since moved onto Trance music, and upload Trance DJ mixes to Mixcloud these days. I would love to either DJ a huge dance party, playing very loud Trance, along with lighting OR have the money to hire a place with a huge dance floor, hire a lighting technician, and send out an invite to all my friends and their friends to attend a Trance happening. I could just get lost in it.
(E) Hire a gay male escort to work me over. It feels like a long, long time since I last had sex with another guy ... 2014 to be exact ... and I would love a younger guy just playing with my body ... just for the memory. – Tim Alderman

—————▽—————

St. Cloud, MN (USA)

I want to dance with more ladies. There are so few places where ladies can go and dance with each other. I can't even go anywhere to dance with my partner.

I want to write one solid lesbian novel. I have outlined a few … just have to sit and write now. If someone could turn it into a movie that would be awesome as well. – Rachel Wexelbaum

—————∇—————

Brunswick, ME (USA)

An LGBTQ Bucket List? I don't think I have even one such thing. I guess, all I can say is that my "bucket list" is more about being more fully human, loving and giving back. If any of that includes anything LGBTQ, good. – Michael Pickel

—————∇—————

Cork, Munster (Ireland)

1. My flatmate Julija, a Lithuanian transgender activist, and I, have made a pact that we will do tandem parachute jumping sometime next year.
2. Venice, before it sinks.
3. I have already been to Westwood Cemetery in Los Angeles (where Marilyn, Truman and Eve (Arden) are buried). So, I guess I only have two items on my bucket list. Although I am nearing the end of the rainbow, my journey is not over by any means. No regrets. – David Clayton

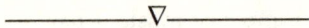

—————∇—————

King, NC (USA)

I would have to say, number one, being married to this wonderful man that I find myself with and enjoying what time we have together, discovering new things about each other and making each other fulfilled and happy.

Two, living long enough to see my children happy, contented, and living their dreams, and finally three, (the easy one to do) traveling with my husband to wherever he'd like to go. – Ron Cline

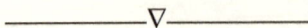

—————∇—————

Palm Springs, CA (USA)

I know this is boring, but I am looking forward to retiring from the 40 hour a week work life and just enjoying time with my husband.
Bucket list? Travel, I guess. He's talked about going to Patagonia on a cruise; I'd like to visit Japan during Cherry Blossom time. – Tony Earl

————————∇————————

Charlottetown, Prince Edward Island (Canada)

1. I want to create a record of "The Secret Social History of Prince Edward Island" (a project in the works), because our social history locally is actively being forgotten.
And less specifically:
2. I want to be a part of the ending of violence against LGBTQ people.
3. I want to be involved in more LGBTQ arts projects.

————————∇————————

Milwaukee, WI (USA)

1. To see world peace and everyone treated equally
2. To find that soul connection and fall in love again
3. Binding federal legislation to punish all those who commit hate crimes against anyone who is different … with NO ROOM for states to amend the federal laws.
– Sherrie Howe

————————∇————————

San Diego, CA (USA)

1. Post-transition, to find myself in a good relationship. Post-divorce, post-transition, making sure I'm in the best possible place to be available. But when that happens, I absolutely want to be ready. Having that really amazing relationship with someone would be number one.
2. Continue to grow and show others outside the trans community the value that we have in everyday life. Whether it's at work, I'm an out trans leather kinky person at work. Within the trans-community I'm the first openly trans-female title holder in San Diego. The options for trans-folks in the LGBTQ community is important. Whether it be leather, drag, whatever

aspect beyond the trans community which is phenomenal in and of itself, but there's so much more self-expression. Being able to explore that and make those roads available for the next trans person.

　　　3. The third one is for my daughter who is four. Yesterday she brought the *I Am Jazz* and Telly Teddy to school for show and tell and told all of her friends that her ———, her other mom, is transgender. And be there for my daughter and help her navigate this very different world, having a mom and a transgender parent is going to be tough. Hopefully for her generation it will be easy. For my journey I'd like to make sure her journey is better.

– Serafine Sawyer

———————▽———————

Des Moines, IA (USA)

I don't have an LGBTQ bucket list in that sense, but I want 1) peace 2) peace 3) peace. – Sr. Freida Peoples aka DJ Chrysler Sheldon

———————▽———————

(Pakistan)

The three things on my LGBTQ bucket list is to write a book about my experience of being an openly queer activist in Pakistan and my asylum journey to the US. To complete my higher education to the level of PhD especially in the subjects I love that is in human rights, environmental studies, and queer literature/ anthropology. Also, do more for my queer siblings back in Pakistan especially through research and activism. – Salman

———————▽———————

Fort Lauderdale, FL

I want something I've written to be a best seller or to be produced on Broadway, to dance with Gene Kelly and to be devastatingly good-looking. None of these will ever happen. I'm too old to have a best seller or Broadway show produced, Gene Kelly is dead, and I'm fat and old (although in Wilton Manors, Florida, that doesn't necessarily rule me out). – Rick Karlin

———————▽———————

OTHER BOOKS BY ...

ST SUKIE DE LA CROIX

Chicago Whispers: The History of LGBT Chicago Before Stonewall
The Blue Spong and the Flight from Mediocrity
The Memoir of a Groucho Marxist: A Very British Fairy Tale
Gay Press, Gay Power – contributor
Out of the Underground: Homosexuals, the Radical Press, and the Rise
and Fall of the Gay Liberation Front
St Sukie's Strange Garden of Woodland Creatures – with Roy Alton Wald
Tell Me About It – with Owen Keehnen
Tell Me About It 2 – with Owen Keehnen
"Who Was Jane Dalotz?" in The Kiss of Death: An anthology of vampire
    stories."
"The Dinner Party or All's Well That Ends Well" in Midsummer Night's
    Dreams, edited by M. Christian.
"Jane Austen Must Be Turning in Her Grave" in Guilty Pleasures, edited by
    M. Christian
"I Fuck the Dead" in Book of Dead Things edited by Tina L. Jens and Eric
    M. Cherry
"Private Dick" in Noirotica 3: Stolen Kisses edited by Thomas S. Roche

OWEN KEEHNEN

Tell Me About It 2 – with St Sukie de la Croix
Tell Me About It – with St Sukie de la Croix
The LGBTQ Book of Days: Revised 2019 Edition
Dugan's Bistro and the Legend of the Bearded Lady
Night Visitors
Love Underground
The Matinee Idol
Young Digby Swank
Vernita Gray: From Woodstock to the White House – with Tracy Baim
The LGBT Book of Days
Gay Press, Gay Power – contributor
The Sand Bar
We're Here, We're Queer
Jim Flint: The Boy From Peoria – with Tracy Baim
Leatherman: The Legend of Chuck Renslow – with Tracy Baim
Doorway Unto Darkness
Nothing Personal:
Chronicles of Chicago's LGBTQ Community 1977-1997 – co-editor
Rising Starz
Ultimate Starz
Out and Proud in Chicago – contributor
More Starz
Starz

www.ingramcontent.com/pod-product-compliance
Lightning Source LLC
Chambersburg PA
CBHW031943090426
42739CB00006B/64

* 9 7 8 1 7 3 4 1 4 6 4 5 5 *